TURKEY AND THE

ARAB SPRING

ALSO BY GRAHAM E. FULLER

Three Truths and a Lie: a Memoir
September 2012

A World Without Islam
Little Brown, August 2010

The New Turkish Republic: Turkey's Pivotal Role in the Middle East
US Institute of Peace, 2008

The Future of Political Islam
Palgrave, May 2003

The Arab Shi'a: The Forgotten Muslims (with Rend Francke)
St. Martin's, 1999

Turkey's Kurdish Question (with Henri Barkey)
Rowman and Littlefield, 1997

A Sense of Siege:
The Geopolitics of Islam and the West (with Ian Lesser)
Westview, 1994

The New Foreign Policy of Turkey:
From the Balkans to Western China (with Ian Lesser)
Westview, 1993

The Democracy Trap: Perils of the Post-Cold War World
Dutton, 1992

The Center of the Universe: The Geopolitics of Iran
Westview, 1991

How to Learn a Foreign Language
Storm King Press, 1987

TURKEY AND THE ARAB SPRING

LEADERSHIP IN THE MIDDLE EAST

GRAHAM E. FULLER

Bozorg Press

Published by Bozorg Press
www.grahamefuller.com

Fuller, Graham E., 1937-, author
    Turkey and the Arab Spring : leadership in the Middle
East / Graham E. Fuller.

Includes bibliographical references and index.
ISBN 978-0-9937514-0-0

    1. Turkey--Politics and government--1980-. 2. Arab Spring,
2010-. 3. Political leadership--Arab countries--History. 4. Arab
countries--Politics and government--21st century. 5. Islam and
politics--Arab countries--History--21st century. I. Title.

DR603.F84 2014   956.104'1   C2014-902341-3

Cover design by Graham Fuller and Margreet Dietz: the tulips—from Ottoman-era glazed mosque tiles—are classic symbols of the Ottoman Empire; the two words in Arabic—*al-thawraat al-'arabiyya*—signify "The Arab Revolutions," a commonly used Arabic formulation for "the Arab Spring."

Manuscript preparation and design by Margreet Dietz

Author photo by Pascale Gadbois

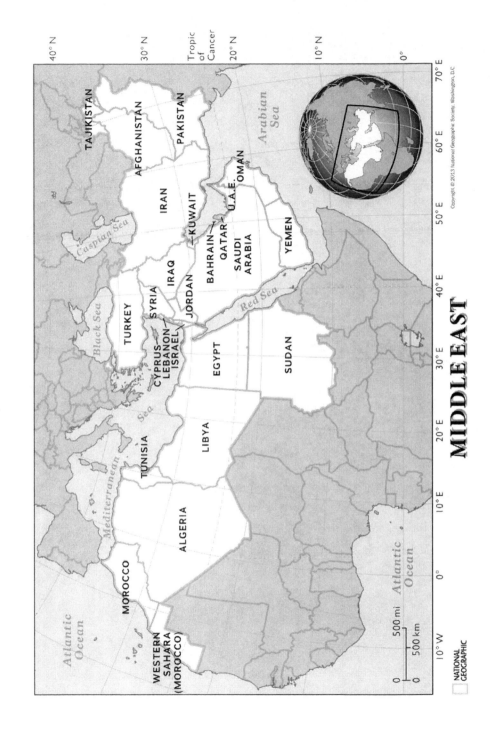

MIDDLE EAST

NATIONAL GEOGRAPHIC

Copyright © 2013 National Geographic Society, Washington, D.C.

CONTENTS

INTRODUCTION

We write about historical events at our own peril. History "changes" looking back from our perspective of the immediate and shifting present. A book about 19th century European history written in 1912, on the eve of World War I, might be upbeat; it would perceive the course of the previous century in quite different terms than a history of the same century written eight years later in 1920—after a horrendous world war. A key focus of the later account would then be to uncover the destructive seeds of a war nobody knew was coming.

Writing about the Middle East presents similar problems, perhaps more so. Its politics are among the fastest moving in the world: war, violent change and endless outside intervention rapidly punctuate events. We write of contemporary events there with some trepidation because we know the revelations of the next few years may change our perception of what was really happening back a few years earlier.

I took up this tale of Turkey and the Arab World in 2010; if published then it might have essentially drawn the following conclusions: Turkey has established itself as a country that has achieved great prosperity, notable democratic deepening and a newly-emerging post-Ataturkist form of social stability, civilian leadership and dynamism that is unmatched in the region. Turkey has become virtually the sole dynamic player in a Middle East that is otherwise controlled by frozen, authoritarian and unimaginative Arab regimes unable to provide leadership or regional vision. Turkey's success under the ruling Justice and Development Party (AKP) has captured the attention of the region.

A book published two years later in 2012 would have noted that several Arab states during the Arab Spring had suddenly revealed prospects for exciting democratic change in a new era—a process in which Turkey was involved and perhaps ready to form new partnerships in a region rediscovering its own dynamism.

But a book that concludes its narrative in early 2014, as this one does, is compelled to note that so many of the hopeful new regional power relationships and ideologies have once again plunged into an unexpected state of flux, uncertainty and even regression. The major themes of this book—the foundations and nature of leadership in the Middle East political order—are now up in the air again, unresolved and more complex than ever. Four Arab governments have fallen in popular rebellion, several more regimes are buffeted and struggling to survive.

Despite all the turmoil and drama of the Arab Spring, it is hard to know how much, if anything, has really changed. Despite early hopes, there still is no Arab leadership on the horizon in the Middle East that offers heartening new prospects for the region. Turkey too, after introducing remarkable innovations in domestic and foreign policy, found its foreign policies pummeled by the Arab Spring—as did the rest of the world. And domestically, by 2013, the Turkish government moved into an unanticipated series of corruption charges and political tensions in which the extraordinary successes of the AKP in power seemed to have run their course; the prime minister lost his vision, élan and political touch; the AKP's inevitable loss of the reins of power now beckons in future elections. Yet Turkey's crises will be resolved via the electoral process. And, for all its turmoil, Turkey still remains the only state that offers a credible model of modern governance in the entire region, including the Middle East, the Balkans, east into Asia, the independent states of the former Soviet Union and south into Africa.

"Leadership in the Middle East" is the subtitle of this book. But what do we mean when we talk about leadership? *Arab* leaders who might possess the potential to galvanize the broader region? Or Turkish leaders whose outstanding accomplishments have changed the region? We can even consider new *Iranian* promise of a dynamic and semi-democratic state that, like it or not, has inspired and influenced the region's populace in the past and is likely to play a dynamic role again as it reintegrates into the region. And what about ideology? Will leadership emerge from an Islamist environment, or perhaps from a nationalist, or even a secular liberal vision? With the region in such turmoil, new trends in the Arab world could emerge from any quarter. Here the Turkish experience has much to offer as well.

I suggest that there has not been any true, coherent, successful regional leadership in the Middle East for many decades. By "true," I mean leadership that deals with the major questions that affect people—not just their daily lives and their pocketbook, but also their emotional or psychological hunger to see the region climb out of the mire in which it has been stuck for decades—perhaps even a century or more. Not just the practical issues of feeding, housing, educating, and employing a growing population, but perhaps also a psychic leadership with a vision—something that addresses who and what the region is, what its identity, ideals and even ideologies might be, and where it wants to go in the world relative to its neighbors and the rest of the world.

Leadership has been lacking for multiple reasons. First is the general absence of democracy and political legitimacy. Few states other than Turkey have maintained a democratic order in which heads of state rise and fall through elections. Without democratic process it is hard to debate and then articulate the national aspirations of the population. Ideologies might stir the crowd, but often end up being manipulated in order to maintain some regime in power; most regimes have failed to achieve true legitimacy in meeting the aspirations of the people. Second, there is no region in the world that can match the Middle East in being on the receiving end of external interventions, invasions, wars, coups, missile attacks, foreign control of energy resources, manipulation of domestic politics, and incitement of domestic groups against each other. Problems aplenty already abound in most of the states of the region on their own, but the external world—mostly the West and especially the United States—have served to hugely exacerbate these problems, perhaps complicating and distancing the process of possible resolution. The region is the ultimate global cockpit of proxy war.

The Arab world has been largely moribund for decades under frozen autocracies in the Arab world. Turkey, on a rather different course since its foundation as a modern state after World War I, has struggled intensely with identity issues, initially utterly turning its back on the Middle East after the fall of the Ottoman Empire (from which modern Turkey emerged.) Indeed, Ankara had largely ignored its Middle Eastern neighbors until the turn of the 21st century. Iran too, despite its semi-democratic government, has been isolated due to its own poor internal governance and a revolutionary ideology which has worried seated monarchs in the Persian/Arab Gulf, as well as inducing the obsessive wrath of the United States for over 35 years. Israel, a state that potentially could have much to offer the region, is rejected by its neighbors, widely despised as a result of its own politics of *force majeure* in the region, for its contempt for its neighbors, and its neo-colonial treatment of the displaced Palestinians as second class non-persons.

In the first decade of the 21st century Turkey thus emerged as a state bearing uniquely credible leadership credentials. This is not about formal, acknowledged leadership but rather as a wielder of influence and a source of inspiration and direction that more closely reflects the character, culture and interests of the Middle East region itself. It is what the Iranians might call a *marja'-e-taqlid*—a source of emulation. The Arab Spring—a series of long overdue popular uprisings starting in 2011 against entrenched dictatorship—raised some hopes for the peoples of the region, yet several years later the process seems to have foundered and run out of steam, at least for the moment, with only marginal, if any improvement. The Arab Spring's turmoil shook the regional order however and exposed the impoverished trappings of autocratic regimes that cling to power with no sense of direction other than ad hoc maneuvering for self-preservation. Iran under newly elected pragmatic leadership in 2013 just may be in the process of emerging anew as it reaches accommodation with Washington, possibly to build a more solid political foundation among its population; at the best, however, it will be some time before Iran can provide any kind of model to others. Yet in many ways Iran is instinctively more closely in touch with the aspirations of the people of the region than most of other regional leaders, even if Tehran has often exploited these aspirations clumsily. One senses a latent dynamism in its society not readily perceived elsewhere.

The quest for regional leadership tests political systems, ideologies, economies, governing skills, grasp of the pulse of Middle East culture, and vision. Reasonable success in governance, credible national independence, genuine exercise of national sovereignty, and positive influence in the region are all prerequisites. Leadership will not come in the form sought by the US or the West, but in its own native form, painfully hammered out over time. The question is how will the Turkish experience affect not only the regimes of the region but, more importantly, the people of the region.

This book narrates the unfolding of two parallel time lines: first, the 12 years of the Justice and Development Party (AKP) in power. The AKP decade, whatever happens to the party in its next years of possibly rapid decline, set Turkey on a new course in both domestic and foreign policy—a course that is virtually irreversible in its main features. The book also follows the course of the Arab Spring beginning in late 2010. These two themes are separate in one sense, but intimately linked in another. Never has the modern state of Turkey been so engaged in affairs of the Middle East. The nature of their interaction is instructive. The book spans just over a decade of dramatic and rapidly unfolding change in both arenas that have powerfully influenced each other. And it sets the stage for the second decade, the twenty-teens and beyond, in which these earlier events will continue to powerfully affect each other. Neither Turkey, Iran, or the Arab world will ever be the same again. Nor will the world ever again be able to relate to them in the same fashion as in earlier decades of lingering neo-imperialist half-life.

The term of all political parties in power, however successful, must at some point come to an end; they lose the upper hand through accumulated mistakes and failures, shifting public preferences and needs, and eventual loss of public satisfaction and confidence, bringing elections and a new party to power. The

AKP is now in such a decline. It is too early to write the AKP off since it still maintains considerable residues of strength and so far has faced little inspired or meaningful electoral opposition. Indeed, the very success of the AKP in power was a surprise—not at all what most of us might have predicted at the outset. The major landmarks of the party are impressive and are there to be evaluated.

This book is not a chronology of events nor a traditional history; rather it seeks to grasp the key themes of this remarkable and fateful decade. It reflects the author's sense of the deep political and cultural currents that he has watched for more than 50 years. It perhaps offers some fresh ways of thinking about the region—often departing from western and especially American mainstream analysis of the Middle East. Too many western analyses are heavily US-centric in character, making judgments and drawing conclusions indexed against US policy preferences and goals. They routinely fail to offer perspectives that reflect the attitudes, values, perspectives, concerns and internal logic of the people and states of the region itself. That is one reason the US has gotten so much of it wrong. The world's sole superpower has rarely heeded regional attitudes—in the conviction that they don't really matter all that much in the face of a superpower's own will and agenda.

But the region has awakened and the US-centric perspective is less relevant than ever before—even dangerously misleading. From my perspective of long time involvement in intelligence affairs, the US optic on the region seems to have drifted ever further away from regional realities and into the fantasies of isolated and increasingly frustrated and impotent superpowerdom. US policies are ever more based on narrow American perspectives and the overwhelming power of domestic politics, often obsessively centered around simplistic polarities of Israel (good) and Iran (bad), lacking understanding of regional dynamics, or any empathy for the aspirations of the people (not regimes) of the region. US policy therefore routinely falls far short of grasping regional forces, and therefore fails—certainly in the eyes of the region—in achieving its own stated goals. All this has comes at great peril and cost to the US in what has demonstrably been a decade of disastrous US Middle Eastern policies.

I also seek to provide some deeper historical, cultural, geopolitical and even psychological background behind events that are otherwise so frequently taken at immediate face value—the spin of the moment obscuring deeper trends. In many ways I challenge the assumptions of the genre of "national security studies" and the "realist" tradition of US foreign policy in which US interests form the primary optic of how foreign events are viewed and in which great power *force majeure* is the key instrument of policy.

The book is roughly divided into six sections. First we look at the broad nature of change in the region and the world over the past decade, particularly the relative decline of US power and influence which changes previous geopolitical calculations. Second, we look at how the region perceives historical leadership in the Middle East going back to the period of the Ottoman Empire, the Caliphate, and particularly the role of Islam as the major legitimizing factor in regional leadership and power. How do nationalism and political Islam interact in that equation in a more modern understanding of leadership today? Third we look at the dramatic changes in Turkey since 2002, the period of the AKP in power in Turkey. I particularly focus on themes that touch upon the role of Islam, Islamic politics, the changing role of the military, and the growth of democratization as stimulated by social and economic factors. I suggest these experiences are of direct relevance to the rest of the Middle East.

The second half of the book looks at the Arab Spring, the nature of the international crises it produced, the swirl of competing proxy interests, and Turkey's own serious involvement in it. Here we particularly assess the nature of the so-called Sunni "Islamist challenge" (especially the Muslim Brotherhood), followed by an examination of the so-called "Shi'ite threat"— what it is and what it is not. Finally we look at major trends that will impact the future including the implications of the Turkish experience for the rest of the Middle East.

A few of the major, less familiar arguments I make in the book include the following:

• The main *ideological* struggle today in the Middle East is not essentially *between secularism and Islamism* as popularly characterized in the West—although that is an interesting side-show. *Nor is it really between Sunnism and Shi'ism.* The primary struggle is *within Sunnism itself.* And it is *not*, as one might expect, even between radical jihadi Islam and conservative Saudi Islam, but rather pits *"democratic Islamism against Muslim autocracy."* [I am indebted to US Ambassador Chas Freeman for this succinct formulation of the thought.]

• Turkey and Iran will likely emerge as the two dominant and dynamic political forces in the region for some time to come; the two will maintain solid, if not always cordial, working relations.

• Contrary to popular expectation, two states with once-close ties to the US in the Middle East—Turkey and Saudi Arabia—may now represent the two competing ideological *polarities* of Middle East politics for the next decade. (*Not* the struggle between Iran and Saudi Arabia as is commonly intoned.)

• Regional *geopolitical* rivalries will persist, lie beneath the surface, and routinely trump ideology and so-called sectarian (Sunni-Shi'ite) confrontations.

• The Left will reemerge in the not too distant future as a major populist force, both in secular and in Islamist guise.

We in the West ignore the increasing power of the attitudes, values, and aspirations of the people in the region at our peril.

PART ONE: GLOBAL GEOPOLITICAL SHIFT

The 21st century has not been kind to the Middle East. It began with the al-Qaeda attacks on the US on 11 September 2001; it was followed by proclamation of the American "Global War on Terrorism" which launched several ongoing US wars in the region; and the decade closed with the start of the chaotic "Arab Spring." The Arab Spring initially opened doors to new hopes and prospects. But it also unleashed complicated new political dynamics whose outcomes could not be predicted. It has been a time of testing, turmoil, and violence, but not necessarily of positive change; the future seems perilous and turbulent.

Faraway places, complex struggles, unclear goals, shifting enemies—it is difficult even for thoughtful observers to follow. Yet it is this same region that is in our face every day on the news, in the headlines, regularly punctuated by dramatic and bloody events. The West is slow in grasping the essential political trajectories of the region, even as the stakes rise. Different partisan observers will offer their own interpretations of what the region is all about; but judging by their lack of policy success they still seem to be getting that analysis wrong. The cost of perpetuating these failures—failed wars, terrorism, humanitarian crises, escalating tensions—is high. This book represents an attempt to make sense of many of these complex issues in the hope that they can be dealt with more wisely and effectively.

The whole Middle East is in the middle of a major new shakedown and reordering of ideological, strategic, ethnic, and sectarian power. In some senses these changes are long overdue—a major reason why the area has plunged into widespread crisis. In all this kaleidoscopic change Turkey still remains the sole stable, dynamic, democratic, prosperous country with functioning national institutions, the only seriously viable model of modern governance in the Muslim world to date.

CHAPTER ONE

THE AWAKENING OF A NEW MIDDLE EAST

I was first drawn to the power of Middle Eastern symbols, images and events at age 17. I now look back at the half century I've been watching, studying, or living in the area and wonder, has anything really changed? In one sense the phrase *plus ça change, plus c'est la même chose* could have been coined in reference to the Middle East: despite change, nothing really changes. At least on the surface. The Arab world has remained mired in its failures, alternating between periodic bouts of chaos, heavy authoritarianism, and seeming frozenness, despite the regular outbreak of violence. Arab governments have been devoid of leadership or vision for decades. Beneath the surface, of course, social change does quietly percolate, but at the top of the system the old rulers have been near-permanent fixtures. Longtime observers could be forgiven for wondering whether the fatigued and sterile status quo would ever change.

And yet, in late 2010, the Arab World did unexpectedly begin to shift. After decades of entrenched dictatorship and repressive state apparatus, the log-jam suddenly broke loose—this time not through another war or military coup but with a small and sad event. On 17 December 2010 in a provincial Tunisian town a struggling pushcart vendor took the horrific step of immolating himself in front of the local municipality—a desperate reaction to the repeated bureaucratic humiliations and the sheer hardship he had suffered at trying to make a living in an inflexible police state.

This event was not likely to have been noted outside the town, or across Tunisia, much less in the region. But his death was in fact an extraordinary catalyst, a tipping point. This specific incident gained unexpected publicity and opened the gates to public expression of long-suppressed anger, frustration, bitterness and a sense of unending oppression that came boiling forth from among the Tunisian population. And, astonishingly, within weeks the repercussions of this tragic spectacle advanced to the very gates of the presidential palace, bringing down Tunisia's longtime strongman Zine El Abidine Ben Ali. Seasoned Middle East observers, myself included, would never have predicted that the seemingly stable police state of Tunisia would be the first place to provide the actual spark for a region-wide conflagration of popular uprisings, one that brought about the collapse of four entrenched Arab dictators within eight months in Tunisia, Egypt, Libya and Yemen.

And the process hardly ended there. Regimes were left teetering in Syria and Bahrain. The whiff of radical change sent leaders in Morocco and Jordan scurrying to implement cosmetic changes. Mali was sucked into the chain reaction of Libyan events and collapsed into the chaos radiating around the region. Algeria grew fearful. And the Kingdom of Saudi Arabia itself showed signs of panic at the prospect of popular change that might shake the rule of the al-Saud; the Saudi king reacted by hastily bestowing a broad range of carrots—as well as brandishing a few more sticks—as countermeasures. And of course two American-led wars had toppled regimes in Iraq and Afghanistan in decade-long struggles whose repercussions are not remotely over in the region. And though Washington's mantra throughout was "ending global terrorism," global jihadis in fact picked themselves up, dusted themselves off despite their setbacks in Afghanistan and the death of their guru Osama Bin Laden, and regrouped to carry out the struggle in new theaters of action across the Middle East.

The western press quickly dubbed these Arab events the "Arab Spring," in reference to earlier popular democratic uprising in some other countries of the world. But "spring" suggests an inevitable cycle of seasons that ends in winter again. Nor does that term accurately predict where these movements are going over the long run. I much prefer the term "Arab Awakening" but the image of spring has been widely accepted in the popular media. Whatever we term it, the Arab Spring unleashed the most significant series of events since the wave of Arab nationalist movements that swept the Arab world in the 1960s. Those events had witnessed the collapse of an earlier generation of traditional monarchical regimes, many closely tied to British and French colonial power.

If the explosive drama of these Arab events caught the world by surprise, it overshadowed another quieter, longer, more gradual but deeper transformation right on the Arab doorstep: the emergence of Turkey as a major regional power. There, bold change transformed the country politically, socially, culturally, and economically over the course of the last quarter century, and even more intensely in the first decade of the 21st century. Its major domestic and foreign policy changes, particularly in the realm of political Islam, are one of the major themes of this book. And they have deep implications for the rest of the whole Muslim world.

These quieter developments in Turkey over the past decade actually far surpass in importance the events of the Arab world—which have been dramatic but have yet to fulfill their promise. And who could fail to note a significant relationship between the Turkish accomplishments of the past decade and the frustrated aspirations revealed in the more recent Arab Spring?

Turkey was not the immediate spark of the Arab Spring, but it offered the Middle East a vivid example of successful change unfolding in a nearby Muslim country. Turkey's emergence opened new perspectives, horizons and hopes to aspiring Arab populations who call for change. Turkey's ruling Justice and Development Party (*Adalet ve Kalkınma Partisi*, AKP) which oversaw the country's remarkable evolution was the essential driver of both domestic and foreign policy change. But after a spectacular decade in power by 2012 the AKP finally began to show signs of serious attrition. A party with Islamist roots, it has been in power longer than any elected party in Turkish history. Even as the party reaches a point of inevitable exhaustion and faces severe weakening if not defeat in new elections, its track record in power has been extraordinary. Its legacy is already powerful and enduring both at home and abroad. Turkey has changed irrevocably. The decline of the party, as is often the case with most successful parties that eventually lose their magic, began to spark major domestic political crises. But those crises, however messy, will almost certainly be resolved through existing democratic institutions—something that cannot be said of the governance of most countries of the world.

Thus, in both the AKP's successes and in its eventual decline and political defeat, Turkey is a bellwether. It has come to command serious attention and genuine respect across the Middle East since the advent of its new government in 2002. Ankara went on to become deeply engaged in Arab affairs in ways few would have predicted a decade ago. Equally important, Turkey's profile and reputation in the West also changed dramatically. It is an irony, but it is an independent-minded Turkey, no longer willing to define itself as just a "western ally," that commands more respect and attention in the West than at any time in history. A case can also be made, in one sense, that the roots of the Arab Awakening lie in the Turkish example; Turkey is the first country in the Middle East to achieve the goals now sought in the popular uprisings against autocracy in the Arab world. It is the first country that recreated its historical identity and reshaped public views and goals via democratic process against the weight of decades—even centuries—of a European- or American-based global order dominating the Middle East.

In this book I argue that Turkish trajectory of change is path-breaking for the Muslim world as a whole. Turkey cannot be the leader of the Arab world in any formal sense, but it is in reality leading the pack in terms of change in many vital respects. That experience cannot fail to have major influence on other Muslim states—and perhaps beyond. That, and not the messy final waning of the AKP's political power and skills, will be the criterion by which history will judge it.

The West naturally tends to look at Turkey through a western optic. Perhaps less well known to westerners is that Turkey in many ways is as much part of Asia as it is of Europe. Turkey's language and ethnic roots are quite Asian, originating in the vast high plateaus of eastern Siberia. The Turkish language is more akin in structure and syntax to Japanese than it is to Arabic, Persian, or European languages. Nor should we forget that the Ottoman Empire, with its capital in Istanbul, was the largest and longest-lasting Muslim empire in the world, its influence radiating out to Asia as well as to the Middle East and the Balkans. It was one of the last great multinational empires of the world—until its collapse at the end of World War I.

A significant part of this book's analysis is oriented towards Turkey. It looks at the new complex interaction between Turkey and the ongoing events in the Arab world and the region—an experience quite new to modern Turkey. Westerners have never known exactly where to place Turkey: as a member of NATO is it a western state? Or, being Muslim, is it part of the Middle East? Or something unique to itself? There are indeed some reasons to consider Turkey as part of the West. But such a view is limited and misleading. Turkey is much more than a western country. It is also a Middle Eastern country, a Balkan country, a Mediterranean country, a Black Sea country, a Caucasian country, and a Eurasian country, now with expanding interests in Africa and Latin America. More to the point, it now *conceives of itself* in these terms, as a state with increasing global involvement—something it has never done since the collapse of the Ottoman Empire, its forerunner. What is the relevance of this Turkish experience to the future of *leadership* in the Middle East: what does regional leadership mean at this juncture of the Middle East in the 21st century? Does the region constitute a coherent cultural and geopolitical region of its own? What has leadership traditionally looked like in the Middle East? Is it still linked with Islam, with nationalism, or both? And can we find clues in past centuries that suggest potential trajectories in the emergence of a "new" Muslim world?

The Turkish experience is immediately relevant to these developments. Since coming to power in 2002 the AKP introduced bold new initiatives across a broad range: unprecedented new ties with neighbors, the opening up and quadrupling of the economy, the doubling of the national income of its citizens, major expansion of its diplomatic and economic ties into Asia, Africa, and Latin America, the taming of the military in its interference in civilian politics, the adoption of a more progressive vision of the role of Islam in society, efforts to establish a regional Muslim identity, aspirations for the shaping of a new Middle East/Asian order, a new dogged independence in foreign policy thinking, a spread of Turkish soft power in the Middle East, an active involvement in a broad range of contemporary global issues, a deepening of democratic participation in the state, significant milestones towards the solution of the burning domestic Kurdish issue, and the gaining of new regional respect. Turkey has done a lot right, much of the world is watching, and most of the rest of the Middle East is envious.

The Turkish experience suddenly took on new relevance with the Arab Spring. Those events, quite unanticipated, confronted Ankara with new problems, unpalatable choices and perhaps even caused it to overreach. As Arab events spun out of control greater domestic anxiety emerged back home in Turkey over the degree of Turkish involvement in these messy new events. And in the Middle East not all Arab regimes are now happy with Turkey's new activism. Nonetheless the Turkish experience still speaks directly to the *people* of the region and their struggles for political and economic progress. Today both Arabs and Turks mutually influence each other in shared aspirations and the creation of a new regional consciousness—with global implications.

As if that were not enough, all these events took place against an even more momentous backdrop—a fundamental shift in the character and structure of the entire global political order. We have witnessed a decisive decline of American power and influence, accompanied by the weakening, timidity, and new introspection of the European Union as a coherent international player, the rise of Chinese power, and the simultaneous emergence of new regional powers of the G-20 that includes the BRICs— Brazil, Russia, India as well as China. Turkey, now the 15th largest economy in the world, is part of that G-20 list of new medium powers. Its increasingly self-confident behavior reflects its new status.

The Arab Awakening also takes place after two to three centuries of anti-imperialist struggle within the Muslim world against western domination and control. That struggle, still unfinished, is one of key popular impulses at the heart of events—even if the "post-colonial" West does not fully perceive it. There is a growing self-consciousness within the *umma*—the community of world Muslims—of its own cultural distinctiveness. It is vividly aware that it has been at the receiving end of aggressive western power, starting sometime in the 16th or 17th century. Indeed, many—but by no means all—of the conditions that created the frozen Arab world can be traced back to the period of western imperial rule. The institutional, geopolitical, and emotional seeds planted at that time remain problematic today.

This, then, is the backdrop against which a Turkish Renaissance and the Arab Spring has taken place. Its repercussions are still emerging as the Middle East struggles to reinvent itself and to redefine its character in the new global environment. The geopolitics of the region are changing significantly; new powers, new leaders, new perspectives, revolution and counter-revolution, democratization and crushing of democracy, new rivalries, new fault lines and new tensions emerge. What is the nature of the Muslim identity or identities in all of this? How will Muslims demand to be governed? And what will be their global orientation in a more multi-cultural, multi-polar world? Although the Arab Spring may now be disappointing to many who hoped for a more sweeping and permanent shift towards democratization, the impact of events has already altered the mentality of the region, and cannot truly be reversed, even if temporarily suppressed. We are only at the beginning.

CHAPTER TWO
GLOBAL SHIFT OF POWER

If the peoples of the Middle East are struggling for domestic freedom against long-standing dictatorship, they are equally struggling for freedom from longtime external intervention, even domination. These struggles now take place in a new context: a global power shift. Western dominance over the greater East has receded further than ever before in over a century or more; the long western rise to global hegemony is reversing itself. A legacy of centuries of eastern ambivalence towards the West lies just beneath the surface of events—sometimes reflecting explicit anti-westernism. Arab nationalist movements, the emergence of political Islam, the role of a revolutionary Iran, the phenomenon of radical jihadi movements and terrorism in the name of Islam—all have partial roots in this legacy.

When the West speaks of the "rise of the East," today of course we think in the first instance of China. The burgeoning of Chinese economic, diplomatic, and military power in less than two decades is the single-most astonishing geopolitical event of the early 21st century. These changes are even more remarkable in light of China's last century—wracked with chaos, dogmatic, violent, and disastrous economic and social experiments pursued for years under Mao Zedong's catastrophic vision of communism. That experience with its social dislocations and deaths of tens of millions of people was in fact far worse than anything the Middle East has suffered. Now India, too, is a rising Asian power. Whether New Delhi's sprawling, decentralized, messy and creative democratic order is superior to the Chinese top-down, hybrid authoritarian system has yet to be proven. But these two eastern powers will eclipse the West economically in another decade or so. And economic power breeds geopolitical influence. New groupings of states now look to shape a new, alternative world order that differs from the one conceived and designed by the United States over the last century.

The rise of new economic powers sets the world on a slow but firm path towards greater convergence in standard of living—a phenomenon that bears long-term political implications as well. As the *Financial Times* noted:

> This convergence should not surprise us. Poorer countries are correcting the huge divergence in incomes that occurred at the start of the industrial revolution when western economies made unprecedented strides in productivity. That was an aberration, albeit one that lasted nearly 200 years. For a neutral observer who wishes the

greatest well-being for the greatest number of people, the reversal of that trend is good news. [1]

And in March 2013 the United Nations Development Programme in an annual report observed:

> For the first time in 150 years, the combined output of the developing world's three leading economies, Brazil, China and India, is about equal to the combined GDP of the longstanding industrial powers of the North—Canada, France, Germany, Italy, United Kingdom and the United States. This represents a dramatic rebalancing of global economic power. [2]

The Nature of Anti-Westernism

The character of anti-westernism has also shifted over time. The last centuries of the non-western world have mostly narrated the story of struggle for national independence from the West and a search for restoration of pride and dignity of formerly weak states in the international order. "Independence" is of course a relative term. While most countries under colonial control eventually were able to gain nominal political independence from their former masters in the 20th century, their newly acquired independence was not all that they hoped it would be. In colony after colony, the former colonial power established political and economic infrastructures that enabled it to exert continuing major influence over the former colony. Local ruling elites were often dependent upon ties with the metropole; the metropole could at any time manipulate vital economic links to which the new state was acutely vulnerable. Continuing political and military intervention by the metropole into its former colonies was commonplace; indeed, western intervention in one form or another has scarcely ceased even today in economic, political, and even military terms.

The history and character of colonialization and imperial domination was not just a tale of purely negative exploitation. The colonized also benefited from the colonizer—the introduction of new technologies in exploitation of raw materials, techniques of industrial and agricultural production, transportation and road infrastructures, modern administrative techniques, modern educational systems and improved health systems. Horizons were broadened as select native elite traveled to the metropole for higher education and training. But in the end, investments in the colony were naturally dictated by the needs of the metropole itself. The colony was perceived as an organic and complementary appendage to the metropole's own larger economy; the metropole was not interested in the overall integrated economic development of the colony on its own. This experience usually led to quite skewed developmental profiles in the developing world. And it hindered the *orga*, development of these states in accordance with their own histories and cultures.

The negative and destructive sides of colonialism are also well known: distortion of the colonial economy to meet metropole needs; frequent recourse to divide-and-rule techniques that pitted sectarian or ethnic groups against each other; this left a legacy of rivalries and resentments still evident in regional strife today. Particularly problematic was the phenomenon of ruling *minorities* placed in power by the metropole for better control. Reversal of those minoritarian orders still wreaks havoc in so many Middle Eastern countries such as in Iraq, Bahrain, Syria and elsewhere. Sometimes when the language of the European metropole was adopted as the language of the elite, it separated and isolated the elite from the majority of the population that retained their native language: the French-speaking elite of Algeria is a classic case of an ongoing cultural and social fracture of Algerian culture and society—between French-speaking and Arabic-speaking classes.

Traditional institutions of education, religion, law and social reconciliation were often suppressed or allowed to atrophy under the colonial West rather than to develop and evolve organically into the modern age; frequently the newly imposed western institutions, not being organically rooted in the country, did not function effectively. International borders were redrawn wholesale as arbitrary new political states were established, destroying old patterns of social and economic intercourse and creating new crises of identity. Raw materials, especially oil, were controlled and monopolized by the metropole until the newly independent countries demanded control over them, often meeting strong resistance from the metropole in the process. Most of these countries were dragged unwillingly into western war projects including World War I, World War II, and the Cold War. These societies perceived the urgent need to rethink and reinvent themselves in the modern period. As a result, issues of national identity and national dignity matter a lot in their modernization quest. These concepts may seem abstract to westerners, but they represent key psychological sources of anti-westernism that emerge out of decades, even centuries of settings where the powerful foreigner dominated the weak natives.

Ottoman Views of European Power and Modernization
As European economic, political and military power increasingly threatened them, Muslims were compelled to address an urgent question: what was the "secret" of western power and strength? Was this an acknowledgment that

ivilization had finally become superior to eastern? It is fascinating
t the Ottoman elite had no problem in accepting the idea of the
of the West—but only as a *temporary and transient phenomenon*.
Indeed, the Ottomans were even willing to acknowledge that the West had
been the first to discover and develop certain universal principles relating to
the development and institutionalization of power. Western attainments
represented merely the winning of a race, reaching the goal post first. In their
view these western skills and techniques were learnable and transferable. For
many Muslims the task seemed merely a matter of learning and reproducing
the western "hardware" of power; less thought was devoted to whether there
was an accompanying civilizational "software" in the West that also required
mastering.

Thus the Ottomans accepted the reality of their temporary weakness, but
did not accept any *inherent* western superiority. According to scholar Ussama
Makdisi, the Ottomans perceived themselves as situated somewhere along a
continuum of development in which Europe was more advanced than the
Ottomans; but in turn, the Ottoman elite was well ahead of other still less
developed segments of the Empire, both Christian and Muslim, and especially
many Arab regions. In this sense, the Ottoman Empire perceived itself as a
kind of conveyor belt of modernization to the less developed areas of the
Empire, or even to other parts of the Muslim world outside the Empire. [3]

At the same time Ottoman thinkers emphatically rejected the concept that
the West's temporary superiority provided any justification for its domination
or imperial control over the Muslim world.

> To modernize the empire, and to make it "the free and progressive
> America of the East," required a massive project of imperial reform
> that could reform state and society at all levels. This began during the
> Tanzimat [reforms] (1839–1876, literally the "ordering" of the empire),
> a period when the Ottoman state sought to redefine itself as more
> than an Islamic dynasty, [but] as a modern, bureaucratic, and tolerant
> state—a partner of the West rather than its adversary. [4]

But there was a proviso here in Ottoman acceptance of European claims of
establishing "universal" concepts of civilization and modernity: it meant that
these proclaimed values of liberty, equality, and rule of law must likewise apply
to *European treatment of the East*. This theme runs deep in Turkish thinking even
today. It is also an important theme in the broader thinking of the Arab world
and in nearly all developing countries that have struggled against western
domination. European *values* are acknowledged and for the most part admired.
But if they are truly universal, these values must apply to the West's own
behavior vis-à-vis others as well, especially in foreign policy.

Cemil Aydın sets forth the deeper context of this intellectual confrontation in his book *The Politics of Anti-Westernism in Asia*; he observes that the West's *behavior* did not reflect adherence to universal values. On the contrary, western power devolved into a racism and arrogance towards the rest of the world that undercut its own thesis. Asian reformers in both the Ottoman Empire and in early 20th-century Japan sought out what was "truly universal" in the features of the western experience, whereas the West increasingly viewed its own "universal values" as the product of western civilizational superiority, granting it the right to exercise its dominant power over others. In this sense the East became more universal in its acceptance of these values and demand for their *global* application than the West did itself. These tensions continue down to today in the "civilizing mission" of Washington and the West in imposing regime change and overturning of "rogue" regimes in the developing world that do not comply with the western order that it claims is "universal."

It was this gap—between a western *vision* of its civilizing mission as opposed to the *reality* of its imposed western imperial order—that ultimately created an Asian quest for "alternative visions of pan-Islamic and pan-Asian thought." [5] These two bodies of thought represented Asian attempts to create its own "universal order" to challenge the western. Indeed, both the Japanese and Ottomans were intrigued by each other's alternative civilizational vehicles. The triumphant military victory of Japan over Russia in the 1904-05 Russo-Japanese war marked the rise of Asia, its first victory over a western power, and the demolition of the idea that imperial power was a uniquely western project.

Here we have the roots, then, of a more emotional debate that is still ongoing, especially prominent after 9/11 when most Muslims insisted in effect, "we don't hate your values, we hate your policies. We want your values to apply to *your treatment of us*." Or, as other Muslims have said, "Your 9/11 has been our 24/7." These views represent a sharp and ongoing rejection of western double standards—a charge regularly leveled against the West by most developing nations today, including China.

Today, as the Arab Awakening unfolds, the West has comfortably assumed that it's all about a struggle of Middle Eastern peoples for "freedom" against their own rulers and a desire to emulate western ideals. Western fascination with Facebook, Twitter and other social media in the Arab Spring should not conceal the reality that for the people of the region, "freedom" also entails *freedom from western control and dominance*. It's about the gradual restoration of power back to the non-western parts of the world, many of them cradles of ancient civilizations in their own right. We see a demand by these states and societies to be treated with dignity and equality as significant players again on the world scene. Not surprisingly, we also see western discomfiture in watching its own former dominance and hegemony fade. While the United States speculates on the problems of dealing with a *rising* power on the international scene like China, from a Chinese perspective in looking at the US the issue is how to handle the problems of a *declining* power and the challenges and risks entailed in its behavior.

One century after the Russo-Japanese war we see a parallel in the rise of China, rapidly rivaling American and European economic and global influence. This phenomenon is gratifying to the non-western world in that it signals a decisive rise of non-western powers onto the global power scene. These powers are forcing open the international game. Turkey is one of those players.

Turkey's Place in the Shift

The emergence of a confident, fully sovereign and independent-minded Turkey fits into this same broad pattern. Turkey is a country that struggled to rise from the ashes of Ottoman imperial defeat at the end of World War I to found a new modern state and identity. To put it in bumper-sticker form, this is about the "return of history" in the Middle East—of an eastern tradition of power that had been put into cold storage by a more powerful West for many centuries. Now we see the gradual restoration of a more "normal" state of global geopolitics whose previous existence may have faded from our shorter-term western historical memories. By "normal" I mean an age in which power and influence is more evenly distributed around the world. Turkey, in the form of the Ottoman Empire, once acted on a global stage for long centuries, but modern Turkey has only quite recently started figuring prominently as an independent player in anyone's geopolitical thinking.

For the West, and especially Washington, it seems very difficult to accept this shift away from its once comfortable and dominant world order. Washington's frustrations with Turkey have provoked many quickie and superficial pseudo-analyses that pose such questions as, what is "wrong" with Turkey that it now behaves this way? Or why has Turkey "become an adversary?" Or, "Islam must be the source of the problem now that Turkey is led by a party of Islamist background." Or, "what elements should we in the West support within Turkish politics that will right this situation?" All these questions have been commonplace in Washington over the past decade. They are equally condescending to the cultures and states that are carving out new geopolitical space for their own historical reasons—and setting the US on a potential collision course with them unless it understands the new realities.

Ambivalence about the West

Yet, for all the understandable Muslim pushback against western imperial power and interventionism, the last two centuries also demonstrate massive Muslim *ambivalence* towards the West. The Muslim world sees both a Jekyll and Hyde character to the western venture and the process of westernization.

Actually, what does the word "westernization" really mean? Muslims for long centuries had been confident in the *reality* of their own cultural superiority. They had received first-hand impressions of the Frankish invaders during the Crusades and remained generally unimpressed; they felt there was little to be learned from them. But in succeeding centuries—while Muslims demonstrated little interest in the West—the balance of power and technology between the two sides began to shift. They failed to perceive the tipping point in western history—when the West began to surpass Muslim civilization. By then it was too late, for the Muslim world, China or Japan to escape becoming the targets of Western power.

How could Muslims defend themselves against this mighty new phenomenon? A complex process we like to call "westernization" began in different parts of the developing world in various ways. But what was its actual nature? When non-western peoples looked to adopt some features of the West, it wasn't so much to assume some kind of western lifestyle; it was more a quest to discover the *secret* of western power. It was driven, in the first instance, by the urgent need for self-defense, to fend off encroachments of western imperialism. Modernization meant power. The goal was not to *be* the West, but to *have* what the West had. The burning question was, how much traditional local culture and traditions would have to be sacrificed to attain those goals?

Muslims weren't alone in thinking this way. These ideas also drove reformers and modernizers in Latin America, China and especially in 19th-century Meiji Japan, that pursued its own quite distinctive form of modernization while still preserving its Japanese character. China today speaks of "modernization with a Chinese face." At the time, of course, the West represented the only existing model of modernization. Westerners flattered themselves in the belief that these efforts at modernization in the non-western world showed that "they wanted to be like us." But in reality they didn't want to be like us, they wanted to be *powerful like us*. It's really all about a *defensive* process, a form of nationalism, a quest for the most efficient means to match the West's success in order to fend off the West, develop productive societies on their own, and to reduce dependency upon outsiders for national security. If we in the West don't grasp this essential point, we misread much of the history of "westernization" in the Muslim world. Today most of them still don't want to *be* us and they don't trust us. They admire western technology and standards of living. They admire many (but not all) western values as seen in western *domestic* life, but they detest the policies they see projected in western *foreign* policies that have taken the lives of many millions of non-westerners as the West imposed its new international order—and it's still not over.

Yet, astonishingly, we in the West still generally assume that our own civilization is essentially benign, even providing a kind of public good for the world—technology, ideas, institutions and a political-economic order that the rest of the world needs and should gratefully receive. But we are relatively myopic if we accept such a view as the whole story. There is no doubt that in the modern era the West has achieved extraordinary heights of civilizational and technological advance as well as unparalleled economic and military power—enough power to impose its views on most of the rest of the world. Much of the world has indeed profited from many of these advances. But that doesn't mean it represents a world order that most people want imposed upon them. Non-westerners admire western democratic institutions, but these values are often exported at gun-point and for self-serving reasons. When asked once what he thought of western civilization, the renowned anti-British Indian resistance leader and pacifist Mahatma Gandhi famously replied, "I think it would be a good idea." A wisecrack to be sure, but what are the impulses that lie behind his remark?

The history of the non-western world has largely been officially written by westerners over the past many hundreds of years. Victors generally get to determine the way history is written. Even in the Muslim world itself, Muslim academicians for long decades over the past century depended upon western scholarship—some excellent, some not so good—to learn and understand their own history. Today all that is changing. Look at the departments of Middle Eastern or Asian history in the West now and you'll find growing numbers of academics who are non-western. They are exploring their own histories—using modern techniques of scholarship—usually with far greater knowledge of languages, culture and attitudes than earlier western scholars. Not surprisingly, these scholars from the developing world bring new perspective to these histories that are now no longer told from the traditional western perspective.

It is painful for the West to acknowledge this new shift in the equilibrium of power away from the West—indeed many are in denial. But the realities are there, and both sides are starting a long slow process of accommodation. These are among the active themes in the emergence of the new Middle East in the first and second decades of the 21st century. They cannot be ignored.

Middle East Leadership

Leadership of what? The term "Middle East" itself is of British colonial origin from the 19th century and it's culturally revealing. It's now time-honored, but it's never been a very satisfactory term; above all it is very eurocentric—east of what? Middle of what? Nonetheless the term has been fully absorbed into Arabic, Turkish and Persian culture and linguistic usage with few other real alternatives in use. The more recent, colorless, but more geographically accurate term "South-West Asia" is not likely to gain much purchase anywhere except among academics and Pentagon planners. But whatever the term, what does it really mean?

In essence the term denotes a region primarily distinguished by its Muslim culture and religion and therefore distinct from the West. Muslims have from very early on been aware of their membership in a collective Islamic culture and community known as the *umma*. But how long will the Muslim world remain a self-consciously coherent place? There are two possible trends here. One is that the Middle East state system with time will grow accustomed to, and even comfortable with its colonial borders; the new "national" identities as established by imperialism within them will take firm hold. In this model, states of the Middle East ultimately come to resemble states in the West, with only a touch of regional character. An alternative trend is that the region will maintain an intensity of Muslim identity that will possess strong *supranational* character.

In my mind there is little doubt that a self-conscious sense of Muslim identity remains powerful. It will define the area as a distinct culture. Yes, Arab nationalism has in the 20th century been a partial rival to the Islamic identity, but only partially. And anyway, Arab nationalism contains within it elements of "Islamic nationalism" as well (see Chapter 14). There is no longer a contradiction between the terms "Arab" and "Muslim" any more than there is a contradiction between "French" and "western."

This book posits that a keen sense of Middle East identity will persist; ironically it has now been much fortified by the US Global War on Terror and western Islamophobia in which Muslims feel cornered. The question is how inclusive will that Muslim identity be in geographical and even ethnic terms?

These are competing elements of sub-identities within the Islamic world. Even Arab Christians often describe themselves as "Christian by religion but Muslim by culture," by dint of living, speaking Arabic, and sharing life in the Muslim world. And if the region retains a strong sense of identity that transcends narrow identification with the individual states, questions of regional leadership arise. Who will contribute to, or drive this leadership? And what kind of leadership will it be? And what will constitute its geographic scope?

PART TWO: LEADERSHIP IN THE MUSLIM WORLD - WHAT IS IT?

Today the Middle East presents a striking vacuum of leadership. A key theme of this book is what kind of leadership(s) Muslims feel they need and where it is most likely to come from, both domestically and internationally. It's revealing to look back at how Muslims tended to think about leadership in the past, and what kinds of institutions they accepted as constituting leadership.

For most of Middle Eastern history it was religious affiliation, and not ethnicity, that characterized the foundation of community—legal communal entities—within empire. Sometimes the two overlapped. As Israeli scholar and statesman Uri Avnery puts it:

> Two thousand years ago, the modern idea of "nation" was unthinkable. The prevalent collective structure was the ethnic-religious community. One belonged to a community that was not territorially defined. A Jewish man in Alexandria could marry a Jewess in Babylon, but not the Hellenic or Christian woman next door. Under Roman, Byzantine and Ottoman emperors, all these dozens of sects enjoyed a wide autonomy, ruled by imams, priests and rabbis. This is still partly the case in most former Ottoman territories, including Israel. The Turks called these self-governing sects "millets". [1]

Similarly in the West, people for nearly two millennia possessed a sense of being part of a grand entity called "Christendom" within which tribes and communities also asserted more local identities as well. At the highest level it was overseen by a pope who engaged in ongoing struggles with local principalities and kingdoms. In the East the global Muslim community too, conceived of itself as ideally constituting a single religious community or *umma* that needed to be protected. Renaissance Italy too, was at least as much driven by Church politics as by secular power. Christians fought for leadership of Christendom—both the papacy and kingships.

Against this background we look over the next two chapters at two different approaches to leadership over the past thousand years in the Middle East: religious and ethnic. The religious approach is represented by the Ottoman Empire, the last, largest and most important empire in Muslim history. The ethnic approach to community and state is a far more modern invention, and represents a narrower view of leadership in the Middle East, typified most prominently by Turkish and Persian ethnicity and, above all, by the transnational Arab nationalist movement. These two types of claim to leadership authority—religious and ethnic—continue to compete in the Middle East. But they are not always mutually exclusive and each one carries broader implications for the Muslim World as a whole.

CHAPTER THREE

CALIPHATE AND UNITY: OTTOMANS AND THE

MIDDLE EAST WORLD VIEW

For the first time in a century, Turkey is returning to a role of active membership and direct participation in the Muslim world. At the same time, issues of Middle East leadership have become more pronounced with the slow re-emergence of more sovereign Arab states with the gradual retreat of western domination and interference. Today we can see certain concepts of the Turkish Ottoman past returning in new form to affect Turkey's active new role within the Muslim world. Meanwhile, the Arab world stills struggles with what it means to be "Arab" within the context of quite artificial states that evoke mixed loyalty.

"The past is prologue" is a cliché, but no less true for all that. The Ottoman Empire was a vast world in both geography and time span. It set an indelible mark upon all regions within the Empire, and most of all upon the Turkish heartland. Certain continuities from the past are more strikingly evident in today's Turkish thinking of the 21st century than they were a century before; these are the elements that make Turkey's recent history more understandable—even predictable. Turkey is engaged in a historic return to the Middle East, or, as its Foreign Minister Ahmet Davutoğlu puts it, Turkey and the region are experiencing "the return of history." But this time it is not as some kind of new Turkish hegemon or imperial power, but rather as a new significant player that can offer a valuable body of experience in modern governance, and even serve as a certain inspiration in a newly evolving Middle East equation. This effect of inspiration is usually more powerful upon populations than upon regimes, many of whom feel threatened by Turkey's liberal agenda.

The Ottoman Empire was the bedrock, the embodiment of the Muslim *umma* for centuries. It was within the Ottoman Empire that the history of most of the peoples of the Middle East unfolded, directly or indirectly, over the last 500 years. The Ottoman sphere of control and influence ranged from the Balkans, the Levant and Iraq, to Egypt, North Africa and large parts of the Arabian Peninsula. Indirectly, the Caucasus, Iran, Afghanistan, Central Asia and South Asia formed part of this broader regional system where Ottoman ideas and actions mattered. Just below the surface lie certain elements of a cultural continuum, an age of shared Muslim history. This is why we often hear facile description of the new Turkish role in the Middle East as "neo-Ottomanism." But even as Ankara rejects this simplistic interpretation of its policies, the legacy and impact of the Ottoman world in molding the thinking of the contemporary Middle East persist. The past offers clues about how a new Middle Eastern geopolitical order might interact.

It's not that people in the region today want to go back to the Ottoman Empire—they do not. They possess negative as well as positive memories of being part of a greater Muslim Ottoman empire—its bad features as well as good. The present re-emergence of Turkey as a new (old) player in the region generates differing reactions across today's Middle East power system. In some ways it is welcomed, in other respects its motives are not fully trusted. It will take time for the role of this new player to be re-integrated into regional politics. But all ethnic elements of the region—Turks, Arabs, Persians, Kurds, Berbers and others—are part of this complex new process of self-reassessment.

The Ottoman vision conceived of the region as an Islamic world—distinct from the West. The Ottoman Empire lay at the center of the *umma*'s consciousness, identity, and even source of defense and self-preservation in the face of western invaders. Interestingly, the Ottoman Empire never called itself an Ottoman *Islamic* empire; "Islamic" was a given. The addition of "Islamic" to the names of various republics and monarchies in the Muslim world today is actually quite recent. Today the use of the title "Islamic" represents more an assertion of identity and a political claim than a statement of the culturally obvious. It was often the West, through its invasions and conquests, that more sharply drew the cultural lines between "us" and "them" in imposing its power and control over the Muslim world. The East was forced to accept the West, often at gun-point. That paradigm has not yet altogether disappeared even today in western strategic thinking.

What was the outlook of the Ottoman world? The Ottomans were of course preceded by many earlier Arab Muslim dynasties or caliphates—Umayyads, Abbasids, Fatimids, as well as Persian Safavids, Indian Moguls, and other regional empires. Still, the Ottoman was the largest and the longest-lived Muslim empire, and, by dint of geographical proximity, the one with the most intense interaction with the West. Islam and Islamic culture was the organizing principle of the Ottoman Empire under the direction of the Ottoman Sultan and Caliph. So the office of the caliph (the caliphate) had much significance in the Muslim world view—even for Shi'ite Muslims. The caliphate was the office accorded the greatest degree of respect within an Islamic order; it signified religious leadership rather than naked political power.

Yet ironically today the concept of an Islamic caliphate seems to evoke irrational fear, near hysteria and invective in the West. Top Fox News Network commentator Glenn Beck spoke of a possible "Ancient Babylon" in Iraq emerging as a new seat of evil and the center of the new caliphate. "When I say that there's a caliphate, that it is a desire of the Islamic extremists in the Middle East, that is not a conspiracy theory," he said. "They want a caliphate."[1] President George W. Bush himself spoke of extremists seeking resurrection of an Islamic caliphate "with greater economic and military and political power . . . able to advance their stated agenda: to develop weapons of mass destruction . . . destroy Israel . . . intimidate Europe . . . assault the American people . . . and blackmail our government into isolation."[2] Donald Rumsfeld stated in Feb 2011: "We are up against a vicious enemy, the radical Islamists are there, they intend to try to create a caliphate in this world and fundamentally alter the nature of nation states". A few weeks after an Indonesian Khilafah (caliphate) conference took place in 2007 in Jakarta, George W. Bush vowed to fight those who seek to re-establish the caliphate. He spoke of America being "engaged in a great ideological struggle—fighting Islamic extremists across the globe." He went on to define these extremists as those who "hope to impose that same dark vision across the Middle East by raising up a violent and radical caliphate that spans from Spain to Indonesia."

There is a good bit going on here between the lines. Washington, like many great powers, maintains a basic antipathy to any form of broad political unity anywhere else on the globe that might rival or limit the unrestricted freedom of American action as a global hegemonic power. For Europe too, the idea of a caliphate has been disconcerting, part of a general atavistic fear inherited from Europe's millennium-long perception of Islam as the "Other," the closest political, religious, and military rival to Christianity for well over a thousand years. That fear includes Europe's contemporary anxieties over problematic Muslim immigration and concerns over imported terrorism. And during the 19th century the British quite explicitly viewed Islamic unity as the primary threat to the maintenance of the British Empire in India and other parts of Asia. So the term "caliphate" seems laden, in both historical as well as contemporary terms, with the idea of *rival power* in the East. The modern adoption of the concept by violent radicals has made the situation worse. Yet the concept of *some kind* of appropriate Muslim community organization remains a meaningful aspiration for large numbers of Muslims.

Who's Afraid of the Caliphate?

On 3 March 1924, one of the most symbolically laden events in the history of the Muslim world took place. The venue was Ankara, the new capital of the recently founded Turkish Republic. On that fateful date, Turkish law-makers filed into the Grand National Assembly and, in solemn ceremony, proceeded to vote for the abolition of the Islamic caliphate—an institution with some 1,300 years of history behind it—and that for the last 500 years had been based in Istanbul. Atatürk was determined to turn his back on the past, on the Empire and all its Islamic offices and trappings in order to build a modern westernized state that could develop entirely western instruments of state power. And so the next day, as a result of the vote, the last Ottoman caliph, Abdulmajid II, boarded a ship in Istanbul with his family and quietly set off into exile, to die in Paris 20 years later—his body, symbolically, to be buried in Medina, Saudi Arabia. The caliphate had ceased to be and, for Turkey at least, the issue was all over. But the Muslim World was sent reeling with the news of the abolition; the implications and ripples were widely felt for a long time to come.

It may be difficult for westerners to quite grasp the psychological import of such an act. The caliphate is, after all, for westerners an exotic concept, poorly understood, and Islamic unity perhaps an object of fear. Today the term caliphate is still invoked in the radical programs of numerous Muslim extremist groups, both violent and non-violent. In mirror image, the term is also exploited in the West by Islamophobic groups to strike fear and to warn of some kind of an impending Islamic takeover of the West by fanatics.

To understand the impact of the abolition of the caliphate upon Muslims we might draw a western parallel: What if the prime minister of Italy were to get up one morning and decide to abolish the papacy as an outmoded and scandal-ridden institution in Italy? Whatever that might mean within Italy, it would surely spark a severe reaction across all the rest of the vast Catholic world: world Catholicism, after all, would not have even been consulted on the matter but would have much to say about it. Catholicism does not belong to Italy, nor did Islam belong to Turkey. And that was precisely the reaction of the rest of the Muslim world: the shock that the "eternal" symbolic role of leadership of the entire Muslim world, through legal fiat in just one Muslim country, had ceased to exist.

For the Arabs in particular, this was just one major event in a series of devastating moments that came with the end of World War I. When the Ottoman Empire fell before Allied European armies, the lands of the Arabs were suddenly cut loose and left on their own. But rather than achieving independence as they hoped, they were summarily taken over as new possessions ("mandates") of European imperial states for several more decades, some until well after World War II. Only Turkish Anatolia itself was able to fight off the imperial intentions of the Allied military powers and to eventually establish a new Turkish Republic—in defiance of western designs.

But what was this institution of the caliphate in reality, and why does the term still have some resonance—at least cultural and sentimental—among many Muslims today? "Caliph" or *khalifa* in Arabic, simply means "successor," designating the individual selected to succeed the Prophet Muhammad—not as prophet, but as leader of the newly established community of Muslims. The first four caliphs were traditionally reported to be selected on the criterion of being pious, wise, and upright individuals. Three of the first four (Orthodox) caliphs died violent deaths in early political struggles. But after the murder of the fourth caliph 'Ali (the son-in-law of the prophet), the caliphate fell into the hands of a military dynasty in Damascus and was promptly transformed into a hereditary office determined by military power. Nonetheless, the office persisted throughout most periods of Islamic history, with the caliphate—sometimes contested, sometimes even non-functioning—still bearing the symbolic power of leader of the *umma*. And the office was frequently combined with the de-facto secular rule of an emir, a sultan or a king. But even if the importance of the office waxed and waned over the centuries, one thing was in no doubt: if there was any one figure in the Muslim world who was regarded as its nominal leader, it was the caliph. He represented the single-most important figure in Islam, especially Sunni Islam.

Thus the caliphate is a revered office in Islamic culture. It is not mandated by the Qur'an, but it represents the *ideal* of an Islamic state—never fully attainable in practice, but a constant and worthy goal for believing Muslims. That ideal envisions unity of all Muslims within a just political and social community and within a strong and independent state based on God-given values—a Muslim version of the American "shining City upon the hill," if you will. Such a state represented a cherished ideal, especially in the face of military invasion and domination by the West in later years.

This phenomenon is perhaps mirrored in the dream of Christian leaders over the centuries of a unified Christendom as an ideal of religious aspiration. After all, the pope had been the single, supreme representative of western Christendom for a thousand years, until rejected by much of Europe in the Protestant Reformation. There is nothing unusual about this dream: nearly all religious communities strive towards greater unity, even ecumenicism, if it strengthens the community and its values.

Muslims always possessed a clear sense of an *umma*. One could travel the length and breadth of the Islamic world and find people familiar with Arabic, who could read the Qur'an, whose local languages contained large numbers of borrowed Arabic words on matters relating to law, philosophy, theology, literature, science and other cultural and intellectual issues. A visitor to most Muslim states would find familiar institutions, habits and customs widely shared across this cultural continuum as well as a deep consciousness of the extent and range of the *umma*. And this *umma* came together annually at the compelling experience of the Hajj, the pilgrimage, where Muslim pilgrims of diverse races, languages and states met with other Muslim pilgrims from all over the world in Mecca, dressed in an identical plain anonymous cotton robe on a basis of absolute equality before God.

In recent times, of course, the term caliphate has been given a more radical interpretation through its exploitation by a few radical and violent Islamic groups including al-Qaeda as a unifying symbol in their struggle against the West. But in the end, for many Muslims the caliphate has been symbolic of the *ideal of just and moral leadership* in the Muslim world. It goes to address the question of what kind of Muslim world Muslims want. And how should its governance and leadership (or leaderships) be structured? To what degree should Muslims work towards unity, and in what areas? Religious? Social? Cultural? Political? Legal? Institutional? How are Islamic traditions and values to be best reflected in society and governance? There may be no consensus, but the question remains valid among Muslim believers.

None of this suggests that Turkey is interested in restoring the caliphate today. Ankara would find the very suggestion ridiculous and irrelevant to its role in the modern world and its vision of contemporary foreign policy. But that does not mean that Turkey does not share with other Muslim states thoughts about how Muslim cooperation and the overall welfare and advancement of the Muslim world might be promoted over time. The question comes as naturally as it does to Europeans seeking to promote the concept of the civilization and well-being of Europe through the unity of the European Union. Or the Pan-American Union in Latin America, or the Organization of African Unity. Or the English-speaking Union, or the Organisation Internationale de la Francophonie with its 77 member states. Or international Catholic organizations, or the World Jewish Congress spread across 100 countries. At the heart of the issue is the *kind* of cooperation and unity to be achieved among Muslims and what its purpose should be.

Let there be no doubt about the argument I am making. There is no caliph today and the caliphate will almost surely never be restored by anybody, mainly due to the complexity of the task. Who would the caliph be? What would be his powers? Who would select him, and how would he be selected? By whose authority? By what mechanism—democratic vote? What would be his country of origin? What would be his authority over Muslims? How would he relate to secular heads of state in the many Muslim countries of the world? Over what range of issues would his writ extend? What would be his term of office? How could he be removed from office? How authoritative would his opinion be, and in whose eyes? How would non-Muslim states deal with him? These problems are not really resolvable nor is there much burning interest among Muslims today to settle them. But there are nonetheless meaningful impulses towards the *ideal* of some kind of greater Muslim unity and cooperation. Leadership *of some kind* in the Muslim world is still viewed by many Muslims as a vital missing ingredient for the strength, welfare and advancement of the Muslim world. But where is the model?

There can be many models, and many leaders. And model does not have to convey leadership. The only country that so far offers a credible, persuasive and meaningful model of overall success for Muslim governance in the modern world today is Turkey. But what kind of contribution is it? How is its contribution to the modern Muslim world viewed?

Leadership in the Muslim World and the Place of Islam
Nearly all Muslims today are engaged in a struggle for a more just, democratic and effective political and social order. But these questions don't emerge in a vacuum but as part of a search for a modern Muslim identity: what does it mean to be a Muslim in today's world? Muslims are not westerners nor do they seek to simply adopt and imitate western views of the social and cultural order. They seek to operate within their own evolving historical and cultural tradition. Indians, Chinese and Brazilians do no less. Identity and culture matter greatly as nations set themselves tasks for the future. And in the context of Muslim culture, what is the place of Islam in modern governance and society?

Turkey has been struggling with both these questions for nearly a century and its views have evolved dramatically. Over this period Turks have developed two differing, even contradictory, models of the relationship between Islam and governance. The first is the radical secular Kemalist model in which the state rigorously controls religion. The second model permits the state to take a far more permissive posture towards the role of Islam in public space, society and governance—reflecting majority opinion. Atatürk's decision to abolish the caliphate aimed at setting the country on a radically secular course in which Islam in public life was to be suppressed and "modernization" was imposed in a forced march. Religion would remain under strict state control, as under the Ottomans, but with one crucial difference: in the Ottoman state the caliph-sultan played a central role; Islamic institutions wielded great power in the political, social and economic arenas with their great foundations, land-holdings, social, medical and educational institutions. In the Turkey of Mustafa Kemal Atatürk, however, the political, social, cultural and legal role of Islam was perceived as a barrier to Turkish progress, a retrogressive force to be largely excluded from the public sphere. This concept of strict secularism goes back to the European Enlightenment with its newfound secular "faith" in rationalism and science; it was dominated by the French Revolutionary view of religion as a negative force to be controlled, contained and marginalized. Today Turkey still debates the question of the precise place of Islam in contemporary social, cultural and political life, even in the context of an officially secular order. Indeed, this issue remains central to a debate across the whole Muslim World.

Debate over the place of religion in governance and society today exists nearly everywhere, even in US politics. Again, the papacy offers a useful parallel for westerners, however imprecise. Most Catholics view the office of papacy as possessing great symbolic importance, even though the pope's word and writ may only be loosely followed, if at all. Yet the pope wields powerful symbolic attraction and regularly draws huge crowds around the world. This was reinforced in 2013 with the nearly unprecedented resignation of Pope Benedict XVI and the drama and theater surrounding the anointment of the new pope, Francis I. The proceedings received huge publicity and detailed coverage in all media as the various contenders from different countries with differing religious and ideological perspectives were considered and compared. The world followed the early statements and actions of Pope Francis with intense interest in a search for clues about his personality, style, and the likely policies he might pursue politically, socially, theologically, and even economically with the Vatican Bank. The whole world followed these deliberations, including a warning from Beijing that it would not accept papal meddling in the community of Roman Catholics and religion in China. The pope may hold no temporal power, but many countries of the world still maintain an ambassador attached to the Holy See, or Seat of the Roman Catholic Church. This is the best parallel by which to view the caliphate. And if the caliphate is gone, what other contemporary symbol of Muslim unity and leadership might there be? Certainly Saudi Arabia's custodianship of the Holy

Places of Mecca and Madina contains little religious resonance for Muslims towards the Saudi regime.

The Image of the Caliphate to the Muslim World

For Muslims, modern history has seemingly been cruel. The Muslim world once led in civilizational attainments—medicine, law, philosophy, science, and martial skills—for many centuries while Europe lay under the mantle of the Dark Ages before the Renaissance and the Enlightenment. And yet the Muslim world would soon lose its vitality, weaken and slowly fall in the face of European imperial power and control. This series of catastrophes sparked deep soul-searching among Muslims as to how and why this reversal of fortune had come about. How could Muslim power and glory be restored? The imperative of defending the Muslim world against western control became the dominant theme of the geopolitics between the West and the Muslim world over five centuries. It is still very much alive today. While some Muslims might dream of an ideal world in the future in which Islam would be accepted by all peoples everywhere, it is only a distant ideal, just as Christendom hoped—many still hope—for the spread of Christianity across the world and the return of Jesus Christ. The chief task of Muslims by the 15th century was no longer expansion, but *resistance* to western power—simple preservation of their own territories, independence, way of life, and the well-being of the *umma* itself. And their religious identity played a central role in play of international politics.

At this juncture in history the Ottoman Empire was the chief barrier to the global projection of western power into the Middle East. As western imperialism advanced deeper into Asia, Muslim rulers even *outside the Empire* whose territories were threatened turned to the Ottoman Caliphate for assistance. The largest group of Muslims anywhere was in India; indeed, there were more Muslims in the populous Indian Mughal Empire than there were in the Ottoman Empire. Yet the diverse and loosely allied Muslim princely states of the Mughal Empire were falling under British control. Although the Indian Muslim Mughal Empire was not part of the Ottoman Empire, Mughal ties with the Ottomans highlight the seriousness with which both sides took the position of caliph. As early as 1453, for example, Indian Muslim leaders were heartened by the news of the fall of Istanbul, the last bastion of the Byzantine Christian Empire, to Ottoman Muslim forces; they viewed it as a positive turn of events that strengthened the position of Islam in the East.

When the Ottoman sultan-caliph later assumed the title of Protector of the Two Holy Places of Mecca and Madina (in today's Saudi Arabia), Indian

Muslim leaders acknowledged the rising religious prestige of Ottoman leadership in the Muslim world. Over time a number of Indian rulers appealed to the caliph to extend his sovereignty over all of India to protect Muslim states against first Portuguese, then against rising British military control in India. With the British defeat of the Muslim Mughal Empire in India, Indian Muslims looked to the Ottoman Empire as the last Muslim bastion capable of halting the spread of European imperial takeovers—the "creeping western threat."[3] Muslims of course don't invariably side with other Muslims against all non-Muslims; rivalries exist among Muslim states as among any others. Muslim powers have often fought alongside non-Muslim powers against common enemies. But the *umma* was a source of potential assistance against non-Muslim enemies.

It wasn't just Muslims that thought about Islamic solidarity. By the late 18th century the British, now fully in control of India, had grown concerned about the influence that Ottoman legitimacy could exert over Indian Muslims as the British expanded their conquest of India. The British thus began to cultivate ties with the Ottomans in order to head off any possible Ottoman willingness to speak on behalf of other Muslims, not just in India, but in Afghanistan and other Muslim countries where the British sought control. The rhetorical power of the Ottoman state to stir the emotions of Muslims abroad grew stronger even as the Ottoman state itself grew militarily weaker.[4] In Central Asia too, various Muslim khanates in the 19th century also looked to the Ottomans as a legitimate source of Muslim help against encroaching Russian imperialism, particularly as the Ottomans found themselves at war with Russia on numerous occasions. Calls to the Ottoman caliph for help reached even from as far as Aceh in northern Sumatra (Indonesia) against rising Dutch imperial power.[5]

> "Naturally the feeling of belonging to a universal brotherhood and of being under the protection of a world power must have given [world Muslims] a sense of security and comfort. However, by the middle of the nineteenth century, in practical terms, there was neither an effective universal brotherhood, nor was the Ottoman Empire the world power that they believed it to be. Thus by the 1870's most Muslim countries had been subjugated by European powers amidst lamentable appeals for help and hopes that the Ottomans would save them."[6]

Europeans themselves were affected by this view. What began as a general *Muslim* belief in the power and moral authority of the Ottoman caliph to protect them had by 1878 morphed into a general *European* acknowledgment that the Ottomans exercised "some kind of formal religious jurisdiction" over all Muslims outside of the Ottoman Empire. This was a western acknowledgment of an existing reality, not some particular concession to the Ottoman sultan/caliph.[7] Russia too, was to recognize the important Ottoman religious influence over the numerous Muslim populations of the Russian Empire, whose loyalty Moscow hoped to win.

At times there was indeed dissension within the Empire. The Ottomans often put down local rebellions among Muslims, in Arabia, Egypt and elsewhere. Usually such rebellions were directed not so much against the Empire itself, as against the sometimes poor character of *local* Ottoman rule in one or another region. Symptomatic of Muslim thinking in India was an editorial in the newspaper Urdu Akhbar in 1876:

> It is no doubt incumbent upon the Muhammadan community to do all it can on behalf of Turkey in its present distressed condition.... It is no secret that all the honour and dignity which the Muhammadans command in India or in any other country is due to the maintenance of the Great Turkish Empire, and if that Empire ceased to exist, the Muhammadans will at once fall into insignificance and be utterly neglected.[8]

Istanbul likewise became the refuge of countless Muslim luminaries fleeing European imperial control over their own countries. Political and literary figures from India, the Caucasus, the Crimea, Russia, the Balkans, Afghanistan, Algeria and other parts of the Arab world visited or remained resident in Istanbul, offering Ottoman officials opportunities to play in the politics of other Muslim countries. The use of new printing technology and the steamship enabled the sultan-caliph to project his influence into other parts of the Muslim world, causing the imperial powers to fear Istanbul as a potential source of "international Muslim subversion" in their own colonies.[9]

As the Ottoman Empire weakened in the decades before World War I, the sultan-caliph sought to exploit his religious credentials to the maximum in order to bolster his foreign influence. Interestingly, he sought to be acknowledged as caliph of *all* Muslims and not just of the Sunni world. He demonstrated concern for the upkeep of Shi'ite as well as Sunni shrines, and sought to remove anti-Shi'ite material from religious textbooks and speeches. He sought rapprochement with Shi'ite Iran, reminding the Shah of Iran that Russia had designs on Persian territories as well as on Ottoman, requiring them to work together against the common enemy of Islam. Iran was partially responsive to these overtures. Note that this was not an era in which sectarianism was the driving force on the part of either of the preeminent Sunni and Shi'ite religious states.

At the same time, many Muslims outside the Empire feared that a weakened sultan-caliph might even fall prey to western control—enabling the

West to *manipulate* Islam for its own political ends. Muslim fear was not ill-founded: influence and manipulation of Muslim public opinion became an essential tool in the imperial policies of the British, Russian, French and Germans. In 1898, for example, Kaiser Wilhelm II visited Damascus and, in his ambitions to project German power into the Middle East and check the British, proclaimed himself the friend of 300 million Muslims.[10] (Today many Muslims are also offended and worried about US attempts to define (manipulate) Islam to its own ends, through the use of selected Muslim clerics recruited to the American cause to preach the virtues of a "moderate Islam"—a term ridiculed by many Muslims as representing an impotent "American Islam.") After World War I the British unsuccessfully sought to set up their own British-controlled candidate for caliph.

With the collapse of the Ottoman Empire after World War I, in 1920 a group of important Indian Muslims formed an All-India Khilafat (caliphate) Commission which urged the British to protect the office of caliphate and encouraged Muslims everywhere to support it. In 1926 leading Muslims convened a conference in Cairo to discuss resurrecting the office but the British suppressed any serious attendance, fearing potential anti-British sentiment arising from it. Once again in 1931 Jerusalem was the site of a Caliphate Conference to discuss the future of the office, again with little result.

Today Muslims in self-exile from modern colonial powers—Chinese control of Muslim Xinjiang, Russian control of Muslim Chechnya and the Caucasus, Bosnians under threat of genocide from Serbs—seek refuge in exile outside their countries; Turkey has been the major choice of exile within the Muslim world.

Yet it's striking that despite the symbolic power of the caliphate, most early modern Islamists such as the Muslim Brotherhood did not place their *practical* emphasis on restoration of the caliphate itself. Nonetheless, the issue took on new life in more recent times in the rhetoric of radical Islamists, both violent and peaceful, over the past 25 years. Al-Qaeda constantly speaks of the caliphate as a long term goal—although subordinate to the more immediate task of expelling western power from the Muslim world. The widespread radical (but non-violent) *Hizb al-Tahrir al-Islami* (Islamic Liberation Party) offers one of the most detailed and systematic presentations of what modern Muslim governance, institutionalized under a contemporary caliph, could look like today. It represents a desire to construct a system of government with *indigenous roots* in the origins of Islamic society rather than simply adopting a borrowed constitution downloaded from some western government website.

For the Ottomans, *religious* affiliation determined the major administrative lines drawn among diverse ethnic and linguistic communities. In this age of ethnic conflict, the *supranational* character of the Islamic vision is striking: ethnicity theoretically has no place in Islamic governance. The Qur'an regards focus upon ethnic identity as divisive. Some Turkish Islamists ask: might not the Kurdish question, for example, be better resolved on the basis of shared Islamic identity than on sharp divisions along blood lines of Turk, Kurd, Arab, and Persian? These are the grounds on which many Islamists even today search for common ground for a solution of Kurdish or Berber nationalism within a broader Islamic framework that would be ethnically blind.

How then, should the West view efforts among Muslims towards greater political unity? Shouldn't strivings towards unity be perceived as a more desirable course than collapse into disunity and division? One of the great blights of the world has been the poisoned European gift of the nation-state and nationalism—concepts that virtually devoured Europe in two terrible world wars and created havoc elsewhere on the globe. The world is still trying to claw its way out of an ethnically-based organizing system for the world in a search for something better than atavistic, raw and manipulable ethnic nationalism. On these grounds voluntary Islamic unity, or smaller-scale unions within the Muslim world such as Arab unity, should in principle be a *progressive* political concept. Should the West oppose the unification, on a voluntary and democratic basis, of Arab countries in some form of association that can promote Muslim or Arab culture, power and the ability to defend itself? This might be superior in principle to a divided Arab world, many of whose borders were designed by ruling western imperial powers. Why should the Arabs, or any other cultural groups, not seek greater unity of purpose when we in the West laud the cross-ethnic EU experiment? Yet patently Washington instinctively fears such projects towards Muslim unity for reasons that are often neither principled nor admirable: they object to the development of strong alternative coalitions capable of challenging western power.

Ultimately, talk of a caliphate is really a way of talking about Islamic unity. The longing for some unity of purpose among Muslims will not go away. Indeed Muslim unity is greatly enhanced in the face of ongoing western assault and routine denigration of Islam. It's as if to say, "if the West fears the caliphate that much, the idea can't be all bad." Muslims want to reconcile a golden vision of the early era of the *umma* with the harsh reality of the low standing of the Muslim world today. It is in this sense that the idea attracts. The concept of the caliphate or some kind of Muslim leadership will therefore not likely vanish, but will undergo constant rethinking and re-evaluation in light of the shifting circumstances. Why *shouldn't* there eventually be a caliphate if Muslims, through a process of serious consultation and consideration, want one? Or seek to create any other institution that could promote Muslim international interests?

In sum, the purpose of this discussion of the caliphate is not to call for its revival, but simply to note the source and power of one of the *organizing principles of leadership* in the Muslim world in the past and to speculate on its implications for today.

The ideal of some kind of unity runs deep in Muslim culture; contemporary discussion of the caliphate, even among a minority, reflects dissatisfaction with current ruling systems. It would be ridiculous of course to attribute the weaknesses of contemporary Muslim governance to the absence of a caliphate, or to suggest that the solution to Muslim problems lies in the recreation of a caliphate. But the quest for greater unity and cooperation within the Muslim world in some form is a task in search of a leader. It is not about absolute leadership, but relative leadership, a model, a kind of authoritative and respected voice that can help break deadlocks, generate ideas, gain international voice and recognition, clarify issues, set the tone, exert muscle, make things happen, demonstrate some successes, speak for the community, be heard.

How questions of leadership will ever be resolved by Muslims is unclear. There will likely be no single leader, nor would Muslims likely agree on one. But Turkey, for historical reasons as well as its contemporary achievements, is one powerful contender to speak on behalf of the welfare of the *umma* and to offer useful contributions and leadership on select issues. Indeed, it is already doing so as we will see in a later chapter. For the first time in modern history Turkey again seems sensitive and aware of the issue of leadership, common Muslim welfare and is interested in furthering the process. Obviously the question belongs to the *umma* as a whole and not specifically to Turkey. Furthermore, large numbers of Turks have no interest whatsoever in Turkey even playing such a role. Many other Muslims do not want them to do so either. Nor need there be one single leader. But Turkish sensitivities to this issue have been heightened through their new contacts with the Muslim world, and as reflected in the new foreign policies of the AKP.

Several key themes emerge then. First, a sense of Muslim solidarity grows in direct proportion to the degree that Muslims feel themselves under siege by the West. Muslims will look to outside support as necessary to protect themselves from external assault and domination. In the absence of support from a Muslim source, they will look to any great power willing to check a potential imperial western rival operating in Muslim regions. During the colonial period besieged Muslims sought aid from their Ottoman Turkish Caliph; failing that, they sought to play off western imperial powers against each other. During the East-West Cold War with the Soviet Union some portions of the Muslim world gravitated to support and cooperation with Soviet policies, not because they approved of communist ideology but because Moscow could serve as a counterweight against Washington that was perceived as supportive of western domination and the champion of Israel. The Arab world in particular felt abandoned by the early Kemalist republic that had turned its back on any involvement with the rest of the Muslim world and that had rejected its own Muslim past—a massive religious, cultural and geopolitical defection in their eyes.

The foreign policies of the ruling AKP in Turkey demonstrate for the first time a contemporary awareness of this phenomenon. Turkey does not formally seek to "unite Muslims" as such; but its foreign policies seek to help preserve the culture and strengthen the societies of the Muslim world in ways that can lead to greater cooperation. In this area Turkey is acting out of awareness of its role as defender of the *umma* in the past. As Foreign Minister Ahmet Davutoğlu points out,

> One strength of our foreign policy, thus, is the ongoing process of reconnecting with the people in our region with whom we shared a common history and are poised to have a common destiny. This objective will continue to shape our foreign policy priorities, and we will not take steps that will alienate us from the hearts and minds of our region's people for short-term political calculations...[11]

Many Muslims of course recognize that Turkey has its own ambitions in seeking to find a new role and project itself more deeply into the Muslim world. But the Muslim world now finds itself at a low point in its ability to resist overwhelming western military, economic, and political pressures. In this context Turkey's increasingly independent voice makes it an object of respect, gratification and hope. Turkey, with all its ties to the West, is now also becoming a culturally, economically and politically integrated part of the Muslim regional equation in ways that we will see. The call for some kind of Muslim joint cooperation and vision is far from dead.

CHAPTER FOUR

LEADERSHIP AND ETHNICITY: TURKS, PAN-ARABISM AND PERSIANS

The Ottoman period reveals the powerful role that Islam and the concept of the *umma* played in shaping the identity of the Muslim world. But in the modern age a new perspective appeared on the scene: ethnic nationalism, representing the effort to forge a Middle East identity based upon an *ethnic* foundation—especially Turkish, Arab or Persian nationalism, and, more recently, Kurdish. Which one will be the more powerful force in our age: a vision of the Middle East based on common religious (Islamic) culture writ broadly, or one based on the power of ethnicity? Ethnicity of course rests on a notably narrower base; in early Kemalist Turkey the concept of "Turkishness," linked to Turkish blood, dominated the new republic with a nationalism that often bordered on chauvinism. That racial form of nationalism has diminished but has not disappeared. In Iran, Persian nationalism dominates smaller ethnic groups and has always been a force in Persian politics; it continues to lie just beneath the surface even in the Islamic Republic of Iran today. Finally the Arab nationalist movement—Arabism or pan-Arabism—emphasized loyalty to ethnicity over shared religious commonality. All these ethnic movements in their narrower forms often end up excluding important minorities within their countries.

Since Arab nationalism represents the largest and most complex of the nationalist movements in the Middle East, this chapter devotes particular attention to it. Like all other ethnic or nationalist movements in the Middle East, Arab nationalism too is of relatively recent vintage—the first seeds sown in the late 18th century under the influence of European ethnic nationalism. The Islamic identity has always been the main vehicle of identity; Islamic thought has always resisted nationalism since Islam inherently disapproves of the force of ethnic identity. From the earliest days, Islamic clerics perceived tribalism and ethnicity as essentially narrow, divisive and secular, degrading the broader sense of Islamic unity and identity. The Prophet Muhammad on his final pilgrimage is reported to have said, "No Arab has any superiority over a non-Arab, nor a non-Arab over an Arab; nor a white person over a black person, nor a black person over a white person—except by piety. The most honorable of you in the sight of God are the most pious and righteous of you."[1] This remains a view shared by most Islamists today.

Yet Arabism is not quite the complete antithesis of Islam, as we shall see. Like many other ideologies, pan-Arabism took on various shadings; nationalist, socialist, Marxist; even Islamist facets of pan-Arabism all coexist. While pan-Arabism has been a powerful intellectual concept in the Middle East over much of the 20th century, its experience in the political arena was checkered. In its initial impact it created a new Arab narrative, stirred the masses to nationalist fervor, created a new political consciousness wider than the local Arab state, and introduced revolutionary ideas into post-colonial governance. But pan-Arabism also ended up being captured by authoritarian rulers and led to damaging inter-Arab struggles for leadership of pan-Arab movements—causing some observers to question whether pan-Arabism is still a viable concept for Arab politics at all.

Yet the impulses of pan-Arabism need not, by definition, be backward or negative. There is no reason why yearning for good governance and democratic process cannot also rank high on the list of Arab nationalist aspirations. Pan-Arabism need not automatically exclude progressive values. Given its inherent links to nationalism and identity, whatever the failures of pan-Arabism have been in the past, it is equally unlikely ever to vanish as an ideology—it represents the commonly shared cultural aspects of the Arab world. But like the restrictiveness of all ethnic nationalist movements, those who are not Arab cannot really be players in the project. Similarly, how much does pan-Arabism automatically work to exclude non-Arab Turkey or Iran from some kind of leadership role in the Middle East—and hence divide the region? Can these three (or more) nationalisms productively coexist? Or does it take Islam to build an ideological roof over all of their heads? "Let's all just be secular liberal democrats together" is not a call—at least now—that will sway the passions of peoples still struggling to break out from western dominance and authoritarian leadership and achieve a new identity.

Pan-Arabism roiled the waves of Middle East geopolitics in the 1950s and 1960s, injecting fear into the imperial powers—Britain, France, and the US. Pan-Arabism was, after all, the major vehicle not only of anti-imperial and anti-western resistance, but also the clarion call for Palestinian rights and resistance against Israeli expansionism. It was also crudely exploited by Arab domestic strongmen to force national compliance with their own political agendas. Thus in the West the very word "pan-Arabism" still evokes negative reactions and numerous commentators are routinely eager to pronounce it dead.

But there is nothing unique about pan-Arabism as a movement. History has witnessed many such "pan" movements over the centuries. They never truly die because they rest on powerful reality: feelings of cultural solidarity among groups of people with a shared language and culture. It was the West that essentially invented the concept of modern nationalism as the founding principle for the new "nation-state" in the 18th century, replacing states that had previously been organized along either religious lines, or loyalty to a specific princely house. It was not a big step to advance from local ethnic nationalism to pan-ethnic movements. Thus in the 19th century we find German nationalist movements that contributed to the creation of a German identity and the unification of Germany. As the force of nationalism grew, theorists sought to rise above the narrow nation state to conceive of a still broader cultural entity such as "the Germanic peoples," who would additionally embrace Dutch, Austrians, Scandinavians, Icelanders, and Germans in the diaspora (in Czechoslovakia, Russia, Poland, Hungary, the Baltic states, etc.) Pan-Slavism was not far behind as it emerged in Eastern Europe. While Russian nationalism had already become a strong force in the 19th century, some nationalists dreamed of a greater unity of all Slavic peoples that would include Poles, Czechs, Ukrainians, Bulgarians, Serbs, Croats, and others. Ironically these forces of Slavic nationalism have particularly foundered in most recent history on age-old religious differences among Slavs.

Peoples outside of Europe soon evolved their own forms of nationalist ideology as the foundation for national resistance against western imperial intrusion and other foreign enemies. Thus pan-Turkism emerged as an ideology in the late 19th century, calling attention to ethnic, cultural and linguistic links among various Turkic peoples as far away as the Uyghurs in Western China, Uzbeks, Kazaks, Tatars, and Azerbaijanis. Pan-Turkism was (and still is) feared by Russia since the bulk of Turkic peoples and states (apart from Turkey) had constituted significant parts of the former Soviet Union and developed threatening breakaway movements. Many Turkic peoples still remain inside the new borders of the Russian Federation. The emergence of Turkish nationalism in the late Ottoman Empire also helped spark the counter-development of Arab nationalism, even within the Ottoman Empire. Numerous other pan-movements came into being in the world as well.

Pan-movements are of course essentially racial in concept; by definition they are based on acknowledgment of racial and linguistic commonalities. They pose the same problems as any other forms of ethnic nationalism; as with all such group identities, these ethnic nationalist concepts are positive or negative depending on how they are envisioned and practiced vis-à-vis others. More liberal or generous interpretations of ethnic nationalism can embrace any who identify with the culture and traditions of the country they live in.

And political power is quick to exploit the appeal of nationalism
its own agendas.

Criticisms of pan-Arabism quickly emerged from the West. F
accurately perceived it as a major organizing ideology against western
dominance. Pan-Arabism was criticized as "artificial," a process that sought to
place a variety of Semitic peoples across the Middle East and North Africa
into one box—peoples who a century earlier would not necessarily have
considered themselves to be "Arabs" even if they spoke forms of Arabic. Yet
of course nationalism is always "imagined"; identity is what you think you are.
Even Egyptians did not really consider themselves "Arabs" at the beginning
of the 20th century, yet within 50 years they came to lead the Arab nationalist
movement. And as with all nationalist movements, the concept of who is a
German, or a Jew, or a Russian, or a Turk is in a state of constant evolution,
expansion and contraction, depending upon how it is employed and the
existing circumstances around it.

Strictly speaking, in the 19th century the term "Arab" applied primarily to
the inhabitants of the Arabian Peninsula. Yet today most (but not all) people
who speak Arabic natively today consider themselves "Arab" and associate in
some way with the general Arab cause. Nonetheless, Arabism has also been
used by regimes and ideologists to suppress other ethnic identities within the
Arab world such as Kurds, Copts, Dinka, or Berbers and to impose a
common "Arab" identity. Lest we become too indignant about this, we need
recall that France in the 19th century ruthlessly crushed—indeed still
discourages—"non-French" identities such as Provençal, Basque, Breton or
Sardinian. The English forcibly worked to erase the Scottish, Irish, Welsh and
Cornish identities. China has engaged in a long-term process of Hanification
of its many minorities, even while nominally recognizing them in the interim.
The workings of the nation state abuilding is not always a pretty thing.

Egypt exploited pan-Arabism as a powerful tool when it asserted
leadership of the movement. Yet states like Iraq or Syria were not ready to
yield to Egypt ultimate leadership of "the Arabs." With the political and
military debacle of pan-Arabism under Gamal Abdel Nasser in the 1970s the
ideology as a political force seemed to fall out of favor. But such ideas never
really disappear; they simply lie fallow, awaiting resuscitation in new form as
circumstances change. Nearly all mainstream political movements in the Arab
world have included, in one form or another, elements of pan-Arabism or
Arab nationalism: we find the Arab Republic of Egypt, the Syrian Arab
Republic, the Libyan Arab Republic, and the United Arab Emirates all
officially employing the word "Arab" in their names. Lying behind the idea is

eep psychological impulse towards unity: for defense, for common cause, common strength and solidarity, and common celebration of heritage. And why not? It is perfectly reasonable that Arab peoples and states should acknowledge much commonality and consult on regional matters, especially as they affect issues of Arabic language, culture, economy and sovereignty.

But regional identities also exist among Arab states and peoples. There are movements for Greater Syria, or North African cooperation, or for unity among the Gulf States. And even *Islamist* movements within the Arab world are not without their unspoken Arab nationalist components. While the Qur'an categorically rejects ethnicity as taking priority over religious identity, in reality concepts of sub-regional identities—the Maghreb, the Arabian Peninsula—operate on a more comprehensive plane than the mere local state, and thus constitute building blocks towards ideas of greater unity among Muslim peoples. Now, any look at the history of Egypt in the 1950s or 1960s demonstrates how Islamists were then political enemies of the pan-Arabist ideas of Nasser in Egypt or of the nationalist leaderships in Iraq or Syria, for example. But the clash was more about *politics and power* than ideology: Islamists represented the only significant alternative political force to rival and oppose the dictatorial policies of the pan-Arab dictators. Otherwise there are often strong ideological grounds for close cooperation between pan-Arabists and Islamists, *most particularly on issues of foreign policy*—when the state or the *umma* finds its cultural and territorial sovereignty threatened by foreign (non-Muslim) intervention. Islam and Arabism culturally overlap to face a common enemy.

Language is one of the keys to the Arab future. One hundred years ago there were multiple local dialects of Arabic, many barely mutually comprehensible. Illiteracy was widespread. Classical or literary Arabic was just that—the language of an educated elite. Yet modern communications brought dramatic change. The Voice of the Arabs from the 1950s beamed radio broadcasts from Cairo to the Arab world, passing along information in neo-literary language (sometimes sprinkled with Egyptian dialect) that contained news vital to the lives and events of the Arab world; they quickly gained mass following. Today that linguistic revolution has taken even broader steps forward with the satellite TV station al-Jazeera. Al-Jazeera began to broadcast in the late 1990s around the clock, breaking old taboos and airing controversial debates and discussions over almost every issue once off limits in the Arab world. Arabs in tea-houses were transfixed at the frank debate about their own lives, the economies, politics, culture, and coverage of war and peace in the Middle East. Most important, it was all in more or less modern literary Arabic. Today there are few Arabs who cannot at least understand literary Arabic, so vital is it to their ability to follow events in the region. And the Arabic language is becoming ever more homogenized among Arabs, making it easier for people in all Arab countries to learn to communicate in literary Arabic as the universal language across the Arab world, even if they use and thrive on local dialects at home. Modern communications thus created one of the vital tools of pan-Arabism. If few people who lived in the Middle East 100 years ago felt themselves to be Arab, today that situation has changed dramatically. The number of people that identify themselves as Arab has grown hugely, with the Arab identity easily rivaling local state identity (such as Jordanian, Omani, or Libyan). And the Islamic identity has grown in parallel along with it. (One might be Libyan watching a football match against Egypt, but Arab when Egypt plays Greece.)

Pan-Arabism therefore exists on several levels. But what does it mean? It describes a cultural linkage among ordinary Arabs across diverse states that had never been felt before, except perhaps a century earlier when Ottoman Turkish was the lingua franca, at least of the Arab elite and the official language of the Empire. Remnants of that era still exist in folk memory and in the Turkish expressions that still dot the speech of many dialects, especially in Egypt and the Levant. Today all Arabs are vividly aware of events in all other Arab countries. The same cannot always be said for Europeans, who might not feel identification with events in all parts of the EU. A sense of commonality among Arabs is greater today than at any time in history—now stimulated by external challenge, threats and war. That is true even when their leaders sometimes stand at odds with each other.

Note too, the unique use of the phrase "the Arab world." Where else in the world does such an expression about a "world" exist—except in the term "Muslim world?" There is no longer any "Christian world" or Christendom (although the term did still exist in the 19th-century West.) We don't routinely talk about a Buddhist world, Catholic world, Latin American world, African world, or East Asian world. (There is a "Western world," mainly a hangover from the Cold War days as the antithesis of the "communist world.") All of which is to say that even culturally speaking there is a global acknowledgment of the existence and power of Arabism, or pan-Arabism.

But what are its limits? Does it permit Cairo or Riyadh or Damascus to set the course for the Arab world? Increasingly not. But one of the key features of the colonial period in the Arab world was western redrawing of Arab state borders following the collapse of the Ottoman Empire. Consider how Greater Syria in particular was carved up into many smaller states out of a greater

Syrian cultural entity with long historical continuity. It is worth pondering: what if there had been no Western colonialism, no European mandates in the Middle East, what would the borders of this region look like today? Indeed, one of the remaining challenges of Arab statehood has been the lurking feeling among populations that the new Arab mini-states are not entirely legitimate or "real" because they are originally creatures of the European powers whose leaders were routinely installed by the West. This state of affairs provides partial justification for leaders to mess in the affairs of neighbors.

The dilemma is serious. The principles of modern western nationalism demanded that Arab citizens transfer their loyalties to the newly created individual colonial states after World War I, which had basically been just regions before. But how could one become a passionately patriotic "Jordanian" overnight when there had been no state of Jordan until 1922, it achieved independence only in 1946, its ruling family was imported from outside, and its very geography recently invented, and half of its population felt themselves Palestinian? The absence of meaningful historical borders among these regions in past centuries helps explain why Arab states today often maintain strong organic and historical interests and ties in the affairs of a neighboring state—where similar ethnic, tribal, sectarian or even clan groups exist—and that only recently had become an officially "independent" political states. Foreign policy in the Arab world still very much revolves about what are really Arab "internal affairs," in which Arabs endlessly consult about possible common approaches to regional issues or even problems of specific neighboring states. Arab states rarely seem to operate independently and without consultation in isolation from each other. National, that is, local sovereignty among Arab states in one sense is probably weaker than among other groupings of states in the world; Arabs recognize the interlocking character of so many policy issues. All of this is a further nod to the power of pan-Arabism. Nor is it necessarily all bad to find grounds of common interest.

Pan-Arabism as an aspiration, an ideology, particularly fell on hard times when Egypt dropped out of the international game after 1981 when Husni Mubarak was essentially corralled and bankrolled into the American fold to protect US and Israeli interests. Egypt thereafter remained largely silent, *hors de combat*, out of the game on many of the grand issues of the Arab world. Saudi Arabia, by dint of its huge oil wealth and possession of the Holy Places, benefited from the weakness of the Egyptian voice to assume a larger role of regional leadership. But Saudi Arabia too was often perceived by the general Arab public as lying within the American sphere of influence, its royal family responsive to American wishes, possessed of a caution and timidity of approach, and the limits of its initiatives safely circumscribed. What the populations of the region craved was an independent voice, a voice that would express bold new aspirations, as well as sharp defense of national sovereignty in the face of unpopular US or European policies. The lack of an independent-minded leader with the charisma to speak out, to act, to inspire as Gamal Abdel Nasser had once done in the name of the Arab Revolution, was strongly felt. Ironically it was the Islamic Republic of Iran after 1979 that first began to fill that vacuum, to speak the language of revolution and defiance of western power, to create its own authentic version of Islamic government, and to voice regional discontent with western domination or intervention.

Some in the West might argue that both Arab nationalist leaders and Iran are simply exploiting anti-western sentiment for political gain. Yet the reality is that some state, some ideology, some leader will invariably emerge to serve as a vehicle of expression for these strong nationalist impulses, aspirations, and popular anti-Western regional sentiments as long as such sentiments have grounds to exist. Nasser himself, once asked about why Egypt was pursuing the Arab nationalist cause with such fervor, replied in effect that "there is a role in the region in search of an actor; Egypt will assume that role." He was acknowledging the existence of deep-rooted and abiding political drives in the region that will always seek expression, regardless. It is naïve for the West to believe that such political sentiments will go away simply because current politicians are wary of expressing them out of concern for western displeasure. Or because their leader of the moment has been overthrown. Such ideas and sentiments will always demand expression in some form when there are reasons for it.

Thus Arab nationalism gave voice to key ideas still central to the thinking of most Arabs: injustices committed against the Palestinians in the creation of the Israeli state; the now 40-year Israeli occupation of the West Bank and Gaza; the emptiness and charade of the US-sponsored "peace process"; frustration with Arab dictators who are autocratic and often incompetent, who are clients of Washington, and who lack the courage to represent Arab public opinion on the international level; anger with the implicitly anti-Islamic character of the American "Global War on Terrorism," and the constant spectacle of ongoing western political and military intervention and wars in the affairs of the Arab world. Whenever any Arab leader even slightly articulates any of these ideas he is quickly hailed by the public, but such outspokenness has been infrequent and timorous. From the point of view of the general population and most of its thinkers and intellectuals, there was no leadership in the Middle East to give voice to its aspirations and grievances or to defend the national honor and interest. And the aspirations were not simply all negative and anti-western; populations sought better lives, a state that accorded them dignity, jobs, education, housing, more freedom, a more representative and engaged state.

Iran since its revolution clearly understood and expressed this dynamic and, in line with its Islamist and revolutionary values, gained much sympathy among the Arab populace in the region. It does not matter all that much that Iran is not even an Arab country. There are indeed strong reservoirs of Persian nationalism in Iran that are intrinsically anti-Turkish and anti-Arab, at least from the old days. But the Islamic orientation of the Islamic Republic of Iran softens the more chauvinistic elements of Persian nationalism so that it blends in more successfully with the broader Islamic cultural character of the Middle East—until the recent explosion of Saudi-financed anti-Shi'ism.

This was the context in which the AKP government of Turkey initially began to articulate many of these same regional concerns and to show its own Muslim credentials for the first time. This shift in Turkish thinking quickly caught Arab attention and rapidly earned Turkey new respect and popularity starting in the 2000s. Ankara was equally concerned too, over the long-term destabilizing aspects of US policy towards Turkey's neighbors Iraq, Syria and Iran. And, as we will see, Turkey's AKP dialed back considerably the strong Turkish nationalist overtones of Kemalism, in new emphasis on shared Islamic values, thus softening Turkey's image and making it more acceptable in the Middle East. Indeed, the larger ideological tent of Islam can include a far greater variety of diverse ethnic groups; but in turn it then has trouble accommodating non-Muslim minorities.

The question today is, what is the future of ethnicity, and especially pan-Arabism in regional leadership? And can Turkey fit into this in any respect? Does the region not require a far broader ideological tent for greater regional cooperation? Indeed, from the perspective of this 21st-century era of globalization, a look back at the two centuries of European-created "nationalisms" makes clear that those narrow ideologies plunged Europe and the world into repeated conflicts and wars. Europe finally learned at terrible cost that nationalism is not a viable basis for the European future. The European Union, for all its faults and stumblings, represents a revolutionary new approach to regionalism and regional solidarity: the willingness of states to cede large elements of national sovereignty in the interests of grander gain. The powerful forces of economic globalization assist this erosion of boundaries.

Why then, should the pan-Arab experiment be viewed as romantic, foolish, naïve, utopian, retrogressive, exploitative, or a joke? Does not the aspiration to greater regional unity accord more closely with the spirit of the times than individual Arab states with irrational borders working in isolation? It was actually the very authoritarian nature of the regimes of the Arab world that contributed heavily to the early failures of pan-Arab efforts towards greater Arab unity. Transitory new political unions—"the United Arab Republic of X"—had been founded at the whim of this or that ruler, "marriages" between states hurriedly consummated at airport unity-signing ceremonies where, as Arab wags had it, one always wondered who was the bride and who was the groom. And these shotgun unions came apart with similar rapidity as soon as the leaders found the union no longer advantageous or effective—all without public consultation. Arab publics were left with a bitter taste in their mouths after such ill-conceived antics.

There is every reason to believe that Arab politics in the coming decades will involve increased demand for democratic process. Arabism and Islam will not necessarily be contradictory but complementary. The old dichotomy of "secular versus religious" will less and less describe a political dynamic that can include both elements in the public quest for improved society and governance. The enemies of democratization and representatives of the old order will continue to attempt to manipulate these values and ideologies in order to divide public opinion and make it easier to control: thus a new surge of fomenting divisions such as Sunni versus Shi'ite, secular versus religious, Turk versus Arab or Persian.

Under democratization Arab foreign policies too will inevitably incorporate a greater degree of public opinion; this has broad implications that directly affect both traditional US hegemony and regional dissatisfaction with hardline Israeli policies that perpetuate expansion of Israeli settlements on Palestinian lands. These criticisms of Israel cannot simply be attributed to "anti-Semitism." It is evident to most of the world, even if not to US politicians, that Israel has come to be dominated by the most right-wing and harshest Israeli government in its history. The US cannot be surprised by growing public frustration and anger in the Middle East and dissatisfaction with the old rulers. The reality is that Arab populations do not willingly accept unelected autocrats beholden to outside powers. They want rulers who will reflect the interests of Arab states, domestic and foreign, as perceived by their own populations. Turkish policies have moved in this same direction which contributed to newfound Turkish popularity among Arab populations at a time of no real Arab leadership. When the first post-Mubarak government emerged in Egypt in 2011 it looked like Egypt had once again begun moving in the direction of new more popularly-based leadership. But with the subsequent military coup against the first post-Mubarak government in Egypt, it seems unlikely the new military government can be responsive to public aspirations; it will likely regress to the bureaucratic grayness of the Mubarak era. Arab nationalist impulses will probably thus be suppressed again, leaving a leadership deficit in the region. Who will fill it?

An Arab Agenda and Turkey

What will produce future leadership of the Middle East region: will it be based on an ethnic, or some religious foundation of Middle East culture? The answer is very unlikely to be an either/or. Religion and ethnicity are not mutually exclusive commitments and, unless a domestic struggle for power is at stake, both factors can be present in the political culture of a future Middle East. Neither narrow ethnicity nor narrow religious identity are sufficient to re-stimulate the rise of the region with new confidence in itself and enjoying greater independence, legitimacy and regional cooperation that has so often been lacking in the past.

Four issues stand out on the Arab agenda for the future. The first is the Palestinian question and the normalization of Arab state relations with Israel. Its urgency and emotionalism are no less than it was four decades ago. Second is the drive for sovereignty, independence and self-determination of the Arab world from outside influences, pressures and interventions. Third is democracy, dignity, and human rights in the Arab world that have been almost completely absent in the modern period—until the first spark of the Arab Spring in Tunisia in 2010. Fourth is good governance: the prosperity, well-being, economic vibrancy, employment levels, and the cultural-educational level of Arab and other Muslim populations. Turkey not only shares a strong interest in all these issues but has considerable recent domestic experience and success to demonstrate in its own right. Ankara shows a desire to share in the evolution of the region as a member and not as a western surrogate watching from the sidelines. The Muslim world is clearly more open and responsive to cultural models and examples coming from within its tradition—in this case, from Turkey—as opposed to imported western plans.

Negative Reactions to Turkey

Turkey over the last decade overwhelmingly became the most popular state in the Arab world and Prime Minister Recep Tayyip Erdoğan overwhelmingly the most popular leader. But for all of Turkey's success in many fields and the general admiration it enjoys in public opinion polls, some negative views exist as well. They can be summed up as follows:

• Lingering negative memories of the Ottoman Empire: While the Empire was in many respects very successful, it also crushed internal rebellion and opposition—as all empires did. A modern Arab nationalist version of history came to dominate the Arab educational curriculum for three-quarters of a century, one emphasizing an Arab nationalist struggle for independence—against the Ottomans as well as against European imperial control. While much of this narrative represents a modern reimagination of history told for nationalist purposes, it has negatively influenced some Arab thinking towards Turkey.

• Distrust of Turkey's Islamic credentials: While the AKP made extraordinary gains in impressing Arab and Muslim populations with the country's successes, Arabs remember that for most of modern Turkish history the government was hostile to Islam and to the Islamic past, and had contempt for the Middle East and its culture in the Kemalist quest to be "western." Has Turkey really changed?

• Distrust of Turkish secularism: While the growing religiosity of the Turkish public is evident, Turkey's official acceptance of secularism (even by the AKP) as the legitimate basis of government makes other Islamists and pious individuals suspicious of Turkish political and cultural goals in the region. Yet many Middle East secularists admire Turkey on the same grounds.

• Distrust of Turkey's geopolitical goals: For most of modern Turkish history under Kemalism, Ankara was intimately linked to western geopolitical goals, including an alliance with Israel for some years in the 1990s. Lingering suspicions remain as to whether Turkey—for all its talk about independent policies—may not have become simply a more sophisticated Trojan horse with an Islamic mask to project western influence and interests into the Middle East.

• Concern by Arab *regimes* over rivalry for influence: Arab *publics* show far greater admiration for Turkey today than the regimes do. Regimes in Iran, Iraq, Saudi Arabia, Syria and Egypt all share suspicions that Turkey has moved into geopolitical roles that could threaten to diminish their own influence.

• Fear of Turkish democratization plans: Authoritarian regimes are highly concerned over Erdoğan and Davutoğlu's open calls for reform and democratization as well as their good ties with the Muslim Brotherhood—all suggest an agenda that threatens the security of authoritarian regimes and monarchies.

- Fear of Turkish non-neutrality in conflict: Over time it will be difficult for Ankara to avoid being drawn into conflict between states in the region and taking sides. Indeed, Ankara has already taken positions that have angered regimes in Syria, Iran, Iraq, Saudi Arabia, and Egypt in very recent years.

- Resentment of any outside intervention: Some Arab nationalist leaders do not welcome *any* non-Arab intervention in the Arab world, Muslim or not.

These themes will recur as we look at some of the details of geopolitical forces at work in the region.

PART THREE: TURKISH EXPERIENCE AS A MODEL

Turkey has undergone a remarkable evolutionary process in the early 21st century that bears major significance for the rest of the Muslim world. This is primarily due to the government of the ruling AKP, in power since 2002. As Turkey's relations have moved ever closer to other countries in the Middle East and the Muslim world, its experience takes on greater relevance for other Muslim states; this is particularly true in two areas of major significance: the problem of the military in politics, and the role of Islam in domestic politics. Turkey has managed both these processes with major success not visible elsewhere in the Muslim world. But all political leadership eventually declines; by mid-2013 Prime Minister Erdoğan showed signs of losing his political touch, probably heralding the decline of his career or even that of his party. The potential unraveling of the AKP nonetheless does not detract from its remarkable accomplishments of its first decade.

In the following chapter we look at the longtime role of the military in Turkish politics and the slide towards an eventual showdown between military and civilian power. We then move on to the so-called "Ergenekon" case—the process by which the underbelly of the "deep, or secret, state" linked to the military was exposed, facilitating the final exclusion of the military from civilian governance. Like Turkey, a high proportion of states in the world suffers from the existence of a "deep, or secret, state" within the state—unacknowledged networks of unelected and unaccountable power operating independently or outside of official state institutions, mechanisms and laws.

The second section examines the evolving role of religion in the Turkish state experience. Turkey has never truly been secular in the western or American sense—meaning neutrality of the state towards religion. But it is by no means an Islamic state either. Virtually every single Muslim state in the world faces a similar challenge: how do the values of Islam best relate to the functioning of state and society? Our discussion touches on three quite remarkable aspects of Islam operating in the Turkish state and society:

• State-administered religion, or the Directorate of Religious Affairs. How does Turkey, an officially secular state, conceive of its official interrelationships with Islam domestically and abroad?

• The Gülen movement, or *Hizmet*, the largest Islamist civil movement in the Muslim world. How did it evolve? What are its goals and how does it operate?

• The increasing struggle among contending forces within Turkish Islamic politics today;

• The new dimensions of religion in Turkish foreign policy today.

CHAPTER FIVE

AUTHORITARIANISM AND THE KEMALIST SPIRIT: GETTING THE MILITARY BACK TO THE BARRACKS

There is hardly a state in the Muslim world that does not struggle with the legacy of a powerful military role in domestic politics. In most of the developing world military dictators have been the rule rather than the exception: the Middle East, Latin America, Africa and countries of Asia have all experienced this problem; even in Western Europe itself Spain, Portugal and Greece were ruled by the military well into the last half of the 20th century. The image of the military *supremo*—uniform studded with decorations, the high-browed military cap, arm raised in salute to the crowds as dictator of the nation—is all too depressingly familiar. Today the military still poses the biggest single barrier to democratic governance in much of the Muslim world and beyond. The army may sometimes stand behind a civilian façade, but it is frequently the ultimate power broker.

What is the Army Doing in Politics?

Actually, the real question is, why *wouldn't* the army be deeply involved in domestic politics? When western imperial control came to an end, newly independent countries of the world immediately faced multiple internal challenges. The colonial power that once supplied internal security disappeared. Struggle for political power within the new states began. At this crucial stage of national development, the military, which had been established by colonial power, frequently represented the most organized, best trained and most advanced institution in society. In still other countries, guerrilla forces spearheaded the national liberation struggle against imperial power. Thus, at independence, military groups usually exercised greater political clout than other groups in society. Military officers, not surprisingly, often represented the most likely candidates for national leadership. They possessed the necessary skills to maintain domestic stability while protecting the often fragile borders of the new state. Its officers were often better educated than most of the population and many top officers had received training in the metropole. They nominally stood "above politics" and possessed a clear sense of mission. Some officers emerged with charismatic power as national heroes of an independence struggle. And above all they held the power to *coerce*.

From this perspective, the dominant role of the military in governance was a predictable, even valuable phenomenon for new states that were young, fragile, untested and possibly threatened internally and externally. If civilian rule existed it was often weak; the military alone had the power to seize control of the state and impose its own leadership and authority across society. Sometimes new civilian leaders looked to the military to back up their rule against rivals. Genuine democratic rule often had little chance. Many states in the Middle East are still struggling with the problem; for them Turkey provides an important case study of a long and difficult process whereby civilian leadership eventually came to establish civil control over the military.

The Turkish Military

You can't build empires without soldiers, and Ottoman Turkey was no exception. Turkish history is steeped in the military *par excellence*. The Turks were a tribal and martial culture for centuries before ever even arriving in Anatolia over 1,000 years ago. The military played the central role in the creation and expansion of the Ottoman Empire over some seven centuries and across three continents. Turks were renowned for their fine military machine. As the Ottoman Empire grew, the sultan moved away from a tribal and irregular basis of military recruitment to create in the 14th century the famed organization of the *Janissaries*, or "new troops." They were recruited primarily from among the Balkan Christian population: selected young boys were pressed into involuntary service, sent to the heartland of Turkey to learn Turkish, convert to Islam, and then to receive military training, enabling them to move into the very highest positions of administrative and military power within the Empire, ultimately retiring with large pensions. They were legally considered slaves to the sultan, owing absolute loyalty to him and to no others. Due to their Christian social origin, they lacked blood ties to Turkish tribal forces or to the Ottoman nobility; they were therefore in no position to play local politics or to pose a coup threat to the sultan—until later. According to British historian Lord Kinross, the Ottoman Janissaries constituted the first regular standing army in Europe since the Roman Empire.

The institution was a brilliant one: it created a powerful and disciplined military force loyal to the sultan. But, as with most well-designed institutions, the Janissaries eventually became entrenched in their own organization, its customs, rituals and methods. Over time they demanded greater privileges. They were eventually permitted to have legal families of their own which predictably created splits in loyalties as their power within the state bureaucracy grew. Ultimately their power and influence came to be feared by the sultan himself.

Military defeat is often the mother of military reform. In later centuries, as the Ottoman armies began to face defeat at the hands of more modern European armies, court pressure grew in Istanbul for bold reform to develop a modernized and efficient army. Ottoman sultans sought to bring the Janissaries under control and to transform them into a modern army along European lines. The Janissaries perceived these efforts as an open threat to their autonomy and power. In 1622 Sultan Osman II was overthrown and murdered by his Janissaries—an early "coup" and act of resistance against military reform; a more pliable sultan was put in his place. Then, in 1807 Sultan Selim III was overthrown by a Janissary coup in response to his efforts to curtail their power. These continuing challenges to the sultan's power proved ultimately fateful in their consequences for the Janissaries. By 1826 unceasing Janissary resistance to reform and reorganization had grown intolerable; this time the new sultan, Mahmut II, was determined to break their power. He deliberately provoked an armed uprising among the Janissaries by announcing the creation of a new modern army. Massed Janissary forces marched against the Palace but this time the sultan was ready: Janissary barracks were destroyed and the rest of their troops slaughtered in street engagements in just one day under withering artillery fire. The sultan disbanded the Janissaries entirely, confiscated all their property and executed the remnants of Janissary forces all around the Balkans. A new western-style military came into being. Yet it soon became evident that the long struggle to limit Janissary power had constituted only round one; it presaged a longer ongoing pattern of serious "civil-military" confrontations that resulted in the periodic overthrow of Turkish governments by the military right down to the last years of the 20th century.

With the destruction of the Janissaries in 1826, military power took on quite new form. Mahmut II proceeded to establish an entirely new and westernized military force that required modern military institutions for training. He established a brand-new military academy and brought in French and Prussian officers to teach Western military and engineering techniques. The goal was to furnish the late Ottoman Empire with a new class of westernized professional military men.[1] But there was a seeming contradiction here: although western military officers provided the training, these new western military techniques from the Ottoman perspective were actually aimed at meeting the ongoing military challenge *from* the West, as well as to put down rebellions among the Ottoman Christian population (often provoked or supported by western powers to weaken and dismember the Empire.)

Ironically, then, it was not ideas of "Oriental despotism" that created a powerful new military within the Ottoman state, but rather a European model—specifically a German one. German military thinking at this point in history had developed ambitious goals for Germany itself: it urged the creation of a military elite that would "go beyond the traditional [military] role in society and help guide the ship of state."[2] But the presence of this new western-style Turkish military in the mid-19th century had come to drive "a wedge between the new military elite and the rest of society." This new military class "appeared as a cloistered elite; it stood apart from the masses— pretentious, Westernized, and overweeningly ambitious."[3]

As the 19th century drew to a close, the very existence of the Ottoman Empire became deeply imperiled. It faced disastrous external conditions: repeated military defeats at the hands of European powers, continued European annexation of Ottoman lands, rebellions by Christian populations, and rising economic pressures. Yet it would be a mistake to believe that domestic political development within the Empire had been dormant during the 19th century. On the contrary, this was a period of intense rethinking and change; the Empire witnessed the birth of several major reform movements and the emergence of greater popular voices and representation within government.

Nonetheless, a series of weak sultans proved unable to meet the rising challenges to the state; these failures in turn encouraged military circles into deeper intervention into policy-making. The officer corps believed that it alone possessed the most comprehensive grasp of the strategic situation— which may have largely been true. But the military's interventions, even in the Ottoman period, came at the expense of growing proto-democratic institutions such as the emerging elected parliament.

These problems are hardly unique to Turkey. Debates about the "efficiency" of democracy as a means of governance, especially in periods of crisis, have been around a long time. Efficiency has never been the chief boast of democracy; democratic rule above all provides a mechanism for checking or removing incompetent or arbitrary rule and replacing it with leaders whom the public supports. But of course in times of emergency and war all governments seek to curtail the democratic process in the name of greater efficiency, "national security," and "protection of the nation."

As the Ottoman Empire crumbled across the Balkans, and as Europe slid towards a world war, a new combination of political forces—diverse ethnic groups and political groupings—joined hands in what is known as the Young Turk Revolution of 1908. The sultan was replaced and Parliament was restored. But, as Princeton historian Şükrü Hanioğlu, points out, while many popular forces joined hands in the revolution, in essence "it was a well-planned military insurrection, conceived and executed in Macedonia by a conspiratorial organization whose leadership harbored a quintessentially conservative aim: to seize control of the empire and save it from collapse."[4] The military—through the well-known Union of Committee and Progress—dominated Turkish politics until the final collapse of the Empire. In doing so it established the foundation for a long era of one-party military-based rule to characterize the new Turkish Republic under Mustafa Kemal Atatürk.

And the military did save the nation: after the collapse of the Empire, irregular military forces under Atatürk took the lead in successfully beating back invasions by Italian, Greek, British and French forces intent upon partitioning the Anatolian homeland itself. Atatürk had emerged as the supreme military figure of this national liberation struggle; by any standard he was a genuine national savior and father of his nation. With the establishment of the new Turkish Republic Atatürk resigned his military status to become President. He nominally banned military officers thereafter from playing a role in civilian politics, but many of the key leaders of the new republic emerged directly out of military careers. Atatürk ruled largely by decree in undertaking a sweeping series of reforms, many of which greatly strengthened the country, but also laid foundations for a prolonged authoritarian tradition. After Atatürk's death a close-knit westernized elite of followers took over the direction of the republic, perpetuating one-party rule. Even while the politicians were civilian, it was the military that made the major decisions in its self-appointed role as "guardian of the Turkish constitution" exercising a "tutelary" or overseer (*vesayetçi*) role over governance. Someone once characterized this as "democracy on training wheels."

Understanding the Kemalist Spirit

Despite their authoritarian, top-down approach, it is hard not to sympathize with much of the early Kemalist spirit. The early days of the new Turkish Republic are filled with a romance and idealism that created a powerful image in modern Turkish history. It is the story of a defeated country—the Ottoman Empire—utterly vulnerable to Allied plans for partition even of Anatolia itself at the end of World War I. The capital city Istanbul was occupied by foreign military forces; the old leadership, including the sultan and the court, seemed paralyzed in the face of military defeat and western demands. Atatürk's story is the bold and exciting tale of his decision to desert from the supine and leaderless Istanbul government and to head, without permission, into the interior to organize an army of national resistance against the foreign occupiers. While the powerless and pathetic Istanbul government of the sultan bowed to the punitive peace treaty of Sèvres—that dictated the loss of Turkish national sovereignty and huge portions of territory in Anatolia— Atatürk's nationalist forces were determined to reverse these conditions. In a series of remarkable campaigns over several years, a new military force created by Atatürk across Anatolia soon established a new nationalist government and proceeded to drive Allied forces out of Anatolia and to reject the treaty of Sèvres. Indeed the very term "Sèvres" has become a watchword in Turkey to this day to signify surrender to foreign forces. Westerners often accuse Turkey of still having a "Sèvres complex"—a deep-seated suspicion of European intentions to cut Turkey down to size and weaken its sovereignty. But the Sèvres complex is not mere national fantasy, it is based on genuine experience. Turkey in the end was one of the few developing countries in the world that escaped western domination or "mandate" in this interwar period. Ankara was well aware of what it had escaped. It directly witnessed the fate of those states in the region that did not escape, including all the Arab states that had once been part of the old empire.

When at last foreign occupation troops had been vanquished and a brand-new government established in Ankara, a new republic was declared; a new treaty was negotiated with Europe that rejected most of the terms of the earlier and humiliating Treaty of Sèvres and restored Turkish territory, dignity, honor and sovereignty. The country embarked on an effort to rebuild itself, create an entirely new republican order in place of the old dynastic order, and to modernize the country as swiftly as possible. The cadre that came together for this pioneering new venture came out of the ranks of an old reformist tradition that had been developing for over half a century within the Empire; but now it gained the power to implement a new order with full authority. The early Kemalist period possessed much of the excitement of the early revolutionary experiment underway in neighboring Soviet Union following the Bolshevik Revolution, though with vastly less bloodshed and totalitarianism.

Intellectuals in particular were galvanized by the prospect of participating in forging a new political and social order to achieve reform, progress, advancement, much of it modeled on the West: it reformed the country's legal system, changed the alphabet from Arabic to Latin letters, mandated new forms of western clothing, created a new national foundation myth, outlined the character of a new racially-oriented Turkish nationalism, oversaw a march towards state-directed industrialization, and established a sweeping new educational and legal system. It was an era of idealism, excitement, hope. It was also largely authoritarian; the sweeping reform, after all, was directed through unchallenged single-party rule. Opposition to the state was swept aside and rebellions were put down harshly. But the progress was real and major accomplishments were realized. A great deal of the coherence and strength of contemporary Turkey today rests on this foundation.

Something of the spirit of this early period and its class divisions are wonderfully portrayed by a number of Turkish novelists. Yakup Kadri Karaosmanoğlu's novel *Stranger* (*Yaban*) tells of a former soldier who had lost his arm in battle of Gallipoli, who volunteers to go to a central Anatolian village to teach in the early 1920s. He is horrified at the ignorance and backwardness of village life, and is overwhelmed more than anything at the psychological abyss between himself and the villagers stuck in their old Ottoman ways. They still revere the sultan, are ignorant of the great Kemalist "National Struggle" underway to save the country from the imperialist armies; and the villagers still pay deference to ignorant itinerant holy men—all of this representing values completely antithetical to the new mentality that the Kemalist social revolution sought to create.

The hero of the novel ultimately despairs at being able to communicate with this alien peasant world and cries out in bitter frustration: "Who understands me? Who will assuage my pain? Who can save me from this affliction, this place of exile? What brother, what sister, what soulmate? Ah, mother earth, how ruthless you are, how stern and indifferent you are to my woes. Am I your stepchild? Or are you my step-mother? If I'm your stepchild, who did I sacrifice my arm for? Why am I, at this moment in my youth, no more than a ruin of a man lying in some country ditch?"

Karaosmanoğlu's novel *Ankara* portrays the idealism of young people who migrated to the muddy new capital city of Ankara in the center of the country, infused with the enthusiasm of bringing education and enlightenment to the backward rural masses in this new social experiment—with overtones of the early Soviet days in the 1920s in which the Bolsheviks sought to bring Russia into the 20th century via forced modernization. It also reflects a conscious awareness by many Turkish intellectuals of the period of pre-revolutionary Russia when young Russian intellectuals idealistically and naively joined the movement "To the People" (*K Narodu*), to go out into the countryside and educate the politically illiterate peasants.

This theme is a constant in Turkish literature for nearly half a century: the unbridgeable gap between rural and urban Turkey, young Turkish teachers imbued with Kemalist values setting out for rural villages and describing their experience and the mentality they encountered. Other novels describe the growing new social drama as villagers start migrating to the city to live, often with "backward" or "reactionary" views of religion and politics. This early spirit of Kemalism was suffused with this idealistic trend, self-sacrificing in some ways, but in the end also showing a condescending spirit that looks down upon the people as a mass that needs guidance, education and change in their mentality in order to become "modern." They need to be saved from themselves. These attitudes tell us a great deal about the problems of the Kemalists in accommodating later political and religious trends in the country—which they perceived as backwardness. Indeed the military continued to see itself down to the present as the "guardian" against such "reactionary" ideas; expression of Islam has been the primary evidence of backwardness.

It was this gap then—between the ignorant, backward and often illiterate countryside, and the educated, visionary, reformist ideas of the new republic—that gave the elite the strong will to "lead" the people to a new and advanced, modern life worthy of the levels of European civilization. Its paternalism brought both good and bad results. The military, as the "guardian" of the regime, stood ready to crush the foes who would take the country back into the ignorance they associated with a reactionary clerical class who opposed Europeanization; they stood on guard too against potential separatist campaigns among the large Kurdish population of the country. The military's role as watchdog became the chief pillar of the new republic.

Let's not forget either, that the sultan and the Ottoman court, anxious to preserve their positions, had quite failed to resist the harsh European surrender terms (Sèvres) at the end of World War I. Only Atatürk and his followers did resist and saved the country. Furthermore, the Kemalist nationalists never forgave the fact that some clerics in the country remained loyal to the sultan-caliph in Istanbul—who had actually declared Atatürk to be a traitor for contravening orders and going to the countryside to organize armed opposition against European forces. This clearly anti-patriotic position of the sultan and many clerics severely damaged their reputation and was one of the major causes of Kemalist hostility and suspicion towards clerics. It was not surprising Atatürk decided to abolish both the sultanate, and soon thereafter the caliphate itself.

But not all clerics could be accused of being reactionary. An immensely popular Turkish novel and TV series in 1983, *Little Agha* (*Küçük Ağa*), portrayed an idealistic young cleric from Istanbul who, in his sermons, initially criticized the Kemalist nationalist movement as enemies of the sultan, only to be persuaded over time of the validity of the nationalist cause and ultimately changing sides. The novel had political and social impact because it created a human face and rationale for a religious individual who, on religious grounds, originally opposed Kemal's national struggle and yet came to understand and embrace the nationalist cause. This novel suggested that religion and patriotism need not ultimately be incompatible among people of good will.

Mustafa Kemal Atatürk died in 1938. But in the hands of his successors his vision congealed into a rigid and sometimes self-serving ideology—making Turkey one of the few countries in the world still to possess an ideology in the name of single leader—Kemalism. As with any founding genius, successors usually fall short of the original leader and the ideology becomes frozen, stale, repetitive and clichéd. Would a dynamic Atatürk today have approved of the nature of "Kemalism" in the decades after his death, in whose name all policies were justified? The most negative feature of Kemal's rule had been its authoritarian character, its hostility to tradition and to the Ottoman past, including Turkish religious tradition and values. Yet this authoritarian streak also needs to be seen in the context of the era. Let's not forget that some of Atatürk's European contemporaries included Franco in Spain, Salazar in Portugal, Mussolini in Italy, Hitler in Germany, Lenin and Stalin in Russia, the militarists in Japan, and in Nationalist China, General Chiang Kai-shek. Atatürk was relatively benign by these standards.

The problem was that the enthusiastic pioneering Kemalist elite ultimately became entrenched and came to believe that their ruling party, the Republican People's Party, held a birthright to rule the country. Thus they perceived the first electoral losses of their party in later years as a dangerous departure from the "correct spirit" of the country's revolutionary tradition. The military, or elements within it, felt therefore compelled to interfere periodically via coups to change the government. Often a sharp word from the military would suffice to compel civilian politicians to yield and follow military preferences, particularly on "national security issues" that the military defined in broad terms.

When the first free elections in Turkey finally took place in 1950, the ruling Kemalist party lost to a conservative opposition leader: Adnan Menderes who, as elected prime minister, sought to undo some of the harsher features of Kemalist rule, including its strong anti-religious character and its statist economic policies. But 10 years later in 1960, after winning three fair elections, Menderes was overthrown by a group of radical Kemalist officers, jailed, charged with corruption and violation of the constitution, sentenced to death and hanged, along with his foreign minister. An immensely popular leader despite his shortcomings, Menderes' fate became the symbol of military determination to crush political leadership that differed in its vision of the future of the country—particularly in respect to the role and expression of religion in public life. The trauma of this event was not forgotten. Today Menderes has been posthumously pardoned with strong support from the Turkish Parliament, his body transferred to a mausoleum in Istanbul and his name honored. But politicians had learned the cost of defying the military's wishes.

Yet the Menderes events actually marked the beginning of a new process over the last sixty years—the gradual unwinding and rollback of authoritarian Kemalist power and its control over the key institutions of state power. In this period the most extra-legal (or rogue) elements of these entrenched Kemalist forces came to be nervously referred to as "the deep state" (*derin devlet*), operating outside of and out of sight of public or governmental control and usually dominating the state. And yet, in the end, these continuing military coups benefitted the military less and less. In nearly every single case of military intervention into politics, the bulk of the electorate returned after the event to vote ever more heavily for political leaders who respect Islam and honored the Islamic past and traditions of the Ottoman Empire.

Does this suggest that the public wants to go back in history and restore Ottoman institutions and implement some version of Islamic law? Not at all. Public opinion polls consistently point in the opposite direction. But a majority now does call for respect for religion and tradition, freedom from military intervention, and an end to discriminatory legislation against religion (such as the banning of headscarves for female university students and public employees). Above all the public wants capable and efficient government and better economic policies. The three great prime ministers—Adnan Menderes, Turgut Özal, and Tayyip Erdoğan—who presided over dramatic Turkish economic growth and the extension of domestic freedoms, have all been personally religiously inclined.

We see something else here as well: the role of class differences in political leanings. The Kemalist tradition has mainly been upheld by an elite with western university education and a knowledge of foreign languages and cultures. That elite largely descended from progressive elements of the Ottoman elite, and frequently had its family origins in the Balkans or western Turkey. Indeed they are often referred to as "white Turks"—European in appearance as opposed to Turks whose faces reflect more Asiatic Turkish blood and a lifestyle that springs from the rural Anatolian heartland. First names in Turkish society can be revealing in themselves, reflecting the social culture of the parents in which the children were raised. Turks, ever since adopting Islam, had given first names to their sons and daughters that are Islamic, usually drawn from Arabic, as do traditional Anatolians and more religious families today—names such as Mehmet (Muhammad), Ahmet, İsmail, Yakup, Aziz, Hamit, Kemal, Fatima, Ayşe, İbrahim etc. Children of families of a modernist or nationalist turn bestow non-Islamic non-religious names drawn from pure Turkish roots—usually qualities of praise or excellence: Erol (Be a Man), Yaşar (Alive), Şahin (Hawk), Coşkun (Exuberant), Ergin (Mature), Güray (Abundant Moon), Oktay (Pair of Arrows), Deniz (Sea), Türkkaya (Turkish stone), Ertuğrul (traditional Turkish hero), Yalçın (Steep), Ünal (Gain Praise)—even aggressively macho "revolutionary" names such as Vural (Strike and Seize), or Savaş (War). This is also a generational issue, with "Turkish" names over time coming to dominate over Islamic names, thereby revealing small cultural facts about the parents.

The elite also benefitted in the economic realm: in the socialist-oriented economy of the early Kemalist period, businessmen from the elite classes developed close, even cozy, relations with the statist economic policies of the Kemalist party and were able to benefit from state funds that privileged them in the statist economy. This all changed in the economic and social revolution that came to a head in the 1980s, particularly under Prime Minister Özal, that began to bring newly-emerging and dynamic classes of Anatolians into higher education, business, and politics. This group is sometimes referred to as the Anatolian Tigers who have now developed a powerful voice in Turkish politics, society and business, along with a more distinctively conservative and more religious lifestyle, while still modern and "globalized" in outlook. This social segment is today a key source of AKP power, as well as of the membership of the large Islamic grass-roots Gülen movement *Hizmet* (see Chapter 12).

This reappearance of traditional and religious values accompanying the rise of modern new social classes in Anatolia provokes continuing military and Kemalist dismay with the emergence of elected governments whose policies are not Kemalist in spirit. The military routinely characterized such parties as representing a "threat to Kemalist secularism," suggesting that they are bordering on the treasonous. And indeed the westernizing Kemalist elite has sincerely believed in its mission as overseers and guarantors of the Turkish constitution and the westernizing policies of Atatürk. These policies were also self-serving in seeking to retain ultimate power in their own hands. It was not until 2011, as we shall see, that the ability of the military to intervene in

Turkish political affairs was largely and decisively curtailed—representing the end of a long struggle of over eight decades—or, in another sense, perhaps even over 150 years.

Nonetheless, despite the blows against democracy in four military coups, the military did have the wisdom in each case to restore civilian rule to the country within a year or two, although with new restraints. In this respect the history of the Turkish military differs markedly from the much worse patterns we observe in so many other developing countries where the military leadership, having seized power, holds on to it and exercises it indefinitely until faced with rebellion or counter-coup. Such has been the case in Syria, Jordan, Egypt, Libya, Yemen, Algeria, Sudan, Iraq, Pakistan, Iran, and Indonesia among other states (as well as in Africa and Latin America) that have been saddled with long decades of military rule.

The military was the main, but not the only source of Kemalist power. Other major state institutions were routinely filled with appointees and bureaucrats from the elite class schooled in the Kemalist tradition. The judiciary was a second key bastion of Kemalist ideology, and generally supported efforts to remove from positions of real power those who did not agree with Kemalist policies. The judiciary has thus been able to harass, indict, or even jail ideological opponents over long years—a habit that has not entirely disappeared even with the shift of power centers.

The problem is perfectly captured in the law passed by the new Kemalist government after the 1960 coup that formally *legalized* military intervention in politics in the name of preserving the Kemalist legacy. The Turkish Armed Forces Internal Service Law explicitly identified "the protection and defense of the Turkish Republic" as a key obligation of the armed forces—to be interpreted as the military saw fit in issues of internal politics. To oppose Kemalism in effect becomes an unpatriotic, even treasonous act.

The military thus pulled off four coups since free elections were established in 1950: it removed legitimately elected governments in 1960, 1971, 1980 and 1997. In 1971 Turkey had unquestionably entered a period of great political turbulence. A severe economic downturn produced social unrest that polarized society between right- and left-wing groups who engaged in armed guerrilla warfare against each other: universities were forced to close, banks were robbed, citizens were kidnapped, and the elected government grew divided and seemingly impotent to control the situation. Kurdish guerrilla movements also took advantage of the growing chaos to develop their own separatist goals. A burgeoning Islamist party emerged that became increasingly outspoken in criticizing Kemalist secularist views, crossing the military's red line of acceptable behavior. Ultimately the military, in a bloodless action, forced the prime minister to resign. Dominated by its own rightist elements, the military began exercising power through a figurehead prime minister who carried out the military's policies, including a severe crackdown particularly against the left and Islamist elements. Even then, much of the 1970s were dominated by disorder, fear, bloodshed, arrests, and executions. (We need to remember here that this decade were a time when much of the rest of the world as well, including the US and Europe, was wracked by student uprisings, anarchist groups, and violent politics.)

Politics were functionally suspended as the crackdown continued. Dissident elements within the military itself formed a Turkish People's Liberation Army that engaged in robbery and terrorism. Martial law was imposed that was to last for two years. Even though civilian rule was eventually restored, well-known old-time politicians were unable to restore order; chaos continued throughout the decade, leading to the coup of 1980.

The build-up to the 1980 coup came under similar circumstances after a harsh and bloody era of civil disorders and conflicts, this time mainly between radical leftists and ultra-nationalist rightists. Running guerrilla battles in the streets took many thousands of deaths. The military actually decided not to intervene prematurely in order to build up public support for intervention to end the anarchy. The economy had seriously deteriorated with runaway inflation. Senior commanders claimed they were also concerned that more radical junior officers might take matters into their own hands. In investigations in later years (see the Ergenekon investigations in the next chapter) questions were raised as to whether radical elements within the military itself might have fostered some of the chaos to justify harsher crackdowns.

This time, in the aftermath of the 1980 coup the military abolished political parties, the parliament, and trade unions for three years. Reprisals against violent agitators, particularly on the left, were harsh. A new, more authoritarian constitution was promulgated in 1982 which gave the military and security organs of the state greatly enhanced powers over national life, including suppression of ideas, ideologies, and personalities uncongenial to the military or Kemalist institutions. The new constitution reinforced the "responsibility" of the military to act against civilian governments perceived to be in violation of the constitution and Kemalism. The military also assumed oversight over university education that quickly resulted in serious intellectual abuses. In the aftermath of the coup, according to the Turkish press, 230,000 individuals were tried, 14,000 were stripped of citizenship, and more than 100 condemned to death. Hundreds of thousands of people were arrested and reportedly tortured, and thousands went missing. An astonishing 1,683,000 people were blacklisted.[5]

Although the left was the military's primary target, the army also moved against some right-wing nationalist forces, especially the shadowy, ultranationalist and fascistic Grey Wolves organization that had heavily engaged in violence during the period of public strife. But even then it was apparent that the ultra-right had close ties with Turkish security organs as well as with organized crime and the narcotics trade. These same irregular and illegal connections would crop up again and again as information was revealed about the unsavory ties among certain extreme elements in the military, violent ultra-rightwing zealots, the security organizations, and the underground.

The continuing and savage ideological strife in post-1980 Turkish society left an ideological vacuum in the country: top officers recognized the need to restore some kind of traditional national values both secular and even religious to guide the country. The new military regime spoke of creating a "morally strict society." Surprisingly, it introduced new themes into the national ideology to complement Kemalism: a "Turk-Islam synthesis"—a fusion of both nationalist and Islamic elements that could serve as foundation for the Turkish national identity. This "synthesis" broke new ground in acknowledging the tension within the state's Kemalist national culture— between secular Turkish nationalism on the one hand, and Islam on the other. The military hoped the new synthesis would bridge this cultural gulf and bring greater national unity. Even today, the Turkish nationalist movement still reflects these contradictions: one wing weaves strands of Islam and pride in the Ottoman past into its nationalist vision; the Kemalist tradition of nationalism on the other hand still hews to a rigid secularism and rejects the Islamic past as nothing less than a threat, even betrayal, of the Kemalist vision of modernity.

One particularly harmful legacy of the 1980 coup is the constitution promulgated at the time by the military. Turkey is still struggling to get out from under the illiberal provisions of this 1982 constitution, and while nearly everyone acknowledges the need to create a more liberal and contemporary legal instrument, political compromise for broad constitutional revision has remained difficult to achieve. The 1980 coup is still the object of much rancor and anger in Turkey. Indeed a landmark law was passed by the parliament in 2010 which retroactively lifted immunity from prosecution for participants in past military coups; this provision raised the risks for the military to contemplate any future takeover of the state. The most important single result of this new legislation came in 2012 when an investigation was opened up against retired General Kenan Evren who had overseen the 1980 coup, an act for which he could now be prosecuted. But the issues are broader, as noted by newspaper commentator İhsan Dağı: "...democracy will still remain incomplete unless the Constitution made by the junta in 1982 is replaced by a new one. It is not only the Constitution; the basic laws of the system are the making of the military regime. The Political Parties Law, Election Law and Higher Education Law were all introduced by the military junta. Thus, the leaders of the junta are on trial, but the junta's laws and institutions are still intact."[6]

The coup of 1980 marked the last overt military intervention by armed force into the Turkish state. But the tradition of coup-making was not over; it would continue in subtler form through back-door imposition of pressures, gradually creating greater public irritation. In 1997, when a coalition government came to power that included the leader of the main Islamist (Refah) Party, Necmettin Erbakan, the military lost patience at the explicitly critical views of Kemalism articulated by Erbakan's party. This time the military high command simply sent him a memorandum ordering him to step down from power. This "coup by memorandum" rather than by tanks in the street, has been described as the first "post-modern coup" in Turkey. It suggests that the rules of game were becoming better known and that actual acts of violence or arrest were not required to overthrow legitimately constituted government. It also suggests that civilian governments still believed they could not stand up against military displeasure. Erbakan and the coalition saw no other option than to resign. But it is striking here that Erbakan, an avowed Islamist, had even been allowed to form a government at all; even the military had to acknowledge the growing tolerance or even sympathy for Islamic politicians in the country. Erbakan could not simply be blocked from office out of hand; the military had to wait until he had taken concrete steps that the military interpreted as crossing their "red line" before pulling the plug on him.

This 1997 coup-by-memorandum marked the last successful intervention by the military, but it was not its last attempt to intervene. As the military's practice of intervention gradually faced increasing public dissatisfaction, Kemalist elements in powerful places within the judiciary more frequently turned to judicial means to block candidates, parties and policies they did not like. After Erbakan's resignation the constitutional court (still under Kemalist domination) went on to legally ban Erbakan's Refah Party the following year for allegedly violating the constitutional provision to uphold secularism. Turkish courts under Kemalist influence have banned at least 16 Turkish political parties over time—on the left, Islamist, and liberal.

The story was not over even then. Several more key showdowns took place in the next decade with the emergence of the successor to the banned Islamist Refah, the new AK Party (*Adalet ve Kalkınma Partisi*—Justice and Progress Party in power today). While the AKP leadership had indeed emerged out of the ranks of Refah, it had also learned a thing or two about presenting itself in a new light, no longer describing itself as Islamist, and focusing on a national agenda directed at meeting specific and concrete national needs. Even then the military and the courts still sought to quickly break the AKP as well. First, the courts jailed the prominent Islamist politician and successful mayor of Istanbul (and later prime minister) Recep Tayyip Erdoğan in 1997 with the charge of violating principles of secularism when he publicly read a poem that seemed to suggest some kind of militant Islam: "The mosques are our barracks, the domes our helmets, the minarets our bayonets and the faithful our soldiers. . ." Yet ironically, the poem had been written by Ziya Gökalp, an outstanding and revered nationalist figure of the 1920s; the text had long since been approved by the Ministry of Education. In reality the poem represented a call to both the nationalist *and* Islamic spirit of Turkey to stand up against European imperial powers. Erdoğan's jailing demonstrated the close cooperation between the army and Kemalists within the judiciary, including its top prosecutors. After six months in jail, Erdoğan was released and went on to found the AKP in 2001, but was personally and officially banned from politics for life by the courts (a sentence soon thereafter reversed.)

Again, in the weeks before the 2002 elections which looked like it would produce a landslide victory for the AKP, the chief public prosecutor petitioned the Constitutional Court of Turkey to close the party down and block its participation in the election, specifically on the grounds that its leader, Erdoğan, had been banned from politics for life. But by only one vote the court surprisingly decided not to close the party and the AKP went on to win a major electoral victory that brought it to power. Erdoğan was later permitted, this time by parliamentary vote, to take over the prime ministership despite the previous ban.

Kemalist public prosecutors still struck again, seeking to ban the ruling AKP's nominee for president of the republic, Abdullah Gül, from assuming the presidency. Gül had been the AKP foreign minister before then and a leading founder of the party along with Erdoğan. The prosecutor's particular objection to Gül was that his wife wore a traditional headscarf, illegal for women in public offices and to Kemalists a symbol of "reaction" that would bring shame upon the office of the presidency at official presidential receptions in an official state building. Furthermore, the president is commander in chief of the armed forces; yet in the military no officer's wife is permitted to wear the headscarf. The Constitutional Court upheld the ban on Gül's presidency, bringing the country to the brink of crisis, until the AKP won a second election by an even bigger margin causing the court to relent on Gül's assuming the presidency. The military had been partly intimidated by the strong electoral backing of the AKP, the first Turkish party in power to actually increase its representation in a second election. Gül, who is openly religious, thus became the first publicly devout Muslim to be president of the country—long a red flag to Kemalist circles. Tensions between Gül as new president, and the military in the early days were palpable and tense at public ceremonies, including the early refusal of a top military commander to salute Gül at a ceremony and the boycotting of his swearing-in ceremony by the Chief of Staff. But the military had been forced to back down once again and the handwriting seemed to be on the wall. Its final grudging acceptance of Gül as president represented a major setback to the Kemalist power structure. But the *coup de grâce* to military powers of intervention would come with the dramatic and controversial Ergenekon investigations shortly thereafter—the subject of the next chapter.

CHAPTER SIX

THE ERGENEKON CRISIS: THE TWILIGHT OF THE TURKISH MILITARY

In 2008 a dramatic domestic crisis between civilian and military leadership burst onto the scene that came to be known as "Ergenekon"—the military code name that referred to a series of military schemes and coup plots that soon came under investigation. By any measure this process marked a decisive turning point in breaking the 80-year-old tradition of Turkish military oversight and intervention into civilian politics. It also represents an indictment of the extra-legal "deep state" phenomenon and its dismantling to a significant degree. While certain public aspects of these frequent military interventions were known, the Ergenekon investigation uncovered a broad range of secret organizations and activities within the military that had not been previously exposed in all its scope. The facts uncovered in the investigation and trials shook the country's institutions to their foundations as the ramifications unfolded and the winners and losers in the political game were revealed.

The Ergenekon case officially concluded in August 2013 when the 275 verdicts were handed down by the Turkish court that included life sentences for some top military officers. The investigations had huge impact upon Turkish public opinion and the political order. Angry domestic debates still flare: does the Ergenekon process represent the long-overdue revelation of some very ugly truths about illegal activities by secret elements within the state over decades? Or is it a nasty fabrication designed to slander the honor of Kemalist, nationalist and military circles? Despite some of the sensational aspects of the investigations, as the weight of evidence mounted against those indicted, it became ever harder to dismiss the magnitude of the hundreds of charges made by state prosecutors, even if some of the charges ultimately turned out to be unfounded or poorly investigated. The full implications of the Ergenekon investigations were so far-reaching that it polarized Turkish politics essentially along pro- and anti-Kemalist lines. It is impossible to understand the future of Turkish politics without a grasp of this critical turning point that has permanently affected the prospects for the military in Turkey.

The term "Ergenekon" itself goes back to ancient creation myths of the Turkic peoples. The word is loaded with nationalistic overtones; it was adopted by the early Turkish republic as a cultural symbol for the propagation of Turkish nationalism and Kemalism that was to form the country's national ideology. Some rogue elements within the military adopted the term to lend deep nationalist character to the coup plans under investigation. Thus the term links a positive symbol with what were dangerous and ugly underground activities. It's worth examining the Ergenekon case in some detail since it tells us a lot about the power of extra-legal organizations that have been able to manipulate the developing Turkish state. It reveals the anatomy of the *derin devlet*, or deep state, a term that anyone following Turkish politics over the years has often heard whispered; it refers to groups of ultra-nationalist elements operating with illegal and criminal intent within, or even with the assistance of, the security institutions of the state over decades. The investigation sought to bring to light the existence of unelected, unidentified individuals operating clandestinely, employing illegal and violent means to attack those whom they perceive as enemies of the state. The phenomenon almost certainly has close parallels in Egypt and Algeria, among other Middle East countries that face similar challenges from their powerful military establishments hindering the democratization process.

The Ergenekon investigations in fact uncovered evidence of extensive murders, including thousands of Kurdish nationalists, some independent state prosecutors, prominent liberals, intellectuals, Christian priests, and even some nationalists, in cases that were routinely described by investigative authorities as *faili meçhul*—perpetrator unknown—and almost never solved. Those murdered were generally reported in the press over the years as victims of vague or unknown "reactionaries" or Islamic fanatics who threaten the state and society. But over the same period a series of small revelations and incidents came to light offering more serious indications that, rather than the actions of fanatic religious zealots, the unsolved assassinations were in fact conducted by actors who were part of networks within the deep state. While the murders of often prominent individuals were there to see, the existence of the deep state could never be established, and its actions were left unpunished. The deep state remained a shadowy concept over the years, producing a degree of paranoia that dark forces seemed to be operating outside of public knowledge or control and rarely discussed in public.

The idea that such fears might be more than mere paranoia or fantasy first burst into public awareness in 1996 with the breaking of a strange and sensational case called the Susurluk Incident—the tip of the iceberg. Susurluk was the scene of a mysterious car crash in western Anatolia that killed at least three people who by all rights should never have been sitting in the same car together: the deputy chief of the Istanbul police; a prominent Kurdish tribal leader (and member of Parliament); and an armed contract assassin who was leader of an ultranationalist secret organization called the Grey Wolves. Investigation of that specific incident indicated that they were all linked in a lurid and complex tangle; the complex interrelationships involved millions of dollars of drug trade in eastern Anatolia moved via the Kurdish liberation organization PKK, rival drug organizations, leading elements of the Turkish *Jandarma* (Gendarmerie—up to its eyeballs in anti-PKK assassination operations), military Special Forces, police and certain Turkish National Intelligence Organization (MİT) officials and some journalists who provided the appropriately-tailored publicity for the military. Apart from the shocking exposure of this narcotics trafficking, murder of Kurdish activists, and high level collusion among key state officials, wilder conspiracy theories emerged, including supposed involvement of CIA or American military elements allegedly working to "support the PKK."

Subsequent investigations—all before the AKP came to power—brought to light an ultra-nationalist plan to secretly instigate selected PKK Kurdish guerrilla operations against the state in order to justify the powers and policies of Turkish security and military organs and their domination of the state. Among their goals were continuing imposition of emergency military rule over large parts of the country—mostly Kurdish areas—and the empowerment of security and military organizations to dominate state decision-making. Even the prime minister of the time was implicated in some of the actions—all secret and extralegal—that involved widespread plans for assassinations among both PKK and anti-PKK factions. The plots seemed to strike at the highest levels: the targets later on included President Özal himself and a top general in charge of the *Jandarma*; both of these leaders had favored a negotiated settlement with the PKK rather than perpetuation of overt and covert violence as the military demanded. Disturbingly, both of these top level officials died under mysterious conditions within the year as did many other potential witnesses to the case. The sudden death of President Özal is now being re-investigated with indications that he was probably poisoned. None of this is to deny that the PKK is a very real organization that has engaged in large numbers of acts of intimidation, terror, violence, military ambushes and separatist rhetoric over the years. But some elements within it may well have been manipulated by those with an interest in maintaining "the security state."

As sensational as the Susurluk scandal was, it clearly demonstrated that illegal, criminal, even violent connections did indeed exist in high places within the state. The deep state suddenly took on concrete character as names, specific organizations, specific crimes, assassinations and other events began to be explicitly identified. The details sketched a picture of its dimensions and the seriousness of the threat to legitimate, lawful civilian governance of the state. Yet at the time no satisfactory resolution of the case was ever reached; while there were many shake-ups within the police and intelligence organizations, no one in the end ever received judicial sentences. A fleeting glimpse of the inner workings of some of these groups had surfaced and then gone underground again. But the deep state could no longer be considered merely the subject of fantasy. The public had just glimpsed the tip of the iceberg. Act Two of the drama emerged a decade later with revelation of the even more sensational and widespread dimensions of the Ergenekon case.

It started in June 2007 with the seizure of a cache of hand grenades in the backyard of a retired military officer—the incident that opened the door to a broadening Ergenekon investigation. Since then, with one seizure leading to another and to the discovery of documents, records, weapons, and operational notes, the full range of the Ergenekon plans began to take shape. Six years later the investigation drew to a close as the full extent of the plans became clearer and the widespread character of its diverse links better known. The long history of such irregular operations by deep state operatives was described in one study by a Turkish human rights organization:

> The operations may look like a film script to a foreigner. Non-Muslims, pious Muslims, Alevis, Kurds and intellectuals have fallen victim to provocations. In the wake of attacks in which the shadow of the deep state was clearly seen, non-Muslims were made to flee the country, Alevis were massacred, thousands of Kurdish villages were set ablaze and later evacuated, and hundreds of intellectuals were assassinated in professional hits, and any era in which tension was high due to such provocations ended up with a military takeover.[1]

The seriousness of these actions, past and planned, by these clandestine military and civilian activists was revealed in the application of the charge of "terrorism" against them. The charge has particularly powerful resonance since the military itself had spearheaded the struggle against terrorism in the country—usually in reference to Kurdish or Islamic circles. These charges, however, reveal that some numbers of officers were involved in acts, or guilty of planning acts, that involved assassination, murder and deaths of civilians in an effort to sow mayhem, instability, shake the foundations of the state, and provide ultimate justification for another military intervention and the overthrow of the AKP government. Operations included cooperation with extreme right wing nationalist groups, running death squads for years in the Kurdish regions of the country responsible for the deaths of thousands of

Kurds suspected of sympathy with the PKK, the conduct of racist and religious assassinations, and even threats against Turkey's Nobel Prize-winning novelist Orhan Pamuk.

Detentions among the military began in mid-2008 when more than 100 officers including several generals were questioned in indictments of 2,455 pages charging 86 people with incitation to armed rebellion against the Turkish government. In February 2009 another 40 officers were arrested and charged with planning to overthrow the AKP government in a plan that was allegedly code-named "Sledgehammer"—*Balyoz*. Among the officers were four admirals, one general and two colonels, some of them retired.

In the ultimate moment of showdown, in August 2011 the entire Turkish General Staff—its Chief and all three of its service commanders—resigned when the government abolished the right of the military to have exclusive authority over promotions of top level officers onto the General Staff. By Turkish law such promotions should have been the prerogative of the civilian government. The former Chief of Staff had planned to promote several officers who had already been implicated in the Sledgehammer investigation; President Gül refused to permit those nominations to proceed in light of the charges leveled against them, thereby curtailing the military's tendency to promote officers hostile towards the AKP. The European Union itself had weighed in on the issue: in discussing the conditions for Turkey's accession to EU membership, it mandated civilian control of military promotions.

By resigning en masse, the top military leadership had expected that such a protest would represent a decisive rebuff against the government for daring to raise charges against military officers. In the past, no civilian government could ever have opened such a legal investigation against the military; it would have represented an intolerable assault against the military and its role as "overseer" of government. Such civil charges against senior members of the military almost certainly would have sparked an immediate coup against the government, even more so if the charges had been based on false allegations and manufactured documents. This time the military, astonishingly, had little meaningful response to the spectacular nature of the charges and the illegal, subversive and criminal nature of many of the incidents allegedly planned. The mass resignations of the top military leadership—in protest and in a test of strength—in fact seemed to constitute tacit acknowledgment by the military of the overall case brought against many of their numbers. This event essentially marked the collapse of military control and intervention in political affairs in Turkey for the first time in history.

Any question marks about the legitimacy of the charges seemed to evaporate when the Chief of Staff, General Işık Koşaner, shortly after his resignation, privately addressed a group of senior officers a few weeks later. A surreptitious recording of his remarks was made and leaked to the press, in which Koşaner, in what was clearly his own voice, basically acknowledged the accuracy of many of the charges against the military. He went on to accuse officers within the military of betrayal by providing the information to the government. Koşaner was unable to refute this clear and damning recorded evidence.

Equally significantly, although the charges were highly sensational, public opinion did not rush to the defense of the military. Most Turks seemed to want to know more about the accusations. Some found the investigations to reveal just what they had long suspected; yet others believed that the AKP had used the investigation to tarnish the reputation of the military. The Turkish public has always expressed its highest admiration for the Turkish armed forces, yet new polling indicated that trust in the military had dropped from 90 percent in 2002 to 60 percent in 2011. Although some critics of the AKP claim that this assault against military prestige was a conspiracy by the party itself, the reality would seem to be that the public was beginning to register its dissatisfaction with the long tradition of military intervention in politics, especially in its repeated attempts to overturn the popular AKP. The military itself seemed finally to have grasped that time had run out on its "overseer" role in Turkish politics. Nobody accused the entire military of plotting against the state, but clearly a number of high-ranking officers appeared to have been involved. Worse, the military had allowed, or turned a blind eye to the subversive and illegal actions on the part of some of its members. The military has regularly acknowledged in the past the existence of radical elements within in its ranks who needed to be restrained from radical actions—such as the 1960 coup, the execution of Prime Minister Menderes thereafter, and threats by radical military elements to seize power in the period surrounding the 1970 and 1980 coups.

The highest-ranking officer of all to be implicated in the Ergenekon case was former chief of staff İlker Başbuğ, who on 6 January 2012 was charged with using military resources to establish websites that spread anti-government propaganda against the AKP up until 2008, an action designed to undermine the government and prepare the public for another coup. A number of journalists close to the military were implicated in these charges in conspiring to support the military campaign to discredit the government. These journalists generally represented extreme Kemalist or ultra-nationalist positions. A number of judges were also detained and charged with working with the military plotters.

According to the respected independent left-of-center investigative newspaper *Taraf*, operation Sledgehammer planned a series of incidents designed to create chaos and facilitate military intervention to overthrow the AKP government. The gravity of these operations can be seen in the nature of the destabilization operations with which the military officers were charged:

• planning and incitement of hatred and friction between Turks and Kurds, Alevis, and Sunnis;

• links with and support to some of the radical and violent movements, both secular and religious in Turkey, over the past decades; this included elements within the PKK, Dev Sol (a murderous leftist organization in the 1980s), Hizballah (a Kurdish fundamentalist group), assassinations of key leftist, nationalist and cultural figures;

• bombings of mosques;

• organization of mass demonstrations;

• the murders of three Christian priests and the assassination of a prominent Turkish-Armenian liberal journalist;

• the planned shooting down of a Turkish military aircraft over the Aegean Sea to be blamed on Greece;

• The newspaper also charged the Turkish National Intelligence Organization with tapping the paper's own telephones over the coverage of the Ergenekon investigation.

Critics of the Ergenekon Investigation

There are many within Turkey who criticize the Ergenekon case as fabricated, politically driven, and designed to intimidate and weaken the military as an institution and to discredit the ideology of Kemalism. In the first instance the Islamic non-governmental Gülen organization (see Chapter 12) is criticized as driving the campaign with its reportedly now powerful representation within police intelligence, the judiciary, and its media support from its leading outlets including *Zaman* newspaper. These critics of the Ergenekon investigation repudiate the cases as the product of paranoia, claim that it consists of evidence based on coincidences, sloppy investigative work and fabrications, and are part of a broader witch hunt against the secularist and Kemalist elements of society. Numbers of journalists were detained for investigation, many of whom were not known to be particularly pro-Kemalist in the past.[2]

Critics also claim that the hostility of the AKP and the Gülen movement to the military and the Kemalists is zealous and punitive, and involves the leaking of illegal wire-tap information to the press about many of the suspects. The long tape-recording of former Chief of Staff Işık Koşaner, in which he acknowledges the truth of a great deal of the Ergenekon charges, is one such case of a surreptitious audio. Although certainly illegally acquired, it was also highly persuasive evidence of military involvement in parts of the Ergenekon case; even Koşaner could not deny his remarks.

There is undoubtedly a lot of bad blood between the Gülen organization and the AKP on the one hand as longtime victims of Kemalism zealotry—and the military, radical Kemalists and ultra-nationalists, and extreme secularists on the other. Islamist-oriented politicians have been removed from power, including the bloodless coup in 1997. Members of the Gülen organization and other practicing Muslims within the government have felt themselves harassed, discriminated, and persecuted judicially over decades. Over the years any military officer who betrayed the slightest hint of religiosity, participation in public prayer, unwillingness to drink alcohol, or whose wives wore a headscarf or did not dress in clear western style fashion was viewed with suspicion and subject to almost certain blockage in promotions if not purged from the officer ranks. Finally, the Kurdish population feels it has been victimized by the military and the *Jandarma* in the killings of tens of thousands of Kurds and the destruction of over 3,000 villages—all of which is well documented. While not all of this is part of a single "plot," it does constitute a long history of extra-legal, underground, and illegal action by elements within the military in dominating the two most critical areas of Turkish politics: Kurdish and Islamic politics. Both of these essentially political issues have been consistently treated by the military as strictly security issues, requiring security and military solutions by the military itself, outside the purview of political solutions by civilian authorities.

Today there is clearly a growing feeling in Turkey that times have changed in regard to military dominance and that the shoe is now on the other foot. There is now considerable public acceptance of the need to prosecute and punish officers if the charges of criminal acts of assassination and murder over the years are accurate.

As some Turkish observers have pointed out, it is not simply the existence of radical elements in the military that alone planned for political and social destabilization and the overthrow of the past and present governments. There has also been civilian collusion, some by extremist Kemalists, nationalists, and rigid secularists, including many journalists. Some of these figures are now under investigation for such collusion when it involved planning illegal activities. Extreme leftist-nationalist journalist Doğu Perinçek is one such individual who has published quite rabid material over the years—which is not illegal—but who has also been charged with cooperating with coup planners to facilitate the plans for a coup—an act which is illegal.

In a watershed article, the iconic journalist, well-known commentator on CNN Türk, and longtime specialist on military affairs, Mehmet Ali Birand, published a startlingly frank self-criticism in *Posta* on 19 May 2011. Birand captures powerfully the mindset of Kemalist-inclined journalists for whom Kemalism was the only accepted national ideology for decades. Birand's self-criticism was stimulated by a book by another journalist who recently wrote: "The mainstream media has always supported coups and played a key role in the realization of the February 28 [1997] coup. These journalists have acted virtually in accordance with the pro-coup mentality in their genes."

Birand writes,

> For our generation the state always took priority, and it was always in the right. And it was the military that represented the state. Politicians were people who were tricksters, liars, who had no care for the fatherland and who were filling their pockets. But the military were honorable, heroes full of self-sacrifice for the fatherland. Besides, our father Atatürk had bequeathed to them the duty of protecting and guarding this country and the secular-democratic republic. The military had the right to supervise the politicians. When politicians messed things up, the military could intervene. Even when we experienced hesitation over certain events, we would write articles calling upon the military to act by saying, "Commander, where are you? The state is being lost."
> For us, (that is to say, a large part of the members of the secular 'mainstream media,') the priority was not democracy or parliament. The General Staff was more important. Nothing could have been more normal than this. We were raised this way. A pro-coup mentality had entered our genes, perhaps without our even being aware of it. We unquestionably accepted the superiority of commanders. We followed the glitter of the uniform with mixed admiration and fear. We treated all coups with understanding. We even supported them. But in the past few years our genes grew confused and we began to view things differently. For the first time the prioritization of the General Staff over democracy and parliament changed. Democracy has taken a step forward. But let's see, will it last? And now I ask all my professional colleagues: is there anyone out there who will confess to all these same things I have just related?[3]

An additional problem has been the Turkish legal system itself. The constitution of 1982, drafted under military supervision following the 1980 coup, put in place restrictive legal measures in which individuals could be detained indefinitely pending investigation. The military regime used these legal tools against those whom they perceived as enemies of the state. Despite efforts to revise it, the standing 1982 constitution still has not been changed; indeed this revision has been a key stated goal of the AKP and enjoys general public support, but the domestic politics have been complex. Thus those hundreds of individuals detained in the Ergenekon investigation were under detention by the same rules created by the military 30 years ago against its enemies. There were undoubtedly many individuals under detention against whom cases were weak or circumstantial. The police almost certainly exceeded their brief in some cases. Indeed, the AKP itself acknowledged that the rush to indict was excessive and that greater caution needed to be applied and the cases of those under detention brought to swifter hearing. Certainly many of those charged have been released or are likely to be ultimately released. Indeed Erdoğan himself in 2013 visited a retired top military commander in the hospital in a gesture of reconciliation and, criticizing the judiciary, commented that whatever the charges against some top officers have been, the charge of "terrorism" was out of place.

A further concern expressed by some is that, with the recently enhanced independence of the judiciary—strengthened in the reforms of 2010, and strongly backed by the EU—the judiciary now has greater freedom to run its course of investigations without external restraints. Police investigations of those possibly involved in support to Ergenekon plotters reportedly created a wave of caution among some writers opposed to the AKP in fear they could be swept up in the detention process, even if eventually cleared. Even the European Commission, which monitors the glacial process of admitting Turkey into the EU, commented in its 2010 report: "The high number of cases initiated against journalists who have reported on the Ergenekon case is a cause for concern. They face prosecutions and trials for violating the principle of confidentiality of an ongoing judicial process. This could result in self-censorship."[4]

Concern over the Ergenekon case extended outside of Turkey. Some of it reflects skillful lobbying on the part of Turkish military officers with close ties to the US military establishment, with the intention of utterly discrediting the entire Ergenekon process and portraying it as a power play by Islamists against secularists in Turkey. Some external observers indeed bought the groundless argument that the Ergenekon case in its entirety is a fabrication. Indeed, I myself initially had significant doubts about the dimensions of the Ergenekon charges. But doubts and suspicions about the case shared by many have been significantly rebutted by the sheer volume of evidence, recordings, confessions, documents, weapons caches, and decades of murky operations involving assassinations, drug running and devastation of the Kurdish regions—all well-known but that have never before been publicly addressed, explained, or systematically linked. None of the above-mentioned judicial irregularities, and even acts of score-settling that may well have crept into some of the procedures, should obscure the fact that the general thrust of the Ergenekon charges would seem to be accurate, necessary, reflect a long familiar list of events, and are long overdue. There can be no cover-up of the reality that radical cliques within the military and their extremist Kemalist associates in the media, judiciary and security organizations and elsewhere in government have in various cases colluded in criminal acts. A decades-long conspiracy of silence has been broken, and an ugly side in Turkey's political development been exposed, hopefully no longer to be repeated. It would be unfair to suggest that the military as a whole has been involved in such acts, but it is evident that in high places the military has not been sufficiently willing or able to police its own and clamp down on radical and violent elements in its midst. The obligation of military intervention "to safeguard the republic and the constitution" has been its dominant and unchanged mentality for too many decades. That is not to say that there will not be more political abuses in the future, from either the military or civilian side of government. But the precedent has now been set: such abuses from the past are now known to the public, acknowledged as unacceptable, and must be brought to light and judged by an independent judiciary.

By now many of those who support judicial investigations into Ergenekon believe that the net of investigation against process may have been cast too wide, with too many people detained on limited evidence, and excessive pre-trial detention (in accordance with the existing Turkish Constitution). One concern is that judicial overreach and judicial error may have served to weaken what is a vitally important case in investigating, bringing to light, and bringing to an end the most egregious actions by the deep state.

Some even accused Prime Minister Erdoğan himself as coming to constitute a new deep state through his own actions against the Ergenekon conspirators. And, since the Islamic Gülen organization has strongly supported the investigations into the military and its political operations, and is well represented within the police and the judiciary, those hostile to the Gülen organization have sought to blame the entire Ergenekon investigations on the Gülen movement. There is no doubt that the military's political operations have targeted and persecuted the Gülen movement for long years. The movement's rise to more prominent status today during the AKP government has now put it into the limelight. And indeed, as we will see in the next chapter, a bizarre new twist has occurred in the Ergenekon case, unexpectedly now pitting the AKP itself against the Gülen organization.

Understanding Ergenekon in a Wider Context

The longtime dominance of the military/security bureaucracy over the state has deep roots in the nature of the Kemalist state but is hardly unique to Turkey. Among Middle Eastern countries the deep state exists virtually everywhere to one degree or another. The deep state is a useful term to identify and describe shadowy, unseen and unacknowledged elements of hard power that operate corrosively within and around the state and from behind the scenes; the deep state targets opposition to the security-dominated state and stymies the emergence of democratic forces and individuals who would challenge its power. . It is able to manipulate state policies on issues critical to the deep state's collective private interests.

Such forces also exist inside western societies in one form or another—where, even if not illegal, their power is not fully recognized as actors within state deliberations. Giant corporations are one such example, security organizations are another. Algeria's deep state, known as *le Pouvoir* (the Power), engaged for years in extreme violence, nominally to stop violent jihadi movements, but also to eliminate other enemies of the state, to provoke instability and even to carry out atrocities designed to be blamed on Islamists. Most recently the provocation operations undertaken by the old Mubarak regime in Egypt —thuggish attacks against Christian Copts, and against demonstrators in the name of nationalist elements—are designed to sow similar internal fear and suspicion, to break trust and torpedo possibilities of cooperation among the political opposition. In the end the Egyptian deep state managed to capitalize on the mistakes of the Islamists, overthrow the democratically elected new government and to restore much of the trappings and personalities of the Mubarak regime.

Ergenekon not surprisingly has divided public opinion in Turkey. An EU poll in 2012 showed that 56.5 percent of the public interpreted the Ergenekon proceedings as a struggle against illegal gangs within the system, while 43.5 percent interpreted it as the AKP government persecuting the former Kemalist ruling class. As liberal columnist Şahin Alpay points out, however, the fundamental division in Turkish society is not between Islamists and secularists but between those who oppose a military-bureaucratic "tutelary" regime and those who support it. Those in opposition to the military certainly include Islamists, but also include religious Sunnis, Kurds who are opposed to PKK violence, and those with liberal secular political outlooks seeking greater democratization. And there are many who are broadly critical of AKP policies but who also reject illegal military action against democratically-elected government.

The major question remains: has military dominance of Turkish politics been decisively brought to an end? Even former chief of staff general Işık Koşaner in August 2011 privately admitted that there had been a coup plan and that the evidence for it had been destroyed. But, as one commentator pointed out, Koşaner did not in the least seem to repent or condemn such actions. Indeed he claimed that "nothing would change even if laws are amended or reformed; the Turkish Armed Forces (TSK) are here to protect the Kemalist republic, which is their 'natural and historical' duty, and no one can say anything to the TSK about this, and that otherwise, this would mean self-denial by the TSK."[5]

The Ergenekon case thus has had huge implications for Turkish politics, the Turkish state and society. The emotions behind the case are powerful since so many people have been touched by it for decades. The Ergenekon revelations stirred emotions and generated clear winners and losers. The victims of the deep state in the past are now among the most zealous in uncovering the truth of the past and demanding justice—in ways that have undoubtedly led to judicial excesses in the opposite direction. But the revelation and exploration of all this material is essential to Turkey's ability to embrace a deeper rule of law in its political life.

Indeed, in 2013 a milestone law was approved by the Turkish parliament: the rollback of the notorious Article 35 that provided justification for the military to intervene domestically in order to protect the Turkish homeland against domestic enemies. The new legislation eliminates a domestic role for the military and limits its role to protecting the nation against foreign threats. The Ergenekon investigations were further legitimized by a ruling of the Turkish Supreme Court of Appeals in October 2013 upholding the convictions of top ex-officers and 361 individuals in the key controversial Sledgehammer portion of the Ergenekon case; that portion accused these individuals of an attempt to "topple the elected government and parliament by force." But the case has not been fully put to rest: recent political struggle in Turkey between the Gülen movement and the newly beleaguered AKP may reopen some aspects of the case to reexamination in what is a basically political and not judicial context (see Chapter 13). In a major development, in March 2014 former chief of staff Başbuğ was ordered released by the Constitutional Court, reflecting an increasingly politicized division of judicial opinion. More disturbingly, key members of Ergenekon-linked death squads were also released on judicial technicalities.

The European Court for Human Rights, on the other hand, often critical of Turkish judicial procedure, in March 2013 rejected an appeal by a journalist/political activist among those sentenced to life imprisonment for his role in Sledgehammer coup planning; in its review of the evidence the court accepted that there were proper grounds for his indictment. EU review of these cases will likely continue.

Relevance of the Turkish Experience to Other States

The military in many countries then, has established a position for itself as "guardian" of the country, and its dominant ideology: Kemalism in Turkey, "Islam" in Pakistan, Arab nationalism in Egypt, communism in Russia and China. The military claims to protect the country against internal and external threats to the state but more likely it is concerned for maintaining the power and privilege of the military and its major holdings within the national economy. In economic affairs the military prefers a statist orientation that facilitates centralized control over governance. The military generally portrays itself as being "above crass politics and self-serving politicians." It often presents its own vision of how to "harmonize" society under its tutelage, in what is essentially a corporatist-fascist vision on the ideological spectrum. But the military often comes to recognize also that direct rule by the military can be damaging to itself when it gets drawn into messy domestic political issues. It will prefer to intervene only selectively.

It appears that the military's hands ultimately can only be pried off the levers of state power when public opinion comes to demand it. The military sometimes still manages to co-exist with democracy in some form by permitting a degree of civilian rule, but it usually draws "red lines" beyond which civilian governments cannot threaten the military's ideology, interests and power. Such was the case in Turkey too. But genuine civilian rule only emerges when a sufficient degree of democratic practice emerges that comes into conflict with military powers. It requires that the public come to see how the military thwarts the people's own political aspirations; the public must learn to speak out, and to stir political opposition in order to curtail military power. If the military is ever to retreat, it is only when it comes under this kind of popular civilian pressure. National disaster under military rule—economic, military, massive corruption, bloodshed, the emergence of chaos—can hasten public disenchantment with the military and facilitate its retreat. But such drastic conditions can also justify imposition by the military of even more draconian controls in the name of "stability." In the end this kind of military domination is not sustainable, but it may take decades before it collapses elsewhere in the Middle East, as it now seems to have done in Turkey. In the end the democratization process requires terminating *all* authoritarian controls in a society, not just military. Turkey's experience, including the rise of a new and vocal bourgeois class, may be instructive, as states such as Egypt, Algeria, and Pakistan now currently witness struggles to lessen military domination, as we will see in later chapters.

CHAPTER SEVEN

ISLAM, POLITICS AND SOCIETY

Most Muslim states face a common challenge: determining the appropriate place for Islam within Muslim societies. Yet it's fair to ask, why should Islam play any role in the society and governance of Muslim societies? One response is that religion in most societies has provided the early foundation for moral values and legal codes. Much of the western moral code has its origins in the Ten Commandments, among other early sources. It is logical that Muslims would turn to their own historical cultural values in establishing moral values rather than to those of a foreign culture. These religious values in the Muslim world can be and are interpreted in diverse ways. But Islam nonetheless remains a key component of cultural identity to most residents of the Muslim world, particularly when they perceive the Muslim world and Islam to be under siege from the West today. Islam cannot be culturally excluded from exerting impact on ideals of governance and society.

The West regularly urges the Muslim world to adopt "secular" policies, but even this term is loaded with implications of cultural struggle. In the US "secularism" describes a *hands-off, neutral* approach by the state to religious affairs. But many supposedly secular states have also been deeply involved in religious affairs, if only in a strictly negative way, such as the "laicism" proclaimed by the French Revolution, the radical and violent anti-church, anti-clerical secularism in Mexico in the 1930s, or by Kemalism in Turkey. These states sought to control and suppress religion and bend it to their own ends. That is not, of course, true secularism. True secularism stipulates that the state stand above the temptation to manipulate religion, stand neutral and equidistant from all religious and non-religious communities, and keep its hands off the free expression of religious or non-religious activity consistent with the liberty of all. At least that is the ideal.

Anti-religious "secularist" policies often evoke strongly emotional responses today when the prominence of religion in politics and society all over the world may be at its highest level in decades, if not centuries. Hostility to the concept of secularism in the Middle East comes primarily as a reaction to heavy-handed western political and military intervention: when Islam forms a key element of Muslim identity then secularism sounds very much like rejection of identity. Turkey's own "secular" approach to these issues is still evolving, perhaps now moving closer to the mainstream Muslim world in its willingness to openly and democratically deal with the question of religion in society rather than banish it. Turkey's experience has huge relevance to other Muslim countries.

In 2002 Turkey became the first country in the world to elect freely and fairly an Islamic Party to national power. As of 2014 the AKP has been in power for well over a decade, thrice re-elected—a milestone in the evolution of Islam in politics, or political Islam. What has been the specific modern Turkish experience in exploring the place of Islamic thinking within democratic governance and political-social institutions?

In simplest terms, after long decades of Kemalist ideology the Turkish state now shows greater tolerance towards domestic Islamic influences—a process that permits Islam to play a more public role in popular culture, ceremony, and sentiment. But Turkey is also a sociologically mixed culture— in ethnic, religious, and sectarian terms. The challenge is how to achieve peaceful balance among contending religious and secular trends within the country without suppression from any side. And finally, how might this experience relate to the political evolution of other states in the Middle East?

What Brings Religion and Politics Together?
Like it or not, the history of the world is a history of the linkage of politics and religion, in either cooperation or in contention. Religion is too important an element in human life, too powerful a motivating force for the state to leave untouched. Religion deals with the most fundamental aspects of the human condition: the meaning of life, ceremonies of death, the meaning of after-life, the source and role of moral belief, spiritual inspiration, sexuality, punishment for moral transgression, the ideals of the good life and the good society, justice, and good governance. Nothing else except sexuality and family has quite the same emotional motivating power upon humans as does religion. Thus the state seeks to harness religious values in supporting and legitimizing the state. But these same values can also serve as powerful instruments for criticizing, even denouncing the state when it fails to meet moral, social or political expectations.

It's no surprise then that the state seeks to ensure that religious institutions and leaders will give their blessing and support to state policies and provide it with a certain legitimacy. We mustn't forget that secular religions can exist as well—ideologies that can similarly capture the state. Communism was one such secular religion, replete with its own world view, orthodoxies and heresies that the Soviet state manipulated to its own purposes.

The temptation for the state to manipulate religion can be great, especially in times of major social stress or war, when the state enlists religion for its own urgent political needs. It will often make appeals in the name of religion, or invoke religion as a banner, as a rallying cry in wartime. Even Joseph Stalin temporarily suspended his persecution and suppression of the Orthodox Church in the Soviet Union during World War II to get the Church's blessing for the national struggle against Nazi invasion. The Catholic Church too, has been deeply involved in politics over long centuries including the blessing of any number of wars. In Israel religion and politics are so deeply intertwined that Israel cannot be called a secular state. Religion everywhere can serve as the banner and justification for a variety of causes, to lend them greater power, appeal and legitimacy.

In the Muslim world too, Islam has served state purposes over long centuries, chiefly to provide the state with a claim to legitimacy—the Ottoman caliphate, for example, or modern Saudi Arabia, Iran, or Pakistan. Islam regularly serves as the banner for anti-imperial resistance by Muslims against non-Muslim invaders. Islamists today still invoke Islam to criticize the legitimacy of authoritarian states that fail to deliver "just governance." The Arab Spring is just one of many examples in which Islam played a major role in the political and social challenge to authoritarian states and the debate over national problems.

In the Muslim world a debate is ongoing, questions abound. Just what is the appropriate place for Islamic values in Muslim societies? Should Muslims aspire to an Islamic state—a relatively modern term? Indeed, what *is* an Islamic state? What would an Islamic state look like, and how would it be constructed? Should an Islamic state be *imposed* as an indisputable good, or should its adoption be subjected to popular vote? A few Islamists claim that the public has no right to vote yea or nay on God's laws. Others say it's all about how you *interpret* God's laws. Still other Islamists might suggest that religious establishments should merely play an *advisory* role in a Muslim state, in seeking to ensure that legislation does not violate the basic principles of Shari'a. But in that case, how are the basic principles of Shari'a and the sources of Islamic law to be understood?

For many decades leading up to the Arab Spring the only serious major opposition to entrenched regimes in the Middle East has come from Islamists. But who are they? The term "Islamist" actually suggests many different things to different observers. At a minimum Islamists believe that the Qur'an and the Hadith (the sayings and doings of the Prophet) have something important to say about governance and society in the Muslim world, and they seek to implement these ideas in some way. That definition is admittedly broad, and deliberately so. Yes, the term includes extreme jihadists like Osama Bin Laden and other violent groups, but Islamism does not have to be violent at all— indeed most Islamists are not violent, however radical their political agenda may be. The term Islamist in fact embraces a spectrum from violent to non-violent, radical to moderate, democratic to authoritarian, legal to illegal movements, modernist to reactionary. Some Islamists form social movements, others form political parties, others eschew politics entirely. Some will cooperate with non-Islamist groups to attain certain political and social goals, others will not. Significantly, most Islamic movements are not actually led by clerics at all; most Islamist leaders today bear advanced degrees primarily in technical fields like medicine and engineering.

This strongly technical background of many Islamists may in itself be an issue. Technicians understandably tend to view problems in concrete, black-and-white terms, as systems to be adjusted and fixed: certain conditions should predictably produce certain results. Yet when such presumptive leaders turn to political and social issues, they often flail and fail, seeming to assume that societies can be fine-tuned like a machine. But of course the essence of political and social policy lies in compromise and choice by fallible individuals among many less-than-perfect options and means. The art of compromise is unappealing to true ideologues—religious or secular—who think in absolutes.

Nor are these issues static. Islam has been undergoing great change over the 20th and 21st century. Actually it is not Islam itself that has been changing, but the *practice* of Islam—as Muslims perceive its practice in new light over the passage of time and emergence of new conditions. We are not talking about reforming the religion itself, but rather changing *understandings* of religion. This is true in almost all faiths—especially Judaism, Christianity and Islam—demonstrating an ongoing evolution in the *perception and understanding of God*. See, for example, Karen Armstrong's *A History of God* that notes, among other things, how Jewish views of God have changed dramatically from when Moses was able to have a direct conversation with God in the burning bush 4,000 years ago, to a later period when God's very name became so holy that it cannot even be uttered.

Further challenge came as the Muslim world began to confront massive western imperial pressure starting several centuries ago; Muslims struggled to make sense of their plight. Why was their once-great civilization, more advanced than the West, now lying weak and helpless before western power? Some Muslims advocated abandoning their culture entirely and adopting western ways. Others felt a compromise could be found between their own cultures and western civilizational advances. Yet others felt the fault lay within Muslim societies that they had abandoned the true precepts of Islam, lost their moral compass, causing God to avert his face from the Muslim *umma.*

Muslims by the late 19th century began to look for precepts within Islam that could be adapted to the contemporary needs of Muslim societies. How could long-standing Islamic ideas be reintroduced into society to strengthen its moral framework and moral compass? What were the core elements of Islamic belief? And how could these ideas be brought into the political order to improve it?

It is in the presence of the Other that we perceive our own distinctiveness. In the face of the West, Muslims became more self-consciously aware of being *Muslims* in distinction to the West. As Muslim states finally began to achieve independence from the West in the 20th century, large numbers of them began to introduce the word "Islam" or "Islamic"—for the first time—into the official title of their states, such as the Islamic Republic of Pakistan. Of course they had been *culturally* Muslim for well over a millennium, but these new state titles represented a *public affirmation* of their cultural affiliation and distinctness from the West. And it was really in the late-19th and early 20th century that Islamic thinkers launched major debates, writings and theoretical discussion about what an "Islamic state" actually is, or should be. The very term carried modern political connotations. It suggested that in a world dominated by western models of state, Muslims should seek their own models drawn from Islamic culture and faith. But beyond the general claim that Islamic Law should rule supreme, there was no blueprint available. The Qur'an did not set forth a theory of Islamic statecraft. But, coupled with documentation of the way the Prophet himself dealt with day-to-day issues of the new Muslim community (Hadith) these two sources did posit a few key values vital to the concept of Islamic governance. A legitimate ruler must be just and upright, must uphold Islamic law, and must rule in close and regular consultation with his people (*mushāwara*). The interests and welfare of the community (*maslaha*) were a key touchstone in decision-making. And the laws of the community must not violate Islamic principles as set forth in the Qur'an or the Hadith, however interpreted.

The debate over what constitutes an "Islamic state" then, remains under intense discussion. But we can still witness a certain evolution of thought over time. Most Islamist movements, for example, have now come to a general acceptance of democratic principles; such principles help to ensure that the ruler remains just and accepted by the people, and can be *removed* from office by the people. Social, legal, and economic justice are perceived as vital elements of an Islamic state. Parliaments can be understood as contemporary forms of the Islamic principle of "consultation." Islamists increasingly have come to accept the idea of elections as valuable mechanisms to achieve these goals. But not all Islamists concur. One major international Islamist movement, the *Hizb al-Tahrir* (Liberation Party) for example, has developed elaborate blueprints for the retention of traditional Islamic institutions (including the caliphate) as a necessary "Muslim" model of governance even while fulfilling modern state functions.

As Islamist movements and parties entered into national political debates, they adopted greater pragmatism. But they cannot skirt some basic questions: Should an Islamic state be founded through democratic process? Or is it legitimate to consider the use of force to establish it—given the supreme worthiness of the goal? How should the leader be selected, or removed? What are the institutions that will promulgate laws? Who will decide on the Islamic legitimacy of laws passed? How are they chosen? What is the position of non-Muslims in an Islamic state? How much is it the obligation of the Islamic state to *impose* morality? In what areas? With what penalties? As we can see, many of these questions are not exclusive to Muslim society; they represent many near-universal questions of governance and morality everywhere. The Islamic Republic of Iran broke new ground in thinking about the application of selective Islamic principles to modern governance and we can witness a rich debate there that is ongoing.

The Turkish case is of particular importance since, starting with the Ottoman Empire down to modern times, that country has had more experience with issues of governance and Islam than any other Muslim state. Over the last decade or more Turkey has developed its own new set of emerging responses to questions of contemporary political Islam. Let's examine the expressions of public Islam as they have developed in contemporary Turkey; they have direct bearing on the evolution of thinking in other Muslim states.

CHAPTER EIGHT

FORMS OF ISLAM IN TURKEY: THE DECADE OF THE JUSTICE AND DEVELOPMENT PARTY (AKP)

"Erdoğan is the only leader who can go to pray in the mosque on Friday—and on Saturday lecture the Muslim Brotherhood on secularism." - Burak Erdemir

Turkey is a secular country. Neither the government, nor the ruling party, nor even the country itself is designated as "Islamic." There is no official state religion, despite the fact the country's population is 99% Muslim. Furthermore, Turkey's legal codes are based not on principles of Islamic law at all but on western legal principles. Yet by other standards Turkey is not secular in the technical sense, that is, a neutral arbiter: the state has long been deeply involved in managing religion in the country.

But let's put this in perspective. Is secular purity to be found anywhere? No legal code can fully free itself from roots in ancient religious moral codes; such codes were, after all, the first "laws" that came into existence in human society; they bore a certain "divine" character to lend them legitimacy. Staunchly "secular" America, for instance, still hotly debates the question of prayers in schools; US coinage reads "In God we Trust," US presidents routinely end their speeches with "God Bless America," the White House and Congress routinely conduct "prayer breakfasts," while God is invoked constantly in the speeches of politicians. America has private religiously-based Christian and Jewish schools that receive public funding. The oath to high offices is taken on a Bible, religious dignitaries are present, and oaths of office (and courts) conclude with "So help me God." England still has a national Anglican church and officially celebrates Good Friday; the UK, along with Canada, officially celebrates Easter Monday as a national holiday. Thus the meaning and practice of "secular government" can vary widely even in the "secular" West. It is along this *spectrum* of secularism that we need to gauge Turkey. Because underneath the secular legal framework, any visitor to Turkey immediately notices the choruses of calls to prayer echoing around any city five times a day and becomes vividly aware of the active role that Islam plays in daily life.

Institutional Forms of Islam in Turkey

As Turkish scholar and writer Şahin Alpay notes, three types of Islam exist in Turkey: "official" Islam (linked to state institutions), political Islam (Islam in politics), and popular Islam (grassroots Islam.) Official Islam is represented by the Directorate of Religious Affairs (*Diyanet İşleri Başkanlığı*), an office within the executive branch of government. Islam in politics is represented by the ruling AKP, in power since 2002 and winner of three successive elections. Finally, popular Islam is represented most prominently by a major grassroots social force known as the Fethullah Gülen movement, or *Hizmet* (Service). Each of these three faces of Turkish Islam is distinct but together span a broad spectrum of Islam in contemporary Muslim society.

In successive chapters we will look at all three forms of Islam in Turkish public life. Future political and social change in the rest of the Muslim world will likely reflect many aspects of this Turkish experience in understanding and practicing Islam.

The first question all Islamists are required to address is, should Islamist movements become involved in politics at all? Should they keep their distance from the state and politics, or become part of the mechanism of state at the risk of becoming politicized or "corrupted" by power? Islamists the world over have gained considerable body of political experience over the past half century, particularly through watching the experiences and mistakes of diverse Islamic/Islamist states like Iran, Afghanistan, Saudi Arabia, and Sudan. Debate over these cases is still intense. Since Islamism (Islam reflected in politics) was officially banned by the Kemalist secular state, the goal of pious Turkish politicians has all along been to permit greater freedom for the public expression of religion in society. Islamists early on addressed issues such as restoring the call to prayer back into traditional Arabic (instead of in mandatory Turkish under the early Kemalists); gaining freedom to wear conservative Islamic dress in public (especially women's headscarves); the right of women to serve in public office while wearing the headscarf; the right of pious Turks to enter officer ranks in the army or security institutions of the state bureaucracy; invoking Islam in public ceremony; acknowledgment of the historical role of Islam in Ottoman Turkish history; and greater freedom for public education on Islam and the Qur'an.

A progression of religious, or Islamic parties have appeared in Turkey over the decades, but they have all scrupulously avoided use of the term "Islam" in their party names—specifically out of fear of violating the constitution. Most of them were shut down within a few months by Kemalist-dominated courts as violating the laws of Turkish secularism. But these parties have regularly regrouped and returned to the political scene each time under new names even if with partially familiar faces; and with each iteration their platforms and rhetoric often adopted a more moderate and pragmatic tone. And over the decades more top political figures in the government felt greater freedom to acknowledge their own religiosity (seemingly never a bad move in politics anywhere). The major turning point came with the strong showing of the Islamist *Refah* (Welfare) Party at the polls in 1995 that won it a place in a coalition government in which Refah's leader, Necmettin Erbakan, eventually rotated by turn into becoming prime minister. This precedent, and the tone of his early policies, quickly led to the 1997 military coup which banned the party and its leader from politics. Yet, typically, the party came back in new guise, this time as the *Fazilet* (Virtue) Party, only to be struck down again soon by the courts. Finally a reformist wing of that party founded yet a new party, the Justice and Development Party (AKP) that quickly secured even broader political support, including from many liberals and nationalists.

Even though the AKP's top leaders—Abdullah Gül (still president of the Republic in early 2014) and Recep Tayyip Erdoğan (still prime minister in early 2014)—emerged out of the ranks of earlier Islamist parties, they rejected the idea that they were a continuation of past Islamist parties. They officially described the AKP as simply a "conservative democratic party, whose conservatism is limited to moral and social issues." Erdoğan himself had previously been a highly successful mayor of Istanbul which had garnered him broad popular support. As his aspirations for national political office grew, Kemalist authorities predictably moved to legally bar him on flimsy pretext from participation in politics for life; the sentence was soon lifted in view of broad public dissatisfaction with the blatantly political character of the court's ruling and the growing power of the AKP in parliament.

Turkish-Islamic Synthesis

Achieving a more public role for Islam in Turkey has been a long process. Despite Kemalism's general disdain for Islam in Turkish public life, in reality Kemalist and military leadership in the 1980s were forced to acknowledge the place of Islam as a valuable anchor or social glue in national cohesion. After the military coup of 1980, for example, the new military regime under General Kenan Evren sought to create a new ideological synthesis that would unite the two major ideological trends within the country to avoid further vicious and bloody internecine fighting. Military regimes in general often lean toward "corporate solutions" in which multiple elements of society can be incorporated and controlled under the state's wing. In this case the military government sought to forge a kind of synthesis of secular Turkish nationalism and Islam—in something of a departure from orthodox Kemalism—in the belief that the two trends had much in common in the composition of Turkish national culture and identity. The military's most immediate goal at that moment was to break the back of violent Marxist, Maoist, and anarchist Leftist movements which were then still strong and at war with equally violent ultra-nationalist, ultra-rightist movements.

It's easy to view this "Turk-Islam synthesis" with a degree of cynicism—as simply part of a military ruse to bring both these ideological forces under its own control in the name of "patriotism." But the concept is nonetheless an important one; it demonstrates that the tired old secular-versus-religious dichotomy regularly invoked in the West to characterize Turkish politics does not really tell the whole tale. Many in the military realized that elements of Turkish nationalism and patriotism could clearly coexist alongside religious and Islamic segments of society; these values were held by people who felt Turkish national pride in being Muslims and descendants of the Ottoman tradition. And even though the military always spoke of itself as the bastion of secularism, its personnel also inevitably reflected cross-sections of broader Turkish society. Believers cannot simply be categorized as "the enemy" or "backward reactionaries" when officers have mothers in the countryside who are pious and wear head scarves, or uncles who regularly pray, or school-mates who have sympathies for the grass roots Islamic Gülen movement. They are all real people representing a large and legitimate force within society even if many officers are not themselves religious. Thus religiosity could not remain forever simply a negative abstraction to the military; it describes genuine aspects of their own personal lives and families. The existence of these trends over time weakened the force of militant secularism within the military corps.

One clear and fascinating insight into this reality was revealed at the 2011 funeral of the "grand old man" of the Turkish Islamist movement, Refah leader Necmettin Erbakan, who had been deposed as prime minister in the "soft coup" by the military in 1997. His funeral attracted hundreds of thousands of mourners in Istanbul, including a broad cross-section of statesmen and even some officers in military uniform. It was clear that Erbakan had achieved status as a national figure and a patriot, even to those who did not share his Islamist views. He was a personally popular and attractive figure, sometimes treated with esteem as *Hoca* or teacher. It was significant that the chief of the general staff himself hailed Erbakan's "great services to our country as a valued man of learning and politics." *The Economist* magazine described Erbakan as "a moderating force on Turkey's Islamists," even though the AKP leadership had broken with him to found its own more pragmatic party. "[Erbakan] disavowed all forms of violence. He sported a suit and tie (usually Versace). When the army pushed him out in 1997, Mr Erbakan did not call on his followers to take to the streets. He infused his message with generous helpings of nationalism. When asked about his humiliation by the generals recently, he responded: 'They are the sons of this country too.' He quarreled with the state, though he was firmly wedded to it."[1]

A former general secretary of the Turkish National Security Council, General Tuncer Kılınç stated: "May God richly commend his soul; Erbakan was a nation-minded (*millici*) leader. We weren't able to understand him; the military did not understand him properly." Another general known for his verbal assaults against Erdoğan said, "If only we had understood Milli Görüş [the National View—Erbakan's Islamist movement.] It was a phenomenon of that era. I really value Milli Görüş's firm stance in the struggle against imperialism."[2]

And again, distinctions between secularism and religiosity blur in this realm of shared nationalism. Islam in principle is hostile to narrow ethnic allegiances or to nationalism when they shatter the higher unity of Islam. But in Turkey nationalism and the state have always sat comfortably with Islam, partly because Islam was part of Ottoman state institutions from early on.[3] In contrast, in the modern Arab world Islamic expression has generally been *anti-state*, partly because many modern Arab regimes have been autocratic and hostile to Islamism, fearing it as the chief rival and threat to the regimes' shaky legitimacy. It is important to understand the nature of this complex coexistence among these three forces—the state, nationalism, and Islam—as they operate within Turkish state and society; they are not always engaged in a simplistic secular-versus-religious clash. The AKP and the military already share a broadly common view of Turkish foreign policy with its expansive vision of Turkey's role in the world and certain shared suspicions towards the West's intentions. It is this factor that gives hope to the gradual long-term political reconciliation of these forces within Turkish state. The grassroots Gülen movement too in its earlier phases was highly Turkey-oriented with strong flashes of Turkish patriotism operating within the more familiar confines of Ottoman and Turkic world culture (see Chapter 12).

Islamists and Economics

Whatever the AKP's ideological roots, its administration of Turkey proved effective beyond most observers' expectations in multiple fields. This party with Islamist roots adopted a powerful and successful economic model that has appeal in a Middle East whose economic orders are weak and supported primarily by oil—which Turkey does not possess. The AKP built upon the economic liberalization and export policies of former prime minister Turgut Özal and former finance minister Kemal Derviş. Its economic success enabled it to win an increasingly greater number of seats in parliament with each new election—unprecedented in Turkish politics; these victories strengthened the party's hands in the political struggle with the military. Its economic success and electoral popularity also strengthened it against the highly politicized Kemalist courts which sought to block the party from attaining power. A successful AKP referendum on reform to the constitution, passed in 2010, further defied the military, strengthened the party, and cleared the way for its final confrontation with military power in politics.

Social Issues

While the AKP denies being Islamic, Islamic themes nonetheless can be found in many of its domestic policies. The party always made clear that its self-described conservatism applied primarily to social issues, particularly for greater freedom for pious practicing Muslims and for the right of women to wear the headscarf (a kerchief or head-and-shoulder covering, not a face veil) in public. Women wearing the headscarf had long been banned from attendance at public universities or from holding jobs in the public sector.

But many liberals, particularly women, distrusted the AKP social agenda as backsliding from bans on public expression of religion. Most prominently, Erdoğan succeeded in passing legislation that permitted female students to wear headscarves on university campus; they had previously been legally denied attendance. For Kemalists the headscarf is a prima facie symbol of Islamic reaction and the issue has become highly charged and symbolic. The fact that President Abdullah Gül's wife wore a headscarf was an affront to them—she was the wife of the Commander in Chief, she would be prominently visible at national receptions at the presidential mansion and hence a national embarrassment. The military proclaimed this to be an almost insuperable barrier to permitting him to assume the presidency even after his election by parliament. Only the force of public opinion expressed in AKP victories in elections forced the military to back down.

Neither Gül nor Erdoğan drink alcohol and have stated that it is fundamentally inimical to good social health. Erdoğan proclaimed *ayran*—a traditional yogurt and water drink—to be the national beverage. City and local municipalities in several parts of the country tightened controls over granting liquor licenses, and on drinking on the streets in public, and in many areas

100

imposed stricter laws regarding hours of sale in many areas, including in entertainment districts in Istanbul, but there has been no overall attempt to ban alcohol. At one point the party even flirted with the idea of criminalizing adultery—on the grounds that it constituted a social evil that weakened family bonds and hence the overall social fabric; any possible punishment was to be limited to fines. Eventually, on reflection, the party dropped the idea. And in 2012 Erdoğan made an effort to ban abortions but then backed off in the face of opposition. Erdoğan himself has angered liberal women when he urged them to have three children and personally criticized abortion. He has also criticized mixed-sex dormitories in universities.

Yet electoral support for the party has not stemmed primarily from such religiously conservative propositions, but rather from the spectacular advances of the economy. Just before the AKP came to power, the country suffered a severe financial crisis in 2001. Yet by 2012 at a World Economic Forum in Istanbul, Erdoğan proudly proclaimed that in the past 10 years under AKP stewardship the economy achieved an average annual growth of 5.3 percent, faster than any country in the Organization for Economic Cooperation and Development (OECD); at the same time, Turkish gross domestic product (GDP) and foreign reserves more than tripled while foreign investment grew over 16 times. Average national income per capita doubled. Early adoption of International Monetary Fund (IMF) recommendations for fiscal and financial reform greatly strengthened the base of the economy. The government made major efforts to promote business and trade abroad and to attract foreign investment to Turkey, particularly from the Arab world and the US.

Turkey's agricultural sector has always been strong and constitutes about 30 percent of the economy. Its industry and service sectors, however, increasingly represent the main drivers of the economy. Textiles make up one-third of national industrial employment, although this sector is now being surpassed in exports by the automotive, construction, and electronics industries. The government has undertaken an aggressive privatization program in basic industry, banking, transport and communication, buoyed by a rising middle class of entrepreneurs. On the negative side, Turkey carries a relatively high current account deficit, with fiscal imbalances that could affect longer term investor confidence.[4]

Scholars have debated the social origins of this spectacular economic growth that the party helped set in motion: did earlier social change in Turkey, which produced a new pious Anatolian entrepreneurial bourgeoisie, make possible the emergence of the AKP, its policies and entrepreneurial successes? Or was it the policies of the AKP that unleashed the Anatolian entrepreneurial potential? The answer is, a little of each; the roots of the phenomenon do go back earlier. But the important economic argument remains: can a more liberalized economy and social order bring about the emergence of a bourgeois middle class that transforms the economy? In this sense the AKP was both the product of social change, and the beneficiary. Such events would probably not have been possible a generation earlier. The Turkish economy had previously been dominated by an elitist bourgeoisie deeply in bed with the long-term statist policies of Kemalist-dominated governments. The economic system was not a truly open one due to the cozy relationships between state and top industrialists; business empires that emerged in that era owed much of their success to state largesse. After the economic privatization of the Özal era in the late 1980s new opportunities emerged for classes that had practically been excluded from the earlier economic order.

This Turkish experience has direct relevance for stimulating potential growth of Arab or Iranian economies in the era of the Arab Spring. None of these other states truly possesses an open or liberalized economy; in nearly all cases the business class is beholden to the state, or represent "comprador bourgeoisie" in Marxist terms. The autocratic state is reluctant to permit the emergence of a powerful and autonomous business class because it would threaten state monopoly of power. Here it is striking that the Egyptian Muslim Brotherhood had studied the AKP model with interest. It certainly understood that its own handling of the economy, and not its piety or Islamic policies, would be a critical element in any political success it might have enjoyed after its election to power. In the event, the Brotherhood, in the face of constant political crisis, was never able to implement a coherent economic policy in its single year in power. In Tunisia, the Ennahda party studied the Turkish experience closely, openly admires it and is equally interested in introducing similar innovations there.

The model of the pious businessman is not of course new to the world. Calvinists in Europe—the source of the Protestant ethic—or the Mormons in the US are obvious immediate examples. As we will see in following chapters, the foundation of the Gülen movement likewise rests first and foremost on new and pious Anatolian business classes. Unlike Christianity, Islam has always felt fully comfortable with commerce, starting with the Prophet's own profession as a merchant. A new fusion of economic liberalism with Islamic values may represent a culturally comfortable new wave in the development of the Middle East. Business acumen does not of course stem solely from pious bourgeois classes, but the combination seems a strong one. And the Gülen movement, as just one example, explicitly encourages business and trade which creates the wealth that drives its programs of education, good works and its growing influence.

The AKP could not have won elections and achieved the successes it has, including its showdown with the military, if its sole political basis had been among pious Islamic business classes. The AKP phenomenon also included a vibrant new trend of bringing together two other social elements as well: liberalizing secular democrats, and Islamic intellectuals. Secular liberal democrats by the mid-1990s had grown alienated from the old Kemalist political system with its tutelary, overseer role of the military that blocked genuine democracy and freedom within the country. Remarkably, these secular liberal democrats broke with the Kemalists and turned to the AKP in quest of the greater political freedom that the party promised. Islamic intellectuals, similarly, were interested in new freedoms of expression and in more creative thinking within the framework of Islam; they found the AKP more open than previous Islamist parties in Turkey.[5] Finally, large elements of the Kurdish population also found grounds for hope that the AKP might bring new thinking to the resolution of the Kurdish situation by deemphasizing Turkish nationalism in the future Turkish state.

Visitors to Turkey become quickly aware that it is often the women of Kemalist backgrounds who are the fiercest in their support of Kemalism and the harshest critics of the Islamists in Turkey—more so than the men. On reflection, this should not be surprising. It is the women who have the most to fear in their personal lives from tradition-minded ("old white male") Islamists. Women in every society feel their freedom has been hard won and nowhere yet fully achieved, not even in the West. They are aware of how traditional life in much of the Middle East and across the developing world has not been kind to women in treating them as second-class citizens and placing them under broad social restrictions—overseen by men. Males often spout religious justifications to support their biases—but of course you don't need religious excuses to find reasons to keep women down, in any culture including the West. Thus "Kemalist" or "westernized" women tend to be the most sensitive to any new policies by governments that might move women back to an earlier era or mindset, on whatever grounds. They distrust Islamists more than they do other elements in society and are more outspoken about it because they fear that they might bring retrogression in women's freedoms. They are also uneasy at the creeping conservatization of modern Turkish society, in which the number of women wearing headscarves has increased over time, particularly in the big cities. They fear not legal, but potential rising *social* pressures to conform.

Several phenomena are at work here. First is the ongoing migration of villagers from Anatolian countryside to the big cities which had traditionally been the bastions of westernized lifestyles. Second, this phenomenon is hardly unique to Turkey or AKP policies: note the growth of conservative and religious views in many societies everywhere, including in the US. But there is no doubt that the AKP has openly supported the freedom of women to wear headscarves in official work places, state offices and universities that was not permitted by the Kemalists. Nonetheless, it is also commonplace to see groups of young women walking together along the streets of Istanbul or Ankara talking and laughing—some of whom are wearing headscarves, some who are wearing western casual clothes, or combinations of both—at great ease with each other. Clothing indeed should not be a political issue, yet governments past and present in Turkey and other Muslim countries have made it so. Hopefully the politics of clothing is losing its impact everywhere.

Women's rights, but rights to do what? It is striking to note that a number of liberal-minded westernized women in Turkey have actually turned out in *defense* of women's right to wear a headscarf. They see the issue as one of freedom for women, in which state-imposed dress codes—of any kind—do not represent liberal governance. They too do not interpret the issue as one of secularist versus religious values, but as an issue of individual freedom, especially female freedom, against the oppressive state, or oppressive males, regardless of the state ideology.

Religious schooling, as in so many countries, is a highly sensitive issue in Turkey as well. School is where values and beliefs are imparted to children, but there is not always a social consensus on what religious values should be included. Erdoğan called for Turkey's religious schools at the elementary level, the so-called *imam-hatip* (imam and preacher) schools, to play a greater and more integrated role in the national education system. These schools offer the standard national educational curriculum, but also have courses on the Qur'an and religion that are popular among religious elements of the population. (Erdoğan himself and a number of his cabinet ministers are graduates of the imam-hatip schools.) He made it a key goal for the AKP to repeal a 1997 law that banned study at imam-hatip schools for all under age 15 and that denied graduates of these schools the right to attend university. That law had resulted in the number of students attending religious schools to drop by 90 percent. In a remark that stirred great controversy Erdoğan justified these goals by saying "we want to raise a religious youth." Justifiably secularists attacked his position saying that this was not an appropriate role for the state. Erdoğan struck back: "Why do imam-hatip schools disturb you so much? Why are you disturbed by vocational schools? Are the students studying at these schools not children of this country? Why are you disturbed when the graduates of these schools pass university entrance examination and study at a university? Why shouldn't a pious generation come?"[6] Religious education remains a hot-button issue between Kemalists and religious segments of the population. Ultimately its symbolism probably matters more than the reality; neither of the two camps is monolithic and both have coexisted for a long time, even as the Kemalists lose their former domination.

The AKP has indeed done much to bring the practice and discussion of religion back into the public arena—where it continues to evolve. Ultimately the liberal and secular charge against the AKP is not so much that it has actually imposed religious values upon the public, but rather that it has tolerated or encouraged the rise of religious belief and practice in the public sphere. Religion still remains a key symbol in a power struggle between former elites and a newly emerging bourgeoisie.

The presence of the AKP in power has spurred new thinking around the role of the state in religion. For most of the 20th century Islamic movements focused attention upon introducing elements of Islamic law into governance; the quest has been to bring virtue to society and the social order. The AKP is the *first Islamic (or Islam-inspired) party to achieve national power by democratic means in the history of the Muslim world*; this event opens up a new dynamic and places new demands upon the party. Entry into politics now forces Islamic parties to focus upon the social and economic needs of society; they can't win elections if they don't. Islamist politics have almost been turned on their head by the electoral need first to meet the *material demands* of their societies in a democratic order. Moral and spiritual values do matter, but where do they rank among the many practical demands placed upon the party?

A major dilemma in the evolution of any religious party comes with the question of morality versus legislation: how much can/should morality be legislated? In a mixed society where not all citizens agree on religious principles and their legal expression, how much can a religious party insist upon imposing its own moral vision? Neither the ruling party nor the state can really play "moral nanny" to society. Morality can no longer be imposed, only laws designed to encourage it. As one Turkish Islamist expressed it to me, "the gates of Hell cannot be forbidden to the public." Thus moral choice becomes an individual matter, between the individual and God. The state cannot protect the citizen from sin. And yet of course, in all societies the state does impose certain elements of morality; a wide range of personal actions are considered crimes and are punishable by the state. States may differ as to which specific actions are considered crimes, but a certain broad consensus exists. We are really talking about a *spectrum* of imposed moral beliefs that become law. Murder? Of course it's a crime. Theft? Yes, but there are more and less grave categories. Drugs a crime? Yes, but which ones? Alcohol? Maybe yes, maybe no. Unmarried sex or adultery? No longer a crime. Sex with minors? Yes, a crime. Abortion: a crime or not a crime? Porn—what are its limits? Over time shifting perceptions of the *public welfare* come to replace morality as the chief criterion of legislation—and it is determined by voters.

The democratic order thus places new demands on Islamist parties and their course of action. This is why some Islamists reject democracy as incompatible with founding the Moral State. Yet with the establishment of the democratic order, even conservative Islamists and ultra-conservative Salafis are now drawn into the logic of politics if they hope to succeed in exerting impact on society. Absolutism on these issues weakens them. They *compromise.*

The AKP gained further popularity through its many social programs, long a foundation of its success at the level of municipal government. Social programs represent an integral part of the AKP's moral and religious outlook. This was evident in its legislation making health care more affordable and accessible, as well as creating housing credits and other improvements in poorer neighborhoods.

A vigorously developing education scene also contributed to social change. Under the AKP the number of universities increased to 174 of which about 60 percent are public, the rest private; there are now some four million university students; two and a half million new university graduates entered society since 2008 with predictable impact on Turkish society. These students are now better educated, better informed, more middle class in their outlook, tastes and demands, replacing a more rural or working class perspective. Indeed, apart from the dynamism that this investment in education brought to the country, these same new graduates from university education are now more demanding in their expectations of government and less accepting of an older paternalistic political style. By 2013 the AKP actually began to face rising challenges from a younger and more politically engaged generation such as in the "green" demonstrations against the government over rampant developer schemes in Gezi Park in Istanbul that grew into a much broader protest movement against aspects of AKP policies. (See Chapter 24). These events emerge partly as a result of the party's own success in creating a more educated electorate.

There are numerous other indicators of party's Islamic orientation. As scholar Ömer Taşpınar notes,

The AKP leadership clearly views the party as a model for other Muslim countries. On June 12, 2011, Erdoğan told thousands who had gathered to celebrate the AKP's landslide victory, "Sarajevo won today as much as Istanbul. Beirut won as much as Izmir. Damascus won as much as Ankara. Ramallah, Nablus, Jenin, the West Bank, and Jerusalem won as much as Diyarbakır."[7]

It is evident in all of this that religious issues in Turkey are in a state of dynamic flux. We see how Islamists are capable of evolution and change in the direction of greater liberalism. And how Kemalists can realize that religious expression does not have to mean reversion to backwardness and ignorance. Turkey is unquestionably far more experienced in democratic evolution than any other Muslim state. Now in the Arab world other Islamist parties seek new openings to operate in an environment of greater political freedom to develop new economic, political and social thinking. But will they be permitted to do so? This will be the subject of later chapters. What is clear is that liberalization, democratization and modernization are far more appealing to the Middle East when they arrive *in Muslim garb from Turkey* than coming directly from the West or introduced by westernized ruling elites.

Despite the AKP's remarkable successes, 13 years have passed and time takes its toll. The party may gradually be losing some of its vitality and vision. Corruption has inevitably crept in; the AKP may now have peaked in its decade-long performance. Prime Minister Erdoğan's blustering, at times erratic and bullying style has recently starting winning him more enemies. Issues of major corruption at the highest levels have rocked the party. This is perhaps inevitable with any leader or ruling party and eventually leads to its loss of vital energy. We'll look at those problems in later chapters.

AKP Foreign Policy

Foreign policy is one of the primary areas in which the AKP has demonstrated a distinct new strategic orientation towards the Muslim world. But these policies are far subtler and broad-gauged than the ill-fated foreign policy initiatives of the AKP's predecessor, the Refah (Welfare) Party. In 1996 for example, upon assuming his turn as prime minister in a coalition government, Refah leader Necmettin Erbakan early on undertook a formal visit to Iran and Libya among his very first foreign policy acts. The visits were provocative to the Turkish military which was incensed at the Islamic symbolism, as was the US with such Turkish high-level hobnobbing with two states it considered pariahs. Erbakan also spoke of creating a Developing Eight (D-8) organization, a pointedly Muslim parallel to the Group of Seven (G-7), that would consist primarily of Muslim nations. Other trips took him to

Pakistan, Malaysia, Indonesia and Nigeria—indicating a new Islamic focus for Turkey. Note that none of these states were monarchies; Erbakan was interested in more "modern" governance in the Muslim world. But in the end Erbakan crossed too many military red lines, and thus was deposed by the coup-by-memorandum in 1997 and banned from politics for life.

Economics was one of the early drivers for Turkish interest in the Muslim world in the 1990s. The AKP clearly followed the pioneering moves of Prime Minister Özal a decade earlier, particularly in opening the Turkish economy to external investment and in seeking trade and construction work for Turkish firms in Muslim countries and in post-Soviet space. AKP foreign ministers—first Abdullah Gül, and then Ahmet Davutoğlu—travelled tirelessly with large trade delegations promoting new economic openings, playing on Turkey's new acceptance of its Islamic identity in ways not seen before. This cultural shift went over well in most Muslim countries, as did Turkey's increasing independence from the West in foreign policy, epitomized by Turkey's refusal to permit the US military to launch its invasion of Iraq from Turkish soil in 2003. In the next chapter we'll take a closer look at the important Islamic as well as independent dimensions of AKP foreign policy. In the end, we should note how Turkish President Abdullah Gül articulated a vision of the place of Islamic tradition in the modern developing world in an interview in 2012:

> Modernity…no longer belongs just to the West. We have managed to fashion it to fit the values of an Islamic society just as the Chinese have been able to style economic prosperity, science, and technology to their ancient civilizational ways.
> I would say that the concept of modernity is itself debatable. More properly, we should talk about fundamental values—social justice, equality, respect for the faiths, languages and ways of others; a governing system and economy that delivers the goods to its people.
> When you approach the issue in this way, and explain to the people that their values are not in contradiction with new ways and means to improve their lives, they take ownership of the process of development. …[But] if the idea of "being modern" is imposed from the top by authoritarian means, it doesn't work. That amounts to social engineering. There is resistance to it because it is seen as importing western values. We have seen this reaction clearly in the Arab Spring uprisings which overthrew authoritarian "modernizers" across the region. The Arabs are now seeking their own path commensurate with their values.[8]

Implicit in these thoughts is a recurring view: the traditional western paradigm of political values, as well as social and economic development is losing relevance, especially as the US has come to place its primary emphasis on freedom of the markets and national security—as interpreted by Washington. These values now fall far short of what the developing world wants or needs.

CHAPTER NINE

FORMS OF ISLAM IN TURKEY: OFFICIAL ISLAM AND THE ROLE OF DIYANET

Since the abolition of the caliphate the Muslim world no longer possesses a single authoritative voice for Sunni Islam. In fact, several different and contesting voices exist, opening up a variety of possible interpretations on Muslim religious issues.

Is diversity of theological opinion a good thing? There are at least two ways to look at it. Consider the Protestant Reformation in the 16th century. When it rejected the religious and political authority of the pope—long the single authoritative theological and political Christian voice—the result was an explosion of new and competing religious voices and sects within Protestantism, dozens, eventually hundreds. Some of them proclaimed extreme new interpretations of Christianity—some even turning to violence—that would never have been previously permitted by the pope. Thus loss of centralized authority can weaken ideological stability and undermine the caution and tradition inherent in a single venerable institution. A case can be made that contemporary fundamentalist movements have increasingly "protestantized" Islam; a variety of radical groups, including al-Qaeda, assert the right to interpret Islam as they see fit, usually in radical ways to justify violence or level charges of heresy (*takfir*—anathematization) against other Muslims.

On the other hand, the disappearance of a single authoritative religious voice can open the door to new thinking, creativity, reform and evolution. Changing times call for new ideas. Intellectual anarchy and debate can promote creative evolution of thought. Which of these courses is the better?

If there is no single authoritative interpretation of Islam anywhere in the Muslim world today, many powerful institutional or individual voices do exist. One is the Grand Shaykh (Mufti) of the Faculty of Theology at al-Azhar University in Cairo who wields significant clout as a major interpreter of Islam and a voice on Islamic affairs. His position commands much respect. But while his views carry weight, they are not universally authoritative for Muslims in any sense. The Grand Shaykh also happens to be appointed by the Egyptian government, a factor that in principle compromises his intellectual independence, especially when the positions he adopts on religious issues have often seemed to conform to what the Egyptian state of the time wants.

Various grand shaykhs have been delivering up fatwas for a long time, almost on demand, to meet the shifting political needs of the Egyptian ruler. This is one reason many fundamentalists seek to break the state's control over religion and over the "state 'ulama" whom they view as corrupted and intellectually compromised.

While the shaykh of al-Azhar is swathed in institutional tradition, not so a key rival, Shaykh Yusif al-Qaradawi, who owes a great deal of his authority to the power of contemporary media. Qaradawi is Egyptian by origin, a longtime leading scholar and intellectual and a member of the Muslim Brotherhood. But his hostility to the Mubarak regime compelled him to leave Egypt long ago and to choose permanent residence in Qatar. With the fall of Mubarak in 2011, Qaradawi began regular visits back to Egypt but soon fell out with the military regime that overthrew the Muslim Brotherhood government of Egypt thereafter. He remains a highly prominent and immensely influential interpreter of Islam. He is followed by upwards of 60 million viewers on the al-Jazeera satellite network on his weekly program *Shari'a and Life*; he also maintains the website Islam Online which offers rulings or fatwas on a huge range of issues relating to Islam in daily life, including personal faith, marriage, sexuality, political participation, economic relationships, and education. There is no other scholar in the Muslim world today whose views are followed as closely as Qaradawi's. Yet this is a self-achieved status—he has no formal title and no one appointed him to anything.

Other large international Islamic organizations such as the Muslim Brotherhood itself also have major impact on religious thinking, although its voice is not centralized. In South Asia the Jamaat-i-Islami or Islamic Association is ideologically akin to the Muslim Brotherhood and it too takes positions on key issues across several countries. There are a variety of local Muslim scholars of less international renown who also maintain important popular followings within their own countries, especially in Egypt, and offer *fatwas* or interpretations on the practice of Islam. Television is their lifeblood.

Due to the power and reach of media today there is probably more talk about Islam and its various interpretations and implications for society and governance than at any other time in Muslim history. Muslims show awakened interest in theological issues that have immediate relevance to their lives and the governance of their countries. At the extreme end of the spectrum we have al-Qaeda whose media impact, direct or indirect, is also extensive— although its every word is probably more closely scrutinized by western intelligence services than by pious Muslims. And while the few extremist jihadi organizations benefit from modern media, they enjoy no monopoly or dominance of the field and are regularly challenged by Muslim mainstream voices that operate in public; mainstream thinkers and institutions have an address, radical jihadis hide out.

In the Shi'ite world, of course, senior ayatollahs represent the sole source of authoritative contemporary legitimacy. But even among ayatollahs there is no single authoritative figure. Shi'ite theologians can be roughly divided between activist and "quietist" ayatollahs depending on the degree to which they support active clerical participation in politics. The late Ayatollah Khomeini in Iran and Ayatollah Sistani in Iraq are each the leading representatives of this polarity, but there are many lesser but still quite influential and independent ayatollahs within the Shi'ite world.

Significant Muslim voices exist in the West as well. In Europe, Tariq Ramadan, from an illustrious family of Egyptian Muslim Brothers, speaks with great influence as a scholar of religion at Oxford, but he is not a cleric and his views are in no way binding. Most of his efforts are focused upon defining the place of Islam and Muslims within European culture and society. He preaches a moderate vision of coexistence and integration between Islam and the western societies. And there are more intellectually radical voices, particularly in the UK, who speak out in favor of restoring the caliphate or of the need for armed resistance against the presence of western armies in the Muslim world.

Apart from these groups, there are few other Muslim voices with major international clout, although Indonesia's two huge main Islamist movements have gained growing respect in the Muslim world since the fall of the authoritarian Suharto regime in 1998.

Turkey and the Diyanet
Given these proliferating and diverse voices on contemporary Islam, Turkey's own voice and actions on religious affairs take on new importance. No one in Turkey issues *fatwas*—a ruling on a point of Islamic law—for the Muslim world, but Turkey is becoming less hesitant about speaking out on questions of interpretation of Islam for the modern world.

Turkey may nominally be a secular state, but it possesses an important state institution that represents official Islam in Turkey, the Directorate of Religious Affairs, or *Diyanet İşleri Başkanlığı*. In fact, the very existence of this institution makes it difficult to characterize Turkey as truly secular. But let's take a look at the transformation of this office over the last eight decades, particularly under the AKP. Diyanet supervises all religious affairs inside Turkey and is developing a significant outreach abroad. Its most important program, the Hadith Project, has major implications for Muslims' understanding of Islam all over the contemporary world.

The Story of Diyanet: Religion at the Service of the Reforming State

State involvement in religion in Turkey is a constant in the country's history; both the Ottoman Empire and its successor, the modern Turkish Republic, have been deeply engaged in the management of religious affairs. But there is a major difference between the two periods: the Ottomans strongly *supported* religious institutions and used them to fulfill state and societal interests; the Kemalist state on the other hand, with its own staunchly secularist ideological approach, directed religious affairs with the aim of *weakening* the power and role of religion in society and eliminating its independent power base. The Ottomans employed the offices of the caliphate and the *şeyhülislam* (grand mufti); the Turkish republic replaced those offices with the Diyanet.

The AKP inherited the Kemalist institution of Diyanet, but that office now takes a benign and supportive role towards Islam in society. Furthermore, Diyanet now uses its office even to project the role of Turkey in Islamic affairs abroad in the interests of the broader welfare of the *umma* (as Ankara perceives it.) Turkey now plays a far more vigorous role in religious affairs internationally than ever before, but Diyanet in no way claims to speak officially for Islam, or in the name of Islam. Still, it is increasingly willing to publicize its own views on theological issues and to impact the interpretation of Islam in other Muslim societies.

Diyanet today exercises three key responsibilities that determine its public face. It officially implements activities relating to "the beliefs, worship, and ethics of Islam, to enlighten the public about their religion, and to administer the sacred worshipping places."[1] Diyanet maintains a huge staff of over 100,000 employees and oversees nearly all aspects of public religious life in Turkey, including directing the religious content of Friday sermons all across the country. Diyanet has also employed many members of the Nakşibendi Sufi tradition—a major Islamist group that has historically comfortably coexisted with the state (except for some early Kurdish Nakşibendi rebellions against the new Kemalist state—more driven by Kurdish nationalism than religion.)

But Kemalist insistence upon tight state control over religion ironically led the secular state to end up privileging mainstream Sunni Islam while ignoring other Muslim and non-Muslim communities in Turkey. Kemalist secularism was never "equidistant" among all religious groups in the country, it favored Sunni Islam. Thus Diyanet's administrative rulings and policies, and its financial grants were not equally shared with the large Alevi (heterodox Shi'a) community, and the much smaller mainstream Shi'ite (*Caferi/Ja'fari*) community who together make up nearly one third of the population. The Alevi situation is especially serious because the Turkish state over centuries has publicly defined the historical origins and character of the Alevi faith in ways repugnant to this large community (25 percent of the population). They demand full legal recognition of their own faith, to be defined by themselves, and to benefit from any state assistance given to any religious community. Diyanet's continued imposition of essentially Sunni administrative rules on non-Sunni communities has remained a source of consistent complaint by non-Sunni or non-Muslim communities, including the unequal dispersal of public funds that went to the upkeep of Sunni mosques but not to other Muslim groups. Diyanet is now taking steps to correct this imbalance.

More importantly, over the past several decades growing popular pressures in Turkey have sought to redefine the meaning of "secularism" away from Kemalist-style state domination of religion towards a "truer" secular posture whereby the state would at least stand as a neutral force among religious communities. A shift has already taken place by which the AKP government has lifted suppression of religion and now encourages it. This change has come about not only through ascent of the AKP to power but also through shifting demographic, economic and social factors that have affected Turkish life beyond the religious sphere. Free market reforms begun in the 1980s have enabled the emergence of a new Anatolian merchant class, or Anatolian tigers, who have transformed the economic face of Anatolia in areas once considered backwaters.

These changes have come more from the bottom-up than top-down. Public hostility has grown against the old Kemalist civilian and military elite. Public opinion shifted against Kemalism's enforced, discriminatory "secularism" that effectively marginalized large numbers of conservative-minded and religious Turks. A renewed pride in the accomplishments of the Ottoman past and the Turkish Islamic tradition is now fully acceptable and no longer treated as suspect and reactionary as it was in the past by military, security, legal and educational institutions. The Ottoman tradition today figures ever more prominently in Turkish popular culture, festivals and arts. This is the context in which we examine one of Diyanet's boldest new forays into religious thought: the ambitious and innovative Hadith Project.

Diyanet—the Hadith Project
The Hadith Project seeks to examine the origin and validity of thousands of Hadith, that is, the thousands of historical accounts that transmit the

Prophet's activities in establishing and administering the first Islamic community and state. The Hadith matter a great deal in Islam. They are second only to the Qur'an in importance. First, the huge body of these reported events serves as a major guide to Muslims in fleshing out the details and the practice of religious concepts often rather vaguely expressed in the Qur'an itself. They are all about what the Prophet said and did in his lifetime. Second, the Hadith are overwhelmingly the *primary* source for traditional Islamic legislation (*fiqh*), far more than the Qur'an itself.

The problem is that from the earliest days there existed a vast number—over 10,000—of these reported Hadith from diverse individuals who claimed to have seen or heard the Prophet say this or do that. Often these sources reportedly got it second- or third-hand from some other source, usually orally transmitted. The problem resembles the efforts in the early centuries of Christianity to identify what texts and Gospels were "authoritative" or not, in a rather arbitrary process that is still debated today. In Islam, the huge body of reported sayings has been gradually winnowed down to some 5,000 today through processes of scholarly analysis, verification and substantiation over the centuries. There is still disagreement over many of them: some are categorized as more reliable and credible than others, and different schools of Islam do not necessarily uphold the same exact corpus of Hadith. Many of the Hadith also appear to be contradictory in nature, requiring resolution by scholars. Again, we are not speaking of *revealed* scripture here, but of human reporting about the Prophet from various sources and times.

The challenge of the task is heightened by the fact that historically one or another political or religious group favored certain Hadith over others, depending on their own agenda. ("The Devil can quote Scripture to his own ends.") Thus many conservatives tend to lean heavily on the Hadith to support their more literal interpretations of Islam, even today. They stand in contrast to Islamic modernists who emphasize the vital importance of *context* in understanding the true intent behind what the Prophet said and did. Thus Turkey's Hadith Project came into being, a modern effort to sort these issues out. This effort comes in the context of another, more radical, but soundly-based "Qur'an-only" branch of Islamic interpretation (non-Turkish) that rejects the Hadith entirely and believes that the true spirit and significance of Islam can be found only in the Qur'an. (This reflects the Protestant *sola scriptura* or reliance solely on the Bible as the source of Christian thinking.) The Turkish project in no way goes that far.

In 2004 an earlier head of Diyanet, Ali Bardakoğlu, wrote an important article entitled "On Updating Our Understanding of Religiosity"

(*Dindarlığımızın Güncelleştirilmesi*)—a carefully crafted expression that makes clear that it is not Islam itself that is being "reformed" but rather Muslims' *contemporary understanding of Islam* and the foundations of their religious thought. Modernists argue that many of the alleged Hadith were dubiously remembered— perhaps even fabricated—even hundreds of years after the Prophet's death in order to justify policies of later times; they claim many of these Hadith have distorted or lost sight of the original spirit and values of Islam, and have even been hijacked by conservative circles who formally resist the application of reason and contemporary textual analysis (as has been applied to Biblical studies) to religious understanding. While there have been many undertakings over centuries by individual Islamic scholars to verify the soundness of various Hadith, this effort by Diyanet represents a major institutional project to do so in the modern era. Diyanet began holding public classes around Turkey to study and think about the Hadith—a major educational outreach with the potential of changing thinking about the true meaning of religion.

Indeed, such an examination could lead to the rejection of the validity of many Hadith often quoted by extremist and violent groups today in defense of their radical agendas. Furthermore, human religious understanding has naturally evolved and advanced over time, providing fresh insight into what the real intentions of the Prophet might have been at the time in making certain judgments in the early Islamic state. In fact, most modernist interpretation of Islam focus on understanding the *context* more than the literal *text* of these reported sayings and doings. The thrust is towards understanding the *spirit and underlying principles* that lie behind certain statements and actions. Modern analysis of these Hadith or traditions of the Prophet help Muslims to interpret in a more knowledgeable way the spirit of these past events as it relates to today, rather than clinging to literal readings of events of a millennium and a half ago. A simple example are the Prophet's reported various statements about the undesirability of wearing silk. At the time silk in Arabia was quite scarce and represented conspicuous consumption. Today silk is widely available to all; the true intent of the statement was to avoid ostentation, not attacking the character of silk itself.

A BBC commentator reporting on the Hadith Project in 2007 excitedly suggested that "the spirit of logic and reason inherent in Islam at its foundation 1,400 years ago are being rediscovered. Some believe it could represent the beginning of a reformation in the religion."[2] But the new head of Diyanet and the Hadith Project, Dr. Mehmet Görmez, was at pains to dispel such sensationalist ideas that the Hadith Project is about "reforming

Islam"—language he knows could be incendiary. When asked about the ultimate aim of Diyanet's project he responded: "There are three aims: firstly, to isolate misunderstandings that stem from the history [of the Hadith]; secondly to make clear how much [of the understanding of the Hadith] is cultural, how much is traditional, and how much is [actually] religious; thirdly to help people today to understand them right." Görmez points out that "there have been no similar studies of the Hadith in the Arab world. Turkey comes from a different tradition. We cannot discard the Ottoman tradition. It was open-minded. We can discuss anything here, and there is a good level of scholarly knowledge in Turkey. For these reasons, it's important to do this work here in Turkey." Thus Görmez links the tradition of objective scholarly inquiry with the Ottoman tradition itself, suggesting both a new theological role for Turkey as well as the restoration of a balanced approach toward religion that has not existed in Turkey since the start of the Kemalist era.[3]

The fact that such a Hadith Project is underway in Turkey today under the AKP will certainly find greater resonance in the rest of the Muslim world. If such a project had been announced by the staunchly anti-religious Kemalist governments in the past, the rest of the Muslim world would surely have rejected it out of hand. Today, because Turkey is coming to terms with and embracing its Islamic past, culture and Islamic roots, the project commands far greater credibility among other Muslims. This Hadith Project may therefore encourage and influence more contemporary and thoughtful reassessments of the foundations of Muslim thinking, just as has taken place in the modern evolution of Christianity and Judaism. The role of the school of theology at al-Azhar University in Cairo, linked to the state, is positioned to play a similar role today. While this change will not come quickly and the conclusions of the Turkish project may not be quickly adopted by other Muslim societies, or even by some conservative religious circles in Turkey itself, it marks an important and significant pioneering step by a "new" Turkey.

The character of the "new" Turkey matters a lot in today's global Muslim society that everywhere feels under siege and facing the discrimination of rising Islamophobia in the West. These conditions—war, invasion by US and NATO troops, foreign occupation, assassinations by drones, popular denigration of Islam, and the entire mechanism of George Bush's Global War on Terrorism—have created the most negative possible context for any liberal rethinking of the meaning of Islam and its prescriptions. Under threat and assault, the natural response of any religious or social group is to hunker down, circle the wagons, go back to its roots, and embrace basic principles as a statement of commitment, solidarity, and loyalty to the very heart of culture and religion. Such stressful conditions imposed by western forces actively undermine an environment in which a more liberal and open examination of Muslim tradition and belief could emerge.

The problem is heightened as non-Muslims in the West itself have taken it upon themselves to dissect and criticize Islam—often for their own narrow political and strategic ends. Muslims are naturally suspicious of the unfriendly and condescending character of many western projects that promise to explore "what is wrong with Islam" and how to "reform and change Islam"; these suspicions are compounded when these goals are usually self-serving, ill-informed, and seek to place the blame for all strategic conflict on the "flawed" Muslim adversary. Let's not forget how difficult it was to find open and frank examination of American foreign policies in the immediate aftermath of 9/11, when reflexive patriotism constituted virtually the only acceptable analysis of events. Perish the thought that long-standing and ill-conceived US policies might have had anything to do with the rise of radicalism and violence within the Muslim world. Societies that feel themselves under siege usually lose their capacity for liberal self-examination. We cannot expect Muslim society to calm and restore the balance of normal life until the West ends its siege, military presence and constant interference into the Muslim world. Only at that point will an atmosphere emerge that is more conducive to liberal interpretation of its own faith.

Look what happened, for example, when the Chechens of the Caucasus found their capital city of Grozny under bombing and siege by Moscow in 1999: they declared the full adoption of Islamic law for the first time ever, including implementation of traditional Islamic punishments such as cutting off the hands of thieves. This was an in-your-face proclamation of resistance and defiance, a forceful assertion of the Muslim character of Chechen identity and nationalism—against Russian and Christian Moscow.

Diyanet's Görmez interestingly links the Hadith Project to what he sees as a more open character of religious thought in the Ottoman past.

> You cannot show me from the 600-year history of the Ottoman Empire a case of a person being stoned for adultery or a thief whose hand was amputated... Punishment is not on our agenda. We are putting the emphasis on belief, on worship, morality, individual and social life, women's rights, relations between the individual and God, between individuals, between people and nature. We have no aim to put issues from history (such as punishments) on the agenda.[4]

Görmez, along with other Muslim modernists, argues that what many people take for "Islam" is actually traditional cultural practice in various parts of the world such as female circumcision, or the stoning of adulterers, both adopted from the Old Testament. Görmez relates the following story to illustrate his point about mixing culture and religion.

> Let me tell you of a discussion I had with Yusuf Islam [the English rock singer and convert to Islam, formerly known as Cat Stevens] whom I met in 1996. He was wearing a thin white cloak. He had a black turban on his head. He had a long beard, while I was wearing a suit. I was introduced as a Hadith scholar... "Are my clothes in conformity with Sunni Muslim teaching?" he asked me. I said: "Imagine a battle between the Prophet and his followers, and infidels. What was the difference in their clothes? They were all wearing cloaks and turbans..." Then I asked him "What if our Prophet had gone to Siberia instead of living in a climate of 50 degrees Celsius? Would wearing fur be considered irreligious?... It was Ramadan and we were about to end our fast. He ended his with dates [according to the Arab tradition] while I ate olives. I told him there are no dates in my country. ...On clothing, I said we should [simply] dress in a way that does not make sexuality obvious.[5]

This anecdote comes at a time when Islam is often culturally "Arabized" in other parts of the Muslim world in order to seem more "authentic": Arab clothing and food, for example, are now widely emulated in Malaysia as being "more Islamic."

The new focus of the Diyanet suggests that its message is not limited to the practice of Islam in Turkey, but intended for the world. In his first speech after appointment as president, Görmez stated that the Diyanet will "act on the principle of service to all the world's Muslims, all the oppressed nations of the globe, all Muslim minorities." The sweep and ambition of this statement is startling. It resembles nothing less than a principle of foreign policy. It also happens to represent a major theme of service (*Hizmet*) that is central to the Gülen movement.

Turkey is indeed quietly striving to establish a position of leadership both through the use of Islamic values as well as its own interpretation of moderate Islam. This interpretation is not simply the product of Diyanet bureaucrats; it comes out of the work of the Ankara School, a group of scholars at the Theological Faculty of Ankara University where intense work on review of the Hadith is taking place. Arab scholars, aware of the sensitivity of the topic back home, often quietly visit the Ankara School to learn of its work and how it might apply to theological review in their own countries. Dr. Mehmet Paçaçi, a faculty member at Ankara University, was subsequently appointed Director of Foreign Relations at Diyanet in 2011, further reflecting the important international impact of Diyanet's work and the effort to place Turkey front and center in this enterprise. Paçaçi believes that the emphasis upon literalism in Islam, while always present in history, is a particularly *modern* phenomenon, one promoted by 19th-century Egypt in a movement that ignored earlier Islamic traditions of open inquiry and revision of Hadith traditions. He speaks of "rethinking" Islam, not as a deviation from classicism in Islam's roots, but as a *return to classicism*. It represents a more rational and individualistic approach to religious understanding than was common in the past.[6]

But can we say that Diyanet's work is in any sense authoritative? After all, it is an administrative office within the executive branch of government. Should a secular state even be involved in theological interpretations? And does its work therefore carry any credibility with Muslims, especially outside of Turkey? In the first instance, Diyanet is working with qualified theologians from the Ankara Faculty of Theology. Diyanet, among its various functions, has always been responsible for the interpretation of religion within the country from the earliest days of the Turkish republic; thus its work in this field is nothing new. There is no denying that Diyanet's work is still at the service of the state. But the state itself has changed dramatically over the past decades in its perception and handling of religious affairs, reflecting change across the entire country. Understandably, the key goal of Kemalist administrations was to prevent the rise of religious radicalism in Turkey. But today under the AKP, Diyanet has now adopted a mission to bring new thinking to old Islamic precepts. Diyanet is now tolerant towards the Gülen movement that had long been an object of persecution by the Kemalist state (see next chapter.)

> [I]t is striking how much Diyanet's religious and moral advice conforms to values promoted by the modern Turkish republic, which are widely accepted by the Turkish public. Diyanet's stance on contemporary issues, such as birth control, in vitro fertilization, organ transplantation, and sexuality, as well as how these subjects should be taught in schools, broadly reflects the views and opinions of a majority of the population. Diyanet accepts and promotes Turkish nationalism, one of the pillars of the Turkish republic, and provides it with a religious legitimacy.[7]

Nonetheless, Diyanet has its detractors within Turkey including hardline Islamists who see it as a creature of the state that is still manipulating the essence of Islam and watering it down for its own domestic and international uses. One prominent Islamist historian Ismail Kara points out that Arabs and Turks reacted quite differently to the abolition of the caliphate: Arabs turned to new schemes for the creation of an Islamic state. But because that avenue in secular Turkey was legally closed to them, Turkish Islamists found hope in Sufi brotherhoods where Islam could be harbored and preserved from the pressures of the Kemalist radical secularists—thereby preserving a spirit distant from the strict Salafi interpretations that emerged in the Arab world.[8]

One of the great political ironies of the Hadith Project is the contradictory attacks made upon the AKP from the right as well as from the left. Both more radical Islamists, as well as hardline Kemalist opponents of the AKP, accuse it of being a tool of Washington, in fulfillment of some kind of "American project" to change Islam and establish US dominance in the Middle East. Yet this ironically comes at a time when neoconservative and Zionist groups in the US routinely attack the AKP as an "anti-western" party that has "shifted Turkey into the enemy column." In this interpretation, the US has supposedly now come to view "moderate Islam" as the best antidote to radical Islam and hence is now in the business of promoting moderate Islamism in Turkey. Even the mere thought of Washington engaging in any such alleged "AKP project" infuriates Kemalists and nationalists who believe Washington is imposing the party on Turkey in order to promote broader US interests in the Middle East. These rather paranoid interpretations overlook long-standing Washington hostility to nearly all Islamists in the Middle East.

One of Diyanet's particular efforts has been to examine and cast doubt upon some Hadith that are considered misogynistic, in the belief that such denigration of women is clearly contrary to the essential spirit of the Qur'an and the Prophet's reforming vision of the time. As Mustafa Akyol points out in his thoughtful book, *Islam without Extremes*, new understanding of the true spirit and message towards women in the Qur'an does not come solely from scholarly work in Diyanet; it reflects the rise of educated professional middle-class women in Turkey who themselves challenge the historical legitimacy of traditionalist Hadith. They draw public attention to the problematic nature of some Hadith that are "historical" and "cultural" in nature (from old traditional males), and are not religious in origin.[9]

Turkey's advanced social development is one of the best arguments for the acceptability of new thinking (or a return to "classical" thinking) in Islam that was previously missing among traditional and ill-educated segments of society. In 2011 Görmez publicly criticized conservative views that place the blame on women who are subjected to rape or sexual harassment if dressed in less-than-modest clothing; "rape and sexual harassment is a crime committed against all humanity," he said. (This same debate is not unknown in western societies.)

In another unusually outspoken statement, in 2011 Dr. Görmez took sharp public issue with a *fatwa* issued in Saudi Arabia that called for the removal or destruction of churches in the Arabian Peninsula – in this case in Kuwait.

> [Görmez] sharply criticized the fatwa as contrary to centuries-old Islamic teachings of tolerance and the sanctity of institutions

belonging to other religions. He emphasized that "the opinion of the [Saudi] Grand Mufti also obviously contradicts the agreements that the Prophet of Islam signed with the non-Muslim communities both in Medina and in the region. It also plainly overlooks the right of immunity given by Islam to the holy shrines and temples of other religions on the basis of the rule of law throughout its history." Görmez underscored the negative impact of the fatwa: "We strongly believe that this declaration has left dark shadows upon the concept of rights and freedoms in Islam that have always been observed on the basis of its sources, and it will not be recorded as an opinion of Islam. … We, therefore, entirely reject the aforementioned opinion and hope that it will be amended as soon as possible."[10]

In another case, in 2012 the National Fatwa Committee of Malaysia passed a ruling stating it was "not permissible for Muslims to participate in any rally intending to oust a government or cause disturbance in the country." Turkey's Diyanet took public exception to that ruling and said "the right to protest the government was given to people as a constitutional right in Turkey." However, the official added that, "evil-minded and illegal actions were not permitted in Islam."[11]

While Diyanet's statement is open to interpretation, it is clear that Turkey opposes the use of state clergy to support governments in power, a principle closer in spirit to those Islamists who fight the abuses of "state Islam." We can assume most of the Gulf countries, other monarchies and even some authoritarian republican regimes in the Middle East are quite unhappy with Turkey's position.

In one of Diyanet's first major educational and outreach initiatives in May 2009 it announced a new focus on the more traditional areas of Turkish cultural influence—the Balkans, Caucasus, the Middle East and Central Asia—in order to provide Islamic education on websites in English, Russian and Arabic. Moving beyond theology into action, Diyanet has undertaken projects to restore mosques in numerous Muslim countries, many of which reflect their Ottoman Turkish heritage, including the largest mosque in Mogadishu in Somalia, in the Balkans, and construction of a new mosque in Moscow. Diyanet is covering costs of restoration for many mosques in Gaza that were destroyed by Israel in air attacks. It also sponsored 250 Somali students to go to Turkey to study Turkish as well as theology, and to be trained as imams for their home country.

Diyanet assists Turkish students to go on the *umra* ("little Hajj," or off-season pilgrimage) to Mecca—raising complaints from secularists, but Diyanet justifies the program as an entirely appropriate part of religious education, "just as Christian students visit the Vatican."[12] It's worth noting that even under Kemalist governments, education *about* Islam has long been compulsory in all Turkish secular schools, as part of understanding the national cultural tradition.

In November 2011 Diyanet organized a five-day conference in Istanbul of African Islamic religious leaders from over 40 African countries—the second African Muslim Religious Leaders' Summit. Görmez noted that the summit "calls for efforts to combat problems such as famine, poverty, scarcity, racism, malignant diseases, and unequal access to education and limitations on the freedom of belief in Africa." Görmez said Africa and Turkey must open new pages for the benefit of future generations. "Islam made us brothers, and the Prophet Muhammad said whoever goes to bed and sleeps, while his brother is hungry, is not a good Muslim. I believe we must provide a common front of building bridges of brotherhood." Görmez noted that the history of Africa has been "grossly distorted by the west. Africa, as seen through the history of colonization, the slave trade, internal wars and helplessness in general, hides the cultural and spiritual richness of the people of the continent."[13] In late November 2011 Görmez met with the Russian Orthodox Patriarch in Moscow and with leaders of the Muslim community in Russia to discuss concerns of Muslim religious education, as well as the design of a new mosque that Turkey is building in Moscow.[14] Görmez also met in Beijing with Chinese leaders to discuss problems of Islam and Muslim populations in China.

A key element of the Ottoman legacy are the Muslim minority communities in the Balkans, whose welfare since the breakup of the Yugoslav state has been at risk. During a visit from Görmez in 2011 the Bosnian Grand Mufti Mustafa Cerić emphasized the urgent need for solidarity of the Muslim Balkan community with Turkey. He noted that "it is not easy to be a Muslim in Europe", and suggested it is far better to "join with Turkey to form a population of 82 million, rather than only two million standing alone"—suggesting that as a Muslim country Bosnia cannot be considered as truly separate from Turkey. In a highly revealing remark, Cerić views this as part of the *"reconstruction of Muslim identity in the Balkans."*[15]

This striking phrase—"reconstruction of the Muslim identity"—is in keeping with the new domestic and foreign policy vision of Turkey. Tradition is re-inventing itself. Ottoman tradition is taking on a new and vital contemporary significance. The Muslim world is rethinking itself in a new context outside the usual western-oriented framework. Indeed, the West tends to be so wedded to its own self-referential interpretations of world events that it is almost impossible for it to note, much less understand, external events in other contexts. Thus Turkish or other countries' actions in the Muslim world designed to strengthen Muslim solidarity are sometimes perceived in the US as hostile or as diverging from the values of "the international [read: US-led] community"—a drift from the norm and even as a challenge to the West. Perhaps the closest parallel to Turkey within the western order itself in this respect is France—the only European culture to maintain a genuinely alternative western cultural outlook and frame of reference—and a leading reason why the US seems so routinely piqued by France and its prickly independent posture on many issues.

In sum, the institution of Diyanet continues the tradition of major state involvement in religion, even in secular Turkey. Diyanet has a representative within many Turkish embassies around the world, indicating its direct interest in ties with local religious groups. This is particularly true among the large Turkish population in Germany where Diyanet seeks to strengthen moderate religious forces against the more radical religious views propagated by a few individual Turkish firebrand clerics.

Diyanet has now become a major instrument in its own right for propagation of a more open and modern interpretation of Islam both at home and abroad. Its credibility among non-Turkish Muslims has been greatly enhanced by the Islamist background of the AKP, by Turkey's "return to the Muslim world," and the AKP's major accomplishments in power. Diyanet thus represents an important pillar of Islam in Turkey's new domestic and foreign policies.

What is the relevance, then, of Turkeys' experience to reform in other Muslim countries? Certainly the Turkish experience has been unique, particularly as functioning as the center of Muslim empire for many hundreds of years during which religion and state were closely fused despite the adoption of many western-style laws.

There is another vital distinction to be drawn here: the role of religion in opposition to the state. In Turkey opposition to the state has rarely taken strong religious form. But in the Arab world the main vehicle of criticism and opposition to the autocratic state has persistently been Islamic radicalism. Some argue that in authoritarian states the mosque was the sole venue where expression of political activity could take place. It is probable that as Arab states become less authoritarian, Islamist movements will lose their monopoly of criticism of the state, especially as Islamists themselves assume power and responsibility for solution of domestic problems. Turkey furthermore has never been truly subdued under western imperial domination; this reality has likely helped reduce the levels of Islamic passion in Turkey against the West. Turkey's longtime adherence to the dominant and moderate Hanafi school of

Sunni Islam also predisposes it to greater application of reason to juridical determinations and interpretations. Perhaps Turkey's evolving democratic practices from 1950—and even in the late Ottoman Empire—have served as a pressure escape valve; criticism of the state could find other avenues apart from religious or fundamentalist form.

In the end, all Muslim states eventually need to rethink the meaning of the Islamic tradition in order to bring the understanding and practice of Islam into greater conformity with the demands of modern society. The process is under way everywhere. Here the Turkish experience is becoming well known to other states and will impact religious thinking in the evolution of Arab societies as well. The role and mission of Diyanet as an arm of foreign policy in Turkey is unlikely to change much in the future, regardless of whatever new political party comes to power in Turkey. It represents an important constituent of Turkish "soft power" in the Muslim world.

CHAPTER TEN

FORMS OF ISLAM: AHMET DAVUTOĞLU –
PIONEERING A NEW TURKISH FOREIGN POLICY

What is surprising is not that Turks are again deeply engaged in the Middle East, but rather how long it took them to get back there. Turkey's foreign policy in the region has undergone remarkable transformation over the decade of the 2000s, exploring entirely new terrain. Consider the bold, slightly presumptuous language used by Turkish Foreign Minister Ahmet Davutoğlu in April 2012 in describing Turkey's role in the Middle East—even during the chaos of the Arab Spring:

> Turkey leads the winds of change in the Middle East and will continue this way in the future…. Turkey is regarded not only as a fraternal country in the Middle East but it is also considered as initiator of new ideas.[1]
>
> Yes, we [of the region] will direct change. And in saying that I'm not excluding ourselves. We too are part of that process of change. If Turkey had not itself undergone a restoration of civil government and if there had been no AKP, the Arab spring equally possibly might not have occurred. If certain events hadn't happened in Turkey, if the negative consequences of the 28 February 1998 military coup had persisted, perhaps it might have been a "Turkish Spring" that would have first taken place. When I say "we will direct change" I'm not singling out Turkey, I mean that the people of this region together will direct this change.
>
> If we speak of a return to the Middle East borders of 1911, if walls were thrown up [between Turkey and the Middle East] between 1911 and 1923, and if we experienced problems with some peoples there at that time—we must overcome all that now and embrace those peoples, show respect for the borders between us. But we also have to diminish the meaning of those borders and build new regional orders. Have there ever been as many wars between Turks and Arabs as there have been between France and Germany? If those two countries are erasing their borders without it being considered some kind of imposed hegemony, why should it be different in our case? Our economic and cultural borders will extend beyond our political borders, but this is a function of geography, it's not some kind of hegemony. … For example, we will see more people of Balkan origin, more Middle Easterners in Istanbul. Just as we Turks now go to Damascus, Cairo and Tripoli, they will come to Istanbul."[2]

This shift of vision in Turkish foreign policy of the 21st century is one of the most dramatic elements of the AKP tenure in power. Its leadership team—President (and former foreign minister) Ahmet Gül, Prime Minister Erdoğan, and above all the chief architect of foreign policy Ahmet Davutoğlu—pioneered a new and independent path for Turkey. They began by establishing several bold milestones, registering significant breakthroughs in relations with neighbors and in the region. These policies are not simply the product of a few new AKP leaders however; they tap into deeper roots in Turkish geopolitics and have *permanently* altered the nature and image of Turkey's role in the world. But what no one could have foreseen was the Arab Awakening process starting in late 2010 which pushed events in the region onto a rollercoaster course—one of the most tumultuous periods in the history of the modern Middle East. Since 2010 Turkey's ambitions have nonetheless struggled to maintain consistency, but have partially foundered in the rough seas of the Arab Spring; indeed, the same can be said for virtually all other countries in the world that have touched the Middle East.

This decade of AKP foreign policy broke new ground and opened new horizons. The experience cannot be unlearned. In whatever way the successes and failures of these policies will ultimately be judged, they have established the outlines and future direction of Turkish foreign policy for a long time to come. Almost any successor government in Ankara will likely pursue approximately the same independent posture with its expanded vision for Turkey's international role. These policies emerge immediately out of the AKP vision, but other key factors also played a role: the impact of domestic change in Turkey, geopolitical change in the region, as well as major shifts on the global scene building for over half a century.

If a young Turkish citizen of today were to travel back in time to the 1950s, he would find himself in an entirely different geopolitical world—in which not Syria or Iran, but Russia was the center of all calculus. Our Turk, for example, might have grown up hearing grandparents say, "If you're not good, the Russians will come and get you." Russia's aggressive and expansionist policies against the Ottoman Empire over centuries were marked by continuous territorial encroachment. Moscow justified all of this in the name of liberal humanitarian intervention—in this case "liberating Christian populations" of the empire from Turkish Muslim rule. Indeed, there was a Turkish expression directed towards its Christian citizens: *Osmanlı ekmeği yeyip Moskofa dua etmez*—"You can't eat Ottoman bread and then pray to Moscow." Even when the Soviet Union replaced the Tsarist Empire in 1917 the Russian expansionist threat still remained Turkey's number one policy priority.

For these reasons Turkey sought admittance into NATO in 1952; NATO backing became the key guarantor of Turkish territorial integrity against Soviet expansionism. Turkey became a key front-line state for the West in the Cold War. Over long decades the country also witnessed hundreds of thousands of refugees, mainly Muslim, from various parts of the Soviet communist empire seek protection in Turkey; these refugees further promulgated the anti-communist message and talked of Soviet efforts to extirpate Islam in their lands. Only with a slow moderation in Soviet policies over time did relations with Turkey begin to relax and improve. Turkey then started to focus on new directions in foreign policy, particularly international trade; with bold new economic liberalization and openings in the late 1980s Turkey's economy began to take off and stimulate new initiatives in Turkish foreign policies.

Fast forward to the mid-1990s. The Soviet Union had collapsed and gave way to the new Russian Federation; communism as a meaningful ideology lost credibility. The Russian empire shrank drastically: the states of Eastern Europe were liberated and eight new countries in the Caucasus and Central Asia—six of them Muslim, five of them Turkic—gained national independence. For Turkey the consequences were huge: it now no longer even *bordered* on Russia, making the prospects of Russian expansion onto Turkish soil remote. NATO at that point lost a great deal of its security value to Turkey; it now primarily represented a significant seat for Turkey in European strategic councils.

The Arab world too was impacted by the collapse of the Soviet Union, but in a different way. During the Cold War Moscow provided diplomatic and military support to many Arab states that felt exposed to Israel's overwhelming military power, western interventions, and a US slant towards Israel. But with the fall of the Soviet Union, Arab states were left without a major international backer and had no choice but to rethink their strategies. New opportunities were there for Turkey as well. With the opening of liberal free market trade under Prime Minister Özal in the 1990s, Turkish business circles embraced new opportunities for labor and construction projects in the Middle East and even in Russia itself. But the major revolution in Turkish foreign policy had yet to come.

Ahmet Davutoğlu and the Proposition of "Zero Enemies"

Ahmet Davutoğlu has been the chief intellectual force and architect behind the AKP's new foreign policies. He grew up in Konya, the heartland of religious Anatolia, studied at a German-language lycée in Istanbul, gained a PhD in international relations, and embarked on an academic career. He then studied Arabic and spent three years teaching in Malaysia where he founded and chaired the Political Science Department at the International Islamic University of Malaysia. These years outside Turkey undoubtedly provided an important intellectual experience, exposing him to an alternative Muslim way of life with sharply different geopolitical perspectives including Malaysia's peaceful, but pan-Islamic perspectives. Even though a pious Muslim himself, Davutoğlu also became a lecturer for four years at the Turkish Military Academy and the War Academy in Istanbul where he was in close contact with the heart of Kemalist-oriented military culture. His mind ran to theoretical and sweeping visions across history, space and geopolitics, a sense of the *place* of the Muslim world in international affairs, and of the historical interrelationships among diverse cultures. All of this created a theoretical foundation for his later practical policy approaches. This broad background led to his appointment as chief architect, advisor and activist in foreign policy to Prime Minister Erdoğan in the new AKP government in 2002 and later as foreign minister in his own right starting in 2009.

Davutoğlu introduced a bold new concept into Turkish foreign policy—a "zero enemies" guideline towards all its neighbors—also known as a "zero problems," or *sıfır sorun* approach. With this concept Davutoğlu sharply challenged the traditional security-based and western "realist" school of Turkish policy—that nations are driven primarily by "interests" and threats posed by enemies. It is worth examining this concept of "zero problems" in greater detail because it touches on some of the US anguish in its views of Turkish foreign policy; it further challenges many sacred cows in US strategic thinking. Davutoğlu's proposition indeed directly challenged the entire course of Turkey's own foreign policies since the death of Atatürk.

What does the term "realist" mean in foreign policy? This debate lies at the heart of the newly emerging global order. In many ways "realism" is a misleading term; it suggests that there is a clear objective "reality" out there which determines national interests and action. But the terms "reality" and "interests," far from being objective terms, are in fact intensely subjective and elusive. What do we mean by "reality"? Whose reality? There are multiple ways to view a situation. What one observer sees as a "threat" may be perceived by another only as an issue requiring attention. Indeed, even a term such as "the national interest," so regularly invoked by realist observers, is hardly a clear concept. Foreign policy debate is *precisely about what the national interest really is*. Is it maximum wealth accumulation for the nation? If so, by what means? With what trade-offs? Or is creation of national power the major national interest? But power how defined: economic, military, or even in terms of national social cohesion and balance? Or is the national interest defined by the ability to dominate the international environment? And if domination, then is it through force of arms and war, or economic power, or leadership by moral example, or attraction as a model? International power can be assessed in many different ways. The existence of the term "soft power" is just one indicator of this recognition. The way the national interest is defined is itself a direct expression of national ideology, providing a rough indicator of how an actor might act.

Turkish foreign policy for long centuries was concerned with genuine direct territorial threats—mainly from Russia and Europe—a reality that cannot be explained away. Beyond that, the dominance of the Turkish military in modern foreign policy for long decades firmly placed "threat assessment" at the heart of its thinking, making it the bedrock of the security state. The military chiefly perceived threats as coming from Russia, from "Islam," from Kurdish nationalists, from minorities, and from unfriendly neighbors. But the way you define a threat can itself change the nature of the situation. For example, is the rise of China on the world stage a threat to the US? If yes, you likely help ensure that the future of Chinese-American relations will be filled with suspicion and vigilance towards the anticipated enemy. We enter the realm of self-fulfilling prophesies here. The same obviously applies to interaction at the human level: if I treat you as a rival and a threat, in all likelihood our relations will be tense and inclined towards friction and conflict. Our *expectations* can facilitate confrontation. If I maintain an open mind towards another individual, relations are likely to proceed more smoothly than when I signal suspicion and hostility. Now obviously, maintaining a positive and constructive attitude cannot, by itself, overcome all foreign policy problems. But it can help to avoid confrontational posture as the default mode of dealing with others.

American foreign policy itself has long been predicated upon "threat perception" and "threat analysis." Other states are readily perceived as "threats"—including popular use of the term "rogue state." Rogue in American parlance tends to refer to any country that resists the vision and architecture of the particular world order Washington has determined upon. Once a country runs afoul of the US and falls into the "enemy" category, it is exceedingly difficult to get off the enemies list. Cases of states with whom the US were not even willing to seriously deal included China for long decades, North Korea, Cuba, and Iran. Venezuela, Syria, Libya, and Nicaragua also fell into similar categories. Yes, problems do exist between the US and such states, but the adoption of enemy labels contribute in themselves to bilateral tensions, often for decades, in a self-perpetuating mode. Indeed, refusing to deal with certain states does not seem to reflect realism at all, but rather a denial or rejection of unwelcome realities—perhaps best dealt with only through overwhelming power to dominate. Turkey too had tended to follow this so-called realist approach with its Kemalist threat-oriented policies towards virtually all its neighbors.

Emphasis upon "threats" can also serve *domestic* political goals in many states. Governments often keep their populace in permanent states of vigilance or anxiety against foreign enemies as a control mechanism—the politics of fear. Some governments like to suggest they are under permanent siege—to compel public support in times of "war" and to demand greater and unquestioned power for the leader. All of this was true of Turkey as well.

It would be naïve to suggest that situations of genuine conflict of interest, dangers and even confrontation do not occur in the international order. But how those interests and "dangers" are perceived, articulated and managed has direct impact upon the very nature of the relations themselves. Washington over recent decades has managed its relations in a frequently truculent, imperious, demanding and confrontational style that contributes directly to already existing genuine tensions. Nor is Washington unique in this. It is here that we see how much Davutoğlu's thinking reflected an awareness of the shortcomings of this kind of approach in Ankara's early foreign relations. And Davutoğlu in particular launched the process by which Ankara gradually distanced itself from this mode of thinking.

Herein lies the heart of the bold shift. Until the end of the 20th century Turkey had poor relations with *virtually every single neighbor*—yes, in part due to the Cold War with the Soviet Union in which the Balkans and several Arab states were Soviet-aligned, including neighboring Syria and Iraq. Bad Turkish relations with Greece led to frequent military confrontations and a routine threat of war between them. And the Kemalist civilian and military elite constantly dwelled on an internal "Islamic threat" to the Turkish secular order and later from the Iranian Islamic Revolution after 1979. Turkey for long decades tended to adopt the same US categories of friend and foe in the region, helping ensure close US support to Ankara.

Even before Davutoğlu took over in 2002 as chief AKP architect of foreign policy, Turkish foreign policy thinking had started to evolve away from the old categories of friend and foe. Ankara was dissatisfied with a whole range of relationships. Washington had not lived up to all that Ankara hoped for—among other things in failing to lend support on the Cyprus issue with Greece, or to provide Turkey with all the hi-tech military equipment Turkey sought. The European Union engaged in persistent foot-dragging in considering Turkey's application for EU membership. The Soviet Union had ceased to exist and was no longer at the heart of Ankara's strategic calculations. Israel did not deliver the full support to Turkey's military and foreign policy that Ankara had hoped for, particularly via the Israel lobby in the US Congress. Meanwhile, starting with Turkey's dramatic opening to free markets and global enterprise in the late 1980s, Turkish business interests had already started to open to the east; Turkey saw that its economic success depended upon expansion of its foreign trade in the region, requiring a change in old attitudes towards the states involved. Turkey's newly emerging mercantile class provided support for the new economic orientation. Turkey had also been fortunate with the appointment of İsmail Cem as foreign minister for the previous five years before the AKP government. An outstanding thinker with left-of-center views, Cem began to soften the harsher security-driven character of Turkish foreign policy, achieved major gains towards acceptance of Turkey as a full candidate member in the EU, and initiated a sea change in relations with Greece, helping set a new tone in outlook.

But Davutoğlu's declaration of a "zero problems" foreign policy suggested more than mere nice words, airport hugs, and expanding ties. In Davutoğlu's view as a scholar of international relations, the philosophy and assumptions that lay behind policies were as important as the policies themselves. Turkey's public adoption of a zero problems foreign policy would represent a clear signal that Ankara was wiping the historical slate clean; its foreign policy priorities would now seek to eliminate all outstanding issues with neighboring and regional states to the fullest extent possible. It was a major shift from the days when Turkish military visitors to Washington used to quip—borrowing an old Israeli line—about how they "live in a bad neighborhood," a perception that ensured self-fulfilling prophecies of regional tension. Turkey now suggested that Ankara too shared past responsibility if the neighborhood had become "bad." It would no longer assume the neighborhood to be inherently hostile and would work to remove existing problems. It would assume that bilateral problems could be worked out through goodwill, active diplomacy and transparency rather than suspicions and a search for "enemies." It was a stance of greater self-confidence and vision that Ankara moved actively to implement.

This new vision had direct impact on Turkish domestic politics as well; to work towards resolution of these issues was to deprive the military of one of its key demands: the right to direct and oversee foreign policy as a fundamentally "security issue" writ large.

Davutoğlu's ideas began to show early and dramatic results, first in the capable hands of then-Foreign Minister Abdullah Gül who projected an intelligent and gracious style sensitive to Muslim sensibilities in the region and an ability to deal effectively with the EU. Within a few years, Turkey's once hostile relations with Syria, Iran and Iraq had shifted markedly towards new dialog and reciprocal actions. Turkey sought to involve itself in mediating significant regional tensions, especially Israel's relations with Palestinian Hamas, with Syria and with the Lebanese Shi'ite movement Hizballah. Turkey recognized and opened dialog with both Hamas and Hizballah, considering them important and legitimate political and social organizations that enjoyed the strong support of their populations. Davutoğlu did not write them off simplistically as "terrorists" but instead insisted upon dialog and the need to include these actors as significant and indispensable political elements in a regional solution—much to the dismay of Washington and Tel Aviv. Relations with Moscow improved hugely as the two states engaged in regular in-depth strategic consultations over a broad range of regional problems and found many common views. Greek-Turkish relations saw a continuing warming. Turkey worked to open new lines of communication with Armenia and began to extend its trade ties more deeply into the Middle East and even beyond into Africa and former Soviet space. Strategic dialog with Moscow blossomed.

In his long and still untranslated encyclopedic study *Strategic Depth: Turkey's Place in the World (Stratejik Derinlik: Türkiye'nin Uluslararası Konumu)*, Davutoğlu introduces a sweeping vision of Turks and Turkey's place in the historical and geopolitical global order. While one can readily quibble with his interpretations of specific historical events and trends, the overall work is bold and pioneering in its vision: it places the role of Turks for the first time ever onto a broad historical and regional canvas. The result is to transform what was a narrowly nationalistic, isolated state in the Middle East into a regional, even global player. The vision has been complemented by Turkey's dizzying new diplomatic dynamism and its high-performing new economic force in the region. Formerly smirking western statesmen were forced to acknowledge, accept and work with the reality of Turkey as an unexpectedly influential new geopolitical force in the region.

Davutoğlu argues that Turkey is a "central" or pivotal country—a term that suggests much more than a simple regional power. Turkey is a country with historical depth of experience in multiple geopolitical arenas extending in all directions including Europe, the Balkans, the Middle East, the

Mediterranean, North Africa, the Caucasus, Central Asia, the broader Eurasian continent and even other parts of Africa. He vigorously rejects the idea that Turkey is merely a "bridge" between East and West—a term that suggests Turkey is a mere transmission belt for western ideas to move into the Middle East. Davutoğlu demands acknowledgment of Turkey as a distinct major power and civilizational force in its own right that cannot be relegated to a single geopolitical or cultural box.

The western press quickly dubbed this approach "neo-Ottomanism," a term the AKP rejects. Still, there is no gainsaying the fact: the Ottoman experience provided Turkey with long experience and involvement in a common civilization and exercise of power in the Middle East, the Muslim world and beyond for over half a millennium. But past imperial experience is not what the region is all about today. It is about shared interests based on many elements of a shared culture that extends into geographical regions well beyond the confines of the old Ottoman Empire. Turkey absorbed—like it or not—traditions of multiculturalism, multi-ethnicity and multi-faith community. Its ties of Turkic culture extend deeply eastward across the former Soviet Union, into the Caucasus, Central Asia and into China with its Turkic-speaking Uyghur people. It has participated in the complex geopolitics of Mediterranean power for centuries. And in particular it perceives a new task in helping define "Eastern" aspirations and interests in the face of a demanding West. It aspires to act across the Eurasian continent. It seeks to place economic and organizational muscle behind those ideas. As scholar Jenny White points out, whereas earlier Turkish Islamists based their vision on an eastern Ottoman model, the AKP eagerly embraced globalization as the critical new economic and cultural force.[3]

While rejecting the term "neo-Ottoman," Davutoğlu states that Turkey is widening the meaning of a Turkish diaspora: "Diaspora is no longer just our citizens. We consider all societies with which we lived for centuries as part of our diaspora." Turkey seeks to embrace states and peoples with whom Turkey feels a natural historical affinity and who constitute natural trading partners. Now, some neighbors states may not always welcome Turkey's new "Ottoman" conceptual background that could, in principle, threaten their own identity. But in a globalized world, multiple identities are the norm; there is no reason why other parts of the region can't benefit from sharing part of their identities through historic ties with Turkish Muslim civilization.

Many peoples can look back at their role in history in ways that transcend present borders. But Davutoğlu sought to operationalize the vision emerging from this intellectual construct. He thinks in terms of historical eras, of the culture, character, and structure of civilizations—Ottoman as well as others; he looks for some resulting deterministic or structural imprint upon their actions. This provides his perspectives with depth, and sometimes tenacity. Yet Turkish academic Gökhan Bacık suggests it can also lead to intellectualism or rigidity:

> To him, states should act in the manner of the historic structures of their civilizations. Therefore, the Ottoman civilization from which the modern Turkish state evolved shapes his diplomatic paradigms. As a person who analyzes world politics through a "civilizations" lens, Davutoğlu contextualizes Turkish-EU relations on a broad historical model—to him, the trade or agricultural details of EU standards do not really matter. Rather, the grander issues of culture and identity are the more decisive arbiters…. Quite unlike Erdoğan's freedom from intellectual paradigms, Davutoğlu's steadfast attachment to his own is, I argue, an obstacle.[4]

At the heart of Davutoğlu's zero problems policy lies the conviction that a series of regional conflicts, confrontations and wars have been deeply destabilizing, damaging and dangerous to nearly all states of the region, with devastating human and social consequences rarely acknowledged in the West. This belief may seem self-evident, but under the US administration of George W. Bush, military means were routinely employed as the instrument of choice to treat foreign policy problems and to achieve US foreign policy goals—including strategic dominance. Washington's Middle East menu was studded with regional enemies: Syria, Iraq, Iran, Hamas, Hizballah, Libya, Russia, expanding Chinese influence—and Islamists and terrorists everywhere. Turkey's new policies directly countered the American approach; "zero problems" meant that Turkey would seek to *negotiate* issues in direct dialog with all these parties and incorporate them into the solution rather than work with Washington in support of pressure, boycotts, sanctions, threats and military force—policies that had, in the end, borne little fruit for the US either. Davutoğlu characterized these policies of Turkey as part of a "proactive peace effort."

None of this is to suggest that, by simply closing one's eyes and wishing very hard, one can eliminate conflict. Or that simply talking about conflicts will resolve them. But it does mean that openness to negotiation and attention to mutual benefit can reap immediate benefits and even change the tenor of relations between states. And indeed, such changes produced early and rapid results for Turkey.

While Washington claimed to act on the basis of "realism," Davutoğlu represented a new take on "realism." The working philosophy behind this stage of Davutoğlu's approach was Turkish acceptance of the reality of existing regimes and political organizations in the region; it would work with them rather than to try to impose change upon them or eliminate them. It accepted the *reality of the status quo* that Washington was determined to change in the many countries it viewed as hostile threats. Washington claimed that it was primarily following policies of "principle" —support for democratization and human rights. But in reality such goals were camouflage, generally self-serving and selectively applied. Washington supported democracy primarily as a weapon by which to dispose of authoritarian regimes and crush popular movements it didn't like; serious promotion of democracy was ignored when it involved friends or was not seen to be in Washington's interest. Elections in Iraq, yes, but in Mubarak's Egypt over long decades, no. Democratic results are fine in principle, but unacceptable when Palestinians elected Hamas to power in Gaza. Israel's self-proclaimed redlines were routinely adopted as American redlines. Authoritarianism was unacceptable in Iran, but it was okay in Bahrain or Saudi Arabia. Condemn Iran for ignoring UN resolutions, but veto any condemnation of Israel for doing the same. In short, US policies demonstrated clear signs of self-serving selectivity, double standards and hypocrisy that destroyed their credibility and undercut any claim that they were genuinely "principled." This lay at the heart of the sharp differences between US and Turkish policies that helped create uncomfortable relations between Ankara and Washington.

One can also argue that such US policies increasingly inhibited Washington's credibility and ability to exercise leadership in the world. The administration of George W. Bush sought to pressure, intimidate, threaten and isolate numerous regimes and movements—even to bring about their overthrow in the conviction that they represented unacceptable obstacles to American interests. More than mere obstacles, their very *existence* as overt challenges to US policies were seen to diminish the image and credibility of American power and dominance in the region. In this sense Washington's hostility to these states and movements was not "realist" at all but ideological and radical—seeking to *change the status quo* via overthrow of states and movements perceived as unfriendly to American interests. And of course these same policies evoked further hostility from the targeted groups.

Turkey's acceptance of the need to work with the existing status quo, on the contrary, can be viewed as the more "realist" policy. Ankara's position was that these regimes and movements exist, are rooted in historical circumstances and realities and often enjoy genuine popular support. After all, in an Arab world in which kings and presidents-for-life presided, it looked like the political status quo might continue for many long years more. Turkey would seek to mediate among existing regimes and organizations wherever it could, press for regional reduction of tensions, and work for multilateral regional solutions. If there were negative aspects to the policies of these states and groups, a good possibility existed that their policies could be influenced by replacing threats and bluster with a search for dialog and cooperation.

Recognizing the need to work with the status quo did not, however, mean fully accepting it. Davutoğlu's own writings make clear that he never believed that the Arab status quo, for instance, was ideal; he has been convinced of the necessity for serious change if the Arab world is ever to emerge from under its ossified and backward status after long decades of dictatorship. In the meantime, however, change had to come through cooperation, suasion, and offering credible carrots and sticks. And solutions must come from within the region. Furthermore, for Ankara these problems were not distant and theoretical; these problem states and groups lay virtually on Turkey's doorstep. Turkey lives with the immediate, destabilizing and dangerous consequences of wars started by outside powers; it had already suffered considerably from earlier such US interventions. Change through violence and war was counter-productive and threatened the interests of all in the region, including Turkey. As President Gül commented in 2012, Middle East turmoil had been quite predictable:

> I spoke of these Middle East events ten years ago: as I said at the 2003 Islamic Conference Organization in Tehran, if we don't put our own house in order either the people will rebel, or there will be intervention from outside. No one can remain a spectator in front of a collapsing house. However well-intentioned outside intervention may be, a situation where the elephant enters the china shop only makes things worse. I don't like to say "I told you so," but if we ourselves don't undertake reforms on our own they can't succeed.[5]

Davutoğlu's policies caught the attention of the region, but enjoyed mixed success on the ground. He engaged in frequent and far-reaching mediation: between the US and the Arab world in the run-up to the US invasion of Iraq; between Israel and Hamas; between the US and Iran as well as between Israel and Syria. But Ankara had only partial success in actually changing policies of these states and groups. In fairness, the task was monumental, especially against the backdrop of continuing US interventionism, desire for military solutions, and constant threats that usually overshadowed and overwhelmed Ankara's initiatives. Ankara believed, for example, that Israel routinely undercut Turkish efforts to negotiate between Israel and its opponents, primarily because Israel did not really want reconciliation at the cost of relinquishing its territorial holdings in the occupied territories. Ankara believed it broke dramatic new ground with Iran when Brazil and Turkey teamed up in 2011 to gain Iran's agreement to new terms for refinement of nuclear fuel; after giving Ankara the go-ahead—in the belief that Ankara could never succeed in negotiations—Washington subsequently rejected the agreement that Ankara did achieve because it had not expected it to succeed.

As the decade of the 2000s proceeded, it became ever clearer that differences between the US and Ankara were profound. Whereas Washington regularly intoned phrases about Turkey as an ally that shared "common values" with the US, the reality was somewhat different. The "common values" spoken of were really little more than motherhood and apple pie— nothing anyone could take exception to, vague concepts like democracy, human rights and stability. But these bland diplomatic declarations masked deep differences—even a fundamental diversion and conflict of interests. Ankara believed that Bush's policies in the Global War on Terror were counter-productive and destructive—even as a way to achieve Washington's own self-proclaimed long-term policy goals. Where Turkey sought negotiation, Washington wanted military solutions; where Turkey wanted dialog, Washington wanted to cut off relations and impose sanctions; where Turkey placed a premium on stability, Washington wanted forceful change; where Turkey wanted to pressure Israel into agreeing to a Palestinian state, Washington wanted to protect Israel's intransigent position; where Turkey believed that major Islamist movements needed to be included in political dialog, Washington sought to crush or eliminate them from the political playing field. All of these American policies directly threatened Turkish national interests—economic, political, and geopolitical—domestic and foreign. These profound differences have placed severe semi-permanent tensions upon US-Turkish relations and cast doubt upon the existence of any truly meaningful shared "common interests."

Trade

Turkey's burgeoning economy is a major driver in strengthening its overseas clout. While there has been much wringing of hands in the US about a possible "axis shift" in Turkey's strategic orientation, any axis shift, particularly in economic terms, is a global phenomenon; the percentage of Asia's role in the global economy is rising rapidly while that of the EU and the West has been in decline. In this sense Turkey's new orientation of trade patterns towards the East reflects that broader change. Nor can Turkey be expected to "come back" to the West; its alignment with Asian economies is growing and permanent, even if Turkey eventually should gain full entry into the EU. The changing nature and profile of the Turkish economy aligns it more with the East (and South) than with the West.[6]

Ankara reported that its exports increased by an incredible 18.2 percent in 2011 alone, reaching a total of US$152 billion in 2013. It diversified the range of its trading partners with a pronounced shift away from the West and towards the East, with Iraq and Saudi Arabia leading the list, along with Russia. Turkey quickly dispatched large trade delegations to Tunisia, Egypt and Libya after the fall of regimes in those three countries during the Arab Spring. It looked to derive trade benefits from its new and positive relations with these states, in part based on the appeal of its Muslim credentials to new Islamist-oriented regimes in Tunisia and Egypt (until the overthrow of the Muslim Brotherhood government) where economic growth is a priority. Since the fall of Mubarak in Egypt Ankara looked to triple its trade to US$10 billion per year although deteriorating relations between Cairo and Ankara after the 2013 military coup may affect it. Turkey also maintains major projects in the Gulf such as building the new Dubai Metro and a new airport terminal in Cairo. In Libya Ankara continues with oil well construction and a new parliament building. The economic benefits of these new relations are clear to see; they also carry undertones of regenerating Muslim cultural identity.

Turkey's defense industry has similarly developed over the past few decades. Interestingly, eight Muslim countries rank among Turkey's top ten customers that include Saudi Arabia, Malaysia, Indonesia, Bahrain, Turkmenistan, the United Arab Emirates, Bahrain, Azerbaijan, Kazakhstan, Pakistan, and Lebanon. Total sales in 2011 topped US$1 billion and are growing. Items include armored vehicles, and a medium-altitude long-endurance unmanned aerial vehicle. Apart from foreign sales, over time Turkey plans to reduce Turkish dependence on US-produced fighter jets, for political as well as economic reasons. As one Turkish exporter commented, "Being Muslim makes a difference. The Muslim buyers see that you are Muslim and take up a better attitude. In the coming years, we expect better prospects to sell our products."[7]

In terms of Turkey's own arms purchases, Ankara shocked the US with a tentative decision in October 2013 to purchase a new missile defense system, not from the US, but from China, and not even interoperable with NATO systems. This decision further marks Turkey's growing independence even in the strategic and security field. A NATO ambassador in Ankara reportedly commented "I have no idea why the Turks do not see the simple fact that the alliance's security threat perception in the next 20 years is based on China."[8] But this is precisely the point: Turkey does not see the principal threat to itself as emerging from China—a highly US-centric view. Ankara is in the process of seeking better relations with China, including membership in the Shanghai Cooperation Organization that includes Russia and many Central Asia states. Turkey may ultimately modify its final decision on the Chinese purchase, but it represents a landmark shift that will be repeated elsewhere in the Middle East in the years to come.

The Organization of Islamic Cooperation

The AKP's interest in Islamic dimensions to foreign policy is revealed in Ankara's increasing involvement in the OIC, the Organization of Islamic Cooperation (formerly Organization of the Islamic Conference). Over the last decade Turkey has taken an active role in participating in and strengthening the OIC. It is the largest international organization in the world after the United Nations with 57 member states and representing 1.5 billion Muslims, one-third of whom live outside of Muslim countries.

For decades the OIC had been an object of suspicion to the Kemalist-oriented foreign ministry which sought to avoid any identification with Islamic organizations or active participation in Middle East affairs. This prejudice was broken in 1997 when a Turkish prime minister first attended an OIC meeting, and in 2003, under the AKP, Turkey first hosted an OIC meeting in Istanbul. More dramatically, Turkey itself assumed the chairmanship of the organization with the election of a Turk, Ekmeleddin İhsanoğlu, to the post of secretary-general of the OIC—which was also the first time its leadership was chosen through democratic process. The AKP has sought to revivify the OIC structure, long characterized by sleepy consensus, ineffectual resolutions, political irrelevance, Saudi domination, and non-transparent administration. İhsanoğlu, as OIC's first elected leader, has worked to make the organization the preeminent voice of the whole Muslim world. The OIC may officially claim that stature, but it still has a long way to go to become a genuine force in international affairs. The aspirations and the structure are there, and we have noted earlier a Muslim awareness of the absence of any serious modern voice that today can speak for Muslims in international relations. The goal is a serious one. Abdullah Gül in 2005 presented Turkey's frank and progressive views on Islamic convocations:

> Turkey continues to voice its opinion that the Islamic world needs to address its problems in a realistic manner and to assume responsibility rather than blame others. In this connection we place emphasis on such concepts as democratization, human rights, the rule of law, good governance, accountability, transparency and gender equality.

İhsanoğlu spoke of a new vision for the OIC, one consonant with Turkey's own foreign policy aspirations.

> The OIC creates the possibility of obtaining political support and cooperation from the Muslim world on the basis of Islamic solidarity. This is especially the case in situations where eliciting support and cooperation can be challenging within the framework of other intergovernmental organizations such as the United Nations, owing to the delicate international political power balances in which the UN operates.

A second key goal is to facilitate economic development in a situation where the "majority of countries of the OIC are non-industrialized countries and 22 of them are among the world's least developed nations." He sees it as a platform for "joint Islamic Action" on issues of vital concern to the Muslim world on two levels: "the OIC as the expression of a historical and sociological reality"—that is, as the representative of the Muslim *umma*. The second is the OIC as a forum and an *agent* of South-South cooperation. İhsanoğlu sees these goals as emerging from the Ottoman experience:

> Looking back to the middle of the last century of the Ottoman Caliphate, we see clearly that it embraced a modern constitution and founded a parliament along with other institutions that are the hallmarks of a modern state. During that period, prominent Muslim scholars and leaders saw no conflict or disparity between these modern institutions on the one hand, and the traditions of Islam and its fundamental principle of governance on the other.[9] [After ten years as president, İhsanoğlu stepped down from his position in 2013.]

Even before the AKP, in 1995 Turkey took the interesting step of becoming a founding member of the Eurasian Council of Islam (*Avrasya İslam Şurası*), that brings together Eurasian Muslim states in the name of promoting tolerance, freedom of religion, freedom from discrimination, peace, reconciliation, opposition to all forms of violence and terrorism on whatever grounds, and to bring about cooperation among their national spiritual boards. The organization is partly designed to head off more radical interpretations of Islam in Eurasia, that includes Wahhabi doctrines, radical interpretations of Islam (such as represented by Hizb al-Tahrir, a radical but non-violent movement with a foothold in many Central Asian states), and especially against violent jihadi movements. All of these movements represent sources of great concern to Russia and China as well as to the West. Turkey brings strengths and cultural links to this Eurasian region more than almost any other competing state. The Gülen movement took a significant role in promoting this organization as well, given its experience in Central Asia.

While Atatürk is remembered in the Muslim world for the abolition of the Islamic caliphate, he was himself still acutely aware of the vacuum created by its abolition. Atatürk himself actually addressed the possibility of reestablishing the caliphate at a later point, conscious of the predicament confronted by those Muslim states that were immediately taken over by western imperialism after the break-up of the Ottoman Empire. In 1927 Atatürk proposed

> that when Muslim communities, living in Europe, Asia and Africa gain their independence in the future, their representatives could come together to form a congress and constitute a council with the purpose of acting together. He further suggested that the 'pan-Islamist federal government' that would thus be established could be named the Caliphate, and the person to be elected as the chairman of the joint council could be given the title of Caliph.

Atatürk also acknowledged that "it would be neither rational nor logical to entrust addressing and managing the problems of the entire Muslim world to one state or one person."[10]

Even with its strong Muslim world focus, Ankara's foreign policy vision roams well beyond. Its post-Ottoman outlook also reflects ties with countries and peoples that were not part of the Ottoman Empire and that are not even Muslim. Here Turkey is probably best suited of all Muslim countries to provide leadership, vigor and vision to the OIC—a forum in which it continues to speak out frankly on the shortcomings of Muslim world governance. It is unlikely that Ankara will ever take up Atatürk's suggestion of resuscitating the caliphate, but the abiding power—even need—of the concept is evident in supporting the concept of a pan-Islamic international forum.

It's worth remembering here a key slogan of Atatürk in his own vision of Turkish foreign policy: "Peace at home and peace abroad" (*Yurtta sulh cihanda sulh*); the very phrase captures the broad international foundations of the Ottoman language with Turkish, Persian and Arabic words combined in these four words. While the slogan might seem unremarkable today, the phrase takes on new meaning where there has been neither peace at home nor peace abroad for much of the last half century of Turkish politics. The AKP policy vision implicitly embraces this slogan of Atatürk in concrete ways that Atatürk's own Kemalist successors never did.

Domestic Turkish Criticisms of AKP Foreign Policy
All foreign policy principles have weaknesses and Davutoğlu's "zero problems" policy is no exception. First, foreign relations are always a two-way

street. I may not believe I have serious problems with you, but you may believe you have serious problems with me. Or I may want a solution but you may find benefit in perpetuation of confrontation, or conceive your own interests rather narrowly. Second, as Turkish scholar Soli Özel has observed, proclamation of zero problems does not in itself constitute a policy, it is more a statement of attitude. I may state my intention to negotiate all problems, but what, precisely, will I, or you, do about it? Third, conflicts can and do routinely emerge between states; even if you declare a desire to avoid problems with the best will in the world, problems may still not be easily resolved. Furthermore, within each state there are differing interest groups that may interpret or prioritize their interests differently. Great powers generally prefer application of their strong suit—*force majeure*—to handle conflict; smaller states may lean to diplomacy—a not undesirable preference.

AKP foreign policies have generally been well-received by the public due to the major economic gains that flow from foreign trade, from Turkey's more independent position vis-à-vis Washington, and from the heightened global prestige that Turkey now enjoys. Davutoğlu personally receives high popularity ratings. It is striking to note that there has been—at least up to the Arab Spring—some reasonable consensus among Turkish political parties on foreign policy issues even if not on domestic. But the turmoil of the Arab Spring tore apart most geopolitical relationships of the region and plunged Turkey into far riskier waters, offering new grounds for domestic criticism, especially on Syrian policy (see Chapter 21). Indeed, even before the Arab Spring there are several critiques that can be leveled at the AKP and Davutoğlu from varying perspectives.

Not surprisingly the oldest, and now main, opposition party—the Kemalist Republican People's Party (CHP in Turkish)—has always been uncomfortable with what it perceives as an Islamification of foreign policy. Almost all parties support the expansion of Turkish economic interests into the Arab and Muslim world, as well as into Asia, Africa and Latin America, particularly in view of the EU's reluctance to accept Turkey into the EU—a coinage whose value is dropping in Turkey. But secularists are concerned that ties with Saudi Arabia, the Gulf states, and Iran may strengthen Islamist forces within Turkey and further erode secularism, however defined. Erdoğan's surprising declaration, to an audience of Muslim Brothers in Egypt in 2011, that he believes in "secularism" for the Muslim world took aback many of Erdoğan's opponents at home, and may have eased some fears that he aspires to reverse Turkish secularism—an emotive charge. Yet at the same time the CHP has also criticized Erdoğan for pursuing an "American agenda" in his foreign policies—truly ironic in view of comments heard in some quarters in Washington that the AKP may have become "anti-west."

A smaller group within Turkish business and foreign policy circles is concerned at some of the tensions in Turkish-American relations under the AKP, especially among a minority that is more American-oriented in their thinking and that believes Turkey's most basic interests lie in close ties with Washington. While the AKP fully understands the importance of ties with the US, it no longer views Washington as the foundation stone of Turkish foreign policy, but as only one among several important relations, interests and polarities. Most Turkish intellectuals, diplomats and political parties today, however, seem to accept as appropriate this shift away from the US-centrism of the past.

Other criticisms of Davutoğlu are more pragmatic. They argue that Turkey is undertaking too ambitious an agenda, that it basically lacks the financial and bureaucratic resources for a policy with such global aspirations and involvements. These voices also argue that Davutoğlu's policies represent a departure from traditional foreign policy thinking and in the long run are not sustainable. Still others would argue that Turkey cannot realistically hope to maintain good ties with all states in a competitive and conflicting world and thus must choose its allies carefully.

Scholar Şaban Kardaş has suggested that the fundamental division between the AKP and its foreign policy critics in Turkey lie in what he calls "conservative globalists versus defensive nationalists."[11] The distinction is interesting but I think misses the mark. The AKP is "conservative" in the eyes of the old Kemalist order primarily because of its religious orientation, respect for Islamic tradition and the Ottoman past. But that religious vision is "conservative" only if the secular authoritarian Kemalists are taken as the standard of "progressive." On an Islamist spectrum the AKP's religious views are quite progressive and liberal. Its vision on social change in terms of social mobility and social services is distinctly liberal, democratic, and oriented towards *change* of the status quo. In foreign policy the AKP's global ambitions are not "conservative" at all but sweeping, ambitious, often generous in vision and path-breaking. So the "defensive nationalists", mainly Kemalists who are indeed basically defensive and nostalgic for the days of strong Kemalist domination of state institutions, may perhaps be in competition with "globalists," but the globalists are not conservative.

Furthermore, the nationalist opposition to the AKP is not at all of one view; it is divided between those nationalists with pride in the Ottoman and Islamic past, as opposed to those with a preference for the narrow, localized, even racially-oriented and xenophobic character of the nationalist Kemalists. It is the Kemalist opposition that is more truly "conservative" in wishing to sustain the older institutionalized Kemalist order and that shows little imagination on how to reorder Turkey's future in a changing world.

The AKP also faces criticism and opposition from the other side of the spectrum—from other Islamist groups. They consider that the AKP has watered down or sold out the Islamic values of the earlier Erbakan parties because of AKP acceptance of secularism as a "model" for the Muslim world, AKP's heavy push for EU membership, and AKP's partial cooperation with the US. These highly conservative Islamist elements are of little electoral significance however.

More significantly, political differences have emerged between the powerful forces of Hizmet and the AKP on certain specific issues. Gülen was publicly critical of Prime Minister Erdoğan's 2010 confrontation with Israel when the prime minister supported an unarmed international humanitarian flotilla to sail from Turkey to Gaza—carrying humanitarian supplies and clearly designed to challenge, even break, the illegal Israeli blockade against the Palestinian population of Gaza and score an ideological victory. Israeli forces attacked the lead Turkish vessel, the *Mavi Marmara*, on the high seas and killed 11 unarmed Turks on board. Gülen criticized the operation as adventurist, risking negative reaction from the US and further damaging relations with Israel. Gülen is known to favor better relations with Israel, primarily on two grounds: a long-term desire to promote tolerance and dialog with Jews in general, and awareness of Israel's ability to negatively influence US policies towards Turkey. Gülen instinctively avoids support of radical approaches on political issues. He also opposes state violence against the Kurds of Turkey—among whom he enjoys considerable following—even in response to PKK violence.

Gülen's cultural outlook, furthermore, emerges from a basic Sunni orientation. While he strongly advocates tolerance, he also displays some ambivalence towards the force of Persian nationalism which is often cloaked in a Shi'ite framework. He was understandably uncomfortable with the often extremist and confrontationalist views expressed by the former Iranian president Ahmadinejad which he believed were dangerously provocative towards the West and to the overall detriment of the image of Islam. His ambivalence towards Persian culture may also be rooted in the distrust that the Ottoman state felt towards Iran for many centuries when Istanbul was the seat of Sunni Islam and Iran the seat of Shi'ism. Gülen believes that Davutoğlu has been too trusting and naive in seeking rapprochement with

Iran and has run risks of angering Washington in its campaign against Iran on nuclear and human rights issues. Gülen is not, however, a sectarian and is not hostile to Shi'ism as such. With the election of a far more accommodating President Rouhani in Iran in 2013 Gülen is likely to breathe more easily.

We can see then, the broad new shifts in Turkey's vision of its foreign policy that not only pursues the principle of reconciliation where possible, but that also contains an Islamic component in its increased focus of interest on ties with the Muslim world and beyond. The foreign policy of Diyanet with its cultural outreach to world Muslim communities must also be considered as an integral part of Turkey's overall foreign policy strategy. Indeed, Gülen's principles of dialog share much in common with the general principles propagated by Davutoğlu and the AKP—except on Syria and Israel.

Yet, as dramatic as the new principles and approaches of Turkish foreign policy have been, we will see how the emergence of the Arab Spring in 2010 imposed new and entirely unanticipated problems of exceptional complexity upon the AKP. Ankara reacted with uncertainty, inconsistency, occasional tactical confusion and on occasion poor judgment within what was once a fairly coherent sense of foreign policy principles.

CHAPTER ELEVEN

FORMS OF ISLAM IN TURKEY - POPULAR ISLAM

Sufism and Popular Islamic Movements

Popular movements in Islam over history have been particularly linked to Sufism, the mystical tradition within Islam that goes back to the early days of the faith. While Islamic scholars and legalists dedicated themselves to constructing a body of law derived from the Qur'an and the Hadith—similar in this respect to the Jewish tradition of emphasis on the law—Sufi devotees believe that the highest goal of the believer is the search for direct communion and union with God. In the Sufi view, infusion with the spirit of the Divine in one's daily life and activities does not replace fulfillment of rituals, but is more worthy than rote commitment to ritual, especially when rituals are compulsory or imposed. In the West the Sufi spirit of mysticism has proven to be the most accessible and appealing face of Islam: the 13th-century Turkish-Persian poet Rumi is the best-selling poet in US bookstores.

How do we judge what the true face of a faith is? Ultimately, what the faith of any religion means, is what the majority of the faithful *believe* it to mean. This is the importance of popular Islam: it reveals the character of its religious practice among believers over time. This, rather than theological scholarship, is the level at which the faith seems to have the greatest resonance among its followers. Nonetheless, all religions demonstrate a tension between the popular practices of a faith on the one hand, and the insistence of orthodox reformers on the other, especially when the latter seek to "correct" erroneous belief and practice, and to bring people back to the "true faith." These reforming urges to correct deviations are present in all religions and they try to set limits on how far popular religious belief and practice can depart from orthodoxy.

So popular Islam provides an important indicator of where the religion is going in the eyes of its followers and the forms it will take. How do Muslims adopt and implement their faith in their daily personal and social lives? The practice and expression of Islam, or any other faith, will vary from place to place and from time to time, depending upon conditions and the social and psychological needs of the community of the moment.

Sufism has also been one form of religious expression in Islam that has provided a refuge to the believer in times when overt expression of religion was difficult. During the harsh anti-religious oppression of the Soviet Union, for instance, Sufism served as a vehicle for preservation of belief and practice in the home when mosques were closed, clerics eliminated, religion persecuted or banned in the public space. Sufism also served historically as the opening wedge for propagation of Islam among non-Muslim populations; Sufism's softer and more universalist countenance gained a foothold in Hindu, Christian, or Zoroastrian societies before more orthodox Islam established a foothold. But Sufism tends to be condemned by extreme orthodox (Salafi) circles as potentially constituting apostasy. Indeed, the strength of Sufism in many *Shi'ite* lands led to Ottoman suspicion of the unorthodox Sufi tradition—until Sufi practice in the empire itself slowly adapted to the new Ottoman conditions. And Turkey, despite being the seat of the caliphate and Sunni orthodoxy, always maintained a strong Sufi tradition even if not immediately evident in public.

Almost all religions contain mystical aspects alongside of more orthodox practice: the Kabbalah movement in Judaism, the many branches of Christian mysticism (especially Catholic and Eastern Orthodox), or the Bhakti movement in Hinduism. The believer yearns to experience God in everyday life and finds fulfillment in a constant consciousness of joy in God's surrounding creation. In this sense, Sufism aspires to certain *universal values in religious expression* that other faiths can recognize; this quest for universal values creates among followers a greater tolerance towards other faiths. In the words of the great Indian Sufi mystic Khwaja Mu'inuddin Chishti, "A friend of God must show affection as does the Sun. When the sun rises, it is beneficial to all, irrespective of whether they are Muslim, Christian, or Hindu."

Not surprisingly, the state and orthodox religious establishments everywhere have often been uncomfortable with, or even hostile to, mysticism and its independent, sometimes unorthodox, even undisciplined ways. That has been the case in Islam as well, where ecstatic Sufi mystics have sometimes felt themselves to be vehicles of God and have even ignored official orthodox control over belief. Sufi literature is replete with tales of Sufi mystics and holy men who show scant regard or awe for civil authority or kings. As one typical Sufi story relates a tale of a dervish, or Sufi holy man:

> A dervish was once sitting alone, meditating in a patch of desert. A great king with his retinue passed by. The dervish neither lifted his head nor paid any attention. The king was furious and said: "These dervishes in their patched cloaks are no better than animals!" His minister approached the dervish, "The great ruler of all the world passed by and you did not stand and bow: why were you so rude?" The dervish replied: "Tell your king that those people to bow to him hope for some reward from him. I want nothing from him and therefore do not bow. Tell him that rulers are there to protect their people, not just to exact obeisance from them. The ruler is the

watchman of the poor, though he has greater wealth and glory. The sheep are not made for the shepherd, rather the shepherd is there to serve the sheep. "When the irresistible decrees of Fate are issued, neither king nor slave remain. Open up the tomb and search these dusty bones: can you tell which was the rich man or which was the pauper?" The ruler was struck by the words of the dervish. He said: "Ask me a favor!" The dervish replied: "I would ask you to never disturb me again." The king begged: "Give me a word of advice!" The dervish replied: "Now that wealth is in your hands, realize before it is too late, that this wealth and this power will pass from hand to hand."[1]

Many rulers have traditionally valued the wisdom, religious insights and even frank political advice from Sufis and other holy men, although the relationship was often uncomfortable since the ruler frequently exercised little power over the holy man. In another Sufi tale, a sultan so respected a Sufi master that he started coming regularly to the master's circle. After a few meetings, the Sufi master asked the sultan to stop attending the circle. "How have I offended you?" asked the sultan. "You have not offended me at all," the Sufi master replied, "it's just that my followers are now looking to please you instead of God. We are not mature enough to have you in our circle."

Strict fundamentalists such as Salafis or Wahhabis in Islam are deeply suspicious of Sufism: in their view Sufi holy men often become objects of veneration themselves to their own followers; in fundamentalist eyes this represents blasphemy, the sin of *shirk*, or dilution of the Oneness of God. In their view shrines and mausoleums of holy men distract from the need to look to God directly; they disapprove of the intermediacy of holy men. Nonetheless, throughout Islamic history there have been many powerful Sufi movements that exerted major social and even political influence. They extend across borders and usually command an international following. And despite their spiritual orientation, Sufi movements have often spearheaded religious opposition and even armed resistance against invading western imperial forces—or sometimes even against Muslim rulers who are perceived as unjust.

The Ottoman state was no exception in its uncomfortable relationship towards Sufi brotherhoods. These movements were too large to ignore, but also lay outside the control of orthodox clerics and rulers. They might or might not support the state on given issues. They were in a position to stir discontent against the ruler when he was perceived as acting unjustly, paralleling many modern Islamist movements with their demands upon the ruler to deliver social justice. Some Sufi movements contributed to forces of regional resistance or local nationalism against central rule. This is the realm of popular Islam, rooted among the people and not among official clerics who are servants of the state. As the preeminent scholar of social movements of Turkey, Şerif Mardin writes: "Turkish officialdom had always been suspicious of the activities of charismatic leaders and self-appointed messiahs who had caused considerable trouble in Anatolia for centuries."[2] We might note that the Pharisees were similarly suspicious of Jesus.

With the inauguration of the Turkish Republic and the sweeping secular reforms of Atatürk, the power and influence of the popular Sufi orders were sharply reduced or outright eliminated. Their orders were banned, their meetings prohibited, and their properties confiscated by the state. While Turks praised Atatürk's accomplishments in rescuing the Turkish state from European imperialism and building a strong country, there was much popular unhappiness with the anti-religious character of these authoritarian secular reforms. Sufi influence persisted, even if discreetly and out of the public eye. Some Sufi movements in Turkey initially even opposed the new Kemalist secularist policies; some of their members were put on trial for violation of the anti-*tarikat* (anti-Sufi brotherhood) laws and for their hostility to Kemalist ideology. Only as democratic practice gradually emerged in Turkey over the past five decades have Sufi movements re-emerged into public view to become tolerated by the state. Here we see again how Sufism serves as an *unofficial social vehicle* for the preservation of religious belief and practice when it was subjected to anti-Islamic Kemalist ideology. Most of these Turkish Sufi orders also possess international ties and operate across borders such as the Nakshibendi, Qadiri and Tijani; these international ties strengthen the movements and make it harder for the state to control them. Many leading Turkish politicians have sometimes been quietly members of these circles.

Interestingly, Turkey has more recently seen a growth of interest in Sufism in unexpected circles. The Kemalist-oriented elite was of course long suspicious of Sufi brotherhoods as retrogressive forces in society. Yet the outlook of Sufism in recent times now seems to be attracting much of this younger elite, serving to break down hostility towards official or orthodox religious belief; it even becomes an entry point into deeper religious inquiry. Ironically, some of this recent interest in Sufism has come in through the "western door" in which the strong appeal of Rumi in the West began to be noticed and then adopted among many in the elite in Turkey. One immediate spark came via a novel, *The 40 Rules of Love*, by a leading Turkish woman writer Elif Shafak, written originally in English and recounting the life and thought of Rumi. The western garb of the novel perhaps eased the way to its greater acceptability among more upper-class and intellectual consciousness and the novel became a best seller in Turkey.[3] While many more orthodox religious

Turks may view it as little more than a popular form of western "new age" writing, the book contributes to the breakdown of ideological prejudice against Islam among a younger generation of the Kemalist elite. Such a trend also reflects a growing interest in spiritualism among more secular westerners in general as opposed to instinctive distaste for organized religion, its institutions, formal orthodoxies, and involvement in often bloody power struggles in the past.

But a new look at Sufi spiritualism through western eyes obscures the much more important story of the impact of modern Sufi tradition upon 20th-century Turkish Islam itself. One of the more remarkable intellectual figures of the late Ottoman Empire was the influential Sufi figure, Bediüzzaman Saïd Nursi. Nursi grew up in a clerical family in the Kurdish region of southeastern Anatolia where he quickly attracted attention for his studiousness, piety and intellectual curiosity. He was well versed in the activities and beliefs of several Sufi brotherhoods. During World War I he was captured by Russian troops in eastern Turkey and was sent to Russia as a prisoner of war for more than two years. After the war he returned to Turkey and continued his writing activities. He was driven by a calling to bring the message of the Qur'an to the people, freed of the complex language of scholarship, but rather conveyed in accessible language and relevant to the daily issues and problems of ordinary people.

In the early days of the Turkish republic Nursi came to view Atatürk's reforms with some ambivalence. On the one hand, he was in full support of Atatürk's patriotic resistance against western occupation of Anatolia after the end of World War I. Unlike some clerics who had opposed Atatürk's "disobedience" to the sultan in seeking to raise an army against western forces, Nursi strongly supported the national armed struggle; in this sense Nursi was a committed "nationalist" and supporter of Atatürk's leadership. He also strongly supported modernization of the country and the importance of education. But he was concerned about Atatürk's wholesale adoption of western institutions and ideas, especially the embrace of secularism, in which he sensed an anti-religious bias and feared it could be corrupting to traditional Turkish Islamic and cultural values. Atatürk asked Nursi to meet with him and reportedly told him that Nursi represented powerful vision and influence that could be of service to the revolution. Nursi was said to have declined to serve the Kemalist revolution because of the distinct anti-religious focus of its secularism and the scant value it placed on Islam. This may have been a fateful parting of the ways; in later years the Kemalist movement came to perceive the Nursi movement as antipathetic to the Kemalist vision and began to treat it as reactionary—which would carry long term negative consequences for Nursi's movement and the derogatory fashion in which Kemalist ideology treated it.

Nursi remained committed to combatting the positivist, anti-religious and materialist message of secularism that was spreading from the West which, in his view, served to corrupt values, weaken faith, and confuse moral orientation. But Nursi also emphasized knowledge and education as keys to personal development, community advancement and broad social enlightenment, particularly at a time when the world Muslim community seemed particularly weak and lagging behind the West.

Over the years Nursi penned a long series of essays, *The Messages of Light*, that were surreptitiously copied by hand in the hundreds of thousands and distributed among his many followers. His was not a Sufi movement as such, and he was not strictly speaking a Sufi, although his movement came out of that tradition. The movement eventually became known as the *Nur* (Light) movement. Nursi was repeatedly arrested by the state, jailed and exiled, partly on suspicions that he might represent a linkage between Sufi movements and Kurdish nationalism which had produced several anti-state nationalist rebellions in the name of Islam. Nursi, himself a Kurd, preached non-violence and spoke out against these rebellions. He soon came to preach tolerance and understanding across faiths.

Nursi saw no contradiction between science and religion: science serves to illuminate the complexity, wonder and glory of God's creation. He, like many other Muslim intellectuals, was concerned that a materialist-atheist vision places exclusive emphasis on science and ignores the vital element of moral and spiritual development. He sought to demonstrate the compatibility of religion with science and rationalism. For Nursi the overriding question was, how do we live in a materialist world and still maintain the power and meaning of faith? He believed his vision was intended not only for the world of Islam, but for all people who seek practical meaning in genuine faith.[4]

Despite the persecutions that Nursi suffered, his ideas spread and left an important legacy in his huge body of writings and interpretations on the meaning of Islam in everyday life—including 6,000 pages of commentary on the Qur'an that are still a source of inspiration to millions. He was a key historical figure who personally weathered the trauma of transition from the collapse of the Ottoman order through western allied invasion to the emergence of a new anti-religious Turkish state. He sought to make sense of these events in the context of emerging modernity in the Muslim world and to reconcile the two. His movement was long ridiculed and reviled among

Kemalist intellectuals as backward, ignorant primitive, and unenlightened. Only in the final decades of the 20th century were the suspicions, strictures and persecution of the Nur movement lifted, enabling his ideas to spread outside of Turkey and to win him recognition as a major modernist Islamic thinker. (Şerif Mardin's work, *Religion and Social Change in Modern Turkey*, remains the definitive and masterful study of Saïd Nursi.) It's worth noting that a leading characteristic of Christian Protestantism was likewise the effort to take theology and scripture beyond the Church and to make it meaningful to the daily lives and practical concerns of Christians. But the Nur movement was to find its most powerful resonance in a successor movement, known as the Gülen movement or *Hizmet* (Service) that we will take up in the next chapter.

CHAPTER TWELVE

FORMS OF ISLAM: POPULAR ISLAM - HIZMET AND THE GÜLEN MOVEMENT

Traditional Islamic values of piety, social commitment, tolerance, social justice and moderation in Islam find themselves overwhelmed in the current fray of international violence, war, injustice, fanaticism, and daily hardship in the Middle East—a key source of anxiety to most Muslims today. This kind of toxic environment contributes to increased insecurity, desperation, intolerance and radicalism. It is precisely these dangerous trends that the Turkey-based faith movement of Fethullah Gülen today seeks to combat. Gülen's movement represents the largest, most powerful and influential Islamic movement in the world today that prioritizes the quest for moderation, dialog and modernity in Islam.

The Gülen movement is a powerful example of popular Islam; it is sometimes referred to in Turkey as the "community" (*cemaat*), or, as the movement calls itself, *Hizmet* (Service.) Hizmet is by far the most significant movement of any kind in Turkey today, in numbers, influence, and impact. As a unique grassroots organization, it is beginning to gain recognition and significance across much of the Muslim world and beyond through its unusual combination of qualities: modern expression of faith through voluntary works and public service to humanity; its embrace of both science and faith as complementary concepts; its program to spread education; its call for religious and ethnic tolerance; its desire to avoid confrontation with the West, and its outreach for interfaith dialog. Gülen works to counter radicalizing trends and to return to the social commitment, social justice and rational inquiry that he believes are inherent in the deepest values of Islam. Not surprisingly, Hizmet's growing size, wealth and influence have also made it a source of some concern among secularists who oppose any strengthening of religion in public life in Turkey and have misgivings about the movement's power, impact on governance, and longer range intentions. Recent open antagonism between Hizmet and the AKP has also emerged that has heightened the public profile of the organization.

The Gülen movement has roots in the Sufi tradition although it is not a Sufi brotherhood. And while Gülen and his ideas are a source of inspiration to his followers, he does not fall into the traditional role of guru (*murshid, shaykh, pir*) of most Sufi leaders. Hizmet indeed shares in many of the values of Sufi belief, particularly the goal of revitalizing Islamic consciousness and the role of spirituality in one's personal daily life. Gülen has also been influenced by the poet Rumi, and numerous modern Turkish religious intellectuals. But Gülen chooses to direct this spiritual impulse into practical, social and organizational form rather than purely devotional directions. The movement's approach is beginning to influence the practice of social Islam outside of Turkey as well.

Unlike Diyanet (the Directorate of Religious Affairs), Hizmet has no formal association with government; it operates as a popular volunteer movement acting independently of, and outside of the state. It has no ambitions to form a political party and sees itself as an organization standing above or outside of politics. Yet its large membership includes many who work in state institutions including in the police and the judiciary, who on the personal level can and do have impact on policy on controversial issues, especially the Ergenekon investigations and corruption in government. But at a time when much of the Muslim world is wracked by turmoil, radical theologies, and even violence in the name of Islamic liberation, Hizmet is a powerful popular counterweight and a significant expression of contemporary and moderate values in Islam.

It was the Nur movement that laid the groundwork for the emergence of the subsequent Gülen movement. Fethullah Gülen himself is the son of an imam, born near the eastern Anatolian town of Erzurum, a stronghold of Turkish nationalism. He joined the Nur movement in his youth and began to preach independently in the İzmir region after Saïd Nursi's death.

> Gülen put Nursi's ideas into practice when he was transferred to a mosque in Izmir in 1966. Izmir is a city where political Islam never took root. However, the business and professional middle class came to resent the constraints of a state bureaucracy under whose wings it had grown, and supported market-friendly policies, while preserving at least some elements of a conservative lifestyle. Such businessmen were largely pro-Western, because it was Western (mainly US) influence, which had persuaded the government to allow free elections for the first time in 1950 and US aid, which had primed the pump of economic growth.[1]

But while Nursi laid emphasis on the meaning of religion in individual personal life, Gülen began to focus more upon society itself through activism in education, service (*Hizmet*) to the community, and active interfaith dialog to overcome religious hostilities. Here Hizmet bears some resemblance to Christian doctrines of "good works"—faith and God's purpose expressed through social action. The movement initially grew slowly in the long years when it was subjected to judicial harassment, show trials and detentions from the courts as a "reactionary," hence "unconstitutional," organization. Over the past decade and a half it has developed with remarkable rapidity as earlier anti-religious strictures in Turkey have been lifted and Gülen's modernist understanding of faith and action, coupled with organizational skill, have attracted greater public attention.

Fethullah Gülen himself is an emotional speaker and teacher with a strong personal following. Yet at the personal level he is a private man: on the two occasions when I had opportunity to interview him I was struck by his retiring manner, sense of personal modesty, courtliness and almost old-world mannerisms. His Turkish is studded with literary and Ottoman phraseology. His remarks on contemporary events tend to be cautious and he makes his points often by indirection. He has a scholar's knowledge of Arabic and Persian and studied English; he appears well informed on world events. He is referred to by all those who respect him as *Hoca Efendi*—"respected teacher"—in an old-fashioned turn of phrase.

Gülen's role as a preacher marked the beginning of his career when his stirring sermons—many of them bearing the influence of Nursi's thinking—had major impact on his followers. He has published over 60 books; his regular talks (*sohbetler*) are available on line in over 30 languages.[2] In them he addresses a range of religious and social issues that go well beyond theology. Like Nursi, he is concerned with the contemporary implications of religion in everyday life: the spiritual crises of modernity, and people's concerns and anxieties. Islamic rituals do matter, but for Gülen the spirit in which they are undertaken, and the way one lives one's life, are of the essence. It is Gülen's emphasis on the spirit that marks his Sufi background.

Yet his vision of Islam is entirely mainstream. He does not place Shari'a at odds with Sufism as some more libertarian traditions of Sufism have done. He believes that Shari'a —literally "the Way" or "the Path"—is best understood not through legal strictures and analysis but through illumination via the spirit of Sufism, a path. He rejects the formalism and especially the literalism of fundamentalist schools but accepts the significance of orthodox ritual.

Gülen's voluminous writings over time demonstrate a distinct process of evolution and broadening of his vision. In his early days he was more concerned about what he felt was the pernicious influence of atheism, materialism, or agnosticism that both he and Nursi felt was often enshrined in popular western culture. He shared a broad distrust of western intentions as they had affected Turkish history and traditional values. He even more strongly opposed communism whose atheistic values he perceived as a long-term threat to Turkey, to Islam and indeed to all spiritual values; both he and

Nursi had observed Soviet repression of Islam in Muslim areas of the Soviet Union. Gülen too had experienced anti-religious persecution—albeit in a less brutal fashion under authoritarian forms of Kemalism—that harassed religious organizations through detentions and court trials where "reactionary activities" were punishable as "undermining the secular state."

Reflecting Nursi, Gülen embraced the importance of science and mathematics in education—disciplines that had once been central to the intellectual life of the Muslim world in early centuries. Today these subjects play leading roles in the curriculum of the network of schools founded by Gülen. He insists that full human potential can only be achieved through combining reason and experience along with conscience and spiritual inspiration. Religion and science are not contradictory: they are but two manifestations, two different halves of the same truth, each complementing the other. To teach the laws of physics in the classroom is to teach the laws of God's universe.

While nominally leader of a huge conglomerate of institutions that are affiliated with or funded by his movement, Gülen's personal lifestyle is extremely modest, now nearly monastic—but his opponents have called him "shadowy." He has been in self-exile and in poor health living on an estate in rural Pennsylvania since 1998 when he left Turkey for health reasons and in the face of yet another trial before Kemalist-dominated courts for "advocating the establishment of an Islamic state"—charges he consistently denied, but it was not the first time such charges had been leveled against him. He was fully acquitted in 2006. He has nonetheless not returned to Turkey since then, keenly aware of the distracting controversy that his presence could spark on the rough political scene there. He nonetheless remains in close touch with events in the world and is in constant contact with key leaders of the movement who visit him in a constant stream. He grants interviews infrequently, but issues periodic statements on current issues he believes to be of importance. His ideas and ideals serve as a source of inspiration to a large number of followers, much as in the earlier tradition of Sufi leader.

As the movement has expanded it has inevitably become more decentralized. Today it embraces large numbers of independent private groups, committees, foundations, centers, and individuals; it receives major financial contributions from large numbers of businessmen who are part of the movement. Hizmet is self-sustaining; it operates loosely and spontaneously as individuals contribute to its advancement in various ways along the broad lines of action that Gülen has set out.

Evolution in Gülen's personal thinking demonstrates a gradual move away from his earlier focus on the Turkish tradition of Islam towards a greater universalism. Openness and tolerance towards other faiths become the key to avoiding social conflict, to achieving social harmony and fulfilling God's desire for humans to employ knowledge for advancement of human welfare. Over the past decades the Hizmet movement has sought cooperation with members of other faiths to participate in many of the movement's public activities. There is no formal "membership" in the movement, no one carries cards or registers, and one does not have to be a Muslim to be a participant—although the vast majority of supporters are, of course, Muslim believers. Hizmet welcomes the support of all those who share common goals and values and who wish to participate in the movement's educational and social work or its sessions of interfaith dialog.

Over time Gülen has expanded his focus to embrace appreciation of *common values in human life*. These values need not come exclusively from Islam; he perceives similar values in other religions as well, particularly in Judaism and Christianity. It is as if the values of Islam were extracted out of traditional Islamic ritual, theology and culture to be re-framed now as *universal values*. These values do not depend on a specific Muslim (or Christian) cultural vehicle. One might perhaps even call it a kind of "non-Muslim Islam"— Islamic values extending beyond specific Muslim culture to achieve common goals in education, community service, interfaith dialog, and the advancement of general human welfare. Indeed, Gülen has spoken of being "human first, and Muslim second."

Thus Gülen's vision advocates not simply development of personal philosophy, but direct social activism, including voluntarism, that ultimately will lead to the building of new societies. As Gülen states, "these new people will unite profound spirituality, wide knowledge, sound thinking, a scientific temperament, and wise activism. Never content with what they know, they will increase continuously in knowledge—knowledge of the self, of nature, and of God."[3] It is indeed this voluntarism and personal commitment to an ideal that drives so many hundreds of thousands of Turks—and others—to adopt a mission, to travel abroad in order to build schools and teach, and to serve social causes inside and outside Turkey. This is far removed from the suspicious attitudes of those Muslims who view the West only with suspicion. Gülen pursues ideas of progress and modernity—not to *recreate* a western way of life but to create a liberated Muslim mindset that can function confidently in the modern world.

Indeed, a basic if unstated concept behind the movement is the *empowerment* of Muslims to operate successfully in a contemporary and globalizing Turkey, and beyond. This goal has received strong backing from traditional social elements in Anatolia, where pious classes and those proud of Islamic and Ottoman tradition can now rise, achieve education and gain modern skills, and enter the world of business, academia and government and have an impact. As German researcher Günter Seufert points out, "Teachers and students within the educational network, their sponsors predominantly entrepreneurs from Anatolia and civil servants from the lower and/or provincial classes, discover in Gülen's teachings a strategy which allows them to expand their professional and social milieus and yet remain Muslims at the same time. Still more, Gülen's beliefs allow them all to combine their personal educational success and increased social status with their faith and the interests of their nation in a legitimate manner."[4]

Gülen's critics call this "Islamization" of society; others might see it as enabling believers to play a strong and practical role in contemporary society, while maintaining their values. Ironically some strong secular critics see Hizmet as potentially a greater threat to the secular ideology of Kemalist Turkey than Islamic violence or crude efforts to "seize the state" since it entails a peaceful evolutionary process of living, practicing and spreading Islamic values through working in society. Gülen does not employ the Islamic term *da'wa* (propagation of the faith); service (Hizmet) through concrete accomplishments replaces that concept.

"Don't Build a Mosque, Build a School"—The Gülen Schools

Islam has a long tradition of philanthropic contributions (*zakat*, or tithe) by the wealthy to aid the poor and to build mosques. Gülen shifts that approach: he has said that Turkey has enough mosques; instead he urges that philanthropic "good works" are more usefully directed towards building schools or hospitals. Through this vision, Hizmet has slowly built a large network of private schools, initially in Turkey and now increasingly around the world, at this point numbering well over one thousand schools. They are not religious schools, nor do they resemble "parochial" (private Roman Catholic) schools in the US. In Turkey the Gülen schools teach the curriculum established by the Turkish Ministry of National Education. They contain no religious instruction apart from a standard course on Islam long mandated by the secular Turkish government in all public schools as part of Turkish culture. Hizmet schools in other countries follow the curricula set by their own governments.

Because the issue of Islam and religious education in Kemalist Turkey has been politically charged for so long, the Gülen schools initially became the object of controversy, especially given the schools' spread and success. Opponents of the Gülen movement accused Hizmet schools of having a "hidden agenda" in seeking to influence children outside of class towards Gülen's religious values. While there is no special religious content in the Gülen curriculum in any country, Hizmet members freely acknowledge that the values, philosophy and style of life and dedication of the teachers hopefully do serve as a model to students. The teachers do seek to impart a moral vision and commitment in the example of their own lives. If the students make any ultimate commitment to the movement later on, members say, they are responding to the positive image and role model of the commitment and world-outlook of their teachers, most of whom are connected to the movement. Apart from education, the schools also stress social values and good conduct; parents praise the discipline, courtesy and seriousness of their students as well as the high quality of the education in modern facilities.

A striking contribution of the Gülen educational movement is its ability to turn secular education and its social benefits into a positive goal for religious families who otherwise might have sought religious education for their children, particularly among Turkish immigrants in Europe. "For decades, Turkish immigrants in Europe ensured that their children maintained their Turkish-Muslim identity by sending their offspring to schools in Turkey. The fact that many are now choosing to tread the path prepared by Nursi and Gülen, namely trusting that the acquisition of secular knowledge will strengthen their children's religious identity, can justifiably be termed "revolutionary."[5] This suggests an entire new fusion of secular education with religious values that replaces the centrality of religious education for pious Muslims; it becomes a vehicle to attain Muslim pride through educational accomplishments in the secular world. Furthermore, it represents a two-way street in social integration: while the movement in one sense might initially be seen to "Islamize" the middle class through focus on the calling to service, it also transforms that same new pious middle class into a social force that understands, and is comfortable operating within, the secular world. This process overcomes the cultural firewalls that exist in so many other Muslim countries between religious and urban secular classes.

The spread of the schools outside of Turkey further attests to this. Initially established in traditional areas of Ottoman influence such as the Muslim states of Central Asia, the Caucasus and the Balkans, they later spread to Christian countries such as Russia itself. Over ninety percent of the students in the Caucasus state of Georgia, for example, are Christian. There is a Gülen school in Moscow. Schools are growing in Africa and in Indonesia. They are invariably highly subscribed and receive a vote of confidence through the attendance of large numbers of children of the local elites. They are self-sustaining through tuition fees.

Instruction is normally conducted partly in English, partly in the local language, while courses in Turkish are offered as well. The teachers are usually volunteers from Turkey who go off to spend a number of years in other countries teaching, and at the same time learning the local language and winning goodwill for Turkey and the schools. And whereas critics have sought to portray the Nur movement and later the Gülen movement as somehow reactionary and obscurantist, the facts would dictate otherwise. Sciences, mathematics and computer sciences rank high in the curriculum. The goal for the students is to be prepared for making their way in modern society for society's greater benefit—a clear universal human value.

And there are practical benefits for Turkey as well: graduates of these schools usually end up with feelings of closeness to Turkish culture, functioning as local ambassadors of goodwill to Turkey in government and business. In many countries the first graduates left the schools over a decade ago and now occupy significant places in the governments and commercial sectors of their country. For businessmen associated with the movement, it represents a valuable business network as well; they have often established the early foundations for a Turkish community in many of these countries and have a ground floor in establishing trade ties. Many cities in Anatolia have sister cities in Central Asia and the Caucasus that facilitate trade and other ties between them. In short, the schools help create a form of Turkish "soft power" that facilitates both diplomatic and business openings for Turkey.

Despite the schools' overall success, they are not without criticism. Some complain that the students admitted to these highly subscribed schools abroad are primarily from the elites of each country. While that may have been initially true in the effort to gain early acceptance from local governments, the schools now reach out to admit qualified students from all social classes; some 20 to 25 percent of the poorer qualified students receive scholarships. Even in the US, for example, a number of schools have been opened by Hizmet supporters in which a high proportion of black and Hispanic minorities are represented who welcome the low-cost educational opportunities offered, especially in technical fields.

The schools early on suffered from the paranoia of authoritarian regimes in Central Asia who have little toleration for criticism or freedom of expression. Uzbekistan, for instance, recalled 300 Uzbek students back from Turkish universities in 1999. The reasons were specifically political: the highly authoritarian regime of Islam Karimov was concerned that Uzbek students in Turkey were becoming politicized in the open environment in Turkey and beginning to engage in anti-Karimov activities abroad. Because political Islam has been a key underground source of anti-regime activity in Uzbekistan—as it is all over the Muslim world—Karimov accused Turkey of fomenting Islamic "fundamentalism and terrorism" in Uzbekistan. The charges are absurd since both the Gülen movement and the Turkish state are outspokenly opposed to violence and terrorism. But in 2000 Uzbekistan shut down all Hizmet schools. Turkmenistan pursued a similar course of anti-Turkish reaction in 2011 although that is now changing. Not surprisingly, the kind of independent thinking fostered by the schools were producing students too independent-minded for insecure and rigid regimes run by "presidents for life"—especially when the well-qualified students then moved into the local government. Rumors were spread that the schools were operating on behalf of the CIA or Islamic fundamentalists. The US Peace Corps and the international Doctors Without Borders were similarly expelled from the once politically bizarre environment of Turkmenistan.

Moscow too has consistently been concerned about the influence of Islamic fundamentalism in the Muslim regions of Russia. But investigation found no links to "fundamentalism" in the Gülen schools. Nor do the Gülen schools wish to be contaminated by such an association. As we noted, many Christian students attend the Gülen schools not only in Russia, but elsewhere in the former Soviet Union. There the schools filled a special gap: under decades of Soviet anti-religious campaigns, communism had come to represent the sole "moral" or ideological value of society. With the collapse of communism and its ideology in 1991 an ideological vacuum opened, revealing a hunger for some new spiritual values. The Gülen schools provided quality education and a balanced and modern antidote to radical Islamic forces that sought a foothold there, a process that found favor in the West.

The Gülen-inspired schools (or "Turkish schools" as they are often known) have now spread to 120 countries, the majority of which are not even officially Muslim, as far away as Africa and Latin America, the United States and East Asia. They have sometimes been established in countries where no Turkish Embassy or Turkish community had previously existed. In the end there can be no doubt that the schools serve the broader Turkish national interest in the goodwill that is created, similar to the American Peace Corps. Hizmet provides a major network of international connections.

An interesting shift has meanwhile occurred in the views of the Turkish government towards the schools and foreign outreach. We now see a new focus in the Turkish military and the foreign ministry on learning non-European languages and cultures. Indeed, in Turkish think tanks today you now regularly encounter young people who have served several years abroad and learned the language of a Central Asian, Middle Eastern or even African country. This was nearly unthinkable a decade ago. The experience and the cultural area knowledge these individuals have acquired create a valuable cadre of international expertise for Turkey. Turkey's rapidly expanding exposure to the developing world has changed the once insular character of Turkish life. Satellite TV now brings programs in multiple languages from the West, Balkans, the Middle East and Central Asia into the Turkish living room. This Turkish opening to the world translates into direct benefits for the government and business. These accomplishments also dovetail well with Turkey's expanding new foreign policies under Davutoğlu.

The Gülen movement has extended its educational activities as far as the US as well where it has established dozens of centers for interfaith dialog and large numbers of schools. Turkish businessmen and Turkish academics have joined to build and staff some 120 charter schools around the country. In fact, in a Newsweek rating of the 10 top charter schools in the US, two were Gülen-inspired schools. Members of the Gülen movement in the US are also active in building ties with state congressional offices in order to promote trade with Turkey and build bilateral ties between Turkey and sister cities through sponsored visits to Turkey.

The Network of Gülen-Linked Institutions

The Gülen movement shows great skills in the spread of its commercial and financial institutions and in the use of modern media to reach to an ever-broader audience. Its members are generally well-versed in technology, economics or business, rather than philosophy or theology. The movement publishes an excellent commercial daily, *Zaman*, whose sales are twice the circulation of any other paper in Turkey; it features a variety of well-known columnists representing views from right to left—although few traditional Kemalists. Its columnists are not necessarily part of the movement. *Zaman* sets high standards for journalism, avoids the sensationalism that characterizes many other major Turkish newspapers and is as objective, or more so, than any other daily in Turkey. It does, however, openly feature articles about

Hizmet, Gülen, and rebuts attacks against them. The owners of *Zaman* also publish the best English language newspaper in Turkey, *Today's Zaman*, which similarly features a distinguished selection of columnists[6]. The organization also supports several large circulation magazines in Turkish, as well as one in English, and operates two major TV stations in Turkey and one in the US in English.

Of perhaps greater importance to the future development of thinking in the Muslim world, Hizmet has opened doors to the Arab world in more recent years. Reflecting a history of poor relations between Turkey and many Arab states over past decades, Arab Muslims had often viewed Turkish secularism with suspicion and a belief that Turkey simply represented the opening wedge of NATO and western interests in the Middle East. The flagship for Hizmet among Arabs is the movement's first magazine published in Arabic, *Hira*—a deeply resonant name that refers to the cave in the Hijaz mountains in Saudi Arabia where the Prophet received his earliest divine revelations. The magazine reaches out to Arab intellectuals to promote debate and discussion on religious and social issues and promote Hizmet's thinking; interestingly the magazine's highest circulation is in Saudi Arabia where, in principle, its ideas should be less welcome in that officially Salafi stronghold. *Hira* has organized meetings and conferences in a number of countries including Egypt, Morocco, Jordan, Algeria, Saudi Arabia, Yemen, Sudan, Kuwait, Mauritania, and the United Arab Emirates, and has invited more than 2,500 intellectuals to Turkey for workshops. Gülen schools have been opened in Egypt, Yemen and several in Morocco and exchanges with Arab scholars are growing. These developments contribute new input into Islamic thinking in the Arab world and help bridge the gap between Turkey and the Arab world, especially as questions of religion still dominate Arab political discourse. Although Hizmet operates entirely independently, there are parallels to Diyanet's official activities overseas.

Shi'ite Iran is probably the one major political region where Hizmet has not established a significant presence. Gülen in the past has seemed less comfortable with elements of Iranian culture and politics; he considered the Islamic Republic of Iran to represent undesirable radical ideas in Islam; in turn Iran has likely been suspicious of the Gülen schools. Establishment of ties between Hizmet and Iran must be a two-way street. But Gülen firmly rejects sectarianism in Islam; inside Turkey Hizmet is promoting openings with the large non-Sunni Alevi community. As Iranian relations with the West improve, both Gülen and Iran may find it easier to explore contacts.

The Gülen organization early on founded its first flagship institution, the Turkish Journalists and Writers Foundation, which organizes colloquiums on major domestic and global issues. For over a decade and a half it has sponsored the Abant Platform, a remarkable annual roundtable of various leading writers and thinkers, professionals, artists, and statesmen in Turkey representing a broad range of views—Muslim, Christian, Jewish, atheist, conservative, progressive, leftist, secularist—to discuss major social and cultural questions of contemporary Turkey and the world. These forums have produced extremely thoughtful and probing summary reports on the discussions and consensus reached among the rotating members of such a diverse group. A key goal of the forum was to encourage the state and society to publicly consider and debate issues vital to the future of a more liberal Turkey and the movement's own future. These topics had generally been considered too "sensitive" to address widely in public debate but they represented issues that Gülen wanted to see aired more broadly, such as Islam and the meaning of secularism; the nature of relationships among religion, state and society; the character and implications of multiculturalism; the role of ethnicity in society; the democratic state under rule of law; the importance of pluralism in social compromise; war and democracy; the political, economic and cultural dimensions of globalization; and the Kurdish issue. This is probably the most far-reaching and thoughtful annual intellectual gathering in Turkey today; these discussions created a more congenial atmosphere for familiarity and understanding of these issues that were generally stifled under Kemalist orthodoxy, enabling the Abant Platform forums to make an innovative intellectual contribution.

The Business World

Members of the movement operate Bank Asya, the biggest Islamic bank in Turkey. (There are thousands of Islamic banks, quite unrelated to Gülen, around the world. Since Islam views interest as a form of usury, Islamic banks instead offer shares in the future profits of their investments and tend to be more socially oriented in their goals of community development. In the US financial institutions such as JPMorgan Chase, Deutsche Bank and HSBC all offer Islamic banking services.) Bank Asya's success has ensured that its customers include a far larger clientele than simply pious Muslims.

Businessmen who support the movement find financial benefits in expanding into overseas investments and supporting the building of schools overseas as a contemporary form of doing good works, but also founding local businesses as part of a Turkish diaspora, and establishing close ties with local elites. The constellation of Gülen institutions does not represent a single huge corporation, nor are they under any central control or unified management. They are made up of individual organizations or businesses put together individually by members of the Gülen movement acting in their private capacity where they see their skills, funds and influence best used.

Interfaith Dialog

Gülen's writings and sermons reflect his belief that in the modern age religion must not be a divisive but a unifying force serving the best interests of humanity. Values of tolerance and the experience of understanding other faiths and dialog among religious communities are essential to mutual respect, to the avoidance of suspicion, conflict, and to the meaningful fulfillment of a religious life. In the US, for example, in addition to the Gülen Institute headquartered in Houston, Centers for Interfaith Dialog exist around the country and the world. The centers encourage meetings, seminars and discussions of shared issues of concern, often highlighting the diverse religious expression of these same values within different communities. They are a key instrument for explaining Islam and combating Islamophobia. During a visit to several Hizmet-sponsored centers in the mid-west of the US I was struck by the active participation of many Christian activists attending discussion meetings and seminars on inter-religious issues; several participants spoke of having changed their views on Islam through meetings and sponsored trips to Turkey.

Gülen himself has met in the past with Pope John Paul II, Patriarch Bartholomew (leader of the Eastern Orthodox Christian community), and the Chief Rabbi of Israel, as well as with major Jewish leaders, rabbis, and Christian priests inside Turkey. Most minorities in Turkey believe the Gülen organization to be sincere and open to the support and protection of minorities. Human rights is a key term used regularly in Gülen's statements. Dialog is the byword among movement members in reaching out to other communities to find common ground in a broad variety of meetings and exchange visits. These activities are not simply socially useful; the movement's followers believe that *such activities in fact represent the expression of Islam.* Many non-Muslims are also committed to helping arrange and attend these functions.

As with Saïd Nursi, a key element in Gülen's approach to Islam is the importance of making Islam meaningful to the here and now, relevant to people's spiritual needs and concerns in contemporary life. It is a way of life infusing daily human relations with new belief. In Gülen's view Islam should not be a utopian faith, but something attainable in this life that will provide insight and understanding as well as psychological comfort and ease. These ideas trace back to the passage in the Qur'an, "God desires ease for you, and desires not hardship" (2:185).

In this same spirit the movement also operates a humanitarian assistance organization *Kimse Yok Mu?* (Isn't There Anybody Out There?) that works to alleviate humanitarian disasters both in Turkey and abroad. These activities also reflect earlier Ottoman-Islamic traditions of philanthropic foundations that supported mosques, Sufi brotherhoods, schools, libraries, hospitals, public infrastructure and homes for the poor. Such activities again parallel to some degree the work of Diyanet overseas. The Gülen approach, however, emphasizes philanthropy as part of a *civic*, and not state, duty, consonant with Gülen's belief in the vital central role of civic society.

The Gülen movement represents an interesting modernist Islamic organization comfortably operating in the material and commercial world as well as the spiritual. The spread of its work to other countries demonstrates how an originally Islamic-focused movement can come to cooperate globally on agreed-upon social agendas. It demands attention because of its effectiveness in functioning at the grassroots, non-statist level, based primarily on volunteers who commit their time, energies and lives to its advancement. Globally it represents the cutting edge of social activism based on Islamic values, exerting positive impact on the societies where it operates, particularly at a time when confusion, anger and violence reign in many places. Hizmet stresses the term *adanmışlık*—personal commitment or dedication. Its strong following suggests the attraction of this concept in today's world. And it often offers good business connections as well.

The Meaning of Modernization

All Islamists face a key question: what is the nature and meaning of modernization? The answer has immediate implications for policy. It's also an age-old issue as we have seen, stemming from 19th century debates in the Ottoman Empire over reform and its relationship to the West. Is westernization the only vehicle to modernity? Does westernization equal modernization? Gülen probably grapples more explicitly than most other major Muslim movements with the practical questions of coexistence between eastern and western cultures. He is not the first to address such questions— they have occupied Muslim thinkers for centuries. But he sets forth a framework of cooperation on the basis of perceived common values among diverse religious believers.

We noted earlier that liberals in the late Ottoman Empire readily accepted the temporary superiority of western civilization in science and technology, in its demonstrable ability to build powerful states capable of producing great wealth and dominating the world. But the Ottomans considered such superiority to be a *transient phenomenon*; the West, for a variety of reasons, had simply "gotten there first" with the first version of modernity. The Ottomans were confident that they and the rest of the world would eventually learn these secrets of success and would attain similar levels of development themselves. The unfolding of dramatic new economic power in the developing world over the last few decades lends much credence to that early perception: western superiority now indeed seems transient.

Earlier Islamist currents of thought in Turkey had been deeply suspicious of the West, its power and aggressiveness, and its attempt to impose a world order of its own making. But the AKP was the first Islamic political party that sharply diverged from earlier Turkish Islamist thought with its new and open *embrace* of globalization, broadly supported by a growing class of religious businessmen in which the Gülen community was a key element. Still, many in the Muslim world continue to condemn the West as driven by an ingrained harsh and materialistic desire to dominate; western populations are perceived in many developing countries as producing societies that lack spiritual foundation—which they believe will be the eventual seeds of the West's undoing. As many Islamists point out, the problem is not that westerners are Christian but that they are *not* Christian any longer in their social values; they seem devoid of spiritual principle.

Gülen believes that the two worlds, material and spiritual, live in vital coexistence, each quality essential to the success of the other. He looks to a vibrant Muslim world that accepts the scientific and rational theories of the West that make material attainments possible. But he also insists on promoting the spiritual values that must *accompany* material gains in order to build a truly solid civilization. He perceives many of these spiritual values in Islam to be currently imprisoned in backward states, dysfunctional societies and poor governance in so much of the Muslim world. A clear spiritual tradition exists in Islam; it must be allowed to creatively shape the Muslim world's search for modernity and material accomplishment—but *within* the framework of its own culture.

Gülen urges Muslims to avoid the twin pitfalls of either uncritical acceptance of the West, or uncritical rejection. The first identifies westernization as the *sole path* to creating a modern civilization, those who "seek uncritically to adopt, and force others to accept, everything Western as superior, progressive, and advanced, with a corresponding devaluation of native or national values."[7] They perceive Islam as an *obstacle* to the attainment of modernization; in the process they risk throwing out their own Islamic civilizational values. This approach ends up approximating the Kemalist blueprint for modernization.

The second trap is the opposite side of the coin: a view of modernity as a distinctively western project *alien* to Islamic culture, leading to rejection of everything about the West. It demonizes the West as the source of all that is wrong about Muslim society. They perceive western use of force to dominate Muslim states and culture as grounds for rejecting *the totality of western thinking* as corrupt. "Gülen holds that both these reactions, that of uncritical emulation and that of angry reaction, are misplaced and that neither is soundly rooted in Islamic teaching."[8]

How then are the two traditions reconciled? "Gülen does not seek a middle way between Islam and modernity; he perceives *Islam itself as the middle way*: 'Islam, being the 'middle way' of absolute balance—balance between materialism and spiritualism, between rationalism and mysticism, between worldliness and excessive asceticism, between this world and the next"...[9] This, in the end, may capture what is truly "modern" about the Gülen movement. This is also why these concepts are directly relevant to the rest of the Muslim world struggling with the same issues.

Georgetown Jesuit scholar Thomas Michel, based on his studies of the members of the Gülen community, concludes that:

> These are clearly modern people, well-trained in the secular sciences, but with a genuine concern for spiritual and humane values. These values they seek to communicate to students by their own comportment. They offer a first-rate education that brings together the latest technological advances with character formation and high ideals. The Gülen schools, in my opinion, are the most effective proof of the validity of Gülen's effort to reconcile modernity with spiritual values. They are one of the most fascinating and promising educational efforts going on in the world at the present time.[10]

Criticisms of Gülen

The success, power and growing influence of the Gülen movement has in turn generated critics. The major source of criticism of Hizmet has come, unsurprisingly, from Kemalist elites who, as a social and political force, have been losing their former political dominance. Radical Kemalists have traditionally viewed Gülen, the Nursi movement and all other religious organizations as subversive, obscurantist, reactionary, and a threat to the secular state that Kemalism and the army are sworn to uphold. They see

Hizmet's success as representing the undoing of the secular accomplishments of the Kemalist state and its anti-religious firewalls.

But times have changed. Society has liberalized, urbanization has burgeoned, new generations and new social backgrounds and a broadened middle class with bourgeois values have all emerged onto the social scene. Attitudes across Turkey have shifted, reflecting these major new demographic and social realities. There is a new level of appreciation and comfort in Turkey with the former religious and cultural Ottoman Islamic identity. There is more relaxation about women wearing headscarves in public institutions, with expressions of public piety, or the existence of religiously-oriented organizations. Even Kemalists appreciate Turkey's successful negotiation onto a globalized economy and greater clout abroad. None of this means there is significant sentiment in Turkey to create "an Islamic state," or to apply Shari'a law; the Gülen movement itself categorically rejects any such quest. Hizmet explicitly accepts the reality of a modern secular Turkish society in an increasingly secular world; it has no trouble in embracing secularism as long as the state remains *neutral* towards legal religious activity and is not hostile to its activities as before. Hizmet members furthermore believe that a moral movement like their own should not depend upon or need the state and, indeed, might even be corrupted by the state through direct association with its power.

Even as classic Kemalist criticism of Gülen has mellowed with time, an unexpected new source of political struggle emerged onto the public scene starting in 2011, this time between the two dominant Islamic organizations of Hizmet and the AKP itself. A strident and escalating series of verbal attacks from both sides created a major political crisis. This confrontation among Islamic groups themselves will be the subject of the next chapter—in a political furor that seemed to be creating potential new political bedfellows all around.

Modern Turkish history recounts, among other things, the story of how religious movements and organizations came to achieve legal status within the state, and to gain social respect in a once fiercely secularized elite society. In ideological terms one may personally welcome or deplore this trend of events. But from the standpoint of democratic practice, tolerance, and pluralism, it has to represent a clear advance over the past.

At the same time, this new diversity of religious groups and organizations expanded the realm of discussion, and created differences and even rivalries among them. Despite much cooperation between the AKP and Hizmet in the early 2000s, by 2013 these differences had broken out into the open in an unexpected, escalating, and surprisingly bitter public confrontation, revealing a new and serious testing of strength between them. The issues had nothing to do with theology and everything to do with issues of political values, policy choices, social power and political influence. Tensions between the two groups escalated as Prime Minister Erdoğan's style of governance began to move in more erratic, volatile, and imperious directions after his electoral victory in 2011 which he seemed to interpret as license to dominate all facets of governance in the Turkish state. The first serious signs of such political miscalculations on Erdoğan's part emerged vividly with the Gezi Park riots of 2013 marking the beginning of his decline as a politician and party leader. As his mistakes increased, he showed signs of losing his once impressive political touch and ability to command respect. Financial irregularity and scandal weakened his once powerful stature further.

The Gezi Park Riots and Their Implications for Future Turkish Governance
On 8 May 2013 a small public demonstration in Istanbul's Gezi Park ended up plunging Turkey into a dramatic domestic political crisis with no advance warning; a modest event broadened into anti-government riots that soon spread across most big cities in the country and lasted for over a month. Public disorders of this kind had not been witnessed in the country for several decades and represented a significant wake-up call to the AKP government. The incident seemed to catalyze a backlog of dissatisfaction with the government on the part of many segments of the population. In the context

of much violent chaos across the broader Middle East it is important to know what the Gezi Park incidents meant, and did not mean, in the broader picture.

The immediate spark was a seemingly ill-considered urban development scheme in a small park in Istanbul's famed Taksim Square area that would have cut down the park's few trees and transformed the area into a site for a large mosque and a commercial mall designed as historic Ottoman barracks. Many perceived it as another developer's land-grab in the booming development fever of expanding modern Istanbul; environmental activists met it with a demonstration. Properly handled, the municipality could easily have defused this early and modest demonstration against the development plans by seeking public consultation and an airing of all the issues in this symbolically "western" bastion of the city. Instead the Istanbul police met the demonstrators with tear gas and undue force causing the incident to quickly mushroom into a significant domestic crisis that exposed weaknesses of the AKP government.

Beneath the surface of the controversy over the park itself lay a significant body of domestic dissatisfaction with Erdoğan personally and with aspects of AKP policies that far exceeded environmental issues. The disorders in one form or another continued on sporadically for several weeks including some acts of violence against public property by some demonstrators. Ultimately several people were killed, hundreds injured by the police violence, and several thousand people temporarily detained. While President Gül spoke of the need for dialog and maintenance of freedom of speech, and the Speaker of the National Assembly apologized for the use of "excessive violence" by police in handling the demonstrators, Erdoğan himself took an uncompromising line, belittled and condemned the demonstrators, and suggested the existence of a conspiracy by foreign hands hostile to the AKP behind the incident. He announced his determination to proceed with the development, leaving the impression of an inflexible and arrogant leader who had lost his feel for the politics of the situation.

As the disorders spread from Istanbul to Ankara and dozens of other cities, some foreign media began to describe the events as a "Turkish Spring," as if reflecting the spirit of the ongoing Arab Spring. Yet such terminology distorts reality and fails to grasp the most basic elements of Turkish politics. The *Arab* Spring was directed against long-standing Arab *dictatorships* and desperate domestic conditions. The *Turkish* protests were against the policies of a government that had been legitimately elected in fair elections—not once, but three times—and had gained the electoral support of about half the country in the face of overwhelmingly weak and unfocused opposition parties.

Nor was the struggle, as much of the western press suggested, about secular versus religious elements of the population, but rather about specific AKP policies, conditions and personalities over a decade.

Apart from poor handling of the situation by the prime minister, the evolution of the incident also suggested the continuing existence of an earlier mentality on the part of a few that hoped to overthrow democratic government once again by extra-legal means—reviving the old days when national demonstrations and political discontent could stir up enough disorder to "justify" a military coup. The continuing antipathy of orthodox Kemalists against religious parties and public religious expression has long been present. But this time the AKP had also gained the votes of Turkish *secular liberals* who supported its steps to move the military out of politics and to establish a greater degree of democratic practice in the country. With the last AKP electoral victory in 2011, however, many political observers came to believe that Erdoğan had perceived his electoral victories as granting him virtual full license to rule as he saw fit—taking elections as representing the totality of democratic process. Electoral victory in a democracy indeed does represent a mandate but not an absolute one; the government is required to rule in the name of all the people including those who voted against it, and to engage in regular consultation with public opinion on diverse issues. Critics of Erdoğan described him as notorious for having a short fuse, an embattled and aggressive political style, and a tendency to governing imperiously, running roughshod over views that differed from his own.

The public at large was particularly angered at supine Turkish mainstream media that seemed to have been bought off by the government; large segments of the media ignored the ongoing serious demonstrations and riots for a long time, sometimes providing no coverage whatsoever—an unacceptable situation in a democracy.

In fairness to Erdoğan, it's important to note that the issue was exploited by many parts of the political spectrum: various opposition elements soon joined the demonstrations as well, each with its own partisan and opportunistic goals apart from the immediate issue of the park. Extreme nationalists hoped to weaken the government in order to derail the government's significant progress in negotiations with the Kurdish nationalist PKK towards an historic settlement of Turkey's Kurdish problem. Radicals on both the left and right seemed to hope that continuing demonstrations and riots might tempt the military back out of the barracks to assume once again its Kemalist overseer role in state security issues. Some members of opposition parties were deeply frustrated that their own parties had done poorly in elections against the AKP and indeed saw no hope on the horizon for any other political party to pose a decisive electoral challenge to the AKP in the near term. Indeed, one of the by-products of AKP electoral success was the parallel weakening of nearly all political opposition: there had been no credible alternative party or leader on the scene with a chance at winning an election in the foreseeable future—until Erdoğan was touched by personal scandal at the end of 2013. In effect, some participants during the Gezi disorders actually hoped to unseat the elected prime minister and his party through extra-legal means—through expanding riots and disorders across the country in an effort to make the country ungovernable, or to goad the government into harsher crackdowns that would gain greater sympathy for the opposition. The military coup in Egypt against the Brotherhood government a few months thereafter was a scenario right out of the playbook of past Turkish military coups, a model of what perhaps a small handful of genuine extremists in Turkey were hoping to achieve through exploitation of the Gezi Park riots.

The disorders wound down within a few weeks, but emotions remained high and the political mood of the country underwent a modest but significant shift. The major question to emerge from it all was what lessons the AKP, and especially Erdoğan, would draw from the experience. Erdoğan had ambitions to be elected as president of Turkey when his term limits as parliamentary deputy (and thus prime minister) ran out in 2015. He also had aspirations to amend the constitution to create a new and enhanced presidential system which would grant him greater powers; the Gezi Park crisis decisively undercut support for that bid. Erdoğan in the meantime has shown marked nervousness, almost bordering on paranoia, about any possible "extra-legal" methods his opponents might revert to in order to diminish or bring him down. The AKP indeed faced a major political watershed in determining what role Erdoğan would play when his term as prime minister ends. There are other contenders for party leadership within the AKP, including current President Abdullah Gül himself and Speaker of Parliament Bülent Arınç. Fethullah Gülen too expressed his disapproval of Erdoğan's inflammatory language and heavy-handedness in handling the crisis rather than seeking conciliation. For many observers the riots and their aftermath marked the beginning of the end of the AKP era.

The AKP and Hizmet: The Path to Confrontation
The AKP over a decade achieved a strikingly positive record of accomplishments overall, surpassing in virtually every respect the

achievements of any previous elected Turkish government. Nonetheless, numerous tasks remained undone: Turkey still required a deepening of democratic institutions and practice, further progress towards solving internal ethnic and sectarian differences, the deepening of social justice, strengthening the independence of the judiciary, and a more equitable distribution of economic gains. There is every good reason to be optimistic about Turkey's overall long-range future. But, while unlikely, Turkish democracy could nonetheless conceivably experience setbacks in three vital respects: an inability to peacefully resolve Kurdish demands; a possible deepening of authoritarian tendencies within the AKP, particularly in the person of Erdoğan; and, least likely, a return of military intervention into governance.

The AKP and the Hizmet movement both made common cause during the 2002 election that brought the AKP to power. Both groups had suffered persecution and judicial harassment under previous Kemalist governments. They shared a broad desire to expand freedoms for Islamic movements, a desire to revitalize Islam, to break the military's hold on domestic politics as well as the Kemalist grip on the bureaucracy. Never before had Gülen supported an Islamic party in elections; he had distrusted the Islamist agenda of earlier Islamist parties that he viewed as unnecessarily provocative; instead he had sympathized with traditional right-of-center secular parties whose softer Kemalist agenda was less hostile to him. But in 2002 Gülen acted in the belief that the AKP represented something new: an Islamic party that had progressed beyond the risky and ideological posture of Erbakan's Islamist Refah party (overthrown by the 1997 military coup) and had come to stand for more pragmatic change. Hizmet's unofficial endorsement of the AKP and its significant bank of votes at the time were quite significant to the party's broad electoral victory. (Figures differ wildly: some speculate that the followers of Hizmet could potentially number as high as eight million; AKP sources in 2014 suggested Hizmet members make up only three percent of the electorate.)

In 2010 Gülen's vigorous and outspoken support for Erdoğan's referendum on constitutional reform also contributed greatly to a strong AKP victory on the issue; that referendum, among other things, gave greater power to politicians to make appointments to the judiciary (as is the rule in the US). This represented a marked shift in judicial orientation. Earlier judges had in effect recruited their own successors. That system in the eyes of many had served to perpetuate the Kemalist hold on judicial philosophy and practice. Kemalists correctly understood that this new constitutional step (that also accorded with EU recommendations) would further consolidate Erdoğan's political power in weakening the old and entrenched Kemalist judiciary structure. Hizmet too strongly supported opening up the judiciary to new and broader judicial philosophies that would lessen restrictions on religious organizations and also open opportunities for Hizmet's own members to qualify.

Turkey's two major Islamic movements took differing approaches to issues of policy agendas however. The AKP, emerging out of the tradition of earlier Islamist parties, naturally acted as a political party; its political platform has inevitably reflected the issues, personalities and political circumstances of the moment. The Gülen movement on the other hand, emerging out of the apolitical Nur movement, focused upon direct social change through revitalization of Islam through personal transformation, social activism and educational programs, avoiding explicit political activism. These differing approaches have produced natural differences of perspective between them. At the simplest level, the AKP as a political organization by necessity is in the business of building electoral power coalitions, and winning elections; like all political parties it seeks to use the instruments of state to its advantage in future elections. Hizmet, in the end, is not a political organization, although Gülen and the movement's individual members do have an interest and stake in political principles and actions as they impact governance, society, and their own programs. Hizmet's main goal is to seek the freedom to maintain and expand its organizational social activity and to ensure that the state does not block its civic freedom of action as it had done in earlier decades. But beyond that, it is also committed to its own sense of good governance that include values of pluralism and human rights for all, a belief in the supremacy of law, a search for social harmony, the need for honest politicians, and maintenance of democratic practice. Gülen himself has been increasingly willing to speak out periodically on critical political issues he believes vital to Turkey's future stability and welfare.

Each of these approaches—political and apolitical—towards fulfillment of civic goals and Islamic values is equally valid, with its own strengths and weaknesses. The political route operates primarily on a top-down basis— through governance—while a social movement emphasizes change from the ground up. Both are concerned with issues of political and social morality in a broader sense. Erdoğan has periodically advocated policies—largely rhetorically—that many liberals consider straying into the realm of personal morality such as the degree of public alcohol consumption permitted, issues of same-sex dormitories, adultery and abortion. These issues, however, involve not just personal morality, but often issues of social morality. The Gülen movement on the other hand has remained distant from legislation of morality. Indeed, contemporary Islamists increasingly now seem to acknowledge that morality imposed by law from above has limited value: morality must spring from personal individual voluntary choice if it is to possess moral value and meaning. The Saudi-Salafi model of enforced public prayers, for example, is out of keeping with contemporary societies; its coercive character generates limited moral worth for the individual if he is only fulfilling compulsory acts of worship and becomes simply an instrument of social control by the state.

Yet we cannot speak of Hizmet as entirely "outside politics" either: over the past decade of greater political and religious freedoms, its members, as individuals, have enjoyed access to corridors of power through filling positions within the judiciary and police organizations—among other institutions—positions from which they were long banned when Kemalists were dominant. Hizmet argues that its members have as much right as any citizen of any persuasion to serve, if qualified, in these institutions; Hizmet also sought to ensure that these institutions never again be monopolized by those ideologically hostile to it or, for that matter, to the AKP, simply on the basis of their Islamic orientations. Hizmet over the years has thereby gained significant influence within some key areas of the bureaucracy, but its members act as individuals and not as a bloc. A high-ranking AKP spokesman in 2014, however, in a heated exchange of charges between the AKP and Hizmet, stated that Hizmet members may represent no more than 15 percent of the judiciary but charged that it occupies "all the control points."[1] The accuracy of this statement is nearly impossible to verify but would seem unlikely, given the diversity of political opinion with the judiciary.

Gülen has furthermore stated that his movement can never be associated with a single party and should be above day-to-day politics. Hizmet's formal programs operate quite independently of the state. And although Gülen has grown increasingly critical of the AKP, it is striking that he has never been anti-state at any point. Indeed, in sharp distinction to so many Islamists in other countries who became hostile to the oppressive authoritarian state in which they lived, Gülen was always a strong supporter of the Turkish state; he never spoke out against it even when suffering judicial harassment. He emerges out of a distinct tradition of Turkish/Ottoman understanding of Islam which did not perceive a contradiction between Turkish nationalism and Islam. During the 1980 coup—a time of broad national disorder and violent threats from extreme leftist organizations–the military perceived Gülen as useful to military rule in helping forge a new "Turk-Islam" synthesis—the state's new ideological order to bring together both nationalism and religion against a leftist enemy.

Gülen also avoids any competition or conflict with the state over religious affairs. He draws a major distinction between Diyanet—an official organ of the state dealing with religion—and Hizmet, an unofficial society-based organization. He remains deferential to Diyanet's authority. He avoids offering religious opinions in public which might contradict any of Diyanet's official interpretations of Islam. Diyanet's official focus, after all, is on religious doctrine and the infrastructure of organized religion. Hizmet does not compete in these realms; it focuses on questions of broader social welfare and the spiritual state of human society. The two organizations thus complement, rather than compete, with each other on issues of spirituality in Turkey. And with the decline of Kemalist political power and Diyanet's new policies of respect and support to religion there is little reason why Diyanet and Hizmet would not share a common understanding, even if separate in their approaches to religion and modernity. Troubles would arise only if, say, the AKP were to decide to use Diyanet in some way as a political weapon against Hizmet.

Hizmet and its Influence in the Bureaucracy

The poverty and polarization of political and religious discourse in Turkey during the long years of Kemalist power was clearly reflected in the Kemalist political lexicon: for decades there were really only two words used in public discourse to describe the political spectrum—either "progressive" (*ilerici*), or "reactionary" and backward (*gerici*). Even the word "conservative" (*muhafazakâr*) as a neutral political term was rarely used. This impoverished and quasi-Leninist political vocabulary was designed to polarize, denigrate and exclude any non-Kemalist, non-statist mode of thinking. The Nur and Gülen movements acted with extreme caution over many decades to protect their existence when they were persecuted, and their images crudely depicted by state-controlled media as *yobaz*—ignorant, fanatic, bigoted and reactionary.

After years of government persecution, Hizmet still remains wary of the possibility of renewed government harassment—something that diminished with the decline of Kemalist power. For that reason it was extremely sensitive to the revelation as late as 2013 of new evidence indicating that the National Intelligence Organization (MİT) under the AKP continued to open files on Hizmet and to share the information with political figures within the AKP.[2] Today, with Hizmet's major emergence onto the public scene, with the broad extent of its media, publishing, business and educational activities, and with the position of many of its members within the state bureaucracy, some Kemalists now believe that their worst fears have been fulfilled, that forces of "reaction" are now reversing the gains of the Kemalist revolution. Strong secular critics of Gülen claim that the movement has now "infiltrated" the police, the judiciary, and other branches of the government. The Turkish police of course have never been entirely free of politics over the years and was one of the leading instruments of some of the Ergenekon conspirators in the past.

Hizmet followers indignantly reject the loaded term "infiltration"; they claim qualified applicants have an equal right to join the military, judiciary or police forces as any other Turkish citizen of any religious or political beliefs; the key criterion is that they serve the state and not personal agendas. They argue that abuse of position by anyone should lead to being fired for cause. But for a long period followers of Gülen indeed did keep quiet about their affiliation because they knew it would lead to immediate discrimination, possible persecution and loss of a job. During periods of stringent military rule most individuals with non-Kemalist political or religious beliefs, including leftist or nationalist ideologies, kept quiet about their political affiliations. Yet the silence of Hizmet members about their affiliation in earlier periods led to charges of *takiye* or "Islamic dissimulation." Today, the movement breathes more easily in society where it has now become accepted, even admired by many. Members freely apply for government jobs. But memory of past persecutions exists and a resolve of "never again" influences their desire to see that prosecutorial and investigative organizations not fall under the control of Hizmet's secular enemies. But could it have been foreseen that the AKP itself would become hostile?

Whose "Deep State"?
The term "deep state" was originally applied to the entrenched Kemalist hold over the military and other significant political or security organizations for decades. The Ergenekon investigations and the setback to Kemalist ruling elites in turn caused Kemalist and nationalist circles to turn the term around and accuse the AKP and Erdoğan of running their own deep state through their newfound power to manipulate the bureaucracy in their own favor—and particularly through the Ergenekon prosecutions. But in reality of course, all political groups contest control of bureaucratic appointments and policies in order to favor their own, even though the image of bureaucratic neutrality suffers thereby.

Now critics argue that Hizmet members have gained enough power within the state to discredit their former enemies. There is no doubt that Hizmet has shown greater zeal in the Ergenekon investigations than even the AKP itself; in the end the AKP felt the need to bring greater political balance to the investigations while Hizmet stood on principle when it believed that laws were broken. But some critics of Hizmet now claim they themselves need to be careful not to be publicly critical of the movement if they wish to retain their positions. The most well-known such case involved prominent investigative journalist Ahmet Şık; his book entitled *The Imam's Army* was critical of Gülen and the Hizmet movement and a court ordered a draft version to be seized in 2012. Şık was jailed for a year on charges of leaking information on the Ergenekon case; he was subsequently released and his book was published, but many Turks believed the case involved spurious charges and amounted to judicial harassment of Şık by Hizmet members. Such cases cause some opponents of Gülen to fear that the judiciary could be used against them. As always in Turkey, judicial abuses on political grounds—such as charges leveled against Gülen himself in the past—have a long history and need to be carefully scrutinized. An independent judiciary, regardless of the views of the diverse individuals who make it up, is essential to future confidence in legal process. And that is one of the struggles underway today in Turkish politics.

Lack of public knowledge on Hizmet's internal workings provokes concerns among those who are suspicious of its ultimate intentions. Critics point to a lack of transparency in the movement as a source for anxiety given the size and influence of the organization. This criticism has some validity. The movement needs to promote greater transparency, both to help dispel suspicions and to serve as a model of an open and transparent financial enterprise for Islamic organizations in other countries. But Gülen is by nature a cautious individual, wary in the face of state harassment and oppression over the decades. The movement's hierarchy is not fully evident to the public, although the relationships and associations among its various outlets and organizations within the movement are publicly known.

Gülen himself has been eager for the state to move forward with a broader reform agenda that includes the complex task of rewriting the authoritarian 1982 constitution. This is a goal Hizmet shares with Turkish liberals and it receives strong EU support as well. The AKP earlier supported such goals itself but since Erdoğan's last electoral victory in 2011 he has drifted towards a more authoritarian and intolerant style as evidenced in the Gezi Park incidents. This reflects a pattern of strongman rule in Turkish politics over long decades; Erdoğan is politically skilful and has increasingly sought to control as many aspects of society as he can while stretching or even abusing the democratic process—and feeling answerable only at election time. He has angered considerable segments of the population with often intemperate remarks on a broad range of issues. He has sought to expand his control over the media and stifle his critics. Erdoğan's combative tendencies were whetted in the course of an important electoral season in 2014-2015—the series of elections that first elected new municipal leadership across the nation, followed by an election to elect a new president in summer of 2014, and finally a new parliament and a new prime minister in 2015. So Erdoğan, always the consummate political animal, is additionally operating in feisty election mode; he has always found offense, rather than compromise, to be his most powerful defense and weapon against political rivals and opponents.

This is one source of Erdoğan's friction with Gülen: Hizmet has come to represent a significant voice and force within society and the bureaucracy over which Erdoğan has limited control. Instinctively uncomfortable with political forces he cannot dominate, Erdogan seems now to view Hizmet itself as a possibly dangerous rival with an important body of voters and an ability to potentially influence many pious Muslims and others against him. This concern grew as Gülen became more willing to assume a watchdog role in publicly criticizing the prime minister for what he perceives as abuse or aggrandizement of power and in calling for stricter constitutional controls over the executive's bid for unlimited freedom of action.[3]

There are many key figures within the AKP, including President Abdullah Gül and Speaker of the Parliament Bülent Arınç, who are concerned with Erdoğan's intemperate statements and actions; they fear his increasingly harsh personal style of governance will slowly damage electoral support not just for the prime minister, but for the AKP itself. It has already led to a serious break with Hizmet—which the AKP as a party neither wants nor needs. On the other hand, Erdoğan's freestyle verbal assaults against his perceived enemies and the financial scandals into which he fell have already alienated many who voted for him earlier, especially among liberal urban populations. Yet the AKP's strong showing in the March 2014 municipal elections, widely cast as a kind of referendum on Erdoğan's record, suggested that the general public still had more faith in the AKP's long and effective record, including in managing the economy, than in any other of the parties. Erdoğan interpreted the municipal elections as full vindication of his personal political record and his rhetoric lost none of its earlier vindictive streak, suggesting a deepening polarization that revolves around the person of the prime minister himself. This confrontational style is certain to keep Turkish politics on the boil until a more conciliatory tone is struck between the prime minister and those who do not support him. Erdoğan seems unlikely to change his approach and abuse of political prerogative in this era of major political, social, economic, and even cultural transition in the country. If the prime minister cannot do it, current president Gül may represent that conciliatory figure, although he has proven very cautious in challenging Erdoğan directly. Gül's future actions as president are a key variable in the future of the AKP and the country's overall stability during an ongoing period of electoral struggle.

The Growth of the AKP-Gülen Rift

An early difference in emphasis between the AKP and Gülen came with the handling of the Ergenekon prosecutions. Both organizations had been direct victims of official and unofficial state persecution. As the Ergenekon investigations moved towards conclusion the AKP sought to reach a pragmatic working accommodation where possible with the remaining elements of military power and other Kemalist elements and institutions. Hizmet members however, and other critics of military oversight in politics acted with greater determination to identify and root out all Ergenekon plotters, dismantle the old structures of intervention and persecution and to bring them all to trial. Erdoğan initially had strongly supported the Ergenekon investigations, but later came to believe that some of the police investigators and prosecutors (many of them Gülen supporters) had perhaps grown overly zealous in detaining too many individuals, some of whom were eventually acquitted. The AKP also had future elections to win, Hizmet did not. As Erdoğan came under growing pressure, particularly from the major corruption charges leveled against his own party at the end of 2013 (see below), he spoke of possibly reopening elements of the Ergenekon and Sledgehammer trials in a bid to regain support from the military and nationalist elements in the country and to lay blame on Hizmet for any excesses. In March 2014 the Constitutional Court released former Army Chief İlker Başbuğ, earlier sentenced to life imprisonment for Ergenekon plotting, on the grounds of "violation of his rights." Nonetheless, Erdoğan's backpedalling on his early position of strong support for the Ergenekon process made him look opportunistic, particularly since the Turkish Supreme Court of Appeals in October 2013 had unanimously upheld the Ergenekon convictions and the European Court of Human Rights declined to hear an appeal of the conviction of several key defendants. It is hardly credible that the entire Supreme Court of Appeals would not contain judges of various political persuasions, including nationalists, Kemalists and Islamists as well as Hizmet members; yet the court's verdict was unanimous. The Ergenekon case thus has not yet struck a balance between needed prosecution of real criminal actions and what may have been excessive investigative zeal; the case remains a much politicized issue.

Disagreements also arose over AKP policy towards Israel, the Middle East and Syria. Public differences went back at least to May 2010 over the incident of the *Mavi Marmara* when a Turkish flotilla seeking to break the Israeli blockade of Gazan ports clashed with Israeli military forces. Gülen viewed the operation as needlessly provocative on Turkey's part. Nor has he favored the AKP's close ties with Muslim Brotherhood parties and other Islamists in the Arab world whom he instinctively distrusts. Conversely, many in the AKP (and the majority of the Turkish public) disagree with Gülen on his avoidance of criticism of Israel or US policies. Gülen has been similarly critical of Erdoğan's continuing assertive intervention into the Syrian civil conflict to overthrow the Asad regime; this critical view is widely shared by a majority of Turks who believe that Erdoğan's Syrian policy has been reckless, risky, failing, costly, and has increased stresses within Turkish society itself. (See Chapter 10 on AKP foreign policy and Chapter 21 on Syria.)

Rancorous relations also developed over Kurdish policies. Secret negotiations between the National Intelligence Organization (MİT) and the Kurdish separatist organization, PKK, brought dissent from the Gülenists who criticized AKP policy and intelligence officials as exceeding the prerogatives of executive independence in their secret negotiations with Kurdish leaders outside of judicial review. Both Erdoğan and Gülen strongly support resolution of the Kurdish question, but Gülen is more critical of both the powerful but illegal Kurdish national movement (PKK) and the legal Kurdish Party, the BDP (Peace and Democracy Party) with their potential separatist agenda. Hizmet itself has gained considerable following among the Kurdish population that rivals the BDP.

Gülen as a matter of principle wants to ensure that executive power is not abused, especially via the National Intelligence Organization where, unchecked, it can be turned against Hizmet or other political rivals of the AKP again. Erdoğan on the other hand fears maximum judiciary independence that can challenge his own executive freedom of action. These are again essentially debates over principles of political process, limitations of executive prerogatives, as well as degrees of judicial independence—long a political football in Turkey. Even here there has been some inconsistency on the part of both Gülen and the AKP: how independent should the judiciary be when it is alternatively in the hands of one or another strong political or ideological influence?

Gülen has joined liberals and opposition parties in publicly criticizing the AKP on the volatile issue of Erdoğan's efforts to stifle press criticism. The Journalists and Writers Foundation, the flagship Gülen institution, in April 2013 issued a strong statement about the importance of freedom of the press—a clear slap at Erdoğan. Quoting EU norms, it put its finger on many of the longtime ills of the Turkish press: the statement noted that "any practice that restricts freedom of the press, such as political oppression, commercial interests, or self-censorship is undemocratic and unacceptable." It also unequivocally condemned "oppression of the media" by politicians or media owners seeking to defend their own commercial interests or to blackball critical journalists; it called on journalists to defend the "honor and principles of their profession."[4] Most other political groups in Turkey equally criticize current AKP power over the press.

Erdoğan grew increasingly concerned over the influence of the Gülen movement as potential rival for influence among religiously-minded Turks, especially as Gülen will likely encourage his followers to withdraw electoral support from the AKP in future elections. As tensions between Hizmet and Erdoğan grew, Erdoğan sent a particularly provocative warning sign: a proposal to strike at one of the foundations of the Gülen institutional networks in Turkey, the private tutoring institutions or "cram schools" (dershane). These schools fill a widely-felt need to help prepare students to meet all-important university entrance standards. Despite rapid growth of universities under the AKP, there still are simply not enough of them in Turkey to meet demand. Hizmet operates perhaps a quarter of the thousands of such cram schools around the country, providing tutoring at low cost to students to help prepare them for examinations. They represent both a source of income and influence for Hizmet from which new supporters for Hizmet can come. The need for cram schools in the country will not go away, even though they vary in quality. Erdoğan clearly called for closing the schools as a way to intimidate and pressure Hizmet; he was likely concerned that the schools create important reservoirs of goodwill towards Hizmet across the country. A public outcry arose against closing the schools while Hizmet remained outraged and on guard. Some within the AKP itself felt this move by Erdoğan was both excessively provocative and unwise.

In November 2013 the leftist press leaked information suggesting that, encouraged by the military, the AKP had been willing to consider extending deep surveillance and control over Hizmet starting back in 2004. Since then

Hizmet has claimed that the National Intelligence Organization has opened files on Hizmet members and made the information available to AKP leadership. Erdoğan and some elements within the AKP worry that Hizmet represents a significant alternative "Islamic voice," a monopoly once largely enjoyed by the AKP.

Some observers have suggested that over time Hizmet might decide to extend its powerful organization into formal politics by forming a political party.[5] In principle of course there is nothing that would bar Hizmet from establishing a political party. But such a step seems quite unlikely since it would contravene all the stated values and appeal of the movement to date. Its functions differ considerably from those of a political party. Politics is all about the art of the possible. Politics requires putting aside many ideals to work in the realities of the daily political environment where enemies are easily made. The open break between the AKP and Gülen by late 2013 indeed provided a perfect opportunity for Hizmet to form its own political party as a religious alternative to the AKP if it had so wished, but it did not do so. To engage in formal political activity would compromise the respect that Hizmet has earned for its social and educational activities. As soon as Hizmet becomes a political party it becomes a larger partisan target for its political rivals. As a political party it would sharply divide the movement itself since its goal has been to remain above politics and to focus on maintaining its own set of ideals and achieving social ends. Sympathizers with the movement could readily differ on their political preferences. Hizmet's strength comes from the wealth, commitment and activism of its followers, not from dispensation of political power. This does not mean that Gülen will not speak out on key national issues in which he feels some corrective balance is required—he has already clearly done so in his growing and publicly expressed dissatisfaction with the emerging irregularities within the government and the dangerous political directions he believes Erdoğan has chosen. The AKP and Gülen have also differed in their approach to the large Alevi (heterodox Shi'ite) community in Turkey. In recent years Gülen began rapprochement with the Alevis and to support their further integration into Turkish life. He was publicly critical of what he felt was AKP insensitivity in 2013 in insisting on naming a large new Bosporus bridge after Sultan Selim—an Ottoman sultan and conqueror who in Alevi eyes was responsible for the killing of tens of thousands of members of their faith in the 16th century. Gülen spoke of common cultural bridges between Turkish Sunnis and Turkish Alevis. "Efforts are under way to build bridges between us, to have a mosque and a *cemevi* [Alevi house of worship] built next to each other in a park; thus old problems should not be resurrected that foment new enmities. Let's not tear down the many bridges that could bring us together simply over one bridge's name."[6] Gülen promoted a project to build a *cemevi* side by side with a mosque in dedicated park area in Ankara to symbolize the communities coming together. Gülen's statements are in direct contrast to some of the harsher earlier remarks by Erdoğan that have treated Alevis in a slighting or critical manner. Much of AKP's coolness to the Alevi community actually stems not so much from religious principles but rather from the traditionally strong Alevi support given to the chief Turkish opposition party, the Kemalist CHP because of its strong secular character. Erdoğan's policies towards Syria with its anti-Asad, anti-'Alawi posture also unsettles Turkish Alevis as well as Gülen who believe the AKP policy towards Syria to be seriously erroneous.

By August 2013 Gülen had taken the gloves off publicly. Hizmet's lead voice, The Journalists and Writers Foundation, accused the AKP of adopting hostile attitudes towards Hizmet; it claimed the AKP now treated Hizmet as a direct threat to the AKP, accused it of working directly against Erdoğan, and that Gülen himself is under US control.[7] The struggle took on proportions of open conflict when judicial prosecutors in mid-December 2013 arrested the sons of three AKP ministers, as well as dozens of senior government officials on grounds of corruption, money laundering and bribery—including the chief executive officer of a state-run bank for reportedly skirting US sanctions on trade with Iran. Erdoğan struck back with accusations that the charges were entirely fabricated and politically motivated; he accused the Gülen movement of operating a "state within a state," and seeking to destroy the reputation of the AKP. He proceeded to reassign all state prosecutors involved as well as 2000 police officers leading the investigations, reassigned the deputy head of the national police force, and recalled police chiefs from 15 provinces, including the Istanbul chief of police.[8]

Erdoğan additionally threatened to "'break the hands" of those who "harm, stir up or set traps in this country." He appointed ten new ministers, seen as solid Erdoğan loyalists, in what had become a no-holds-barred war with Hizmet. The charges against those in the government and those personally close to Erdoğan were particularly stinging since the party has sought to maintain a clean (*ak*) image. But several senior AKP officials tendered their resignations, one suggesting that Erdoğan had been fully aware of the irregularities he sought the minister to implement. Erdoğan was accused of letting "a small oligarchical group whose intentions were not clear" rule the country; his intent was clearly to stifle all investigation of his party and its officials while blaming it all on Gülen followers as constituting a "parallel structure" within the state. Erdoğan proceeded to pass new regulations designed to limit judicial prerogatives into investigations without informing the government in advance, banned journalistic contact with the police, and ordered prosecutors to stop in their tracks. In response, the High Council of Judges and Prosecutors (HCJP) called on the executive to "respect the judiciary and not to intervene in the ongoing investigations... It was Erdoğan who had campaigned relentlessly to change the HCJP back in 2010 and it is the same Erdoğan now who wants to change the rules."[9]

In the face of mounting public doubts about his account of events in the multiple corruption cases, Erdoğan redoubled his efforts at vilifying the entire investigative process as a plot against the AKP, and even against Turkey; he brought increasingly intemperate language to bear in accusing first and foremost the Gülen organization of organizing the assault against the government, but also "foreign hands" that included the US and Israel, whom he charged with in effect seeking to mount a coup against him. Osman Can, a member of AKP's central committee, in speaking about the investigators on 6 January 2014 said: "My opinion is that they are criminals—the police and the judges and prosecutors. ...If you can destroy this organization [Hizmet], you can save democracy."[10] Erdoğan went on to describe Gülen as having created an "empire of fear" and engaging in treachery in what amounts to a coup plot in the form of a corruption probe. He called on Turkey's ambassadors to foreign countries to describe "the true face" of the Gülen organization and the "dimensions of the danger" to the world. "The target here is not the government or the party but the country and its national interests," he said. "The target is Turkey and 76 million (people). It cannot be explained other than by treachery."[11] In March 2014 Erdoğan personally made phone calls to the leaders of many countries where Hizmet schools exist urging them to close them.

The corruption issue, one of the biggest in decades, escalated further when surreptitious tape recordings appeared on YouTube carrying conversations that purported to be between Erdoğan and members of his family on issues of bribery, secreting of funds, and other revealing and incriminating dealings. He claimed that at least some of them were fabricated or manipulated, but the revelations have been damaging to him and to the party. Embarrassing leaks at election time discrediting candidates is a staple of Turkish politics; in this case Erdoğan has chosen to blame Gülen in particular for fabricating charges. While it is quite likely that some members of Hizmet in the police or investigative offices have participated in revealing this material, Erdoğan has many enemies in many parties at this point; Kemalists, nationalists, liberals and others would gladly participate in efforts to weaken Erdoğan and the AKP by release of such incriminating material.

More deeply, however, the struggle rotates around the amount of independence the police and judiciary may have in conducting investigations, and the degree of control the government should exercise over it. In his anger, Erdoğan threatened to close down YouTube, Facebook, Twitter, and other forms of internet media that might carry anti-Erdoğan information; he passed legislation placing the judiciary under executive branch, gutting its independence—a huge step backward in Turkey's quest for transparency and democratic practice. These are, in some senses, the same issues that were so emotionally debated at an earlier time when the Kemalist political order entirely dominated these institutions, and that the 2010 referendum was designed to overcome. Ruling parties are always uncomfortable with independent police and judiciary procedures, but at this point Erdoğan seems to have escalated the issue into a deeper crisis that can only damage him and his party as it stonewalls any and all investigations into AKP wrongdoing and shifts the blame onto enemies.

If Gülen should urge Hizmet members to withdraw votes from the AKP in upcoming elections, the question remains as to what party Hizmet might find congenial, if any. Gülen has said he will not endorse any political party, although his opposition to the AKP at this point is well understood. Gülen focused his attack primarily upon Erdoğan himself and his immediate entourage rather than upon the AKP as a whole; the party itself, however, faced serious divisions over the prospect of divisive and increasingly erratic leadership by Erdoğan in the years to come. When at some point the AKP reaches the end of its long years of (mostly) innovative and successful policies and loses its control over the government in an election, Hizmet will still continue its grassroots work, independent of the fate of the Islamic political party. Members of Hizmet are in any case free to participate in politics in their personal capacities, but not to offer political opinions in the name of the organization. Nor does participation in Hizmet guarantee that their members will all vote the same way. Indeed, the greater the electoral diversity within the movement the better, since it permits the movement to further evolve, in either "liberal" or "conservative" directions.

Meanwhile, secularists hostile to all Islamic trends in Turkey have tended to seize upon disagreements between the two Islamic organizations in the hope that they express a weakening of one or both forces. The opposite is more likely true: the differences between them suggest a broadening and widening of the Islamic trend in the country, taking diverse directions and offering alternate courses of development and policy choices for the future of public Islam in Turkey. These could be potentially healthy trends as they create widening pluralistic perspectives on religion, governance and society in a free atmosphere. Some trends will succeed and some will not. In the ugly standoff between Erdoğan and Hizmet it is likely that Erdoğan has been the bigger loser. Many who are not supporters of Gülen condemn Erdoğan's behavior and find his self-serving attacks upon Gülen not credible; meanwhile Gülen stands on a strong position of principle on the issue of criticizing corruption in high places.

Leftist Islam?

Apart from Hizmet and the AKP's secular opponents, the AKP as a political party also faces elements of political opposition from still other Islamic groups—especially from the cadres of predecessor Islamist parties. Erbakan's Refah Party (overthrown and banned in 1998 for allegedly violating the secularist constitution) was ultimately succeeded by the present Islamist *Saadet* Party (Felicity). AKP's own leadership, as we have seen, similarly broke away from Refah to form the more pragmatic AKP. Saadet directs a number of criticisms against the AKP today: that the AKP has abandoned Islamist precepts in accepting the principles of economic globalization, has succumbed to the lure of the EU (only to be rebuffed by the West), works to serve American interests in the region, ignores growing domestic corruption even within the party itself, is insufficiently Islamic, and has lost sight of the plight of the poor. Saadet does not have a large constituency, but disillusioned Islamists could switch votes to Saadet.

A further sign of growing populist ideas among Islamist thinkers is evident in the presence of a growing "Islamic Left" in Turkey. One of the more explicitly anti-capitalist trends among the Islamists was represented by Turkey's HAS Party (*Halkın Sesi*—The People's Voice) led by Numan Kurtulmuş. Kurtulmuş comes from a distinguished scholarly family associated with the Islamic cause over several generations. He himself is an economist who earlier was a member of predecessor Islamist parties to the AKP, the Virtue Party (*Fazilet*) and Felicity (*Saadet*). In 2010 he founded HAS in order to advocate greater attention to issues of social justice, greater Islamic openness to broader social elements within Turkey including the left, calls for a more just distribution of wealth, and a demand for greater Turkish sovereignty and independence from the West. He believes HAS represents "a coalition of people from different backgrounds, including leftists, nationalists and conservatives, united around the idea of bringing a new mentality to Turkish politics," based on greater transparency in internal party politics. The party rejects the label "Islamic Left" because "Islam should not be labeled," but the goal is to serve the people, and not serve the state as he believes most Turkish political parties have done.[12]

The appeal of such a political position ironically emerges from the very success of the AKP in one sense: with the doubling of GDP in a decade, large corporations have thrived and a strong new and successful capitalist class has emerged. Inevitably there have been economic winners and losers. The presence of this new call for social justice within the ranks of the religious emerged dramatically in the demonstrations in Istanbul on May Day in 2012 when marchers from the traditional quarters of Istanbul joined the red flag of secular leftists as they unfurled their own black banners of Islam calling for "God—Bread—Freedom." A political scientist at Koç University, Murat Somer, commented: "The AKP was born of the marriage between moderate Islam and global capitalism… The younger generation of some Islamists has a different take on social justice. They focus more on economics and a class-based understanding."[13] Perhaps sensing the power—and even danger—of HAS arguments, Erdoğan persuaded Kurtulmuş in 2012 to dissolve HAS and join the AKP with Kurtulmuş as a vice-president of the AKP. While presently co-opted, Kurtulmuş's party and ideas will certainly survive and possibly break away at some point in the future to become an independent party again, possibly taking some members from the AKP with him, especially as corruption charges around Erdoğan grow. When Erdoğan statutorily must step down as prime minister in 2015, Kurtulmuş is one possible candidate to succeed him.

In HAS, leftist concerns for social justice combined with Islamic concepts in a fusion that can be traced back to the ideas of modern Iranian sociologist and revolutionary Ali Shariati, whose writings in the 1970s sought to forge a synthesis between Islamism and revolutionary socialist nationalism. Shariati was part of a movement "Socialist Adorers of God." (Recall that the generals behind the 1980 coup in Turkey came up with a state-sponsored synthesis of Turkish nationalism and Islam.) Shariati argued that capitalism has damaged the developing world in two main respects. It served as the engine for western imperialism that took over the developing world. And then, through its propagation of materialism, consumerism, and marketism, it also began to undercut the independence and *cultural identity* of all peoples, rendering them weak and vulnerable to powerful external economic forces. Though Shi'ite by background, Shariati interpreted Islam—Sunni or Shi'ite—more broadly as a force that *by nature* struggles against human oppression. His ideas find strong parallel in Christian liberation theology prominent among both Catholics and Protestants on the Left in Latin America, where religious values provide more powerful justification for defense of social justice than does materialistic Marxism.

A second prominent figure on the Islamic Left in Turkey is İhsan Eliaçık, a professor of Islam who speaks out regularly in writings and on television on behalf of socialist views—though he does not identify them explicitly.[14] Eliaçık fights for equality of women, for greater distribution of wealth, and shows hostility to the dominance of capitalism. He thinks more in terms of an *economic struggle* between the rich and the poor rather than a struggle between secularists and the pious. He is deeply suspicious of capitalism as a key instrument of western control of the non-western world.[15]

The Gülen movement also fits into this new social framework. Gülen is definitely concerned with social welfare as an integral part of the message of Islam, although he is far from anti-capitalist. Indeed, the financial strength of his movement rests entirely on the new Anatolian capitalists of pious businessmen. But Hizmet is well aware of the profound importance of social justice and overcoming the suffering of the less fortunate. In this sense it shares something in common with the Islamic left. All of this bespeaks an Islam in Turkey that is focused less upon religious prohibitions and more upon the welfare of the umma in both material and spiritual needs.

In sum, the Islamic intellectual scene in Turkey today is vibrant, even strident, at the official, party, and grassroots levels. Public understanding of Islam is evolving in new directions that suggest greater awareness and sensitivity to the actual conditions of the Muslims living in the world. They espouse programs for action that move beyond mere piety, or simply "blaming the West," to seek to change conditions on the ground—involving both mental shifts and new social mobilization and action. These trends are of great importance to the rest of the Muslim world as well but they are hindered by authoritarian rule and chaotic quest for change—as we will see in coming chapters. Turkey is one of the few countries with lively and open debate about how to understand the place of Islam in political, economic and social life. Indeed, divisions, even hostilities among Islamic parties and movements suggest great diversity among them and demonstrates that their politics can be just as harsh as politics among other political parties. It also demonstrates that liberal fears of some kind of Islamic monolith operating in society are without foundation. As long as these political competitions and rivalries among political parties—Islamic and non-Islamic—are debated and resolved at the ballot box or in the courts, the political order is functioning as it should; issues of public concern are out on the table for voters to decide. Indeed, political turmoil that is resolved within the framework of democratic institutions is a key sign of an essentially healthy political order.

CHAPTER FOURTEEN

THE CHALLENGE OF THE "ARAB SPRING"

The outbreak of popular uprisings, or revolutions, in 2011 marked the start of a longer process known in the West as the "Arab Spring" or, more appropriately, "Arab Awakening." These revolutions unleashed a chain of events that—varying from country to country—heightened ideological confrontation, overthrew several entrenched regimes, and introduced certain elements of greater democratic process; but these processes also opened the door to civil strife and armed civil conflict, attracted external intervention and sparked counter-revolution. Long-existing fissures were reopened at virtually every level: political, social, ethnic, sectarian, ideological, strategic, regional and global. The distinct agendas of external players at work further skewed the reform process. As the Arab Spring democratization process continues to unfold the stakes remain high, and has created a new systemic crisis in the region. New political forces have also appeared on the streets: youth, women, social media, and challenges to *all* authority. Sharper divisions have emerged among Islamists themselves. The outcome is in flux but events have already badly shaken the old order. What has been politically learned cannot be unlearned; there is no real going back despite the reassertion of familiar autocratic techniques in Egypt and efforts by Saudi Arabia to reverse many of the changes brought about by the process.

Above all, even though religion is not really the true source of conflict, these events show how quickly religion becomes a major vehicle and rallying cry for expression of differences. Religion and sectarianism, much ballyhooed by some as the "eternal" source of conflict in the region, actually only stand as surrogates for a deeper struggle for power and influence, both domestically and internationally.

That there were deep problems and discontents across the region was well known, but no one anticipated the time or place of the actual spark of conflagration. From the opening tremors against the regime in Tunisia the Arab Spring quickly posed an old dilemma to western states: at what point should they abandon support to their longtime authoritarian allies as their leadership begins to lose its grip, commit serious errors, and start to totter? When should western patrons cut their losses, abandon clients and throw in their lot with new opposition forces? Change sides too soon, who knows, the dictator might succeed in suppressing the rebellion, leaving you with disastrous bilateral relations in its wake (as in Syria). Move too late and the *new* regime will resent the belated support that you lent to its popular struggle. Should one operate from "principle"—and if so, what principle? Every case is different.

The following set of chapters highlight the problems of revolutionary change. We'll particularly look at the challenges the Arab Spring posed to the main regional players—Turkey, Saudi Arabia and Iran—as well as to the US. Each power has struggled to meet these challenges in its own way and none with great success. But the patterns of regional relations are shifting.

• Turkey was torn between acting on the basis of a "principle" that soon became contradictory: on the one hand maintenance of overall good relations with all neighbors where possible, and, on the other, support for democratic change. And all preferably without western intervention.

• Iran has been primarily driven by sympathy for revolutionary change against pro-western autocrats, to weaken the strategic power of the US in the Middle East, and a desire to break out of its own encirclement and isolation imposed by the US. Iran maintains close relations with other Shi'ite populations in the region (especially in Iraq) where these populations can be useful, but *sectarianism cannot be considered Iran's chief preoccupation*—except when driven into it by extremist Sunni voices.

• Saudi Arabia has established its own "principled" approach: shoring up and preserving monarchy in the region as top priority, coupled with a desire to crush the forces of any revolutionary ideology in the region—Sunni or Shi'ite.

• The US has met most of these challenges with a "pragmatic" or, more accurately, an opportunistic approach, lacking any general principle except an ill-thought-out "pursuit of the national interest," as perceived at the moment. Such a policy of opportunism might be defensible in principle had it been successful; instead it was implemented in a narrow, inconsistent, ill-informed, ill-conceived, unrealistic, and ultimately unproductive fashion that ended up only damaging the US national interest, standing and clout in virtually every single country.

The Course of Revolution

Let's take a quick look at the first four revolutions of the Arab Spring—Tunisia, Egypt, Libya and Yemen—and see how external parties treated events.

Tunisia

Tunisia was the unlikely venue for the opening shot of the "Arab Spring." Indeed, of all Arab states Tunisia had seemed to be one of the least likely to experience rapid regime collapse. Yet it was the first to fall into rioting and disorders that in January 2011 led to the astonishingly rapid abandonment of power with minimum struggle by longtime dictator Zine el Abidine Ben Ali. The post-Ben Ali scene established a familiar scenario that would be played out in several other states. The forces that publicly rallied to demand Ben Ali's departure were initially led by secular groups with demands for greater freedom in terms of governance and economic well-being. But this group actually represented a small part of the opposition's political spectrum; it was media-savvy, and its political vocabulary rang familiar to the West, but ultimately came to be dominated by Islamists of various stripes—the longtime opposition force in waiting. Thus there was little doubt that within a short period the large, powerful and organized *Ennahda* (*al-Nahda*, Renaissance) party, a branch of the Muslim Brotherhood party, would come to dominate the post-Ben Ali political scene. Its leader Shaykh Rashid al-Ghannushi had been living in exile in London for over 20 years and enjoyed strong credentials as a prominent moderate Islamist intellectual and active, non-violent regime opponent.

Our three main Middle East players also established an early pattern. Turkey rejoiced at the collapse of a harsh dictator and welcomed this solid first step towards democratic rule in an Arab country. Turkey had few economic interests at stake in Tunisia but the AKP felt ideological sympathies for Ennahda. Under Ennahda's new leadership Tunisia sought to break away from near-total domination of its economy by France and to develop new markets in the region. Its leader Ghannushi was a great admirer of the AKP party; he stated that he viewed it as a kind of model for the development of his own party and the country. Although Turkish ties to Tunisia were modest, Tunisia had been part of the Ottoman Empire for some three centuries, a fact readily visible in the many buildings and other cultural legacies of Ottoman heritage still to be seen there.

France, to the contrary, as the most active western player in the situation, supported Ben Ali throughout all the rioting virtually to the bitter end of his rule. Washington remained hesitant and undecided. While it had been nominally critical of Tunisia's violation of human rights, it viewed Ben Ali as a useful pro-western force and ally in the struggle against terrorism. Washington played no meaningful role in the transition. Saudi Arabia however was deeply distressed at the fall of a friendly autocrat who had upheld the regional status quo. Worse from Riyadh's perspective, the successor regime to Ben Ali was linked to the Muslim Brotherhood and thus viewed with deep suspicion. Riyadh's preferences were made crystal clear when it welcomed Ben Ali to take up exile in Saudi Arabia. (See more detailed discussion of Saudi Arabia and the Muslim Brotherhood in the next chapter.) Most of the rest of the Arab world was astonished at this unexpected course of events in Tunisia and was uncertain how to interpret it. Iran, interestingly, did not view the event in sectarian terms. To the contrary, it welcomed events—both the fall of a pro-western dictator, and also the emergence of popular forces under a new government linked to the Muslim Brotherhood.

Egypt

Only a few weeks after the Arabic al-Jazeera satellite channel began projecting images of Tunisian youth demonstrating in the streets the same images began to crop up in Cairo, in much larger demonstrations. But the Mubarak regime put up harsher resistance against the demonstrators than Ben Ali had.

Turkey's Erdoğan and Davutoğlu were politically acute in sensing the shifting political dynamic in Egypt early on and welcoming the prospect of democratic change. Erdoğan, in dramatic terms laden with Islamic resonance, publicly called upon Mubarak to step down; his statement struck a chord across the region. In Egypt, as in Tunisia, Ankara had few entrenched interests and had never been close to the Mubarak regime; indeed, Mubarak had tended to look upon Turkey as an interloper in regional affairs, disliked its ties with the Muslim Brotherhood, and its possible challenge to Egypt's (long-forsaken) leadership role. With the withdrawal of army support to Mubarak's regime and Mubarak's ultimate collapse after more weeks of rioting Erdoğan's early stance was vindicated. He had sympathized with the demonstrators and reformists from the outset, they had prevailed, the Muslim Brotherhood was in a strong position and Turkey had good ties with it.

Washington, on the other hand, was dismayed by the rising demonstrations against Mubarak whom it viewed as a loyal US client responsive to US interests. Washington dithered, tried to gently persuade Mubarak to make a few concessions to reduce domestic tensions, but ultimately stood by him very nearly to the end. Washington was also concerned that the Muslim Brotherhood might well emerge as the most powerful political force in the country apart from the army.

Saudi Arabia was even more aghast at the collapse of Mubarak, a key ally, so soon after the Tunisian events; it publicly expressed its anger that Washington had so readily acquiesced to his fall. Riyadh again stood for maintaining the status quo and was even more deeply disturbed that the Muslim Brotherhood again was the primary beneficiary of the revolution. Iran, on the other hand, warmly welcomed the fall of another key US ally in a popular revolution, and expressed its sympathies and desire for good relations with the strengthening Muslim Brotherhood.

The Egyptian public compared the boldness of the Turkish position with the procrastination of Washington. When Erdoğan visited Egypt in September 2011 months after Mubarak's fall he was greeted as a hero; he was proclaimed by many as the most popular world leader in Egypt. With these policies Erdoğan and Davutoğlu had for a second time taken the major step of vocally supporting popular uprisings against dictatorship in the Middle East. But it also represented a *shift away* from the non-intervention policies of earlier years when Ankara made clear its willingness to work pragmatically with all existing governments. Its preference for democratic change quickly took precedence over the reality of defending the status quo. In Egypt too, Turkey's position was win-win; it had little to lose and much to gain in what it believed were both principled and realistic policies.

But what is "realism?" Was Washington "realistic" in protecting its interests by seeking to support Mubarak in power throughout the crisis? Certainly in terms of its rhetorical commitment to democracy, Washington was not "principled" in supporting this authoritarian client to the virtual end. Wouldn't it have been more "realistic" to see that the regime had run its course? Does realism simply consist of guessing accurately which way the wind will blow? And how would we describe Erdoğan's call to Mubarak to step down in the name of the people's aspirations—as a "realistic" statement, based on a sense of "the forces of history?" Or did it stem from "idealism" in supporting the principle of democratic change against autocracy? These terms, so regularly invoked, fail to capture the full political complexity of choices and thus lack analytical usefulness.

Libya

The third state to burst into flames was Libya where the situation grew more complicated for everyone. Inspired by events in Cairo, an armed uprising broke out against leader Mu'ammar al-Qadhafi in the eastern Libyan region of Benghazi in mid-February 2011. For the first time the disorders of the Arab Spring posed slightly tougher choices to Ankara—between protecting its large commercial ties with Libya as established under the Qadhafi regime, or supporting democratic change. Turkey had 25,000 Turkish workers in Libya and US$23 billion in Turkish investments and projects there. It also hoped to keep open the chances of maintaining good commercial ties with a successor government. Erdoğan initially condemned any discussions of western military operations against Libya as "absurd," and Davutoğlu sought to arrange domestic talks among parties within Libya. Turkey's opposition to western military intervention in the region was particularly based on the chaos and negative repercussions of past US invasions in Iraq and Afghanistan and the resulting massive human and material damage inflicted upon them.

But by late March 2011 the UN Security Council, the EU, and even the Arab League had all come out against the Qadhafi regime and in favor of western military intervention. At that point Ankara clearly grasped that events had moved beyond its control and that its preferred approach to Libya had been overtaken by events. Pushing back against the French desire to take the lead in military operations, Ankara saw NATO as providing better political cover for the operation; as a NATO member Turkey at least possessed a veto over its operations and eventually participated in several NATO operations against Libya. NATO, too, valued Turkey's participation as providing valuable "Muslim cover" for what was basically a western operation. Qatar, too, quickly joined in the operation with more robust military support, providing further Muslim backing.

Western operations rapidly and predictably led to classic "mission creep," nominally starting with defense of civilians and then evolving into taking sides and active bombing of Qadhafi's military forces and military infrastructure across the country, killing numerous civilians and unleashing civil conflict. Libya became the scene of full-scale NATO war for regime change—well beyond anything the Security Council had authorized or what Turkey, or Russia, had wanted.

For Washington, what distinguished the Libyan case from Tunisia and Egypt was great distaste for Qadhafi; he had been a longtime foe, only slightly rehabilitated in more recent years, and long disliked in the West for his quixotic and bizarre dictatorial rule, his meddling in African affairs, his broad stance against "imperialism," his flirtation with developing nuclear technology (later abandoned), and especially his own earlier support of terrorism and the egregious bombing of Pan Am flight 103 over Lockerbie, Scotland, in 1988. The US now sensed an opportunity to bring him down.

Any claim by Washington, however, to support principles of democratization and reform had been discredited by its earlier silence, for example, in Tunisian and Egyptian events, and above all silence in the face of an ongoing ugly repression of Shi'ite calls for democracy in Bahrain—where the US Fifth Fleet is based. And of course, Washington had long ago refused to recognize the victory of Hamas in legitimate and honest democratic elections in Palestine in 2006 and even sought to overthrow the elected Hamas leadership by force. Washington maintains quiet on autocracy and repression in Jordan and Saudi Arabia as well.

Turkey remained reactive to events, torn over principle as well as tactics. Only in early July 2011 did Ankara became convinced that further negotiations were useless, openly called for Qadhafi to step down, cut all remaining diplomatic relations with the Qadhafi regime, recognized the new interim government and offered economic aid to the new government. Making the best of the situation, Davutoğlu flew to Benghazi, plunged into a street crowd and hailed them in Arabic, praising their accomplishments, invoking the shared Ottoman past and praising the name of an earlier Libyan hero who had struggled against Italian imperial rule of Libya. Turkey's line clearly played on themes of Muslim solidarity and Libyan historical pride.

Turkey's slow response on Libyan policy was criticized in the West as opportunistic and unhelpful. Here we gain further insight into Ankara's preferred approach to civil conflict: first, proposals for face-to-face dialog, and a call for negotiations to be followed by multilateral diplomatic action. Ankara hoped that negotiations could lead Qadhafi to either bow to major internal reforms, or else step down peacefully, as did Ben Ali and Mubarak. Qadhafi, with his characteristically poor political judgment, believed he could crush the rebellion; he did, however, correctly perceive the crisis as an existential issue for him. A negotiated solution seemed unlikely; by mid-October Qadhafi had been savagely beaten to death by a street mob.

Second, Ankara was initially strongly opposed to the use of western military force against Qadhafi, rightly fearing a long and bloody affair with unpredictable consequences—as in Iraq and Afghanistan. Indeed, three years later the repercussions of this western-assisted overthrow still spill out across the region, leaving Libya badly divided, facing possible political breakaway of eastern Libya, chaotic, without central leadership, dominated by militias, tribal forces and radical Islamist activism, and radiating instability to neighboring North Africa and the Sahara. Despite its initial reluctance to support the rebels Turkey did not lose out in the new Libya: the new government welcomes continued Turkish investment and close economic ties. Europe meanwhile seemed determined to demonstrate that it still possessed the ability to project power into its neighborhood.

Turkey was not alone in its discomfort in the Libyan dilemma: Iran, Russia, China, Brazil, South Africa and the African Union all opposed western military intervention. Iran was torn: it strongly disliked Qadhafi but also opposed western military interventionism on principle, even as its allies in Syria, Lebanon and Iraq all opposed Qadhafi. European powers were concerned that Libya, as a significant oil producer for Europe lying just across the Mediterranean, posed potential problems of instability and refugee flight as well. But now Syria was to throw nearly everyone's policies and principles into a cocked hat.

Syria

The Syrian crisis came to pose the greatest challenge of all to external players in the Arab Spring, confronting them with a nearly insoluble situation. The Syrian crisis turned Turkey's foreign policy principles topsy-turvy and ultimately plunged Ankara's foreign policies into disaster. Yet AKP's earlier policies towards Syria had been one of its major success stories—eight years of hugely improved relations and the development of close working ties with Damascus. With the first public demonstrations against President Bashar al-Asad, Erdoğan and Davutoğlu believed they could persuade him to initiate rapid early reforms that would satisfy the initial demands of demonstrators and show Turkey's positive influence over the regime. But despite the countless personal interventions by both Erdoğan and Davutoğlu to push Asad into concessions, and Asad's promises to do so, he turned to harsher repression and inflexibility. As the death toll in Syria began to rise initially into the tens of thousands, pressure from the West rose on Ankara to demonstrate the fruits of its good relations and alleged clout with Asad to stop the repressions. Unable to change the situation in Syria despite major efforts, and embarrassed at their impotence, Erdoğan grew increasingly disillusioned and finally broke with Asad in bitter denunciation with a full call for regime change even by force. Turkey threw its weight behind the external armed Syrian opposition group that soon based itself in Istanbul while Ankara came perilously close to engaging in military intervention itself, at least to create a safe haven for Syrian refugees within Syrian territory. Ankara was supported in this goal by Saudi Arabia and Qatar who were vociferous in calling for a military end to the Asad regime. The West, too, fully supported these efforts. Erdoğan, violating his own opposition to armed western intervention, finally called upon Washington for strong military support, at least via provision of heavy weapons to the opposition.

By May 2012, however, the momentum for imposing change on Syria had begun to recede. Asad was seen in the West, in Israel, and in Turkey itself, as strongly entrenched. More importantly, the implications of post-Asad chaos were potentially devastating for the surrounding states of the region—Turkey,

Iraq, Iran, Jordan, Israel, Lebanon—diminishing any enthusiasm on their part for stronger action. The external Syrian opposition groups based in Istanbul were disorganized, ideologically fractured, riddled with personal rivalries, and unable to cooperate. The Russians and the Chinese both stood in strong opposition to western armed intervention in Syria. Most importantly, there were ominous signs of rising extremist Islamist jihadi organizations like al-Qaeda joining the armed struggle against Asad, all outside the control of even the more moderate Syrian Muslim Brotherhood. Radical Islamists gained strength at the expense of the moderate Islamists or secularists and, worse, showed themselves to be the more effective and ruthless fighters in the anti-Asad struggle. Ominously, the sectarian implications—Sunni versus 'Alawi/Shi'ite—began to spill over into Iraq and Lebanon, and to affect Turkey itself.

Domestic opposition inside Turkey against intervention grew stronger as the Syrian conflict destabilized the long border areas with Turkey, attracted Islamist jihadis into the struggle, carried violence over the border onto Turkish soil, and stirred up domestic sectarian tensions within Turkey. Yet Davutoğlu remained firm and unapologetic and ambitiously spoke out in defense of his policies in a Grand National Assembly address on 26 April 2012: "A new Middle East is about to be born. We will be the patron, pioneer and the servant of this new Middle East." Yet Turkey backed away from itself launching actual military operations against Syria; a policy of wait-and-see dominated even as Erdoğan and Davutoğlu maintained their rhetoric of a "principled policy" of support for democratic change in the Middle East. As the Obama administration grew ever more leery of any likely desirable outcome of Asad's overthrow, Ankara felt more isolated in its call for strong action. In an admittedly extremely difficult situation it was clear that Ankara had moved too far, too fast, too confidently and was caught out in what became a lose-lose situation for almost every single player in the region, while opening the door to deep sectarian conflict region-wide (see Chapter 21). The Syrian crisis sharply divided the entire Arab world along political, strategic and sectarian lines, with grave implications for all and seriously damaged Turkey's hard-won good relations with Iraq and Iran.

With Asad's apparent use of chemical weapons against Syrian civilians in August 2013, Washington declared that Asad had crossed a "red line" and prepared for a risky punitive missile strike against the regime. Then, unexpectedly, Russia proposed that Damascus give up all its chemical weapons under international supervision; Damascus agreed. Washington quickly accepted the option to cooperate with Moscow to see if such a deal could in fact be brokered. Asad was thus given a new lease on life while the moderate armed opposition against him foundered. Turkey and Saudi Arabia had still been arguing for military intervention against Asad but were both left high and dry by Washington's decision to try the diplomatic route. The Syrian case represented the most outspoken advocacy by Ankara for both armed intervention and western military involvement in Asad's overthrow, quite in opposition to its earlier principles. Meanwhile Erdoğan faced growing domestic opposition against further Turkish involvement in Syria and apparently was forced to the conclusion that its gambit on Syria had failed and that he should cut his losses.

Yemen

Although the least well-known "revolution" of the Arab Spring in the West, its direction in Yemen in some ways is the more encouraging of the uprisings. Yemen is dirt-poor with a larger population than the much larger neighboring state of Saudi Arabia. Yemenis are an alert, dynamic and skilled people, unspoiled by oil, with a significant labor diaspora around the Middle East. While its last ruler 'Ali 'Abdullah Salih had ruled as president for 33 years, he was not able to exercise quite the despotic powers the other fallen dictators possessed. Yemen has always been a messy, individualistic, chaotic country whose many divisions—tribal, regional, religious, and ideological—create a rough balance of forces in which no element has been able to wield truly dominant power. It has enjoyed periods of semi-democratic rule. Even President Salih had to rule through a wily form of balancing these multiple factions against each other to hold on to power. But a remarkably politicized public had grown weary of Salih's rule, and of the entrenched corruption and nepotism around him.

The Yemeni version of the Arab Spring, too, began with anti-regime demonstrations that continued for many months, some of whose elements were neutralized, bought off, or balanced off. Saudi Arabia in particular has long enjoyed considerable power over politics in Yemen through the huge financial payments made to politicians, tribal and regional elements to discourage them from rocking the boat. Few Yemeni leaders can long survive without some sort of accommodation with Riyadh.

In Yemen, too, the Muslim Brotherhood represented the single-largest opposition force, acting through its political party *al-Islah* (Reform). More strikingly, the most prominent single public figure in the opposition, a leader of the moderate wing of Islah, is a woman, Tawakkul Karman; she is also a politician, journalist, women's rights activist, and was (jointly) granted the

2011 Nobel Peace Prize. Unlike in Saudi Arabia, women are active in Yemeni politics and have a significant place in the moderate wing of the Brotherhood. Indeed, the Brotherhood holds a major place in the opposition movement but does not dominate it due to the presence of a large socialist movement based in southern Yemen, and other secular and tribal forces.

After demonstrations and struggles and some bloodshed for over a year, President Salih was finally removed from power after long negotiations involving arbitration efforts by the Gulf Cooperation Council members and efforts by the US. Salih had enjoyed powerful support from Washington ever since 9/11 when the US sought and received a nearly free strategic hand in Yemen in its Global War on Terror. Counter-terrorism has overwhelmingly dominated the US interest in Yemen since that time, a narrowness of focus that has damaged its image among much of the Yemeni population.

The inability of the Yemeni central state to extend its powers all across the land remains a constant issue in domestic politics and ultimately facilitated the ability of al-Qaeda to gain a foothold in the country, especially in the south from where the Bin Laden family originated a century ago. Known as "Al-Qaeda in the Arabian Peninsula" (AQAP), the organization has been active in its recruiting and was the source of several terrorist attacks against US interests, including at least two attempts on US soil. The Yemeni government has had only limited success in weakening AQAP which in part reflects southern Yemeni political resistance against the government in San'a that is dominated by the culturally distinctive northern part of the country. A more volatile situation is created by frequent US use in recent years of drone attacks against AQAP activists in Yemen, including Washington's notorious execution by drone of two American citizens of Yemeni origin, one of whom was a major propagandist in AQAP. Regular drone attacks against Yemenis, and the deaths of a high proportion of innocent civilians in the process, has stimulated much outrage in Yemen, sparked tribal oaths for revenge, and strengthened the popularity and support for AQAP.

After the fall of President Salih and his replacement by a member of his own party, Yemen at present is engaged in a serious process of political dialog among dozens of leaders from all elements of Yemeni society, including tribal, Brotherhood, Salafi, socialist, Shi'ite and Sunni, north and south, women and professional figures. This group is engaged in trying to write a constitution for the country that would accommodate a broad range of views and interests. It remains to be seen whether a compromise constitution can be forged, and if so, whether it can be implemented among the diverse political factions in the country. Yemenis with their traditionally looser political arrangements, however, are better prepared for such compromise solutions than many other countries that are marked by deeper and harsher autocratic traditions or ideological grip.

Despite its poverty and relative paucity of resources, Yemen has long been the focus of proxy struggles and wars of regional powers. In the 1960s it was the scene of a fierce proxy war between Egypt and Saudi Arabia. A Yemeni civil war in 1994 between north and south included heavy Saudi backing of the more conservative north. During the Arab Spring Yemen was the scene of a Saudi-Iranian-Turkish rivalry for influence. Neighboring Saudi Arabia is the most important external player, whose profuse infusions of cash to various players in the Yemeni establishment have kept Saudi control high. Riyadh may be uncomfortable with the Brotherhood overall, but the Yemeni Brotherhood is one of many Yemeni political groups that receives Saudi subventions to keep it favorably disposed towards Riyadh. The Brotherhood is also backed by one of Yemen's two huge tribal confederations; it is therefore likely to remain a major but not necessarily dominant political force among a broad range of competing factional interests that must be accommodated.

Iran has a longtime interest in Yemen, partly because of its dominant Zaydi ("Fiver") Shi'ite population, a sect which is actually closer to Sunni Islam in belief, and is distinct from Iranian "Twelver" Shi'ism. Iran more recently lent support to the Huthis, a Shi'ite insurgent group in northern Yemen that has long resisted dominance of the capital San'a. Iran openly supported the struggle against President Salih whom it perceives to be an instrument of both Saudi and US power. (Salih is nonetheless a Zaydi Shi'ite, as was much of his government.) Tehran has also supported the deep- and historically-rooted left-wing separatist movement in south Yemen as an effort to undermine a pro-US and pro-Saudi government in San'a. Iran at the same time is of course strongly hostile to al-Qaeda's influence in Yemen.

Turkey today is playing a greater role in Yemen than at any time since the fall of the Ottoman Empire, of which Yemen was a significant component. Turkish interests and activities there create frictions with Saudi Arabia which seeks to maintain Yemen as a private Saudi fiefdom. Ankara openly supports the Brotherhood party al-Islah and spoke out in favor of the uprisings against Salih's 33-year rule in order to promote a more democratic order. Tawakkul Karman, the feminist Brotherhood figure, is herself of distant Turkish origin and Turkey recently granted her honorary citizenship. While the successes of Turkey under the AKP are widely admired in Yemen, Turkish ties with the Brotherhood in both Yemen and Egypt have created some opposition to Turkey among opponents of the Brotherhood in Yemeni politics. Turkish-produced small arms have also entered the country—already rife with small arms—in considerable quantities, but Ankara declares they reflect commercial deals outside of its government control and do not represent policy.

Turkey has built a major technical training school in San'a and provided significant medical and food assistance to the country, as well as aid in the transportation sector. The Hizmet movement has also opened schools in the country. Ankara's policies towards Yemen conform to Turkish stated principles of diplomacy in the region: to support democratization (against Saudi wishes), support economic advancement (rather than economic control as conducted by Riyadh), support for moderate Islamism in the form of the Brotherhood as opposed to radical or Wahhabi Islamism, and to expand Turkish influence deeper into the Arab world.

Assessment of Davutoğlu's Policies

The well-known Turkish commentator Cengiz Çandar was one of the first to express Davutoğlu's dilemma in 2011 in an article entitled "Moving from 'Zero Problems' to Problems with Everybody"—more witty perhaps than fully accurate.[1]

In one sense Çandar was right however: the first stage of Turkey's zero problems policy had been the easier one. At a time of weak leadership among most of the Arab states, Ankara's policies signaled a desire to wipe away the former preconditions and mindsets that once stood in the way of good relations with neighbors. Turkey's very identity once so closely tied to the West had demonstrably evolved into a new independence of outlook and action; these changes helped convince regional states that Turkey was no longer acting as a surrogate of western power. With Ankara's new and open approach and its embrace of its Muslim and Ottoman past, neighbors responded positively, willing to translate the new goodwill into concrete gains. The Arabs and Iran welcomed Davutoğlu's pragmatic willingness to cross the ideological and religious lines that had dominated Middle East politics for so long. A willingness to work with existing regimes set Turkey apart from the heavily charged ideological approach of the West. New trade initiatives presented further win-win opportunities to nearly all states in this first stage.

But it's impossible to remain on everybody's side all the time. Conflict often demands choosing sides when diplomacy seems to fail. Turkey, like the rest of the world, faces the same complex decisions in cases of shaky autocratic regimes threatened with democratic change. Unsurprisingly, some of Ankara's decisions hinge on its view of its interests in each case. But what was more enduring in the Turkish case was its general *principled predisposition against the use of military force for regime change*, and particularly via western military intervention. It was here that Ankara's shift in policies towards Syria was a marked and damaging departure from the old approach: faced with the failure of diplomacy, Turkey did come to accept the use of force against Asad and even eventually to welcome western military intervention, at least through provision of arms and training. Erdoğan was further driven by a desire to prove his value to US President Barack Obama who had skillfully courted him. Nor did Erdoğan wish to actively break with Saudi Arabia and Qatar in their military support to the Syrian oppositionists. Ankara still wishes to play a leading role in a post-Asad Syria—but meanwhile Syria's future is partly in the hands of international negotiators including Russia and perhaps even Iran.

Ankara under almost any circumstances will eventually emerge as the most powerful player in a future Syria. Meanwhile it will need to decide how far its principles can be applied as tougher decisions arise in other places—uprisings in Bahrain, stirrings in Algeria and elsewhere as autocracy falters in the face of increasing popular discontent. Davutoğlu, Gül, and Erdoğan are all on record stating that Middle East regimes must acknowledge the need for reform, greater public participation, and greater democratization. But how are such principles to be implemented?

If nothing else, the Arab Spring made one thing clear: the fall of dictatorships and the move towards some degree of democratization opens Pandora's Box; it is a deeply destabilizing process. Any process of democratization cracks the old political and social order wide open; old grievances and wounds are reopened, and demands pour forth demanding satisfaction. Expectations and aspirations rise. The old rules vanish and all parties seek to shape and manipulate the chaotic new situation to their own advantage. Chaos may be undesirable, yes, but the old order was equally dangerous and ultimately unstable since it simply postponed treatment of long-standing political, social and economic frictions. What had been long suppressed is now out on the table and all parties must deal with it, like it or not. Emotions at the start will inevitably run high as domestic forces jockey for power within the new order. But over time things are likely to calm with each new political baby step that enfranchises more members of the population to a greater degree than before. This process of change is a never-ending one in any society, even advanced ones.

This, then, was the rough course of four revolutionary changes of government in the Arab world. But as we look out across this wounded and shaky region, let's try to discern some of the underlying geopolitical factors that are likely to determine the future course of events, most particularly political Islam, Sunni and Shi'ite revolution, sectarianism, and ethnicity.

PART FOUR: ISLAM AND SUNNI REVOLUTION

CHAPTER FIFTEEN

ISLAM AND REVOLUTION

Where does Islam, especially political Islam or Islamism, fit into the scene of revolution and change in the Arab Spring? "Islam" is regularly invoked by both Islamists and their enemies as driving their agendas, yet in reality most of the major change underway in the Middle East today is not directly linked to Islam. *Instead, competing actors use competing views of Islam as banners in their calls to action; these banners disguise the real nature of their involvement in what is all about revolution, counter-revolution, and the creation of political power.*

What is the Arab Spring so far, and what is it not?

• First, the main *ideological* struggle today in the Middle East is *not essentially between secularism and Islamism* as perceived in the West—although that is an interesting sideshow.

• *Nor is it really between Sunni versus Shi'ite Islam.*

• The primary struggle is *within Sunni Islam itself.* And it is not, as one might expect, even between radical jihadi Islam and conservative Saudi Islam.

• In the formulation of former US Ambassador Chas Freeman, the primary struggle pits *"democratic Islamism against Muslim autocracy."* These forces are represented on the one hand by the Muslim Brotherhood as a relatively moderate movement for Islamic change within a (still-evolving) democratic context; and, on the other, by Saudi Arabia that champions preservation of monarchy and even a rollback of democratic process via counter-revolution.

• The irony of this scene is that Saudi Arabia is thus often allied with *radical jihadi Islamists* to combat the moderate Islamists of the Brotherhood who seek more democratic order. How could such a bizarre situation have come about?

Islam and Revolution

In most societies the state historically seeks to maintain some control over religion: the state uses it to gain legitimacy for itself, while the state's enemies seek to use it to pinpoint regime failure in order to delegitimize the state. Most Muslim states maintain ranks of state-appointed clerics, (*'ulama*, or religious scholars) whose main function is to support the policies of the state. But of course such clerical service to the state ends up compromising the intellectual integrity of those same clerics. A much smaller number of clerics prefer to stand as independents outside the shadow of the state. Maintaining independence as a cleric is a tough challenge when the state controls the purse strings of religious institutions, and when the state is skilled in repressing upstart priests. Religious *movements*, on the other hand, are even more difficult to control than clerics since they enjoy mass following, and lack definable institutional structure making them harder for the state to capture. (This phenomenon has been as true in the history of Christianity as in Islam.)

The term "Islamist movement" covers a broad range of actors and ideas but nearly all seek some kind of political or social change. Most describe themselves as "reformist," or "revivalist," advocating "re-Islamization." In using these terms most movements seek to *return to the basics* of some idealized past, to some "original" or "true" Islam that they perceive has been corrupted by power, by non-Islamic traditions, or by lax religious practice. The Wahhabis of Arabia in the 18th century represented one such early movement, stirring up tribal opposition against the Ottoman-supported state, and demanding a return to an austere and purified Islam through literal interpretations of the Qur'an and the Hadith. (Geopolitical resistance by these desert Arabs to Ottoman rule also explains a lot of this early Arabian resistance. The Wahhabis had absorbed the desert into their bones, giving the movement a strong bedouin and tribal flavor, less comfortable with urban Islamic society.) The modern Saudi state emerged out of a fusion of desert tribal chiefs and the religious leaders of the Wahhabi purification movement. While the Saudi 'ulama today are expected to be responsive to Saudi state needs, the state cannot entirely ignore the *'ulama*'s moral authority if the state wishes to preserve its own patina of religious legitimacy.

But Islamism, or political Islam, can also lean in a second direction of calling for change and reform by seeking *new ways* to understand, interpret and revitalize the faith under contemporary conditions. We have seen this already in Turkey's official Directorate of Religious Affairs (*Diyanet*) in which official new thinking about old sources of legislation is under way. This may represent the most progressive example in the Muslim world of religious authority operating under state tutelage. Or in the faith-based good works of Hizmet as a civic organization. But what of the *'ulama* or clerics who are *independent of a government payroll and control,* and who choose to speak out against the state in the name of reform, Islamic justice, and good governance? And what happens when Islamists enter into democratic politics? They are then compelled to win votes from a majority of the population—an exercise that imposes a new pragmatism upon them.

The Muslim Brotherhood

We examined earlier the way Islamism evolved within Turkish politics. In today's Egypt we see such a similar process in mid-evolution with the political rise of the Muslim Brotherhood in electoral politics and its fall through military intervention. The Brotherhood had already evolved politically quite some distance since its beginnings early in the 20th century. The founding statement of belief of the Muslim Brotherhood is austere: *"Allah is our objective; the Qur'an is our law, the Prophet is our leader; Jihad is our way; and death for the sake of Allah is the highest of our aspirations."* For those who seek blanket ideological condemnation of the Brotherhood and Islamism, that statement is all they require to demonstrate its alleged in-built extremism. Indeed, Osama bin Laden and al-Qaeda would probably have no trouble with that statement—as far as it goes. Yet the statement is almost entirely rhetorical; it captures nothing of the character of the Brotherhood and its actions over recent decades, and especially today as it tangled for the first time with the complexities of national power and policy. That statement of faith says little about how it translates into political programs, actual policies and political tactics on the ground with real human beings. Some in the Brotherhood still speak of aspiring to institute Shari'a law (undefined) and even a "global Islamic state," but these ambitions remain distant and vague ideals.

The fact is that the Brotherhood has undergone a major shift towards pragmatism and accommodation with the realities of the state system in the Middle East today. Its recent disastrous encounter with electoral politics and the power of the military in Egypt now pose greater demands upon the Brotherhood to rethink its electoral strategies and tactics. Indeed, a number of observers of political Islam, including myself, have long argued that the *very political process itself* exerts a powerful impact on non-violent Islamist groups who seek a piece of the political pie within some kind of democratic process. Political process forces them to deal with the realities of public opinion and to adjust their political program accordingly. A key slogan of the Muslim Brotherhood, for example, has been "Islam is the Solution" (*al-Islam huwwa al-hall*); this may be fine as a rhetorical call, but only becomes truly meaningful when voters know how it translates into quite specific, concrete policies. Those *policies* will be the ultimate criterion by which the public will decide whether to vote for them or not, regardless of how "Islamic" the movement may be. And the Brotherhood failed that test—at least in the first round. But the story is far from over.

Political Islam can be most simply and broadly defined as an effort to draw inspiration from the Qur'an and the Hadith in some fashion in order to construct contemporary Muslim society and governance. This definition is obviously broad. Its forms can vary widely from violent to peaceful, authoritarian to democratic, reactionary or progressive, dogmatic or flexible, across a wide spectrum of behavior and belief. However defined, political Islam has been the primary vehicle of political opposition to authoritarian rule across most of the Muslim world in the 20th century. Why? First, because it springs from the roots of native Islamic culture; it is not borrowed from western culture. Second, its moral foundations are rooted in Islam, lending it a certain legitimacy. Its movements are also able to function and operate informally out of mosque networks when other meeting places for opposition groups are often banned. They usually maintain practical social programs— food, health, education, housing, women's issues—at the grassroots level in local neighborhoods designed to improve living conditions for the poor. They have demonstrated an ability to win elections within student and professional societies. They have often demonstrated skills in municipal administration. They often possess powerful and modern organizational capabilities. They maintain informal links with similar organizations across borders. The Muslim Brotherhood organization, for example, while not centrally directed, possesses branches in most countries of the Arab world, as well as in many non-Arab Muslim countries with similar programs and outlook, under a variety of names. This international character strengthens its clout and claim to being a pan-Islamist movement. That said, the Brotherhood is not monolithic, and functions differently in different countries without centralized leadership or coordination. In Egypt it foreswore violence and terror over half a century ago; those few advocating violence broke away to form independent organizations.

The Arab Spring was obviously a particular turning point. US scholar Vali Nasr commented that the "Arab Spring became the Islamist Spring." But it should hardly be surprising that this is so—at least in the first stage. Given the prominent place of the Brotherhood and other Islamist opposition movements in opposing authoritarian power, Islamists have done well at the polls, especially in the first free elections after the fall of authoritarian orders. They are respected and often have little serious organized political opposition. This has been one key reason why Washington has often been leery of elections in the Muslim world and concerned for potential turmoil and change in politics after the fall of authoritarian leaders. The real question is not whether they win the first election, but how they will do in successive elections after having to deal with the complex realities of running a country.

Egypt shows that the public wants results fast and its tolerance operates on a short fuse.

What was striking in the Arab Spring was the early participation of youth, women, and westernized liberal political activists, especially in manning the barricades against regime forces and employing social media as a tool of organization. While important, liberal political activists actually represent only a small segment of the political spectrum. They were inexperienced and poorly organized on the political front and quickly became dominated by the Brotherhood and other Islamists. There was no doubt that the Brotherhood would remain one of the most powerful forces lying beneath the surface of events visible on the TV screen.

At the same time the Brotherhood initially hesitated before rushing into the fray; it hung back assessing the course of events and preserving its options. It was cautious about committing itself to early action that could lead to familiar retaliatory crackdowns by the state against them. And indeed, their fears were justified. But as the power of popular political opposition to Mubarak grew the Brotherhood decided to swing its weight behind the revolution. And it did well at the ballot box; after all, few other political forces had led a long and consistent opposition movement against a series of Egyptian authoritarian regimes, had gone to jail, been tortured, and even died for the cause.

In this sense it is simply wrong to claim, as some liberals do, that the Brotherhood "hijacked" the revolution in these countries. It is true they were not at the immediate forefront of the first street action, but they were far from absent, and possessed all the infrastructure, experience, grassroots political organization, will and support to ultimately dominate the political scene once the regimes collapsed.

In most countries Islamists had long benefitted from the "luxury" of being out of power where they could criticize the authoritarian state without having to bear the challenges and burdens of governance. All that changed. *Any* political party that comes to power now must face rising public discontent with existing social, economic and political conditions, even if those conditions were inherited from previous authoritarian regimes. Even if the Islamists should possess genuine administrative skills, the heavy weight of a failed past is not quickly turned around.

Islamism as Revolutionary Force?

The Brotherhood did not come directly to power in Egypt via "revolution." A popular uprising sprung up across a wide political spectrum of revolt against the old Mubarak order; it was only with the withdrawal of military support that the regime fell. It was only under the transitional military government that the Brotherhood had the chance to win a plurality in *legal elections*. The Brotherhood's ideological vision had certainly been revolutionary towards the old Mubarak order, but so was the vision of the secular liberals. Both of them called for the overthrow of an illegitimate regime. Neither of them executed a coup against Mubarak as such—that was the army's role. The important question is *how* the Brotherhood comes to power: *when victory for the Brotherhood comes through democratic processes, its exercise of power is unlikely to be "revolutionary" in character and may even be cautious, even if many do not like their overall orientation.*

Authoritarian orders rarely give way voluntarily to democratic change, except perhaps very gradually, as may be the case in Kuwait. Therefore all autocratic orders, republican or monarchical, fear ideologies—whether religious or secular—that advocate change of regime. Only in this context was the Brotherhood's call for change essentially "revolutionary." It opposes authoritarian rule, both monarchical and republican, both of which have often denied participation to the Brotherhood (and to other parties) in the political order. In principle the Brotherhood opposes even monarchy itself, as does Islam: rulers do not "own" their lands—the meaning is inherent in the roots of the word for "king" (*mālik*) in Arabic. On practical grounds of self-preservation, however, the Brotherhood wisely avoids expressing such views explicitly in monarchical states like Jordan, Kuwait, Saudi Arabia or Morocco where it must survive. It presses for social justice where little has existed under monarchical or non-monarchical regimes. Far from rejecting democracy as a western invention as do some other Islamist movements, the Brotherhood regularly calls for elections—that it comfortably interprets as a contemporary form of the Islamic concept of *mushāwara*, consultation between the ruler and the people. It has favored elections because it had confidence in its demonstrated ability to win votes and has done so routinely for years in trade union and student elections in university.

Now, it is striking that the dynamics of the Arab Spring have first and foremost challenged *republican* regimes more than monarchies. No monarchies have fallen in the Middle East for over four decades, an issue worthy of analysis in itself. But the revolutionary challenge to monarchies remains strongly implicit, and the growing public call for greater democracy has placed the Brotherhood in a more confrontational position towards regional monarchies than ever before. Monarchies sense that. This is particularly important as Saudi Arabia emerges as the leading force of counter-revolution in the Arab world, seeking to protect the ruling monarchies against the further onslaught of revolutionary forces of the Arab Spring, religious or secular. The reality is that the challenge from the Islamists is a far more powerful force than that of the secular opposition, at least so far. But let's now look at the dynamics of the relationship specifically between the Brotherhood and Saudi Arabia over time—a dance of the wary.

The Brotherhood and Saudi Arabia

Saudi policies towards revolutionary movements, both Islamic and non-Islamic, are complex and tactical—all aimed at regime preservation. To the extent that the Saudi royal family has survived many tumultuous periods over many decades, its policies have been demonstrably successful in that respect. Saudi strategy can be roughly summarized as follows:

• Maintain the image of Saudi Arabia as an "exceptional" country—by definition and character inherently religious, therefore *fully legitimate in Islamic terms*. Custodianship of the Holy Places of Mecca and Medina are key legitimizing titles of the king. (Yet Islamists bluntly challenge the Islamic legitimacy of the royal family and the significance of any such "custodianship" titles.)

• Do not allow radical movements, religious or secular, to take aim at the kingdom. Use checkbook diplomacy where possible to buy them off and shield the kingdom from attack, regardless of whomever else the radicals attack elsewhere.

• Support the most fundamentalist (non-violent) Islamist forces everywhere (Salafi) that reject the very principle of democracy as a western and blasphemous idea, but ensure that those forces remain in tune with the kingdom's own Wahhabi outlook, practice, and its interests.

• Oppose *radical secular* forces in the Muslim world (nationalist, leftist), but buy good relations with them if need be.

• Maintain good relations with the West and remain indispensable to it to keep western power on the Saudi side; oil policy, finance, arms sales and security arrangements are key tools in this project.

• Support all monarchies as inherently less dangerous forms of government and more oriented towards preserving the status quo than are republics.

While these general principles are clear, they can on occasion be contradictory; how they are prioritized involves complex tactical decisions. This is sharply revealed in the intriguing case of relations between the kingdom and the Brotherhood, characterized by shifting and often rocky relations over time. In the 1960s the Saudis granted refuge to thousands of

Muslim Brothers who fled persecution in Egypt under the kingdom's primary enemy and leader of revolutionary Arab nationalism, Gamal Abdel Nasser. While living in the kingdom many members of the Egyptian Brotherhood gained important positions in the education system and especially in schools of theology, finance and medicine; they themselves also absorbed much of the conservatism and apolitical character of the Wahhabis; meddling in politics is heavily discouraged by the regime. Later however, many Brothers were attracted into the *al-Sahwa* (Awakening) movement in the kingdom in the 1990s that emphasized anew not just the forms but the *implications* of Islam in governance, was critical of the monarchy's policies and called for reform. Members of al-Sahwa argued that the Saudi model fell far short of the Islamic ideal given the corruption and hypocrisy of behavior of the royal family. Saudi Arabia sought to bring al-Sahwa under greater state control via carrot and stick: increased state financial support to their clerics along with greater state control. Despite al-Sahwa's public declarations of loyalty to the kingdom, the ultimate commitment of this school of thinkers is not to the royal family over the long term; over time it will gravitate instead towards the views and policies of other Brotherhood movements and parties in the Muslim world. Indeed, the Brotherhood's ideological center of loyalty is not to the concept of monarchy at all, despite co-existence and political caution within the kingdom for many years.

The Brotherhood was an object of particular suspicion to the powerful former Saudi Minister of Interior and later Crown Prince Nayif bin 'Abd al-'Aziz (died June 2011) who was unusually outspoken on the topic. After 9/11, when the kingdom came under strong US criticism for the large number of Saudi citizens that participated in the attack, Prince Nayif charged outsiders with responsibility for inciting the behavior of the Saudi terrorists and bitterly criticized the Brotherhood.

> All our problems come from the Muslim Brotherhood. We have given too much support to this group... The Muslim Brotherhood has destroyed the Arab world....Whenever they got into difficulty or found their freedom restricted in their own countries, Brotherhood activists found refuge in the kingdom which protected their lives...But they later turned against the kingdom.

Apart from the Muslim Brotherhood in Sudan that ultimately supported an anti-Saudi Islamist regime, Prince Nayif particularly singled out for denunciation two other major Islamist figures: Shaykh Rashid al-Ghannushi—leader of Ennahda who became prime minister after the Arab Spring in Tunisia in 2011—and Necmettin Erbakan—then leader of the Islamist Refah Party and briefly prime minister in Turkey in 1997—as well as several other leading Brotherhood politicians. All of them had been ideologically sympathetic to Saddam Hussein's invasion and seizure of Kuwait in 1990 which at the time they interpreted as a "progressive" anti-monarchical and anti-western move.[1]

The Brotherhood's political positions on the Arab Spring further upset the Saudi monarchy. As we have seen, Riyadh had been appalled at the fall of secular dictator Ben Ali in Tunisia who was immediately granted refuge in the kingdom. Riyadh's concern was all the greater when Ben Ali was replaced by the selfsame Brotherhood leader, Ennahda's Shaykh Rashid al-Ghannushi— who openly advocates free elections and multi-party democracy. Saudi anxieties increased manyfold with the subsequent collapse of Mubarak in Egypt from which the Brotherhood emerged as the primary beneficiary (see Chapter 16 on Sunni Revolution and Egypt).

But it would be simplistic to sum up the Saudi position as simply "counter-revolutionary"; its tactics are tactically far more sophisticated and flexible. For example, as insurrectional forces emerged in Libya and Syria in the Arab Spring Riyadh showed initial ambivalence but soon ended up actively *supporting* the forces of rebellion in both. The Saudi rationale was driven by two main factors. First, defense of the institution of *monarchy* represents a bottom-line ideological interest for Riyadh; monarchies are more reliably conservative in their policies and are non-ideological. Since the uprisings in both Syria and Libya were against *republican* regimes they were hence more acceptable. Of course the old regimes in Tunisia and Egypt had also been republican, but there are better and worse republican regimes in Saudi eyes. Furthermore, unlike Mubarak and Ben Ali, the republican leaders of Libya and Syria had long and openly proclaimed themselves to be part of the *revolutionary* camp of Arab world politics—often flamboyantly so, and hence a dangerous presence on the Arab scene. In addition, bad blood has periodically existed on the personal level between the Asad regime in Syria and most Arab monarchs: Riyadh has disliked and distrusted the Asads due to their regular vocal championing of revolutionary causes in the Arab world, especially Palestine. Such Arab nationalist and pro-Palestinian rhetoric made Saudi commitments to the Palestinians appear lukewarm. Riyadh has also been engaged in a long-standing rivalry with Syria for influence over Lebanon. The fact that Iran has been Asad's chief ally in the Middle East only increased Saudi desire to overthrow Asad and his entire 'Alawi (quasi-Shi'ite) regime. Riyadh maintained the same suspicions and dislike of Qadhafi's revolutionary rhetoric and his routine contempt for the kingdom's policies over the years.

In Jordan, Morocco and Yemen too, the Brotherhood is the primary (legal) political opposition to the monarchy and constantly issues calls for greater democratization, confident of their own eventual strength at the ballot box. Neither in Jordan nor Morocco nor the Gulf states does the Brotherhood actually call for an end to the monarchy. The Saudis are aware, too, that the Turkish AKP emerged out of Islamist roots sympathetic to the Muslim Brotherhood. Thus, Ankara and Riyadh stand at opposite ends of the spectrum on the overthrow of both Ben 'Ali and Mubarak; Erdoğan's impassioned call for Mubarak to step down —couched in strong Islamic language—was very unwelcome in Riyadh; equally unwelcome to Riyadh was Erdoğan's later denunciation of the military coup against the Brotherhood government. To make things worse, Riyadh regularly supports fundamentalist Islamist *rivals* to the Brotherhood: Salafis and Wahhabi-style groups in Egypt (and elsewhere)—groups who (until recently) were ideologically opposed to democratic process as an un-Islamic western invention.

So the Saudis over many decades have become masters of managing revolutionary turmoil and ideological ferment in the region. While yielding only minor concessions towards reforms in the kingdom itself, it has not shrunk from skillfully forming tactical alliances with radical Islamic ideological groups outside the country to play them off against radical *secular* groups. Thus it supported the Brotherhood strongly for many years inside Egypt as a tool against the secular forces of Nasser's revolutionary Arab nationalism. Riyadh also provided cash and even arms to many more radical Islamic movements in Pakistan and Afghanistan against the Soviet Union and other leftist enemies perceived as even more dangerous to the kingdom. This type of "check-book diplomacy" (or riyal-politik) has been quite effective in buying "protection" from radical Islamic groups who might otherwise turn their ideology against the kingdom itself. It was on this basis that religious elements in the kingdom had unofficially ended up supporting Osama Bin Laden and al-Qaeda in its early pre-9/11 days as a form of insurance against attack from them. In the end, of course, al-Qaeda did turn its revolutionary rhetoric and violence against the kingdom itself. Thus Riyadh's tactics have often been a risky game, but over the years they have succeeded fairly well in protecting the kingdom; most radical Islamic movements have avoided criticism of Saudi Arabia as long as the kingdom remained a source of financial support. These financial ties also provided the Saudis at least a partial voice in the policies of those radical forces, even as the West strongly criticized the kingdom for it. Palestinian Hamas is a case in point, which, despite being a branch of the

Muslim Brotherhood, received Saudi support for years until Hamas broke with the mainstream pro-western Palestinian leadership Fatah.

With the ascent of the Muslim Brotherhood to power in Egypt in 2012 the kingdom moved warily towards dealing with the government given Egypt's huge strategic importance, while behind the scenes it supported the Egyptian army to overthrow the Brotherhood. Riyadh stepped up its surveillance over the activities of Brotherhood members at home and supported the legal prosecution, especially in the United Arab Emirates, of dozens of Brotherhood activities on flimsy charges.

The kingdom's dramatic support for revolution in Syria against the Asad autocracy starting in 2011 has little to do with any support for democratization and everything to do with its hatred of Asad and an (exaggerated) fear that Syria represents Iran's stronghold in the region. (See Chapter 21 for more detail on the kingdom and the civic struggle in Syria.) All of this has been an exercise in choosing the lesser of two (or more) real evils.

The dilemma—and risk—for Riyadh ballooned in 2012-2013 with the rising power of radical jihadi forces (including al-Qaeda links) over secular forces in the joint armed opposition against Asad in Syria. Riyadh was confronted with a series of not very appetizing choices. It was forced to work with both secular forces among the insurgents as well as those jihadi forces who were not explicitly anti-Saudi—at least at the moment. Riyadh may well have to live with the reality of Brotherhood and/or jihadi power in Syria in the future and can only hope that its traditional check-book diplomacy will help blunt any revolutionary tendencies against the kingdom. The kingdom will be compelled to support the most reactionary Salafi groups in Syria, as they have done in Egypt, to weaken Brotherhood power, but such support will only increase Brotherhood hostility towards Saudi Arabia. These calculations may ultimately prove to be disastrous to Riyadh.

Even Salafis cannot really be relied upon as ideological allies to Riyadh over the longer run, despite their ideological similarity to Wahhabism in the kingdom. Wahhabism in the kingdom is beholden to the Saudi regime in the end. But Salafis outside the country, for all their denunciation of democracy over the years as a "western import," have shown that when democratic process opens up and becomes an important element in the power game, they too feel tempted to drift into electoral politics. This trend has been evident in Kuwait for over a decade, and more recently in Egypt where the Salafis demonstrated a surprising willingness to engage in pragmatic political bargaining. Even for the Salafis the Wahhabi kingdom is hardly their model of clean and ideal Islamic government.

In the end, Saudi policies are driven by one supreme concern: the preservation of the rule of the al-Sa'ud in Saudi Arabia, the only country in the world to be named after its ruling family. Islamists who support the Saudis will receive Saudi largesse; those who do not, will not. For all the kingdom's rhetoric about being an Islamic state with "the Qur'an as its constitution," these claims are unconvincing to those Islamists not on the Saudi payroll; few Islamists view the kingdom as an ideal Islamic state due to its corruption, its close ties with the West, and its general timidity in public defense of Muslim causes lest it discomfit the West. Most Saudi clerics are in bed with the ruling family while the Saudi elite are among the most egregiously hypocritical in calling for austere social practices inside the kingdom while lavishing money on profligate lifestyles in the fleshpots of Europe, Morocco and the Gulf. In 2011 the Saudi *'ulama* further damaged its Islamist credentials by passing a fatwa stating that public demonstrations against the Saudi regime are "anti-Islamic."

The Muslim Brotherhood thus represents an affront to the Saudi regime because it supports democratic change (a revolutionary challenge to the kingdom) and it represents a form of Islamic legitimacy that the kingdom lacks, despite the king's claim to being "Custodian of the Holy Places." The Brotherhood actually gained greater following among the public in the kingdom after the military coup in Egypt against it, including on massive Twitter exchanges not only across the kingdom, but around the Muslim world. The Brotherhood may ultimately emerge the stronger over the long run as a result of the military coup and subsequent bloody repressions against it by the Egyptian army.

Overall, time runs against the Saudi regime. But while that may be true, the kingdom has nonetheless weathered such dire predictions by western analysts about its imminent demise for many long decades. Internal pressures and demonstrations against the kingdom have so far shown little success in truly changing the political order. The kingdom has met internal dissension with a fairly successful blend of carrots and sticks. It has made some modest institutional reforms such as permitting a partially elected Consultative Council, but the council has not brought about serious change in the way politics is done. Furthermore, the more recent use of social media within the kingdom has increased the propagation of information on internal events, including increased criticism of the royal family; social discontent is at a high level, because of growing poverty and disparity of income, as well as broad resentment against the privileges accorded to a huge royal family and the social strictures on women that have economic consequences for families and the workplace.

The regime is clearly aware of the growing ideological challenge against it from many fronts. Interestingly, in 2011 Saudi Arabia took an unusual step towards legitimizing its own religious sect and ideology by declaring the Salafi (Wahhabi) tendency in Islam to now constitute a distinct official school of jurisprudence (*madhhab*) in its own right—joining the four venerable existing classical Sunni schools and the Shi'ite school (*Ja'fari*). This is the first time such a claim of independent status as a formal religious school of Islam has been made by Salafis; previously they had always been part of the conservative Hanbali school. This proclamation suggests an upgrading of a Saudi ideological struggle on behalf of its own austere interpretation of Islam on a global level; but the step is buttressed more by its powerful financial resources than by the force of ideological power. In the end, however, Saudi opportunistic support to radical elements, both religious and secular, increases the threat that they will eventually combine to overthrow the Saudi monarchy itself. It's a dangerous game—in what Riyadh views as dangerous times.

Enter Qatar

The calculus of Arab Spring geopolitics was further complicated by the bold new activism of a relatively more recent player on the Middle East strategic scene: the tiny Emirate of Qatar (pronounced "Gutter," not "Catarrh" in Gulf Arabic.) A small and vulnerable peninsula attached to the northern Gulf coast of Saudi Arabia, it possesses only a tiny native population of a quarter of a million; the other four-fifths of the population are expats.) Nonetheless Qatar now exerts a regional clout vastly greater than its size would suggest. Its wealth, imagination and boldness has enabled it to stir the political waters of the region and insert a new factor into the skein of reform, revolution, and Islamist politics across the Middle East. It has annoyed many greater powers in the process, including Saudi Arabia and the US, as it has proceeded to punch above its weight with much independence of action. Qatar wielded money and/or weapons to intervene significantly in Libya, Syria, and Egypt; more importantly, it has established itself as a key patron of the Muslim Brotherhood everywhere, so hated by the Saudis.

Contradictions abound. Qatar backed forceful change in these three regimes, while being a hereditary monarchy in its own right. Its progressive image stands in contrast to its own Wahhabi form of Islam, Qatar's official state religion, that operates in far more moderate garb than in the kingdom. Of all the GCC states, Qatar acts more independently of Saudi Arabia than any other state (with the possible exception of Oman). The tensions between the two countries over many years ran deep but had remained manageable. By March 2013 the fissure between Qatar and its neighbors began to widen with important long-term ideological implications.

Qatar's maverick approach to the Arab world was first heralded by the dramatic appearance in 1996 of a new global media force, the Arab world's first satellite TV channel al-Jazeera, that went on to revolutionize Arab public discussion of regional affairs. Al-Jazeera astonished the Arab world with programs that broke open taboos long kept in place by the state-controlled television outlets in individual Arab states. Suddenly Arab viewers were treated to the spectacle of open debate and hot discussion on a great variety of topics that included airtime given to opposition movements in the region whose voices were suppressed at home. Islamist figures were given particular prominence, particularly those representing the position of the Brotherhood; the pros and cons on a broad variety of issues were aired in emotional debate—secularism versus Islam, the legacies of Arab nationalism, the sources of terrorism, the merits of westernization, and close examination of various crises in the region. The greatest tribute to the success and even relative objectivity of the channel was its regular condemnation by virtually every Arab regime at some point or other. A joke ran that "Qatar is a small Gulf state whose capital is al-Jazeera." Saudi Arabia was particularly offended and several years later launched its own rival satellite channel, the more anemic al-ʿArabiyya, whose popularity fell quite short of al-Jazeera due to its more timid examination of regional issues and its general reluctance to criticize the West. (Wags satirized the views of al-ʿArabiyya by calling it al-ʿIbriyya, "Hebrew.") Al-Jazeera's coverage of most countries of the Middle East was relatively uncensored, except for its coverage on Qatar itself, of which there was virtually none. Perhaps al-Jazeera's sharpest impact on the world was its unapologetic reflection of interests and attitudes of the people of the Middle East who had formerly been required to view their own region solely through the eyes of CNN or BBC in Arabic that earlier had dominated global coverage of Arab and world affairs. It pioneered the presentation of news from a new non-western perspective, as it now does with its bold new English-language channel in the West that has garnered much interest and praise for its freshness.

Qatar promoted its profile further in seeking diplomatic solutions between warring parties in numerous Arab countries including in the Darfur region in Sudan, between rival Palestinian factions, rival Lebanese groups, and Yemeni factions. Qatar has walked a gutsy but fine line with Washington: al-Jazeera's uncensored coverage of US wars in the Middle East infuriated Washington (who bombed al-Jazeera offices in Iraq and Afghanistan) as do Qatar's good working relations with Iran. Yet this is counter-balanced by Qatar's official dialog with Israel and its hosting of the huge US military airbase at al-'Udayd as a forward operating base of US Central Command in support of US military operations in Iraq and Afghanistan. Qatar enjoys diplomatic ties with both Hamas and Hizballah, both designated as "terrorist organizations" by the US, but it has also maintained official trade relations with Israel since 1996. Qatar's foreign policies represent a remarkable balancing act that in many ways parallel Turkey's own complex and multifaceted foreign policies under the AKP. Indeed, the AKP government has all along enjoyed close relations, including economic, with Qatar.

While the phenomenon of Qatar in itself is remarkable, the most striking issue is its bold approach to questions of Islam and revolution. Typically showing a willingness to work with most regional forces and factions, the emirate of Qatar welcomed the Arab Spring revolutions in Tunisia and Egypt (both strenuously opposed by Riyadh) and reportedly provided considerable financial backing to Ennahda (a branch of the Muslim Brotherhood party in Tunisia); Ennahda leader Ghannushi made Qatar his first foreign destination in an official visit. Qatar also supported armed regime change in Libya and Syria. In Yemen Qatar has emerged as a strong backer of the Muslim Brotherhood party (*al-Islah*, Reform), and of prominent politicians and military men with allegiance to the Brotherhood that have upset the calculus of Saudi influence there. By providing Yemen with major funding, it has partially eclipsed Saudi power that long depended on the desperate poverty of the country to buy influence and make it a Saudi fiefdom, a fact much resented by Yemenis. Qatar played a significant role in the negotiated change of leadership in Yemen (a change that was also supported by Saudi Arabia). Ideologically, Qatar maintains close support to the Muslim Brotherhood in Tunisia, Egypt, Libya, Yemen, in Qatar itself, and elsewhere. The leading Muslim Brotherhood intellectual and most popular television commentator on Islamic issues anywhere, Egyptian Shaykh Yusif al-Qaradawi, resides in Qatar. Qatar became the primary source of financial support to Hamas (the Palestinian branch of the Muslim Brotherhood) after Hamas shifted its headquarters out of Damascus in 2012 under Saudi and Qatari pressure, thereby losing its Iranian funding.

While maintaining its support for the Muslim Brotherhood Qatar simultaneously maintains good ties with Salafi groups, and of course can demonstrate its conservative credentials with its own state brand of Wahhabi

Islam. Qatar provided more weapons to anti-Qadhafi rebel groups in Libya and to anti-Asad groups in Syria than any other Arab state (at least until mid-2013). It provided vital financial backing of more than US$5 billion to the Muslim Brotherhood government in Egypt before its fall, even while growingly critical of the Brotherhood's seemingly ineffective domestic policies. Qatar also consulted closely with Ankara on strategies to bring about Asad's fall in Damascus and the two states have been much on the same wavelength.

Qatar's vision and ambitions may be surprising for such a small country, but its policies are backed by its tremendous gas wealth and a population that is one of the most quiescent in the Gulf, undoubtedly influenced by having the richest per capita population in the world. Qatar seems to act in the belief that it can keep nearly all enemies at bay, not just by money like the Saudis, but through its foreign policy activism, its bold support for the popular al-Jazeera, and, like Turkey, open dealing with almost all regional and international powers. But its political resources are not unlimited. Unlike Turkey, Qatar lacks the large and experienced diplomatic staff necessary to carry out its ambitious goals. Its regional ambitions sometimes rankle other states, especially Saudi Arabia that regards it as an annoying and even troublesome upstart. But Qatar has even been willing to run the risk of seriously alienating its GCC partners through its strong support for the Muslim Brotherhood in the region. And after a change of leadership in al-Jazeera in 2012, the network was widely perceived as becoming a mouthpiece for the Brotherhood in its coverage of Egyptian affairs—a fact resented by Egyptian liberal factions and the military. Qatar seeks to widen its international footprint by bidding to host the 2020 Olympic Games. As it has pressed its case, it has also come under greater human rights scrutiny for the poor living conditions of foreign workers living in Qatar—on a par with similar shameful conditions for foreign workers all up and down the Gulf.

A broader question emerges here: Qatar's leadership seems to demonstrate the belief that political Islam will play a significant role in the future governance of the Arab world. It furthermore seems to believe that the *future belongs to a modernist and pragmatic form of political Islam like the Brotherhood rather than to a Salafi/Wahhabi one*. This belief is markedly distinct from the Saudi, UAE, and even Kuwaiti view that the Brotherhood represents a long-term threat to monarchy and authoritarian rule in the region. This Brotherhood vision of political Islam calls for the role of Islamic principles in governance (however defined), for some kind of democratic political process, and for growing acceptance of political and religious pluralism. Qatar has anticipated, for example (and accurately in my view), that Hamas will eventually win out over the corrupt, ineffective and delegitimized Palestinian Authority that is supported by Israel and the US. The military coup against the Brotherhood in Egypt in July 2013 was therefore a severe short-term setback to Qatari strategy and has equally weakened Hamas. Qatar will by necessity adjust to the new realities of military-dominated power in Egypt but is unlikely to abandon its general policy of support to the Brotherhood over the longer run, confident that its own nimbleness of policy will help shield it from Islamist critics.

In my view the Saudi fears of the Brotherhood are, from its own perspectives, instinctively correct. The Brotherhood's approach to issues of Islamic governance basically does threaten the Saudi political and social model—one based on explicit rejection of democracy, rejection of pluralism and of open political discussion—while supporting a narrow Salafi theological vision. There are indeed contradictions: Qatar, too, is a monarchy (or emirate), does not practice democracy and limits political discussion in the emirate; it does not practice at home what it preaches outside the country. But it seems to have made the judgment that the Brotherhood, under present circumstances, represents the best balance between Islam and modern governance within the Islamic tradition. And Qatar shows it can comfortably work with secular democracies as well.

Meanwhile Qatar has set another precedent. In June 2013 the Emir, Shaykh Hamad, in good health at age 61, voluntarily abdicated in favor of his son Tamim, 33. The position of the new emir seems secure: public discontent, much less dissent, has been virtually non-existent. Qatar under its farsighted former ruler Hamad had plunged into open contact with the world in attracting many foreign universities, institutions, and outstanding world architects to build a variety of modern structures including the stunning Museum of Islamic Art in Doha. The key question is how long the new emir will be able to maintain Qatar's ambitious and maverick foreign policies in the face of opposition from most other Gulf states and especially Saudi Arabia. The chances are that he will; to concede to the Saudi line on most issues now would be tantamount to Qatar's loss of identity and ultimately even its independent political existence.

Although never overtly expressed, Qatar indeed has legitimate reason to fear future expansion of Saudi geopolitical power. As a small peninsula attached to the Saudi Arabian mainland, it could be overrun in quick order and absorbed by Saudi military forces at any time in the event of conflict. Qatar is working on building a strong, independent, and internationally-supported identity and presence that will help protect it in the future from

Saudi expansionism, including the big US air base. For all the talk by GCC rulers about the "Iranian threat," the real physical threat to Qatar and other Gulf shaykhdoms over the longer run does not come from Iran. It will come from an expansionist, possibly post-revolutionary and more assertive regime in Saudi Arabia, a country that has already twice in two centuries seen its Wahhabi forces sweep to the shores of the Gulf. The Gulf emirates maintain only a tenuous hold on the independence of their slim and tiny coastal states over the longer term. While other Gulf states may be angry with Qatar's independent stance, they would support it against any possible Saudi takeover—a move that would only presage a Saudi takeover of other vulnerable Gulf states as well.

Turkey's view of the Muslim Brotherhood in the region shares many parallels with Qatar. Turkey sees the Brotherhood as capable of democratic evolution and growth, much in the same trajectory as Turkey's Islamist parties over the decades, and hence a process worth encouraging. Qatar finds Turkey an attractive and non-threatening model; the ties between the two countries rest on ideological as well as economic and strategic views.

The Brotherhood and the Future

A grand question remains: how much do Islamist movements, especially the Muslim Brotherhood, represent the "wave of the future"—or at least as one inevitable stage in the future? If they do, how much should this development be resisted, or managed, as they evolve in the political arena? Shortsighted determination on the part of regional governments to throttle Islamists in the cradle is very likely ineffective if not dangerous, and may only serve to strengthen the Islamists in the eyes of large numbers of their supporters. Indeed, suppression of Islamists has largely been the western preference in the region up to now, with only slow and grudging accommodation to reality as it has evolved in Turkey, then Tunisia, and a brief awkward first phase in Egypt.

Second, we need to remember that "Islamism" comprises a broad spectrum. Debates and struggles mark their evolutionary process. Moderate Islamism in the long run is the most effective and authoritative brake against more radical forms of Islamism. And hopefully the future of Islamist movements will be determined by the citizens of the region via democratic process and not by outsiders.

Third, the reformist, even revolutionary aspect of Islamism will remain. Authoritarian rulers have legitimate grounds to fear it on that basis; but dictators equally need to fear reformist or revolutionary ideas from secularists as well. Both work against autocracy over the longer run. The ultimate issue is not whether we trust Islamists to be democrats, but whether, given the political culture of the region in the past, we can trust any group to continue to be democrats once in power.

A prominent part of Middle East politics in the coming decade, then, will not be mostly about "secularists versus Islamists" but about various trends within the Islamist movements and their backers, in a proxy war for power. The Brotherhood, for all its shortcomings, is the most likely to continue evolving in the direction of moderation and adaptation to democratic processes. Islamism excluded from power can demonstrate revolutionary force; in power, however it is obliged to assume problems of incumbency. Regional autocrats who fear democratic change from Islamists will likely continue to manipulate radical or even jihadi forces to weaken the Brotherhood. Perhaps temporarily, but unwisely. The Brotherhood is far from being a spent force, despite all the pronouncements to that effect from around the Middle East.

CHAPTER SIXTEEN

CAN EGYPT RESTORE ITS REGIONAL LEADERSHIP?

If the concept of an "Arab world" remains strong among Arab citizens, we might legitimately ask, who then leads it? Most might name Egypt: it has an ancient historical position, size, with overwhelmingly the largest population in the Arab world (80 million), and far and away the greatest cultural clout among Arabs. But some might look to Saudi Arabia, with its massive oil wealth, population of 30 million, and possession of the Holy Places of Islam as the most important Arab power behind the scenes over recent decades. Elements of serious rivalry have existed between Egypt and Saudi Arabia in the past, although their relations have been close since the 1970s when Egypt abandoned the revolutionary path—some might say abdicated from any leadership role—and sought cooperation with Washington in return for regime security. But Saudi Arabia for all its wealth and public piety has lacked vision: it has moved with tactical agility and even good sense on occasions, but overall its policies reflect a largely defensive and reactive posture in a quest for regime stability rather than providing genuine regional leadership and meeting the broad political and social needs of the general public.

Egypt began to view itself as the "natural leader" of the Arab world certainly ever since the first era of "Arab Revolution" in the 1950-60s when concepts of Arab nationalism as a state/ideology reached full flower. Yet ironically, for most of its history Egypt was not really grounded in an "Arab identity" at all; Egyptians viewed themselves as just that—Egyptians—with their own unique history and culture based on the eternal civilization of the Nile. It was the 20th century that created Arabism as a political movement across the region and drew Egypt into the fold.

The Arab nationalist movement involved far more than assertion of cultural identity; the voice of Arab nationalism spoke out against traditional western domination and Egypt became a key fixture of the new "Third World" non-aligned movement during the Cold War. But that powerful Arab nationalist voice in the 1950s and 1960s was dealt a dramatic setback with Egypt's defeat at the hands of Israel in the 1967 war and later with the subsequent peace treaty with Israel at Camp David in 1978 in which it withdrew from any further "struggle" for Palestine. Another 30 years passed under the stultifying and passive rule of Husni Mubarak in which Egypt largely abandoned even the pretense to a regional leadership role. Egypt's claim to regional and global leadership through Arab nationalism had become a thing of the past. Three competitors remained as claimants for leadership of the Arab nationalist tradition: Damascus under the Ba'th regime of the Asads, Libya under Qadhafi, and Iraq under several nationalist leaders culminating in Saddam Hussein's Ba'th regime. All three were harshly autocratic and hardly represented ideal states to the region.

This was the Arab context in which Turkey's vigorous new policies under the AKP in 2003 began to find positive response among the people of the Arab world; the region had been starved for a voice that reflected some of the Arab public's earlier and deeper aspirations for genuine sovereignty free of western domination, a bolder voice, regaining of national dignity and greater ability to force Israel into accepting an honorable settlement for the Palestinians. The fall of Mubarak in 2011 galvanized the Egyptian scene, and it appeared for a while that, under new and popularly elected leadership of the Muslim Brotherhood in 2012, Egypt was set to re-emerge as a significant, more confident and autonomous player in the Middle East—one in which Turkey would no longer be the sole activist. But with the overthrow of legitimate governance in Egypt in 2013, the return of military-dominated government heralded a return to the authoritarian features of the Mubarak era—or worse—and probably to an inward, self-consumed Egypt once again. It remains to be seen whether Egypt is ready and capable of resuming any kind of Arab leadership role on the international stage that its population had hoped for; the new regime seems to have no coherent ideological vision of its own other than establishing a firm military grip on power.

Egyptian ties with Turkey go back a long way. Egyptian political and military culture has been considerably influenced by Turkish-speaking peoples for nearly 800 years, creating a special relationship—not always cordial—between Istanbul and Cairo. The dominant ruling class of the powerful Mamluk Empire based in Cairo in the 13th and 14th centuries was drawn from a Turkic-speaking "slave" or soldier class. Egypt was a key element of the Turkish Ottoman Empire in the Arab world; Egyptian names, elitist families, Egyptian architecture, and even Egyptian colloquial speech still bear signs of centuries of Turkish influence.

But with the nascent ideology of Arab nationalism in the 20th century both Turks and Arabs sought to create new nationalist narratives for themselves, each one quite critical of the other. During the height of the Cold War period the two countries diverged further when Turkish policy was under heavy NATO influence while Egypt was a client state of the Soviet Union until the mid-1970s—Syria and Iraq for a longer period.

The AKP achieved great popularity in Egypt, particularly after Mubarak's fall: in a Gallup poll of January 2012, 60 percent of the Egyptian public saw closer relations with Turkey as "a good thing"; 41 percent said the same of ties with Iran, while only 28 percent desired better relations with the US.[1] The dynamic and independent-minded policies of the AKP represented a new regional force and gained respect in global councils; it had a flourishing economy, spoke up for Palestinian rights (in a way that Mubarak never dared do), sought to mediate between Israel and Palestinian Hamas, and demonstrated its independence in being able to reject American pressures when needed in the name of its own national interests. Turkish "soft-culture," including Turkish-made TV soap operas dubbed into Arabic, was an immensely popular export item in Egypt.

Just before demonstrations began against President Mubarak in the spring of 2011, Turkish Prime Minister Erdoğan was the first to unequivocally call for him to step down, employing memorable language replete with Islamic images:

> From here, I would like to make a very sincere suggestion to Egyptian President Mr. Husni Mubarak and caution him: We are human beings. We are mortal. We are not immortal. We will all die and be questioned for what we have done in our lives. As Muslims, we will all end up in two-cubic meter holes. ... What is immortal is the legacy we leave behind; what is important is to be remembered with respect; it is to be remembered with a blessing. We exist for the people. We fulfill our duties for our people. When the imam comes to us as we die, he will not address us as the president, as the head of state, as the prime minister, or as the minister.
>
> I am now talking to the trillionaires: the imam will not address you as trillionaires. He will address us all as simple men or women. What will depart with you will only be the shroud. Nothing else. Therefore we must know the value of that shroud; we must listen to the voice of our conscience and to the voice of our people; we must be ready either for our people's prayers or for their curses. Therefore, I say that you must listen, and we must listen, to the people's outcry, to their extremely humanitarian demands. Meet the people's desire for change with no hesitation.
>
> I am saying this clearly: You must be the first to take a step for Egypt's peace, security, and stability, without allowing exploiters, dirty circles, and circles that have dark scenarios over Egypt to take initiative. Take steps that will satisfy the people.... In our world today, freedoms can no longer be postponed or ignored.

Erdoğan's dramatic appeal to Mubarak was the first such clear public call by any foreign leader urging him to step down. Turkey up to that time had not enjoyed particularly good relations with Mubarak who suspected that Turkey nourished ambitions in the region that could eclipse Egypt. Above all, he was angered by the AKP's good ties with the Egyptian Muslim Brotherhood, Mubarak's primary domestic opposition.

The subsequent fate of the "Egyptian Revolution" underwent three distinct and different phases: the post-Mubarak military interregnum before the presidential elections of 2012; the first freely elected presidency in Egyptian history; and then a coup by the Egyptian military one year later that destroyed the legitimate foundation of new Egyptian governance, forcibly removed the Muslim Brotherhood government from power, arrested its leadership and over 2,000 of its members, closed down its social programs, banned it from the new political order and placed its leaders on trial for terrorism, treason and espionage, and officially declared the Brotherhood a "terrorist organization." Saud Arabia quickly followed suit with a similar declaration.

From Mubarak to Muslim Brotherhood to Mubarak Regime Redux

Mubarak's fall was followed by an interregnum under military supervision; in a chaotic transitional period a full range of competing political forces was unleashed—the Brotherhood, the ultra-conservative Salafists, nationalists, liberals, and the powerful "dregs" or "losers" (*fulul*) of the old Mubarak regime. The military itself proved inept in this period and uncertain about how to control the new forces on the scene beyond preservation of its own fiefdoms and privileges, and especially its massive holdings in the economic sector.

Stage two began with the first free presidential elections in over four millennia of Egyptian history in May-June 2012. The Brotherhood itself found difficulty in coming up with a candidate who met all legal requirements, finally emerging with its third choice, a dark horse, Muhammad Mursi, who went on to win a clear but narrow majority to become president. Almost no members of the Muslim Brotherhood had previous experience in governance—in sharp distinction to Turkey where the key members of the AKP had successfully fulfilled roles of leadership in municipal politics or governance in its predecessor parties. The Algerian Islamist FIS party—similarly denied the fruits of an impending election victory by the military in 1991—had also fielded many candidates with successful municipal experience.

The election of a president from the Muslim Brotherhood in Egypt marked a critical milestone in the evolution of political Islam in the Middle East. An earlier milestone, as we have seen, was the ascension of the AKP as an Islamist-rooted party to power in Turkey. When the day comes, as it may soon, that the AKP is voted out of power, there is no doubt that it will turn over the reins of governance. At that point Turkey will have completed the full political cycle: the ascension of Islamists into power by democratic means, their tenure as a ruling party, and their eventual departure by the same means. Such a cycle exemplifies the first *normalization of political Islam* in the Middle Eastern political development, a learning process for Islamists as well as society. Egypt had now begun that process, on the heels of Turkey and Tunisia. It required the Brotherhood to put to the test its longtime slogan— "Islam is the solution"—and force it to develop concrete and successful policies or be voted out of power by a disappointed public at the end of its term.

But the election of a Brotherhood candidate to the presidency frustrated many other elements who participated in the public revolt against Mubarak— liberals, democrats, nationalists, minorities, many of whom had an exaggerated sense of their own strength. Liberals in particular had been encouraged by superficial western press coverage that mainly saw youths twittering on social media as the unstoppable future of the country. As the Brotherhood moved to consolidate its position within the limited confines of its electoral mandate, it ran into immediate opposition from a diverse coalition of secularists, liberals, Salafis, youth, religious minorities, the military itself, and powerful elements of the former regime that had been deposed. The Brotherhood furthermore acted as if it had full mandate to rule as it saw fit, and treated opposition elements highhandedly. Soon public disorders and demonstrations of dissatisfaction from the former anti-Mubarak activists appeared back on the streets and were openly promoted and orchestrated by the military itself. By mid-2013 it grew clear that some of the anti-Brotherhood forces in Egypt were willing to engage in violence and sabotage in the name of creating sufficient chaos to induce a military takeover and dislodge the Brotherhood-dominated government. The process that led to the coup in Egypt resembled the techniques of classic buildup to military takeover as practiced by the Turkish military on numerous occasions. In the end the elements of disappointed or hostile opposition from numerous sides of the Egyptian political spectrum reached a high enough level that the military felt it had a mandate to terminate the Brotherhood's government well short of its constitutional term of office.

Worryingly, liberals themselves seemed unabashed in short-circuiting due process by calling for a coup. In justifying their support of extra-legal means to overthrow the Brotherhood, liberals argued that "political Islam" is by definition a failed project, that it can never succeed, that it represents a dangerous and fruitless experiment and should never even be given the chance to be put to the test. Their argument is that, by its very nature, political Islam is doctrinaire; it is inflexible because principles "received from God" are immutable and cannot be altered; since political Islam claims possession of the absolute truth it is therefore inaccessible to compromise or change; it will seek to impose Islamic law on everyone; and it is inherently undemocratic since its source of legislation and power is "God-given" rather than based on the will of the people. In practice, the argument goes, Islamist movements are intolerant, authoritarian, rigid, unable to change, often violent and bloody, and therefore must be excluded from power, by force if necessary.

These arguments indeed do identify some legitimate concerns with the issues of mixing religious with political power. They also characterize, in part, some of the problems of the Brotherhood and its structure and organization that render it less flexible. These arguments, however, are in part based on a vision of Islam (and religion in general) that is itself fixed, inflexible, embedded in a characterization of religious essence, a *theoretical* vision of political Islam rather than one based on observation and practice. In daily reality the practice of Islam, including in politics, reflects the diversity of human character and individual politicians, and demonstrates all the variables created by time, place, circumstance and personality. The practice of Islam, even in politics, is far from immutable. Reality becomes far more complex than either the Islamists or their enemies are willing to concede. The Brotherhood, for all its mistakes, demonstrated much pragmatism and flexibility in dealing with many of the new political realities of the country in which religion itself was rarely invoked in essentially a struggle for power.

The Brotherhood's critics raised some legitimate concerns. For example, Mursi was elected as a member of the newly-founded Freedom and Justice Party (FJP— reminiscent of the Justice and Development party in Turkey, AKP)—the party indeed could never have been founded as long as Mubarak was in power. The problem was that the distinction between the party and the ruling council of the Brotherhood was not clearly delineated. People voting for the FJP as a party did not necessarily want to vote for the Brotherhood as such. The AKP, for example, is entirely autonomous and tied to no religious movement or structure. Many felt that Mursi took his orders from the leadership of the Brotherhood rather than acting as an independent president. That nexus between the party and the movement would inevitably have come under pressure with time.

How much would the Brotherhood change under the new conditions as a player in democratic politics and the allure of electoral process? Good question, but the same arguments apply to almost *any* political movement that is driven by principles and ideology: doctrinaire communism, socialism, or free-market true-believers. What compromises will it make? And what guarantees are there that any party will not proceed to establish a new dictatorship; and, indeed, that is precisely what the old guard of Mubarak proceeded to do after overthrowing Mursi.

Assessments of the Mursi government are highly polarized by their respective partisans inside and outside of Egypt. The first reality is that the objective conditions confronting Mursi in Egypt would have daunted any newly elected leader. Egypt with all its disparate elements was feeling its way through a chaotic political environment of transition for which there was no precedent. Competing national forces sought to manipulate, contest and establish favorable new ground rules for themselves in a desperate attempt to gain and hold elements of power within the state—and all this within a system whose very rules were being written as they went along. The Brotherhood, having been suppressed, oppressed, and largely excluded from the political order for nearly a century, was determined not to let the hard-won victory slip from its hands; it therefore sought to amass as much institutional power as it could by way of insurance against hostile opposition. (In the end its fears became perhaps a self-fulfilling prophesy.) Mursi took his 51 percent presidential victory as license to run the country as he saw fit with only limited inclusion within his government of other national political forces (who were mainly hostile to it.) He sought to place the Brotherhood's imprint on as many institutions as he could.

Yet Mursi's control in the end was really quite limited: most of the power institutions of the state still remained in the hands of elements of the former Mubarak regime: the military, the judiciary, internal security, intelligence, and police. These forces were determined to break the Brotherhood and prevent it from controlling the state's institutions and policies. Mursi faced daunting economic and social problems—unemployment, decaying infrastructure, poor social services—that were the legacy of the longtime economic failings of the Mubarak regime. The bleak scene was further exacerbated by the year and a half of political chaos preceding elections which effectively destroyed tourism, slashed the inflow of foreign exchange, discouraged foreign investment, and damaged the prospects for foreign aid from forces, institutions and states that did not wish Mursi well. As the dean of American scholars on Islam, John Esposito, pointed out,

> The international community—the US, IMF, a variety of European countries, Saudi Arabia, and the UAE—were all lukewarm at best and aggressively obstructionist at worst in assisting the Mursi government

to address the daunting challenge of an inherited failed economy and high unemployment. Yet within days after the coup, Saudi and the UAE were quick to promise billions of dollars in aid."[2]

A variety of domestic opposition forces had consulted with military leaders as early as seven months before the coup on how to remove Mursi from power.[3] A large cross section of the opposition was determined to bring Mursi down by any means as soon as possible. Although Mursi treated it with kid gloves, the military was determined that no civilian leadership should threaten its power position in the "deep state." Mursi also handled issues relating to Israel with extreme caution and deference to the reality of US preferences and existing treaties. While often imperious in his determination not to be squeezed out of power, Mursi can hardly be described as radical. Too late, he sought greater inclusion of rival political forces in government at the point when those opposition forces were determined to weaken him by isolating him and refusing to help broaden his political base. Unfortunately for him, Mursi made numerous policy mistakes which facilitated the military's task in crafting the preconditions for a military coup against his government. Extremism, however, is not one of the credible charges against him. In the face of large—and heavily orchestrated—demonstrations against Mursi, the military demanded he step down. Mursi offered to further broaden the ruling coalition, but refused to step down as the legitimately elected president of the country. The military was in no mood for compromise and skillfully manipulated conditions for an extra-legal coup.

One of the reasons the previous Mubarak regime was so highly regarded in the US was his willingness to pursue policies in the US interest. Yet these policies did not reflect Egyptian or Arab public opinion and they still do not today. After the fall of Mubarak and the major shifts underway in global geopolitics it may be difficult for future Egyptian rulers to pursue quite the same Mubarak-style foreign policies of the past. Even before Mursi was elected, ties with Israel immediately cooled. The new military regime itself had not prevented anti-Israeli rioters from storming the Israeli Embassy in Cairo in September 2011, and Egypt even then suggested that its peace treaty with Israel must be a two-way street that requires equal efforts from Israel to alleviate Palestinian suffering and to create a Palestinian state. Cairo cancelled a significant natural-gas agreement with Israel—all before the Brotherhood came to power. The Muslim Brotherhood was initially ambiguous in its statements about possibly putting the Camp David peace treaty with Israel to a referendum; any referendum would likely reflect popular Egyptian belief that Israel has exploited the treaty to gain time to expand settlements in the occupied territories, and to sideline Egypt in an endless and meaningless US-managed "peace process."

Egyptians still seek leadership to bring resolution to the Arab and Palestinian issue, and so far have had to look abroad—Russia, the UN, or the EU, or even Erdoğan—rather than to any existing Egyptian or Arab leaders in the hope of change in dynamics. When, for example, Israeli forces killed 11 Turks at sea on the humanitarian flotilla mission to Gaza in 2011, Turkey expelled the Israeli ambassador and demanded—and eventually received—an apology. But when Israeli forces killed five Egyptian soldiers by error on the Sinai border, Egypt took no diplomatic action against Israel. Timidity and absence of vision in foreign policy towards the whole Arab world's future will deprive Egypt from any role of leadership in the region.

Even under the new military-dominated government, Egypt will still be preoccupied with a complex set of domestic challenges: seeking to define the power of the military, establishing the nature of elections to come, drafting a new constitution, defining the role (if any) of the Islamist parties in politics, and dealing with labor and social welfare problems, unemployment, education, a shrinking economy, plunging economic investment, and youth discontent. Egypt's GDP was US$256.7 billion in 2012 and falling while its credit ratings also plunged. According to the World Bank, Egyptian "economic growth remains weak, with a high fiscal deficit and gross public debt (domestic and external) rising to nearly 100 percent of GDP at end-June 2013. Low growth rates pose a danger to mounting social frustrations, as they will not suffice to deliver the needed jobs and opportunities."[4] All of this requires fundamental shifts in political infrastructure and a new political psychology.

The Brotherhood at present is legally excluded from the Egyptian political scene under new military rule. But it must itself undergo profound introspection and change to adapt to a new Egypt, including the inclusion of younger generations in leadership positions, a move away from a hierarchical and ageing leadership, and adoption of new political doctrines that are more fully inclusive of the population at large, including minorities. This will be a formidable task when the Brotherhood itself is now an illegal organization. The primary question is how long will Egypt remain *hors de combat*, distracted and out of the game, ineffective in influencing the direction of Arab politics?

A prominent "leftist-nationalist-Islamist" commentator, Talal Salman commented

> Egypt must also have a competent leadership made up of qualified people who will put forth a national plan that the Egyptians would support but that also would inspire the Arabs in other countries. Egypt should not care only about itself because isolationism will kill

the Egyptian revolution. In the 1950s, when all the Arabs looked to Egypt for leadership, Egypt was neither greater nor militarily stronger than it is today. Back then, the Arabs looked toward Egypt because they lacked leadership at home. So the Arabs responded to Egypt's call and moved to support the Egyptian revolution. Today, the Arabs are again without leadership and they are once again looking toward Egypt to supply it.[5]

Egypt living under military rule and Saudi subventions is unlikely to supply that leadership. The primary foreign policy questions for Egypt are likely to remain Palestine, Israel, Syria's raging civil conflict, chaos in Libya, an Iraq seeking a new place in the region, and relations with a prickly Sudan. Earlier, during Erdoğan's visit to Cairo in October 2011, Egypt and Turkey had signed a new strategic agreement that had potentially significant implications for the shape of a future Middle East; less than two years later and in the aftermath of Erdoğan's outspoken hostility to the July 2013 military coup, it is questionable whether any meaningful strategic relationship between Turkey and Egypt can continue. But, if suspicions and a sense of rivalry could be overcome, a combination of Egypt and Turkey could create a powerful new force in the region in the economic, political, diplomatic, and military spheres. The Turkish experience in these areas could offer some avenues of development to Cairo. Such cooperation is unlikely however, given Turkey's commitment to democratization, defense of the legitimacy of the Brotherhood, and Cairo's open and defiant capture by military rule and denunciation of Turkey.

Egyptian Islamists can of course be expected to generally sympathize with Turkey's policies; but a leading *populist leftist-nationalist* and Nasserist figure, Hamdin Sabahi, a candidate for the presidency in 2012, also strongly supported closer Egyptian ties with Turkey—as well as with Iran: "Egypt is in need of an independent president that doesn't make his decisions based on the US or Israel... We also need to form an Arab triangle with Turkey and Iran. In the past, we have fought with Turkey and Iran, because we were acting as mediators for Israel and the US."[6] In contrast, one of the candidates for the presidency in Egypt in 2012, Egyptian secular nationalist Amr Musa (and former Mubarak official), declared in a political campaign speech that the "Arab Middle East will not be run by Iran or Turkey." He did not mention Saudi Arabia or the US.

The Counterrevolutionary Coup

Just as Erdoğan was virtually the sole major leader in the world to call upon Mubarak to step down, Turkey was one of the few credible countries to speak out immediately and explicitly against the military coup. Washington and the

EU, for example, dithered and proved unwilling to describe the overthrow of a legally constituted government as a coup. If Washington had so declared it, it would have been compelled by law to cut off military aid to Egypt, an act which would have cost it leverage. Most US commentary did not seem displeased at the extra-legal removal of the Brotherhood from power, even though it had so far proved much less problematic in power than the US had feared. Washington only expressed gentle pro forma hopes for a return to democratic practice and briefly suspended military aid.

Ankara's stand, however, was more principled. It had regularly supported evolution towards greater democracy in the Middle East. Furthermore, the Egyptian coup scenario sent chills down the AKP spine since it was a scene right out of Turkey's own modern history: four Turkish military interventions over a 40-year period, each time removing legally elected governments. As Prime Minister Erdoğan commented on the western response to the coup against Mursi,

> Isn't the West [supposed to be] siding with democracy and making efforts to implement democracy in countries? This is a test of sincerity and the West failed the test again. There is no such thing as a 'democratic coup'. ...You rule the country for 30-40 years with a single party but then you can't tolerate a president elected freely. It is against democracy.

He also struck out against the EU that has constantly made Turkish entry into the EU conditional upon the establishment of legitimate, fully civilian government in Turkey:

> The European Union disregarded its own values once again by not calling the army's coup a coup... Mursi made mistakes; he can make mistakes. Is there anyone who did not make any mistake? ...Every military coup...took Turkey 10 years back in time... Egyptians should read Turkish history well.[7]

Erdoğan burnt bridges further in an emotional attack upon the respected Grand Shaykh of Al-Azhar University, a major center of Islamic theology, by saying that "history would curse him" for his support of the coup. He also decried "the massacre of innocent Muslims" [not "citizens"] in the government attack against Brotherhood supporters in Rabi'a Square that killed over 150 people. Iran, on the other hand, more cautiously described the Egyptian coup a "cause for concern" although the new Egyptian military regime immediately criticized Tehran for interference in its internal affairs. Ankara had also hoped that the Mursi government would succeed early on in retiring the military from a dominant political role in Egypt but such an expectation was wildly unrealistic. Foreign Minister Ahmet Davutoğlu nonetheless quickly characterized the course of Egyptian events in sweeping conceptual terms [italics are mine]:

> The 25th of January Revolution in Egypt [overthrowing Mubarak] is the first great revolution of the 21st century... [But] no matter what the reason is, overthrowing through illegitimate means [the Mursi] government which took office through *democratic* elections and, what is more, overthrowing it by *a military coup is unacceptable*... It is essential ...to preserve the achievements of the 25th of January Revolution, not only for Egypt but also for the future of the region...*As a universal principle*, we have supported the demands of the brotherly peoples of the Middle East for a democracy protecting human dignity and... the rule of law and open and transparent elections...We have never discriminated against any country, any ethnicity or any sect, and we never will.[8]

Erdoğan's critics at home claim his policies made Turkey the big loser in the Egyptian military coup. Indeed, the dominant forces of the new Egyptian regime—the military, police, intelligence organizations, the courts, members of the old regime, Salafists and liberals—dropped all further expression of admiration for the Turkish model; for them it now signifies toleration for mainstreaming Islamist parties to come to power via democratic means. As the Brotherhood everywhere became the target of vituperation by both Egypt and Saudi Arabia, Turkey fell under greater suspicion for its ties with Muslim Brotherhood elements in the Syrian opposition and with Hamas (in Gaza). Saudi King Abdullah, meeting with the Egyptian head of state in October 2013, in quite extreme language accused the Brotherhood of "terrorism, delusion and sedition."

On the other hand, Turkey may well gain over the longer run from its position of principle. Those in the region who believe in the right of Islamists to compete in elections, to win or lose, will find a champion in Turkey in this regard. Interestingly, Iran took a similar position on the Egyptian military coup: far from denouncing the Muslim Brotherhood as a "Sunni organization," Iran has always been quite comfortable with the Brotherhood as representing an Islamic voice independent of the West; Tehran maintained long and close ties with Palestinian (Muslim Brotherhood) Hamas until Hamas denounced Asad in the Syria civil war.

Eventually, of course, Erdoğan and Davutoğlu are pragmatic enough to recognize the need to accept the coup in Cairo as a fait accompli. Over the longer run, however, no one believes that military rule represents the longer-range future of Egypt, or that the Brotherhood is finished. Indeed, overthrow by force of the legitimate Brotherhood government over the long run may well strengthen sympathy for it among many in Egypt and outside.

Furthermore, the Brotherhood may now feel spared of the need to face its own failures and undertake the required soul-searching. It can rightfully claim that it was victimized, and, as in Algeria, illegally denied the fruits of its election victory. It will raise questions among younger Brotherhood members and other Islamists as to whether the legal electoral path to power is anything more than an illusion and therefore turn to extralegal or violent means. No serious observer of the Middle East can believe that Islamism is now "dead," as some rushed to proclaim; this is merely the beginning of another round in a long contest in which the Brotherhood may for the time being gain more politically from being victimized than it might have from failing in the risky game of governing. It will unquestionably be forced to evolve pragmatically in the process as well.

The Cairo events interestingly now place Turkey and Iran in the same camp on Egyptian events (although not aligned with each other), while Cairo, Riyadh, and the UAE stand as the centers of counter-revolution and war against moderate Islamists—along with most Gulf states and Arab monarchies and even the Algerian military regime.

Whither Egypt?

A major question mark is where Egypt is going: can the military-dominated regime construct a new vision, an ideology designed to strengthen its moral and ideological prestige in Egypt and outside? Observers have pointed out an astonishing disconnect between General 'Abd-al-Fattah al-Sisi as the new head of the Egyptian military regime and his writings as a colonel during training at the US War College in 2006 when he demonstrated considerable Islamic leanings. At that time he identified the Palestinian problem as central to the emotional heart of the Arab, and even to the Muslim, world. As longtime Egyptian specialist Robert Springborg suggested:

> To judge from the ideas about governance that he put forward in his thesis, Sisi might see himself less as a custodian of Egypt's democratic future than as an Egyptian version of Muhammed Zia ul-Haq, the Pakistani general who seized power in 1977 and set about to "Islamicize" state and society in Pakistan.
>
> In his thesis Sisi argued that "for democracy to be successful in the Middle East," it must show "respect to the religious nature of the culture" and seek "public support from religious leaders [who] can help build strong support for the establishment of democratic systems." ... Secularism, according to Sisi, "is unlikely to be favorably received by the vast majority of Middle Easterners, who are devout followers of the Islamic faith." He condemns governments that "tend toward secular rule," because they "disenfranchise large segments of

the population who believe religion should not be excluded from government," and because "they often send religious leaders to prison." …"Democracy cannot be understood in the Middle East without an understanding of the concept of the Caliphate."[9]

Sisi's ideas may have shifted now that he has come to power and ordered the sweeping arrests of Brotherhood leaders following the massacre of many of its followers. But interestingly the "old" Sisi reflects the abiding concept of the central place of the caliphate, at least as a Muslim *ideal* of unity and social justice. Time will reveal how much Sisi will work for a fusion of Islamic ideas along with Egyptian nationalism—in theory they are not incompatible. In the end however, *Sisi wants Islam but without the political power of the Brotherhood,* and he wants to keep Islam under tight state control. Secularists will be uncomfortable even with this formula. Interestingly, it is the AKP in Turkey that has actually achieved some version of this fusion of nationalism, secularism, democracy and Islamic values. But Sisi can't look to Turkey as long as Turkey embraces the Brotherhood and champions democracy.

While Sisi in 2006 emphasized the existing symbolic weight of the caliphate, we find the Saudi-controlled press counter-intuitively fulminating about just such a concept as a point of attack against the Brotherhood. An editorial in the Saudi-controlled *Asharq al-Awsat* at the outset of the Mursi government denounced it for dangerously working to reestablish the caliphate as the main goal of the Brotherhood everywhere and the international threat that this poses.[10] Thus does the ultra-orthodox Wahhabi-Salafi state call the Brotherhood kettle black.

Egypt's future is not just determined by the military of course. The decisions the Brotherhood itself takes over the longer run will also have much impact. Will it undertake long-term violent action against the government? Or will it submissively seek to be readmitted to the circles of power? The Brotherhood will likely undergo considerable inward searching before a new policy emerges. It may well divide over issues of future policy. Fahmi al-Huwaydi, a leading Egyptian intellectual affiliated with the Brotherhood, suggested that, while acknowledging the undemocratic nature of the military coup, the Brotherhood must examine and acknowledge its own errors as the prerequisite for further political development. In Turkey political setbacks to successive earlier Islamist parties were indeed part of the forge from which the modern AKP emerged, each time refining its message more closely to electoral reality. There is no reason to believe that the Brotherhood will not follow something of this same path with time, generational change and perhaps splits within the movement. Indeed, that is one of the points of the democratic process: it creates the pressures that fashion the policies of all ideological parties—witness its mellowing impact on the Labor Party in the UK after being voted out of power for nearly 20 years until 1997, or on the radical right Tea Party movement within the Republican Party in the US which is beginning to face hostile demographic realities.

Differences between Egypt and Turkish Environment

No two societies are identical; solutions for one state do not necessarily directly apply to another. To what extent can the Turkish—and AKP—experience hold relevance for Egyptians?

First is the question of democratic experience. The firm establishment of democratic institutions and free and fair elections in Turkey are the fruit of democratic practice for over half a century—and four "corrective" coups by the military. Nonetheless the history of the Turkish republic demonstrates a gradual rollback of military interference in governance. By 2011 the Turkish military had been—seemingly decisively—expelled from domestic politics and back to the barracks, the culmination of some 60 years of effort and changing times.

In Egypt since 1958 the military has never been seriously challenged by civilian authority; all of its presidents came out of the military. Now, after the 2013 coup the military may be more transparently in control than any time in 50 years. At the same time, in the wake of the anti-Mubarak revolution, Egyptian civilian politicians have acquired a greater taste for challenging the military. Although a grand coalition of the old regime, secularists, nationalists, liberals, the military, police, security services, Christians and radical Islamists did come together to drive the Brotherhood from power illegally, many elements of this coalition, particularly the liberals, are already growing disillusioned with their choice as the military regime moves against all political opposition to the government. Most of these elements were not so much bitter enemies of the Brotherhood as they were bitter that each of their groups had done so poorly in the elections while the Brotherhood succeeded; they furthermore feared the Brotherhood would represent the new face of Egyptian authoritarianism. Instead that new face now turns out to be (secular?)-military.

Any downgrade of the role of the military can only take place when there is strong and active public resistance to military power in governance, supported by credible and legitimate public institutions to support democracy. In Turkey it took a powerful combination of Islamists, middle class, *and* liberals to finally banish the military from politics. In Egypt, authoritarian rule had long prevented such liberal institutions from emerging. It will be hard for Egypt to leapfrog such political and societal experience in a short period of time to attain the Turkish stage of political development. But it does suggest that the liberals could ironically come to find an ally in the Brotherhood against the military in the future, particularly if the Brotherhood shows signs of learning from its mistakes.

But in comparing the Egyptian and Turkish cases, we need note other key factors that contributed to the slow rollback of the Turkish military that are missing in Egypt. First, in Turkey the process was long—60 years. Second, Turkey benefitted from its membership in NATO where the accepted political ethos opposed a military role in politics—an influence lacking in Egypt. At that time the desire of most of Turkey's population to join the European Union meant that the EU could exert reformist pressures upon Turkey that included disallowing a political role for the military. Finally, the growing participation and democratization of the Turkish social order brought a new generation and class of Turkish voters onto the scene that was increasingly uncomfortable with overt military interference against governments they themselves had elected.

More than just politics are at issue; economic interests too come into play. The Egyptian military has built a powerful economic stake in the country. It controls upwards of 40 percent of the Egyptian economy with its ownership of key industries, agricultural institutions and other projects. As the *New York Times* reported,

> The Egyptian military defends the country, but it also runs day care centers and beach resorts. Its divisions make television sets, jeeps, washing machines, wooden furniture and olive oil, as well as bottled water under a brand reportedly named after a general's daughter, Safi. The brand is owned by Egypt's military, which operates a wide variety of businesses. From this vast web of businesses, the military pays no taxes, employs conscripted labor, buys public land on favorable terms and discloses nothing to Parliament or the public.[11]

Military control of such a large segment of the Egyptian economy is not about to disappear. Even in Turkey the military share in the economy is still high, however, despite its reduced political role.

> Already boasting of its fame as the most privileged army in the world with far-reaching connections in the economy, the TSK [Turkish Armed Forces] is running a center that commands economic assets amounting to US$50 billion. The Turkish Armed Forces Assistance Center (OYAK) has now grown into a giant holding incorporating 60 companies and affiliates. The areas in which these companies operate are incredibly diverse and include automobiles, cement, iron and steel, finance, energy, mining, agricultural chemicals, foodstuffs, construction, transportation and logistics, private security and

information technology. OYAK even has investments abroad,
including cement plants in Romania and Cyprus and two companies in
Spain and the Netherlands.

Obviously Turkish military influence in the economy is significant, even if it is
run for the benefit of its members. But, in grand perspective, there is no
absolute purity in this regard. There are few major states in the world where
some kind of military-industrial complex does not play a major political and
economic role, even when not overt. Such a role may be more obvious and
explicitly "corrupt" when it goes into the pockets of military members in
developing societies; in western societies the cozy relationship between the
state and the military-industrial complex is more institutionalized and, even if
not technically illegal, can be similarly corrupting, corrosive to the democratic
process, and costly and damaging in its influence upon foreign and domestic
policies.

Worse, in developing countries, military and state control of the economy
tends to stifle the emergence of an independent entrepreneurial class; it was
the gradual emergence of just such a class that provided the backbone for the
new democratic forces in Turkey. In fact, some observers believe that the
Islamists in Egypt cannot anytime soon emulate the Turkish Islamists who
evolved into the highly pragmatic AKP. Dr. Şebnem Gümüşçü, for example,
argues that it was the major economic opening of the Turkish economy under
President Özal starting in the 1980s that led to "facilitating the growth of a
strong devout bourgeoisie with vested interests in liberalism and democracy
and increasing its power within the broader Islamist constituency. ... In
Egypt, in contrast, the way the state-implemented economic reform prevented
the formation of a strong and independent devout bourgeoisie that could be
assertive in political Islam."[12]

In Egypt, Gümüşçü argues, the absence of a liberal free market system
deprived Islamists of buying into the system and thus they remain trapped in a
strictly *political/ideological approach* to Islam via politics that is still essentially
statist in its instincts. In this view then, Egyptian Islamists are thus less likely
to evolve quickly in a liberal direction in keeping with a secular democratic
order, and will be forced to operate within the political/ideological part of the
spectrum to achieve power again—thus missing the opportunity to evolve in
the same way as did the AKP. Note how Hizmet too emerged out of a
burgeoning new pious bourgeoisie. Finally, the experience of Islamists in
Turkey in running major municipalities imposed an important appreciation of
pragmatism and administrative expertise upon AKP politicians that Egyptian
Islamists lacked.

Working towards secularism is also a key issue. During Erdoğan's trip to Egypt in September 2011 he received a huge public acclamation, but he also took the occasion to deliver an unexpected message to an audience filled with Islamists; he advised Egyptians that they

> should not be afraid of secularism....The Turkish state in its core is a state of freedoms and secularism. The world is changing to a system where the will of the people will rule—why should the Europeans and the Americans be the only ones to live with dignity? Aren't Egyptians and Somalis also entitled to a life of dignity?"[13]

> "I am a non-secular Muslim," [Erdoğan] said, "but I am the prime minister of a secular state and I say, 'I hope there will be a secular state in Egypt.' One must not be afraid of secularism. Egypt will grow in democracy and those called upon to draw up the constitution must understand it must respect all religions, while also keep themselves equidistant from the followers of all religions so that people can live in security."[14]

While the remarks about dignity resonate deeply with a Muslim audience, many Egyptian Islamists were reportedly upset and critical of Erdoğan's endorsement of secularism, despite their admiration for him. Erdoğan defended his position and said later that the term "secularism" was incorrectly translated into an Arabic word (*'ilmaniyya*) that also commonly implies "irreligiosity" which is not what secularism is all about. In making his remark Erdoğan reflected a long-standing debate within Turkey itself about the meaning of secularism. It was the Turkish Kemalists who first imposed the French concept of secularism (*laicité*) which is, in fact, inherently anti-religious and the term has been in bad repute among all Islamists. Turkish Islamists came to realize that secularism should refer to the state being *above* religion, a neutral arbiter among all religious and non-religious communities. Despite AKP support for this understanding of secularism, the concept still disturbs many Islamists in other countries who reject the idea of a neutral state and indeed wish the state to positively promote religion. But the very success of the AKP in office offers valuable experience to the Muslim Brotherhood as they seek to reformulate their ideas in the post-coup environment.

A Saudi human rights activist Dr. Hamad Al-Majid commented:

> This success of Erdoğan's Justice and Development Party (AKP) in Turkey became an inspiration to other political Islam movements, to the extent that the Muslim Brotherhood in Egypt almost replicated the name with its own Freedom and Justice Party (FJP), while Abdelilah Benkirane's Justice and Development Party (PJD) currently heads the Moroccan parliament. However, the Brotherhood has neglected the differences between its own experience and that of Erdoğan's, particularly in terms of gradual progression. The Muslim

Brotherhood's FJP in Egypt, which was formed immediately after the Egyptian popular revolution, entered politics from the top, rather than starting from the grassroots. This is a key difference, and mistake, when compared to Erdoğan's experience.[15]

Turkey glimpsed the prospect of much deeper ties between Turkey and Egypt after the fall of Mubarak. Davutoğlu struck an enthusiastic tone after the visit of the prime minister to Cairo in September 2011, after Mubarak' collapse. He even spoke of establishing an "axis" between Ankara and Cairo, to help bring about a new order and to spread greater democratization.

> This will not be an axis against any other country—not Israel, not Iran, not any other country, but this will be an axis of democracy, real democracy... an axis of democracy of the two biggest nations in our region, from the north to the south, from the Black Sea down to the Nile Valley in Sudan.[16]

That vision obviously died with Egypt's military coup; democracy is hardly in the offing in Egypt for some time to come. Nonetheless, the fall of the Mubarak order had already opened the door to new thinking, including on religion. A group of intellectuals and theologians of the prestigious state religious institution of al-Azhar issued a text shortly after Mubarak's fall entitled "Document for the Renewal of Religious Discourse." The document raised discussion of a range of sensitive religious issues including "rethinking fraternisation between the sexes; opening the doors to women right up to the presidency of the republic, guaranteeing the right of Christians to have access to positions of prestige (even the presidency), purifying and reinterpreting the sayings of the Prophet (the Hadith); bringing people to God through wisdom and thanksgiving and not with the threats" and putting a halt to fundamentalist Wahhabi influences from Saudi Arabia.[17]

Note the parallels between these proposals and many of the issues under review by the Directorate of Religious Affairs (*Diyanet*) in Ankara. While Egyptian intellectuals and religious scholars do not need to visit Turkey to discover such ideas, they are being proposed and implemented more vigorously and publicly in Turkey than in any other Muslim country. It would be naïve to suppose that Egypt will quickly embrace these new approaches, particularly given the strength of the ultra-conservative Salafi forces within Egypt who remain recipients of much Saudi largesse (and benefited from the fall of the Brotherhood.) But the doors have been opened; hopefully a debate will evolve. Even if dramatic change is not immediately forthcoming, it is hard to believe that exchanges between religious figures in Turkey and Egypt will come to an end once Ankara comes to diplomatic terms with the new Egyptian political reality.

The Military and Security Issues

The Egyptian military also heads the powerful General Intelligence Service which has always kept close tabs on all aspects of society. Even civilian elements of the old regime were required to defer to the military on "security issues." The military never yielded control of these "power ministries" to the elected Brotherhood government. Today the threat *du jour* in Egypt is identified as the "terrorist" Muslim Brotherhood itself, while the military is the "guardian of the state" against it. The military has employed astonishingly intemperate language against the Brotherhood, perhaps the most vehement in Egyptian history, referring to the need to "cleanse Egypt" of "vermin."

Saudi Arabia is in full agreement. But one may ask how long the Egyptian military leadership will be able to exclude the Brotherhood, now officially banned, from a role in politics given its longtime continuing prominence within Egyptian society. Egypt for the first time in its history did freely elect a president, like him or not, and the pressure will be to return to such a procedure. Nothing can be quite the same again, including the Brotherhood. The public is better informed than ever before and has now tasted participation in street politics as well as in electoral politics. How long will the "liberals" in Egyptian politics—their ideology based partly on political ideals, partly on lifestyle preferences—prefer to seek allies in an authoritarian military than among the anti-military Brotherhood? And how long will the Salafis be able to coexist with the military as well? The military is blunt about its priorities; retired major general Abdel-Rafia Darwish said it all when he noted that the "reshuffling of the National Defense Council prevents the president from interfering in military affairs. 'What if the president is a civilian?' he asked. 'He might take a decision that is wrong and that could harm the military.'"[18]

The Struggle for the Arab Identity

Egypt embraces at least three aspects of national identity: Egyptian, Arab, and Islamic. These identities are all present at the popular level, but are also adopted periodically by the state for manipulation. They are not mutually exclusive. The Egyptian identity is a powerful one, given the ancient and distinctive historical and geographical character of the Egyptian state along the Nile; it is the one that the large Coptic Christian minority especially identifies with. But "Egyptianism" has not been a major element in the character of the Egyptian state in the modern era. Egyptian nationalism was usually wrapped up within *Arab nationalist* impulses, particularly under Gamal Abdel Nasser for whom they were nearly indistinguishable. And when Arab nationalism led by

Egypt collapsed in the late 1960s, Islamist ideas took its place, but still maintaining many similar goals.

Despite all the turmoil in Egypt since the fall of Mubarak, a recent professional poll conducted by well-known scholar and polling specialist Shibley Telhami at American University demonstrates that the Islamist and Arab identities still run deep. Significant soundings taken in August 2013, after the overthrow of the Mursi government, indicated that

> First, citizens identify less and less with their countries and identify more and more with Islam and as Arabs. Second, Egyptians see themselves as the most religious people in the world. … Over the past decade, the rise in people identifying primarily as Muslim was not all or even mostly due to expanding Islamist aspirations. Instead, it resulted mainly from declining identification with the state, thanks to government failings on domestic and foreign policy. … When Egyptians are asked which country they would want their own nation to look like, their top choice has been Turkey, a democratic Islamic nation ruled by an Islamist party. And in 2011 and 2012, Egyptians and other Arabs identified Turkish Prime Minister Recep Tayyip Erdogan as the leader they most admired outside their own country.[19]

Yet among the interesting charges leveled by the Egyptian military (and some Egyptian liberals) is that the Brotherhood is "anti-Egyptian," and espouses a "foreign ideology." That despite the fact the Brotherhood first emerged in Egypt and matured in Egypt over nearly a century ago as the center of Brotherhood activities in the Arab region. The military (and many liberals) make the case that the Brotherhood's commitment to Islam runs counter to commitment to Egypt. It is true that some Egyptian Islamists in the past have indeed contemptuously dismissed Egyptian nationalism as an idea, but that was when Egyptian nationalists were in power and oppressing their Islamist rivals. It is otherwise hard to make the case that the Brotherhood is a "traitor" to the Egyptian cause, unless local nationalism and Islamic allegiance are seen as totally contradictory. In Arab history the two have rarely been viewed as incompatible—unless you're fighting over the same presidential chair.

If one belongs to an Egyptian minority, especially a Coptic Christian, the argument does make more sense; Christians fear a strong Islamic identity will weigh more heavily upon them. One such liberal commentator stated that

> Whether entirely fair or not, it is significant that Egyptians came to perceive the Muslim Brotherhood as 'colonisers of Egypt' who want to erase layers of national cultural character and treat Egyptian liberals, Christians, and the non-Brotherhood as 'national minorities'. Minorities, whose presence could be 'tolerated', but whose input should never constitute the core character of the new Egypt. …The Brotherhood's failure to transform itself into a viable political party

was detrimental to its political survival; it was the Freedom and Justice Party as arm of Ikhwan [Brotherhood] and not a genuine political party like AKP [in Turkey].[20]

In Egypt the liberals joined hands with the Islamists to overthrow Mubarak and establish a democracy, yet abandoned the Brotherhood and democracy after one year to join hands with the military. Arab nationalists now may well find themselves joining ranks with the military; they fear the Brotherhood, not because it is religious, but because it has been a *potent rival* to the Arab nationalists whose own star blazed and then burned out four decades ago (although the concept itself never dies.) This complex intertwining dance among ideological forces reveals just how simplistic any "secular versus Islamist" description of Middle East politics is.

As Giuseppe Merone points out, neither the Islamists nor the nationalists support a program that the West will be comfortable with. Secularists are more inclined towards the nationalists and likely have a more radical domestic agenda with greater "leftist" character. Both absurdly suspect the Islamists of carrying out a hidden "western agenda."[21]

What is the future role of Egypt in the Middle East today? I suggest a few more enduring characteristics that will likely influence the future.

• Egypt will be one of the main factors in promoting or hindering the future of change in the Middle East over the next decade. If the Egyptian military is intent on preserving its position in politics and the economy, it will fall strongly under Saudi aegis due to financial dependence upon it. The military under such circumstances will act to suppress demands for bold change and will probably support some kind of regional status quo, perhaps tinged with modest Egyptian nationalism. This is not what the Egyptian or Arab population wants; Egypt will likely remain sidelined from significant regional action, much as it was under Mubarak.

• Neo-Mubarak, or even counter-revolutionary policies will be sharply challenged by both Islamist and Arab nationalist trends. Previously Mubarak and the Saudis prevented either trend from emerging as a force for genuine change. And although each of these trends is a strong rival to the other in one sense, they share elements of revolutionary vision; both look to change in the status quo. Arab nationalist trends often have strong ties to the Arab Left. A neo-Mubarak or Saudi counter-revolutionary policy in Egypt will permit neither. Only Syria under the Asads, and Iraq under Saddam, managed to maintain a revolutionary image in the region while harshly suppressing Islamism. The Saudis, furthermore, face complex problems in supporting radical fundamentalist Salafi forces against the Brotherhood over the longer run: in the end the Salafis too are likely to turn against both the regime and the Saudis, unless bought off.

•   US influence has waned dramatically. Cairo, now under military domination, and has gained major Saudi and Qatari funding of over US$12 billion; these sums now dwarf US subventions of US$1.8 billion, making Cairo financially far less reliant on Washington than in past decades. Cairo has also moved to renew arms deals with Russia; Moscow is likely to play an enhanced role in Egypt.

•   Through the revolution and months of street demonstrations the Egyptian public has become more engaged in genuine popular politics than in decades. Given the lack of public experience in participatory politics, and the absence of functioning democratic institutions, a degree of disorder is inevitable as new and old competing forces sort themselves out on the national scene. It will be harder than before for the military to maintain an iron hand.

•   The Muslim Brotherhood can be suppressed but not eliminated from the political and social scene.

•   Foreign policy, especially of a more radical nature, will probably take a back seat to domestic issues—although political leaders the world over have often used foreign policy adventures to distract its citizens from domestic problems. The most logical foreign adventure would be against Israel, but the US would not permit that, nor would Saudi Arabia. A military adventure to overthrow the longtime Islamist regime in Sudan is a possibility, as is an invasion of eastern Libya. Both are unlikely but not inconceivable.

•   The Egyptian economy will demand priority attention from any future government in stimulating the GDP, creating jobs, raising standards of living, and improving the social infrastructure. Creation of a more open economy—one of the early keys to Turkey's economic success—is a necessary step, but will take time given the hugely statist character of the Egyptian economy. The Brotherhood is open to commercial expertise but has had little opportunity to develop these globalized skills compared to pious Muslim businessmen in Turkey. The Salafis are likely even less skilled in globalized economic affairs.

•   The new military regime has already taken major steps towards unprecedented cooperation with Israel on security issues against jihadi operations in Sinai and in closing logistics tunnels between Egypt and Gaza, where Cairo now joins Israel is seeking to crush Palestinian Hamas. Foreign jihadis are now drawn to Sinai as a place to combat both Israel and a Cairo that is "soft on Israel." Indeed, these radical jihadis equally loathe the

Brotherhood as apostates from "real Islam." While Egyptian and Israeli anti-Islamist policies may coincide, such policies will run strongly counter to Egyptian and Arab public opinion and will further delegitimize Egypt's new regime under military dominance.

• Radical jihadi activity within Egypt is likely to reemerge in a struggle against the military-dominated regime. The younger generation of Islamists in Egypt remains a wild card. Youthful elements within the Brotherhood and the Salafis might be attracted to participate in it. The Brotherhood proper is likely to abstain from participation in violent politics. But the likelihood for greater political violence in Egypt will grow, and the corresponding government suppression of it will call for a tighter police state.

• Egypt is unlikely to return to a meaningful alliance with Washington and will probably oppose US regional interventionism. The US will have extremely limited voice over Egyptian affairs.

• Liberal elements in Egypt will possess only limited influence on the political scene and they will not automatically be pro-western. Turkey may thus represent the most acceptable model of regional "liberal" influence.

• Egypt will likely try to restore some degree of leadership over regional issues but will be ineffective. Iraq historically has often been a rival to Egypt, but now with its Shi'ite-dominated government it has less "Arab credentials" for the moment to pose that challenge. If Iraq remains strongly and unequivocally in a close alliance with Iran, Egypt will see Baghdad—a major former center of pan-Arabism—as a rival or enemy. Syria could prove to be a bone of contention between Iraq and Egypt, in which Ankara's role could provide important balance.

• Egypt will be unlikely to adopt a long-term strongly hostile posture towards Iran—except under Saudi pressure. It may see ties with Iran as a useful balance in Egyptian relations with Riyadh and Baghdad. Egypt has few genuine grounds to be driven by sectarian views.

Meanwhile, the short-term prospects for Egypt are dismal. As Amnesty International reported in early 2014, "The Egyptian authorities are using every resource at their disposal to quash dissent and trample on human rights… Three years on, the demands of the [anti-Mubarak] '25 January Revolution' for dignity and human rights seem further away than ever. Several of its architects are behind bars and repression and impunity are the order of the day."[22]

Egyptians will find little to choose from in the current polarizing atmosphere in which the prospects for political violence loom ever higher on the political horizon.

Turkey and Saudi Arabia may have now come to represent the two competing *ideological polarities* of Middle East politics for the next years to come. This view certainly runs counter to conventional analyses that pose Saudi Arabia and Iran as the deadly rivals. Ironically, both Turkey and Saudi Arabia are the two states with closest ties to the US in the Middle East. How did this situation of polarity come about?

Turkey today represents an ideological and diplomatic activism that supports democratization, moderate and contemporary interpretations of Islam, modernity, globalization, non-sectarianism, the need for evolutionary change, and a preference for diplomatic solutions. Despite hiccups and periodic skirmishes in governance, none of these commitments in Turkey have been seriously overturned. Saudi Arabia on the other hand stands for status quo, a closed traditional society, preservation of monarchy, a radically conservative form of Islam, rabid Sunni sectarianism, opposition to democracy and regional polarity. The two states of Turkey and Saudi Arabia today share little in common except a concern for the future of the *umma*—which they conceive in quite different terms; they also share an interest in strong economic ties and stability in the region. Tensions of a strategic, political, religious, and cultural nature between them cannot be negotiated away, but both states are likely to maintain, rather than break, this uncomfortable relationship due to mutual benefits. We are witnessing perhaps more starkly than ever before a struggle for the future of Muslim politics as well as of political Islam in the Muslim World.

History reveals centuries of tensions in the relations between Turks and bedouin Wahhabi Arabs of the Arabian Peninsula. The challenge began when the Ottoman sultan-caliph conquered Egypt in 1517, thereby falling heir to the coastal lands all along the Red Sea and to the title of Protector of the Holy Places of Mecca and Madina. The Hijaz coast was culturally quite distinct from the austere bedouin desert culture of the Najd, the Arabian interior where the Wahhabi movement set roots. The Hijaz was cosmopolitan, urban, the destination of the globalized Hajj, scene of the annual comings and goings of foreign pilgrims from all over the world to the Holy Places, a commercial hub and the route to "Arabia Felix," Yemen. The Ottomans ruled the Hijaz for some 400 years, but ultra-conservative bedouin Wahhabi forces from the isolated Najdi interior repeatedly attempted to conquer the Hijaz for themselves and drive out Ottoman power, only to be driven back by Ottoman/Egyptian troops—until the final conquest by Wahhabis in 1924. Thus there is a history of contestation between the Najdi Wahhabis, who were never incorporated into the Ottoman Empire, and Turkey, which represented the anti-Wahhabi center of Sunni power in the region. The struggle involved territory, political and religious authority, and theology.

For most of the modern history of Turkey, Kemalist Ankara had scant interest in anything going on in Saudi Arabia, until an expansion of trade relations that blossomed in the 1980s, primarily involving major Turkish construction work in the Peninsula. Saudi Arabia enjoyed a poor reputation in dominant Kemalist circles, standing for everything the Kemalists hated: the quintessential fundamentalist Islamic state, a rejection of secularism, compulsory prayer, the seclusion of women, and the heart of repressive and socially backward Islam. Saudi banks and investments in Turkey were viewed by the government in Ankara with suspicion as possibly providing financial support to Turkish religious groups and "reactionary forces." Saudi tourists in Istanbul, their women entirely shrouded in black, epitomized the Kemalist visions of the reactionary character of Islam. Even for many other Islamists in the world, including the Muslim Brotherhood, Wahhabi Salafism and the Saudi royal family are not models for an Islamic state. But state-to-state relations remained fully correct, and Turks regularly made up the biggest annual contingent to the Hajj—much to the embarrassment of Kemalist diplomats serving in Saudi Arabia in an earlier era. Turkey's current president, Abdullah Gül, however, lived in the kingdom for eight years in the 1980s when he worked for the Islamic Development Bank in Jeddah, and thus has good personal ties to the Kingdom.

Despite Ankara's support for overthrow of old regimes in Tunisia, Libya, Egypt, Yemen and Syria, there were still contradictions in its policies on regime change in the Middle East. Significantly all of these states were republics; they had overthrown monarchy many decades ago. Thus while Davutoğlu called for regional countries to move "with the tide of history," he did not apply this principle to any of the existing monarchical states, which admittedly were relatively quiescent. Davutoğlu was finally compelled to face the apparent contradiction; he ended up drawing a major distinction between two groupings of states. He described the first group of states as caught up in the turmoil of the Arab Awakening—Egypt, Syria, Libya, Tunisia, Yemen—as states that had been "resisting change." Davutoğlu then conveniently categorized the monarchies as "states not needing change."[1]

This slightly strained distinction seemed to relieve Ankara of any obligation to come down against the monarchies—at least for a while. Even here, Davutoğlu clearly ignored the situation in Bahrain which is a classic case of a "state resisting change" in the face of ongoing uprisings over more than a decade. Ankara's policies on this can hardly be called "principled" or consistent. The unstable and intensifying uprising in Bahrain of course goes back at least a decade or more before the Arab Spring. It had started out as democratic protests demanding greater democracy by both Shi'a *and* Sunnis against the autocratic Sunni ruling al-Khalifa; the regime gradually manipulated those joint democratic protests into a sectarian struggle which caused Sunni opposition to drop away, leaving the Shi'a protesters isolated. This situation enabled the al-Khalifa regime to claim that the discontent of the oppressed Shi'ite majority—who make up at least two-thirds of the population—had all been stirred up by Iranian subversion. Yet well-documented grievances on the part of the Shi'a are broad and deep, including exclusion from significant positions in the government, lack of representative government, ghettoization, harsh tactics used against Shi'a protesters, and a government program to import large numbers of Arab Sunnis from Jordan and elsewhere to receive Bahraini citizenship and actually change the sectarian balance among the population. Saudi Arabia strongly backs a policy of no concessions to the Shi'a in Bahrain, and certainly no democratization process.

To reinforce these policies, in 2011 the Saudis sent a military force of 1,500 troops to Bahrain at the "request" of the Bahraini government to help maintain order in the face of prolonged demonstrations by the country's Shi'a. The Saudis were deeply concerned, not only with the possibility of overthrow of a monarchical regime but, worse that a Shi'ite majority would come to power. In May 2012 Saudi Arabia officially announced a plan to create a new Union of Gulf States among GCC state members. At a subsequent summit, however, many members of the GCC proved reluctant to adopt the plan and politely declared it needed additional thought and planning. The Bahrain regime was the only GCC member that showed full support for the proposal that could, in effect, bring about de facto annexation of Bahrain by Saudi Arabia: the two states are already linked by a short causeway—a symbolic, even binding umbilical cord. The Saudi proposal for the union was also designed to strengthen GCC ranks against Iran; not all members share the same degree of hostility to Iran, especially Qatar, Dubai, and Oman. Several other GCC states are unlikely to accede to a Saudi plan that can only reduce their own political, economic, and strategic sovereignty.

Bahrain thus remains a difficult issue for Turkey. It qualifies as a regime that is very much caught up in a struggle for democracy; by Ankara's own measure the protesters should merit its support. Yet Ankara has so far not been willing to confront Saudi Arabia on this issue which could push their relations close to the breaking point. Washington too tried to persuade the Bahraini al-Khalifa regime to liberalize, but is unwilling to push too hard, especially given the presence of the major US naval base in Bahrain. It remains to be seen whether Ankara will speak out on the Bahrain issue.

Egyptian turmoil intensified Saudi-Turkish confrontation. Turkey strongly backed the Muslim Brotherhood in its electoral victory in 2012 which dismayed Riyadh. The Saudis then quickly blessed the 2013 coup against the Muslim Brotherhood government and launched a major new international campaign against "terrorism"—the new code word for the Muslim Brotherhood in Egypt. Erdoğan rhetorically asked Saudi Foreign Minister Saud al-Faysal, "How could a country claiming to uphold Islam and Shari'a support the overthrow of an elected Islamist president who came to power after fair elections?" But of course that is precisely the point: the threat to Riyadh is "fair elections." More significantly, Riyadh finds it intolerable that another Sunni state or organization like the Brotherhood should claim any kind of religious legitimacy in the Sunni world, especially when it flirts with democratic governance.

In principle then, Turkey does not basically support either the anti-Shi'ite or anti-democracy goals of Saudi Arabia. Turkey and Riyadh are not likely to enjoy an intimate or comfortable long-term political alliance, temporarily shared policies in Syria notwithstanding. Nor will Ankara likely allow itself to be drawn into a position of overall championing the Sunni cause over the Shi'ite—a decision which would diminish its moral clout and put it on a full collision course with Tehran.

Turkey's Economic Ties with the Gulf

Trade between Turkey and the Gulf states took off during the 2000s, surging from US$1.5 billion in 2002 to US$11.9 billion in 2011 with a peak of US$14.2 billion in 2008. Areas of trade particularly targeted for the future are transportation, construction, petrochemicals, energy, tourism, and agriculture; both sides seek to liberalize visa regimes and establish a free trade agreement. The quality of this recent boom reflects cultural as well as economic factors. As one Arab business executive commented, the Gulf countries used to trade a lot with EU countries, but now "the emerging market is here. Moreover, Turkey is like our country regarding people's values, the understanding and warm feelings."[2]

Turkey already has garnered US\$7 billion in construction projects in the UAE alone. Qatar has invested heavily in the Turkish economy to the tune of many billions.[3] Saudi Arabia was expected to invest hundreds of billions in the Turkish economy. These vital infusions of cash naturally place pragmatic constraints on any ideological aspects of Turkish foreign policies in the Gulf. Now in chaos, Egypt will no longer be an attractive destination for Gulf tourism and Turkey will be the net beneficiary.

Supporters of the GCC push the ideological polarization further; some go so far as to claim that the GCC has now come to represent the heart of Arab world politics. This position was breathlessly articulated by Kuwaiti professor 'Abdullah al-Shayji who proclaimed that

> the GCC has emerged as the engine and the unrivalled leader of the Arabs. Today, it is the undisputed leader of the Arab world. Even the sweeping change of the Arab Spring catapulted the GCC into playing a leading role and helped it to steal the show from traditional powerhouses like Egypt, Iraq and Syria, which are all at critical junctures, embroiled in their own revolutions, bloodletting, feuding and the fear of foreign intervention. The GCC put out the fires in Bahrain and Oman, and negotiated an agreement in Yemen. It rubbed shoulders with NATO in Libya. GCC states have led the Arab League and UN Security Council efforts to stop the mayhem in Syria.[4]

Al-Shayji urges the GCC to move beyond soft power now to "an alliance with more teeth and muscle."

These claims of Gulf leadership raise the fascinating question: which form of government—monarchy or republican—has been more "successful" in the Arab world—and which will represent the future? This is an old debate (even aired on al-Jazeera) and is not easily resolved. First, successful monarchy tends to be located in *oil-rich states* with smaller populations where regimes have been able to maintain high standards of living and to keep people largely apolitical via subventions. Iraq with its huge oil reserves is one notable exception with its anti-monarchical revolution in 1958; the oil-rich monarchy of Libya fell in 1969. Non-Arab but energy-rich Iran is also a major exception with the Shah's fall in 1979. Monarchy remains intact only in two non-oil states—Morocco and Jordan; both are politically challenged however and are recipients of direct aid from oil states. Furthermore, most remaining monarchies are preserved in the small states of the Gulf, (only Saudi Arabia is large), where a sea of income goes to benefit a tiny native population. Thus a rough correlation exists between oil wealth, smaller population, and stability.

Second, revolution has tended to come to states with *more advanced and differentiated social orders* that have been exposed to a variety of ideologies. Iraq, Egypt, Iran, Syria and Yemen fall into that category. Finally, one can argue that the *republican regimes fell short of their own rhetoric* and their peoples' aspirations: their publics had been exposed to the concept of popular governance, yet open politics had been routinely crushed in virtually every single republican state—and crushed by *secular* forces: Algeria, Iraq, Libya, Syria and Egypt. In this sense, the republican states, many of whom do not have oil, may be more exposed to the idea of change and to elections, however rigged they may have been. Furthermore the publicly-espoused revolutionary rhetoric and ideals of these states clash more sharply with the reality of domestic political privilege and repression. And while monarchs are not expected to rotate in power, republican leaders are but did not. Finally, monarchy bases its legitimacy on something more than mere competence in ruling—such as ties of the ruler to some religious line.

In the end, al-Shayji's claim that the GCC is the "undisputed leader" of the Arab world seems far from the mark. The GCC is not about to take over leadership of the Arab world; counter-revolution is demonstrably not a policy for the future of the Arab world or most of its citizens. It is difficult to argue that monarchy represents the wave of the future in the Arab world, or anywhere else; republicanism, for all its shortcomings in practice, seems to conform more to the "tide of history." With the Arab Spring a newer generation in these republican states has at least glimpsed the possibility of something more, and demanded change. In almost no Arab state does monarchy offer a political vision even if it has offered some degree of stability for several decades supported by its huge wealth. Most would argue that transition to republicanism is in the long run inevitable and probably for the better as long as it can ultimately lead to greater democratic participation. Preferably, monarchy can evolve peacefully towards constitutional monarchy, as many citizens of monarchies have called for, although there is little precedent for that in the Muslim world. It may just be slowly taking place in the merchant state of Kuwait. In this context, Davutoğlu's facile distinction between those regimes "resisting change" and those that "don't need it" does not pass serious analytical test. But Ankara is pragmatic, and as long as there are no uprisings, Davutoglu is free to say that the need for change among monarchies does not (yet) exist. Yet even here Bahrain remains a dramatic and embarrassing exception.

It is furthermore difficult to claim that the economic power of the GCC will lead to innovative decision-making on its part. Both Saudi Arabia and especially Qatar have been surprisingly bolder in their recent actions of supporting the overthrow of the Asad regime. Yet, except for Qatar, *political* dynamism has rarely been the hallmark of GCC or Saudi policies over the years; despite often spectacular use of their massive oil wealth to build shining new cities and important turnkey culture they remain politically timid in their firm support of the status quo; notably, until recently, none has been willing to seriously buck US policies that are unpopular with their own citizens. Except for Saudi Arabia, the Gulf states are not "normal" states: the natives make up only a tiny part (10 percent or so) of a population dominated by a huge expat service community; their small native populations make both administration and distribution of largesse far easier. Today the GCC likely runs a risk even in supporting revolution in Syria where the likely successors will be Islamists, more or less radical, who will never be pro-monarchy. Some of them can perhaps be bought off for a while with GCC economic aid, but over the longer term the monarchies must beware of whom they bankroll—as they have learned from bitter experience in the past, including with Bin Laden. Fear (never articulated) of Saudi dominance stands in the way of serious joint GCC policies; the organization is headed for harder times and greater divisions, especially as the "Iranian threat" recedes.

In addition, for all their talk the GCC states do not seek military confrontation with Iran. They know that war with Iran is not popular among Arab populations and could create a highly destabilizing environment for everyone. Nor does Iran necessarily seek confrontation with them. Under Ayatollah Mohammad Khatami as president in 1997-2005, for example, Iran's policies sought rapprochement and coexistence with Arab states; those policies were later countermanded by the erratic, shortsighted and often foolishly impulsive policies of President Ahmadinejad, much to the discomfiture even of much of Iran's elite. Those days are now gone and a new, more moderate president, Hassan Rouhani, is in charge who already seeks improved ties with the Arab Gulf states. Even the kingdom's boldness against Iran rings hollow: as the West reaches some accommodation with Tehran on nuclear and other issues, Riyadh is compelled to dial back its confrontational language and restore a reluctant and uncomfortable modus vivendi with Iran—one that has characterized most of the entire modern era.

The Flowering of Salafism

The dynamic appearance of Salafism on the *political* scene in Tunisia, Egypt, and Libya is one of the surprises of the Arab Spring. Prior to then, Salafis (pronounced Sálafi, not Saláfi) had generally expressed contempt for politics, especially "western" political mechanisms such as elections.

Salafis maintain an ultra-fundamentalist set of beliefs closely akin to Wahhabis in Saudi Arabia; their chief goals are creation of an Islamic state that is ruled fully by Shari'a law; literal interpretation of texts, and denunciation (or anathematization—*takfir*) as "unbelievers" those Muslims who do not subscribe to their views. They bear a strong anti-Shi'a streak. Salafis are scarcely interested in converting Christians to Islam; their chief focus is upon converting those they see as lukewarm and misled Muslims to an ultra-orthodox form of Islam. Radical jihadis, too, generally hold Salafi theological views but insist on an additional so-called "religious obligation" to carry out armed jihad. But most Salafis are not jihadis even if most jihadis are Salafis. Nor are they a unified bloc; differences of emphasis emerge among them on such issues as political participation, acceptance of democracy, the use of political violence to achieve their goals, and whether Muslims should ever be targeted by violence. Most Salafis see political violence as just another form of undesirable political involvement and condemn attacks on civilians. Nonetheless, some of the more violent jihadi movements have developed within, and subsequently broken away from, Salafi movements.

When for the first time genuine democratic options emerged within the political order in Egypt and Tunisia even the Salafis could not remain indifferent to the siren song of power. After the fall of Mubarak, elections had become the new vehicle for apportioning power within the state and society and Salafis did not wish to be left out. (They reacted in a similar way decades earlier in Kuwait when offered a chance at partial political power in parliamentary elections—an option they took.) Thus do elections "corrupt" principles, as many of them had feared; they ended up joining the game that they had scorned.

As a new political scene dawned in Egypt a large wing of Salafis formed the *Nur* (Light) Party. It was not always clear whether they saw the Brotherhood as ideological allies or as political rivals, but in electoral politics candidates inevitably become rivals. The Salafis gained an astonishing 27 percent of the seats in Parliament to become the second-biggest Islamist force in politics after the Brotherhood, and gained a voice on the constitutional committee. And yet, when the military went on to overthrow Mursi a year later the Salafis prominently supported the coup *against* the Brotherhood. In the eyes of many Islamists, Salafi support for a military coup against Islamist government was an act of utter opportunism if not treasonous; Salafis had revealed their readiness to weaken the broader Islamist movement for the short-term gains of sitting at the table with the military power brokers. They had showed themselves to be more corrupted by politics than the Brotherhood. Yet other Salafis condemn the Brotherhood as apostates.

Having made their choice, it remains to be seen whether the military regime will actually permit the Salafis to maintain a position of power or influence in any new government. It will probably include them if it judges them to be weak and manipulable and able to provide useful Islamist "cover" in the military's struggle to crush the Brotherhood.[5]

But just what is the nature of the rivalry between the Muslim Brotherhood and Salafism? The Muslim Brotherhood has been the largest and most successful international Islamist movement of the 20th century. Much of its strength lies in its appeal to Islamic tradition, and to Islam as the ideal source of inspiration for social justice, good governance and democratic process. The movement's commitment over generations gained it respect and a strong following, especially in the face of harsh oppression by the state; its appeal grew with its important social programs operating at the neighborhood level. Apart from the Hizmet movement in Turkey, the Brotherhood is the only major international grassroots organization that operates within many Muslim societies. It was the primary vehicle for expression for many of the angers, frustrations and goals of large segments of society. Now, however, fairly or unfairly, the Brotherhood has been judged by its enemies as a threat; it is perceived by its Salafi rivals as a failure and theologically weak; and is perceived by many of its own followers as a disappointment—at least in its first and only year of managing the country in on-the-job training. The Brotherhood has now been politically "blooded." Can it still serve as the same powerful vehicle for expression of much repressed popular sentiment? Meanwhile, the Salafis themselves lack any coherent and realistic policy platform, and possess even less governing experience or even theories of governance, and are still uncomfortable in the political realm. But they could once again produce new ranks of terrorists in the country. And if the Brotherhood in Tunisia, Libya or Tunisia proves unequal to the task of governing, the Salafis may be the primary beneficiaries as the last alternative of pious but frustrated and angry Muslims who have nowhere else to go. But they have a long way to go before even attaining the political experience and sophistication of the Brotherhood. The potential for violence in societies now repressed anew remains high, especially from Salafi circles.

A central theme of this book is the abiding character of certain aspirations and beliefs of broad sections of the Muslim East public. The Brotherhood may be suppressed, its members arrested or even killed and eliminated from the political scene, but that does not mean that the ideas it has stood for will go away, as even General al-Sisi acknowledged in his earlier writings. Certain political, economic, social and even ideological demands within a society will invariably find appropriate vehicle for their expression. As the spokesman for the Brotherhood commented a few months after the coup:

> The Brotherhood has existed for more than 80 years, and subject to several crackdowns, yet it came back stronger. It's not about an organization but an idea. It's the adoption of the basic principles of Islam, which are deeply rooted in Egyptian society. Even if the Brotherhood disappears, somebody else is going to take that idea and call it by some other name.[6]

Social, economic, political and even psychological needs *continuously exist* within the population, even as those needs evolve over time. The *ideological vehicle* by which they are expressed may differ considerably from time to time, place to place, but such needs will always seek an adequate vehicle for expression. The chosen vehicle may become discredited, but the needs do not go away. (A classic case in point is the parade of ideologies lying behind the permanent Palestinian quest for liberation, independence, and statehood over time. In the 1960s the Palestinians expressed their aspirations through the reigning ideology of Arab nationalism; when that movement foundered, Palestinians then adopted Marxist-Leninist vehicles to the same ends. And finally, with the general weakening of leftist ideology the Palestinians turned to Islamism— same goals, differing vehicles.)

If the huge Brotherhood organization remains absent from the political scene in Egypt under the military, how will the Salafi movement fare? Certainly for the Saudis and many in the Gulf, the Salafis are their anointed political instruments in the Muslim world, enjoying full Saudi support. More recently the Salafis have become the Saudis' designated vehicle to weaken, displace and destroy the Brotherhood. But if political frustration on the part of pious and conservative Muslims should mount as a result of the coup against the Brotherhood, will the Salafis become the preferred, the more radical vehicle? Where the Brotherhood once institutionally dominated Islamist forces across the region, the emergence of new Salafi power over the past few decades, especially after US wars in Iraq and Afghanistan, raise new challenges to the Brotherhood and to the Islamist movement more broadly. Will they now simply be perceived as having sold out to military power and Saudi money, at least in Egypt? Will the Brotherhood come to represent the "progressive" force among broad Islamist movements? Or will it attempt to cling to the old formulas even in failure, prompting renewed Islamist opposition against them from Salafi forces, or even "leftist" Islamic forces?

Such a split among Sunni Islamist *political* forces is a significant event in modern Islamist politics. Its implications extend beyond Egypt. The struggles are reflected in the free-for-all and violent politics of Iraq. In Tunisia the Salafis are the major religious opposition to the moderate, Brotherhood-linked Ennahda party. They gained surprising strength after the Tunisian revolution, and, as in Egypt, could not resist new opportunities to gain greater power via participation in democratic processes. They too have been the recipients of much Saudi cash. Thus the Salafis became a key thorn in the side of the moderate Ennahda government, pushing it towards more extreme religious positions on Shari'a issues on the one hand, some of its elements turning to violence and even assassination of liberals while denouncing the very Islamic legitimacy of Ennahda on the other. In Tunisia Salafis gained appeal among a younger population that faces difficult economic and social problems that Ennahda had not so far been able to alleviate. Ennahda has meanwhile outspokenly evolved more in the direction of the Turkish AKP model, as a conservative democratic party with sympathies for freedom for Islam in public space.

Although conditions are different, in Pakistan too Salafi-oriented parties (particularly of Deobandi orientation) have seen their voices rise over more moderate Islamist parties. The question then is, are Islamist parties inclined to make common cause? Or to become bitter rivals? The greater the number of supporters for Islamist trends become, the greater the divisions among them are likely to be. What political coalitions and deals will they make in order to benefit the party? With major Saudi financial power behind the Salafi movement globally, the Salafis can actually damage the appeal and power of the more moderate Brotherhood that has engaged in "compromise." But one thing has become clear: Egyptian military fear of the Brotherhood rests far more on its *political drawing power and organizational skills* as a political rival than it does on the Brotherhood's theology or ideology. The military's denunciation of the Brotherhood today verges on the hysterical and the absurd, particularly on the spurious charge of the Brotherhood as a terrorist organization. That argument has now become hard to sell even in the West. Indeed, while most Salafis themselves are not terrorists, most terrorists are ideologically and theologically closer to the Salafis than to the Brotherhood.

R4BIA – *Whither the Brotherhood?*
After a period of initial political failure, the Brotherhood is still licking its wounds. It does not yet acknowledge even a decisive political defeat—at least in the eyes of many of its followers. Nothing exemplifies that more than the

emergence of the R4BIA movement. R4BIA, or *Rābi'a*, is the symbol of the massacre of Brotherhood supporters in Rabi'a Square in August 2013 in demonstrating against the military coup against Mursi—figures vary greatly but between 1,000 and 2,000 people were massacred by the military, all civilian. (Human Rights Watch described it as the most massive killing of civilians in modern Egyptian history.)

R4BIA's symbol is a black palm facing forward with four (*arbi'a or rabi'a*) fingers raised and spread against a yellow background, as in a traffic sign. The name commemorates the event and the square, but it also memorializes Rabi'a al-'Adawiyya, a female Sufi saint and poet in 8th-century Basra who propounded the idea of Divine Love. The image quickly went viral around the Muslim world and beyond in social media, symbolizing righteous resistance in the struggle against oppression everywhere. A song has now been written, based on a poem written in prison by martyred Egyptian Brother and thinker Sayyid Qutb decades ago, and the image adopted by millions of Muslims now serves as a symbol of hope and resistance.

My brother, you are free behind these gates.
My brother, you are free within these chains.
For if upon Allah you do rely,
The intrigues of his slaves can bring no pains.

As one R4BIA website states:

The blessings of R4BIA have been spreading rapidly around the world, and they bring with them a new spirit, fresh ideas and a novel sense of brotherhood. Conscientious human beings in more than 30 nations, who stand against all kinds of injustice and inequity, express themselves through the R4BIA sign, flag, logo and slogans. An act of mercy roves the earth in full flood, an act which is diverse in ethnicity, color, sect, and faith, but remains united around the same sign.[7]

Significantly, the symbol was seized upon early on in Turkey and heavily propagated from there, including public use of the hand gesture by Prime Minister Erdoğan, but has since spread around the Muslim world to take on ever-broader meaning of struggle for justice, honor and dignity. This event continues to demonstrate a continuing serious engagement of Turkey in Muslim world politics. The Brotherhood's defeat in Rabi'a Square may thus have produced a potent symbol that may serve it—and perhaps other Muslim movements of struggle—effectively in coming years if it continues to draw the same emotional response from millions, even non-Muslims, around the world.

How will the military regime in Egypt manage issues of Islam in Egyptian national ideology? It will be hard to preempt Islamic symbols for themselves, but they may try to use compliant Salafi groups to that end. In the unlikely event that the Islamist wave has crested—it is not a single wave and it comes in many shapes and contexts—what ideological alternatives remain? As we noted in a previous chapter, it is quite possible that the Left, long underrepresented in the Middle East since the 1970s, will become the resurgent populist and ideological force to join forces with, or displace, the Islamists.

There is no doubt Riyadh will be able to use its wealth to help prop up the status quo in selected places in the future, but its efforts at broader regional leadership can come only in the absence of any other acceptable dynamic claimant. The GCC cannot base its policies indefinitely on fear of a hostile Iran as the rallying point for tighter security under Saudi dominance. Furthermore, in the longer run, Saudi Arabia represents a greater threat to the independence of the Gulf states than does Iran. Saudi Arabia under some future Saudi religious/nationalist revolutionary regime, in some invocation of "manifest destiny," could well seek to extend its borders to the waters of the Gulf again. In such a case, Iran might well be the power to which the small Gulf states might appeal for protection—or perhaps more likely to Arab Iraq, or even to Turkey. And Turkey represents the only forward-looking, advanced and democratic model that has successfully integrated a form of moderate Islamic in the region. Egypt under the Brotherhood for a while looked like it might have been a challenger for regional vision, but that prospect is now out of sight for the indefinite future; the new military regime in Cairo is unlikely to develop a bold leadership role for the Arab world. It has no viable ideology to stir men's hearts and dares not embark on a radical vision of the future. Forward-looking leadership among Arab states still seems missing in action. Turkey remains the one state still seeking to identify and implement a modernist vision for the region consonant with its cultural roots.

PART FIVE: SHI'ISM AND REVOLUTION
CHAPTER EIGHTEEN
SHI'ITE REVOLUTION – SPECTER AND REALITY

What is Sectarian Conflict?

Struggles between Sunnis and Shi'a seem to dominate the Middle East political landscape today more than at any time in many centuries. Most western reporting treats these sectarian tensions as if they represented a timeless fault line across all Middle East politics. Yet to analyze the Middle East through sectarian eyes is to miss much of the true dynamics of the region. The theater of sectarian clash often masks the real forces that drive the region. Religion becomes the lazy person's touchstone in seeking to understand political and social divisions. Focus on theology neglects the greater importance of *quest for regime preservation.* Over the last few decades Iran has somehow become the focus of nearly everyone's external security concerns, in ways that really have little to do with Shi'ism per se and everything to do with regional geopolitics and domestic regime security.

Theology is rarely the real issue behind strife between contending communities in the world. At heart are basic unresolved fears and rivalries over power and resources that characterize most *communal* problems. These inter-communal problems flare up with particular intensity in times of painful political transition from old political balances to new ones. *Balance of power among communities—any communities—*is invariably destabilized by violent regime change, war, economic crisis, or new democratic openings in the political process. New winners and losers emerge. We observe this phenomenon most prominently in Iraq, Bahrain, Syria and Lebanon where ruling communal *minorities* have long suppressed communal *majorities*. Events demonstrate how these transitions are invariably painful, disorderly—even revolutionary in impact. Rising black and Latino political power in the US today sparks tensions that revolve primarily around preservation of white privilege, now threatened.

But what do we mean by "communal" as opposed to "sectarian" (religious) strife? The difference is subtle but it is significant; how we understand it affects our *diagnosis and treatment* of the problem. "Sectarian clash" suggests we are essentially talking about problems that have to do with religion, theology, and religious practice—people who hate each other because of what each believes. Such religious diagnosis suggests the problem is so deeply rooted that it is all but insoluble. But if we describe the problem as "communal" then sectarian clashes come to resemble other conflicts around the world susceptible to arbitration.

The nature of communities—their origins, evolution, character, and importance—has been much analyzed. A community is fundamentally based upon a *common, consciously acknowledged and shared identity*; that identity can rest upon any major shared feature as long as that feature helps maintain a coherent community at a particular time and place in history. We all possess multiple identities based on nationality, ethnicity, language, gender, religion, class, profession, ideology, and regional roots. We all implement one or another facet of our identities at different times and places, even in the same day. But which of these facets of our identity will dominate at a given moment depends upon changing circumstances in our lives. A Jew in liberal Weimar Germany in 1920 might describe himself as a German, a Berliner, a professor of sociology, a Jew, a socialist, a male. That same Jew in 1936 would have only one identity that mattered: Jewish—with life or death implications under Nazi power.

The creation of communities goes back to the dawn of human history: what factors caused a given group to bond together at some point for common welfare and protection against another group? It begins with concepts of some kind of kinship, bonds, things in common, that in contemporary nation states often expand into "national kinship." But that same sense of kinship, as it expands and takes in more people, can also grow less meaningful, more fragile or even break down along particular fault lines. For example, when a subgroup within a society comes to perceive that its very welfare, even existence, is at stake, it might rebel, or seek to separate, or be expelled, from the larger community of interests to which it used to belong. It may seek a *reformulation* of kinship. When did southern Americans in the 1850s begin to perceive that they were no longer Americans, but *southerners*? At any given point, what makes for *inclusion* of certain groups and to *exclusion* of other groups in a community? There is no clear single answer; we are observers of a shifting scene. At the beginning we could imagine a group of caves in one part of a prehistoric valley standing against caves in another part. Over time, language, dialect, way of life, economic needs and practices, rivalries, migration and other factors lead to formation of larger groups that may alternate between cooperation, competition and even violence in their dealings among themselves. And the boundaries, even the names, of those groupings can and do evolve and change. Some groups are absorbed into the larger society without a trace left behind. Yesterday's enemies can become today's allies and vice versa. "Eternal" hostility between French and German was an arguable geopolitical truth in 1939 but today it is not.

Sunnis and Shi'a

The origin of the Sunni-Shi'a split goes back to the struggle over the successor (*khalifa* or caliph) to the Prophet as the leader of the early and rapidly expanding Muslim community. 'Ali, the son-in-law of the Prophet, known as a righteous man and first male convert to Islam, was passed over for the post, reportedly against the Prophet's wishes (according to Shi'ite tradition). Opposition came mainly from the large tribal federation, the Quraysh that had opposed and tried to destroy the nascent Muslim community. Technically the argument was whether the caliph should come from the Prophet's blood line (as 'Ali argued), or by selection from among top community leadership. From the outset, then, trade, kinship, economic issues, turf and power, were at stake in the appointment of the first four caliphs. After 'Ali's sons and grandsons were slaughtered in battle, the partisans (*shi'a*) of 'Ali withdrew to form their own distinct community for protection and preservation of the cause. Thus the origin of the Shi'ites had little to do with theology and everything to do with clan, tribal and regional struggles for power and influence, although later each side sought religious and moral justification for their positions. Religion becomes the banner, the ennobling cause masking classic power struggle. But whatever the origins, over time the Shi'ite community took on strong and distinct characteristics, identity, symbols, beliefs, lore, customs and traditions that still exist. This identity was reinforced through conflict with Sunni communities and suffering: identity can be as much reinforced by the hostile views of others as by the way you define yourself. But in the end we are still talking about generic issues of separate communities—community A versus community B; you can fill in the blanks about the characteristics of each as you wish. Clan, sectarian and communal problems the world over often lose genuine and serious substance, but the communities have firmly come to exist, feel passion, and seek to preserve themselves from threats and to advance their own interests—whatever they may choose to call themselves. They may even draw strength and unity from feeling that they are besieged. But the communities become no less real for all that.

And the level of intensity of the communal ("sectarian") struggle rises and falls with time and events. For example, intermarriage between Sunni and Shi'a in Iraq under Saddam Hussein was commonplace; since Saddam's overthrow and the rise of Shi'ite power, the political displacement of the minority Sunnis with its associated anxiety and anger, such cross-sectarian marriages are now virtually unthinkable. But circumstances will inevitably shift once again at some point as other identities, apart from sectarian—ethnic, political, social, regional, ideological, and professional—regain new roles. In the meantime, *frozen sectarian identity in a time of transition of power* creates great emotional trauma and is exploited by all parties.

In most cases of serious Shi'a-Sunni violent conflict in recent decades— Iraq, Bahrain, Lebanon—it has been *Shi'ite majorities* denied a legitimate role in the state commensurate with their numbers. Only in Syria were roles reversed: a Sunni majority was denied its proper proportional role of power vis-à-vis the 'Alawi (quasi-Shi'ite) ruling minority (some 12 percent). In every case newly inaugurated democratization processes exert revolutionary impact upon the communal order: it opens each country to radical political and social change as it shifts power from group A to group B, Sunni to Shi'a—or the converse in Syria.

In the swirling environment of today's Arab Spring several states— especially Saudi Arabia—have sought to reduce complex regional and political factors down to simple sectarian struggle, deliberately masking other more critical issues such as domestic social and political discontent and demand for reform under authoritarian regimes. But placing a religious spin upon communitarian rivalry suggests that such problems contain an essentially *insoluble ideological nature*. At that point each group may like to believe that it is closer to God's Truth than the other, suggesting that political reform is quite irrelevant, that there can be little room for compromise over such vital issues of principle and faith.

As we think about communal conflict we get into even more complex issues, too lengthy for discussion here, of the *psychology of discrimination*, bigotry and exclusion: what are the psychological features that lead one individual to draw lines and seek to exclude others, while another is led to embrace inclusion of others as much as possible? Such roots of discrimination and prejudice lie deep along racial, linguistic, religious, ethnic or gender lines. Elements of ignorance and fear also make up part of the psychology. In Sunni Islam, Wahhabi/Salafis tend to be particularly rigid, doctrinaire and exclusionist. Rejection of Shi'a is not their sole concern, but nonetheless a major one. Salafis over much of the 20th century also issued blanket condemnations of Shi'ism, especially in Iraq; they brandished the slogan about the three enemies of Islam: *Shi'iyya, Shiyu'iyya, Shu'ubiyya* (Shi'ism, communism, (anti-Arab) nationalism)—triple factors corrupting Islam in the eyes of Salafis.

The Iranian Revolution of 1979 was the key political event of the late 20th century in the Middle East, laying down a new milestone in the ideological arena and opening sectarian considerations anew. That will be the subject of the next chapter on Iran and the "Shi'ite Threat." It's important to realize that the Iranian Revolution laid down a new milestone in the political and ideological arena of modern Middle East politics. It represented the first genuine popular revolution in the Middle East in a very long time. Iran's new leaders saw it as the vanguard of political, social and economic change, now embodied in the structure of the first modern Islamic state. Far from limiting themselves just to a symbolic declaration of Shari'a law to qualify as "Islamic," Iran's new rulers moved into new territory in setting forth a detailed set of principles and institutions designed to put Islamic concepts of *modern* governance into practice. And remarkably, Iran did not style itself a caliphate or an emirate, but as a republic with an elected parliament—both institutions rejected by many early Islamists as western and "un-Islamic."

This precedent galvanized Islamists across the region, Sunni and Shi'a alike. Although the constitution also contained certain more typically Shi'ite features of political thought (such as clerical rule and the role of a Supreme Leader providing religious oversight) the scope of the experiment was bold and relevant to *all* Islamists. With its outspoken resistance and hostility to centuries of western imperialism, the new Iranian state struck Muslims of the region as a new experiment; it was admired for its boldness, determination and self-confidence, particularly at a time when such boldness had largely disappeared among Arab rulers. Even Sunni Islamists were impressed and in many ways politically sympathetic, especially the Muslim Brotherhood.

The 1979 revolution heightened the role of Iran as an active geopolitical player in the region. But it also heartened the region's many communities of Shi'ite minorities who had been largely excluded from the Arab political order. For the first time in the modern era Iran offered an example of *Shi'a* placing a stamp upon regional affairs. Oppressed Shi'ite communities believed Iran was the champion that had their back if need be.

It's important to note that the new Islamic Republic of Iran did not even perceive itself as a *Shi'ite* force, but rather as an *Islamic* force. It sought good relations with Sunni Islamist movements, particularly the Muslim Brotherhood in Egypt with whom it felt a kinship in its call for an Islamic state and resistance against western domination. Tehran even reached out to establish relations with *non*-Muslim Third World liberation movements, drawing on contemporary radical Shi'ite thinkers such as 'Ali Shariati, who fused elements of Marxism into his concepts of Islamic and especially Shi'ite concepts of social justice. The new leadership proclaimed the relevance of the Islamic Revolution to *all* Muslims; it went on to identify itself as supporting all the "oppressed of the world" (*mostaz'afin*) —a radical concept that moved well beyond mere promulgation of Islamic law (which is not revolutionary in character at all except perhaps in its ideals.) Sectarianism was not on Iran's agenda, except to express concern for oppressed Shi'a of the region as well. As recently as January 2014 former Iranian president Mehdi Rafsanjani noted: "Who the first caliph was or wasn't is a historical matter of little use to us now, and we will not reach any settlement on it. How we do our ablutions or how we pray is not a rational reason for turning it into a difference between us, and it has no justification in the Qur'an or the Sunnah [Hadith]". Thus Rafsanjani perceives these "religious" issues as essentially minor issues today that have been politicized but can be depoliticized at will.

Thus, apart from the rise of Iran to new political prominence, the new Islamic Republic posed a major *ideological* challenge to the rest of the Middle East in overthrowing monarchy and calling for protection of national sovereignty in the face of western power. Worse, from the perspective of Sunni rulers, oppressed Shi'ite populations now felt their identity newly empowered through the Iranian Revolution. There was more than enough here to worry all kinds of autocrats and sclerotic kings.

Today Iran figures in the region in even more complex ways. The Arab Spring—coupled with the US overthrow of Saddam's Sunni Iraqi regime in 2003 and the ascension to power of the Iraqi Shi'a, the democratic openings in Iraq, and ongoing rebellion Bahrain, the sectarian struggle in Syria—all have reopened old issues of sectarian balance, especially in the Gulf. In addition, decades of US geopolitical antipathy to Iran had encouraged insecure Gulf Arab leaders to curry favor with Washington by climbing on the bandwagon in demonizing Iran as the prime source of regional problems. Iran's revolutionary vision and rhetoric (not its theology) still upsets traditional regimes. And although Tehran itself had lost some of its cachet among Arab publics with its more reactionary domestic policies during eight years of the capricious President Ahmadinejad, all that began to change again with the 2013 Iranian elections that brought to power a new and far more attractive and moderate President Rouhani. Iran and its new negotiations with the West may be in the process of emerging from isolation. In the meantime Turkey's AKP had distinctly stolen much of Iran's previous political appeal with its own much more successful model of a democratic, sovereign, independent, progressive, and flourishing Muslim state.

This section of the book focusses on the role of Shi'ism in the current regional struggle. We will examine the real nature of the Shi'ite challenge as it involves Iran, Iraq, and Syria—what that challenge really is, and what it is not.

CHAPTER NINETEEN

THE CHALLENGE OF SHI'ISM: IRAN AS GEOPOLITICAL THREAT?

The sheer geopolitical weight of Iran—size and population—as a force in the Middle East represents a potentially intimidating presence to its smaller and weaker neighbors and rivals. Its landmass dominates the Gulf. It is vastly bigger, has a far greater population (76 million), is more broadly developed politically and economically (in terms of self-sufficient diversification) than any other state in the region except Turkey. It also possesses a powerful sense of historical identity going back 4,000 years. Iran's regional weight commands attention—and that would be true even if it were not ethnically largely Persian or Shi'ite in character.

But Iran is of course non-Arab and its language Indo-European—totally unrelated to Arabic or Turkish. And while Islam first emerged in the desert heart of the traditional Arab world, Iran represents overwhelmingly the *most important non-Arab source of cultural contribution* to Islamic civilization—in philosophy, theology, science, literature and the arts.

For all its power as a state, however, Iran throughout history has been only a modest presence in the actual waters of the (Persian/Arab) Gulf. It has not historically been a sea-faring nation compared to the Arabs. The Arab side of the Gulf has not been truly conquered or controlled by Iran for nearly 1,000 years and Iran has never represented a significant military threat to the Arabian Peninsula compared with other regional forces like Iraq or Wahhabi Arabia. The lands that Iran historically has contested involved control of parts of Mesopotamia (Iraq) and Anatolia—with Rome, with the Byzantines, and the Ottomans for over 2,000 years. Modern history demonstrates that Iran has not engaged in territorial aggression or posed ongoing significant *military* threat to the smaller Gulf states with the exception of three small islands in the Gulf that are under adjudication with the UAE. Tehran has increased its military capability in modern times—as have the small Gulf states. Despite the government's strong and self-proclaimed Islamic character, Iran also maintains a strong Persian nationalist tradition; its foreign policy behavior is unlikely to change significantly even under a non-Islamist nationalist government.

Iran, the Arab World, and the Nuclear Issue: a Shi'ite Bomb?

When the Iranian or "Shi'ite" threat is invoked by Iran's enemies today, the issue of Iran's nuclear capabilities comes up first—at least for Israel and the West. It is one of the factors behind "sectarian" struggle in the region. Yet the reality of the issue is open to debate. While Iran is determined to master the nuclear cycle—its right as a signatory of the Non-Proliferation Treaty—no reliable source claims that Iran has actually developed a nuclear weapon; even to alarmists that event is perpetually a "few years off down the road." Tehran's very intentions in this regard are debated among western intelligence agencies and in Israel. There is no question that a nuclear weapons capability on Iran's part would challenge the absolute freedom of both the US and Israel to conduct military operations in the Gulf region with impunity. A few argue that a nuclear weapons capability presents an existential threat to Israel. Many others argue that it does not realistically do so since Israel's retaliatory capability would be utterly devastating to Iran and Iran knows it. A few hardliners in Israel and the US claim the regime in Tehran is led by "crazy mullahs" who would not hesitate to launch nuclear weapons against Israel and welcome an apocalyptic war which would "hasten the return of the Shi'ite Mahdi" or Redeemer. Most knowledgeable political and military observers of Iran however reject that argument outright and believe Tehran is quite pragmatic and rational, even if outspoken and occasionally provocative in its views. Clearly a nuclear Iran represents no existential issue to the US, but would serve to constrain US freedom of military action in the region. Indeed, Iran's chief offenses to Washington over the years have been: 1) the humiliating capture of the US Embassy in 1979 and the holding of American hostages for several years, and 2) Iran's persistent rhetorical defiance of US policy wishes and resistance to US strategy and goals in the region, and 3) its support for forces which Washington and Israel view as hostile, such as Shi'ite Hizballah in Lebanon and Sunni Palestinian Hamas. In Washington's eyes that has been enough to characterize it as a "rogue state," and George W. Bush proclaimed it part of an international "axis of evil." Iranians in turn point to the overthrow by the US and UK of its first democratically elected prime minister, Mohammad Mosaddegh, in 1953 because of his nationalist policies that led to nationalization of British BP oil concessions in Iran.

The more relevant question to our discussion here is the impact of Iran's nuclear development upon the Arab world where it has, in effect, taken on the emotional baggage of a potential "Shi'ite bomb." There are two distinct viewpoints on this in the Middle East: that of the Gulf Arab *regimes*, and *popular Arab attitudes*. They diverge. On the one hand, Gulf regimes are almost

271

unanimously opposed to Iran's nuclear projects (including those unrelated to weapons), see them as a dangerous projection of "Shi'ite power," and urge Washington to put an end to it. At the popular level, however, attitudes differ. It is highly instructive here to look at Turkish attitudes on the Iranian nuclear issue as representative of rational regional strategic calculations. In my view Turkish attitudes represent the most realistic view of Iran's place in the long-range security order in the Middle East; they also reflect popular attitudes in much of the rest of the Arab world.

The Iranian Nuclear Issue in the Eyes of the Region

Turkey in principle should be one of the states most concerned at the course of nuclear developments in Iran. The concerns that Ankara does have are of a different order than US views. Indeed, the heart of the nuclear issue between Iran and Turkey is not really bilateral at all; it is more about *how Ankara relates to US policies towards Iran.*

Iran has the right, according to international law and the Non-Proliferation Treaty, to develop a nuclear capacity to refine nuclear fuels within set guidelines compatible with production of nuclear energy and civilian use (usually some five percent of uranium enrichment); Iran has enriched some uranium to the 20-percent level for its research reactor but is not known to have advanced refinement beyond that to weapons-grade purity which requires some 90-percent enrichment. But for Washington the issue is not about whether Iran has the *right* to refine uranium at all, which it does, but rather *how far Washington will acknowledge that legal right* and will accept internationally established safeguards on Iran. Washington distrusts Tehran's intentions in refining at all, even within international guidelines and controls. Grounds do exist for this distrust, but much of it springs heavily from three decades of vocal invective and distrust on both sides. In this sense the nuclear issue is primarily a political issue and not about nuclear rights as such. Washington believes that Iran may eventually develop a nuclear weapon. Iran says it will not, and Supreme Leader Ayatollah Khamene'i has issued and reconfirmed a *fatwa* stating that development of a nuclear weapon is against Islam. (The credibility or firmness of that commitment is certainly open to debate, but the statement does represent a repeated solemn statement couched in religious language by Iran's supreme leader.) And as Iran is working legally at much lower thresholds of nuclear enrichment, the International Atomic Energy Agency (IAEA) does not believe Iran is currently developing a nuclear weapon—nor does US intelligence for that matter.

Putting Tehran's statements aside, it would appear quite logical that over the long run Iran might seek to develop at least the *near capability* ("threshold capability") of producing a nuclear weapon. Going back to the 1970s, the shah of Iran, then America's closest ally in the Middle East outside of Israel, declared that, as a great nation and people, Iran "deserved" nuclear weapons. Indeed the US closely assisted the shah in building nuclear reactors in Iran in the 1970s. As the *Bulletin of the Atomic Scientists* noted, "The same [Iranian] nationalism [under the Shah] that emphasized Iran's 'full right' to reprocess and rejected 'second-class' status foreshadowed Iran's present-day claims about nuclear 'rights' under the Non-Proliferation Treaty. Moreover, US enmity toward Iran after the 1979 Islamic Revolution significantly increased the regime's interest in nuclear deterrence."[1]

Iran is surrounded by the nuclear weapons of Russia, Pakistan, India, and Israel as well as the presence of US nuclear weapons in Turkey and on board US naval vessels on Iran's doorstep in the Gulf. The long-range rationale for Iran is clear: possession of some kind of minimal nuclear weapons capability would serve to deter outside powers that sought to intimidate, or attack, Iran. For now, however, Iran's ongoing legal enrichment of uranium at or below the 20-percent level is very likely for use as a bargaining chip with the West in return for dropping economic sanctions and ceasing to isolate Iran. Its nuclear research does enable Iran to develop mastery of the general range of nuclear technology it would require for such time as it might eventually decide to develop a weapon.

Iran can have little doubt that its national stature, independence and freedom of regional policy would gain immeasurably through possession of a nuclear deterrent. The reality is, however, that *any* nationalistic and independent-minded government in Iran will likely pursue the same goal of a nuclear deterrent. Furthermore, even anti-regime Iranians share the belief that Iran has the *right* to do so. For the international order the heart of the issue really should be, *what kind of government* in Iran will eventually possess a nuclear deterrent? Look at the case of Russia: a drastic change of ideology there with the fall of the Soviet Union hugely changed US perceptions of the "threat" of Russian nukes, even though they still exist in plentiful numbers. No one in the US lies awake at night worrying about British, French, or Indian nukes—that is because of reasonable foreign confidence in the *nature of the government* that possesses them. With this in mind we might ask, have western policies been wise in insisting on isolating, pressuring and threatening Iran over 30 years? Or might it make more sense for the West to work towards normalization of relations with the regime that might enable it eventually to comfortably coexist with Iran and perhaps diminish the grounds for any weaponization of Iran's nuclear capability in the future? Or even to live with an Iran with nuclear weapons that is no longer an object of suspicion and harsh rhetoric? The US has repeatedly said it will not permit Iran to develop a nuclear weapons capability (although reality will eventually force a change in that position.) Israeli politicians never cease to cast the nuclear weapons issue as an existential issue for Israel (though many top Israeli intelligence officials do not). We also have numerous precedents of nukes in the possession of other dangerous leaders: what of a nuclear Stalin in the Soviet Union, or nuclear Mao Zedong in China, or nuclear Kim Jong Un in North Korea, or even a nuclear Pakistan with its jihadi movements and thriving extremist Islamist parties?

These are Washington's calculations from afar that help set the tone of the controversy. But what about Turkey and other regional states closer to Iranian nuclear issues? Strikingly, while insecure autocrats in the Gulf, and especially in Saudi Arabia, constantly harp on the Iranian "threat," public opinion in the Middle East does not see it quite that way. The reasons for the intense discomfort of the Gulf *regimes* have more to do with their feelings of domestic insecurity than with any direct external military threat. Countries such as Egypt (under Mubarak) and Jordan periodically spoke of a "Shi'ite threat" but the charge was scarcely convincing: neither country remotely borders on Iran, neither is likely ever to be attacked by Iran, and neither has any meaningful Shi'ite populations. At least with Saudi Arabia, given the geopolitical configuration of the region, it is not entirely inconceivable that it could one day find itself in military conflict with Iran—but even that prospect remains unlikely after long decades now of frosty relations and periodic political friction that never moved towards military conflict.

On the political level what these American-dependent authoritarian regimes have feared most is the *populist* character of Iran—its championing of popular revolution and its embrace of the Arab nationalist Palestinian cause in a more enthusiastic and effective manner than the leaders of these Arab countries have done themselves, and whose popular legitimacy is already shaky. Iranian support for popular mass liberation movements such as Hizballah and Hamas in Palestine opens fears in the Gulf of possible new such mass movements—more Arab Springs of the kind already witnessed in Tunisia, Egypt, and Yemen where pro-US dictators were overthrown. Saudi Arabia, as leader of a self-proclaimed monarchical bloc, is intent upon protecting monarchy from popular revolt across the region. And the Islamic Republic of Iran symbolizes support for popular Arab causes and defiance of

Israel and Washington—policies well-received among Arab populations. In the process the timidity and weakness of the autocrats—both monarchical and republican—have been revealed and highlighted. The same perception interestingly exists even among Indian Muslims—Shi'a as well as Sunni. A *non-*Muslim Indian diplomatic commentator observes:

> The Indian Muslim takes a dim view of the US' global policies. The Indian pundit may look at Iran as a Shi'ite country, but for the Indian Muslim, Iran signifies strategic defiance of the US. No matter the lavish funding of the Muslim ulema in India by the Gulf Arab monarchies … average Indian Muslim opinion equates Tehran as the voice of justice, honor and resistance."[2]

At the popular level *Arab publics* do not perceive Iran as a significant threat. While Arabs in general may not especially care for Persians, Arab citizens do not seem to fear Iran, even a nuclear one. And indeed, from their own position of weakness they have admired Tehran's guts over the years in challenging the dominance of US and Israeli policies in the Middle East. Remarkably, in a Brookings Institution Poll in six Arab countries in 2010 that included Egypt and Saudi Arabia, 57 percent of the Arab public believed a nuclear Iran would result in a "positive outcome" for the Middle East.[3]

Turkey poses a different case of course; its government does not carry the baggage of domestically unpopular autocratic rule. Its government is popularly elected and it has articulated frank criticisms of Israeli occupation policies that no other serious current leader in the Middle East has been willing to do. Through this stance Ankara has upstaged Iran's own past role as leader of "resistance" to Israel's treatment of Palestinians; Ankara now offers an alternative model of an independent foreign policy for the Middle East that is far more credible and successful than the Iranian version. (For Israel is it good news, or bad, that a far more rational, moderate, and credible state has now gained prominence in the Middle East and launched serious critiques of Israel's policies?) In the meantime Iran was clearly unhappy with its partial loss of regional prestige among Arabs under President Ahmadinejad, only made worse by Tehran's strong support to the Asad regime against domestic Sunni opponents in Syria. Iran is nonetheless very likely to regain some popular support again under Iran's new President Rouhani.

Turkish *public opinion* on Iran reveals much the same ambivalence and differs sharply from the position of the top military brass in Turkey, especially in past years. During an earlier decade of strong Turkish military influence over Ankara's foreign policy the generals indeed opposed close Turkish relations with Iran—precisely because they felt it might encourage Islamic radicalism in Turkey itself. We have noted how former Islamist leader

Necmettin Erbakan in 1996 chose to make his first foreign trip as prime minister to Tehran, much to military displeasure and before his overthrow. (Note how Turkish mainstream Sunni Islamist Erbakan was not deterred by any sectarian considerations in courting Shi'ite Iran.)

Second, it is worth noting that Turkey's major nationalist party, the Nationalist Action Party or MHP, mostly quite secular, has also nurtured significant elements of sympathy for Iran—again, precisely on the grounds of its defiance of the West. Turkish scholars Kibaroğlu and Çağlar note that "The nationalists in Turkey applaud the Iranian leadership and their 'dignified' policies for protecting Iran's rights and national interests against the world's 'only superpower.'"[4]

Thus *internal* Turkish political issues have had a direct bearing on Ankara's policies towards Tehran. Kibaroğlu and Çağlar suggest that Turkish (Sunni) Islamists welcomed Iran's potential quest for a nuclear weapon on the grounds that it would "terrify Israel" and force Israel to deal with Muslim states with greater respect. There is no doubt that should Iran develop a nuclear weapon, it would require Israel to maneuver more cautiously in the region. Again it is striking that Turkey does not seem to fear that Iran would use any possible future nuclear weapon against Turkey, especially when there is no history in modern times of military conflict or high tension confrontation between them. As the two scholars note, "the majority of Turks do not believe that Iran, as a friendly Muslim nation, would want to threaten Turkey with its nuclear weapons, today or in the future, especially when Israel is considered Iran's prime target." Furthermore, most Turks see Iran as insisting on preservation of its own dignity in the face of dominating western powers—towards whom Turkey itself holds ambivalent views.

Prime Minister Erdoğan has been cautious, as have nearly all senior Turkish government officials, to stress all countries' rights to develop the technologies of nuclear energy, and Turkey will be shortly doing so itself. "Turkey officially recognizes the right of Iran, a member of the Treaty on the Non-Proliferation of Nuclear Weapons, to develop nuclear technology, provided that it remains on a peaceful track and allows for the application of full-scope safeguard inspections by the IAEA in a way that would lend the utmost confidence to the international community about its intentions." Turkey is an elected member of the International Atomic Energy Agency board; should any serious evidence arises demonstrating that Iran is clearly on the path to weaponization, Turkey will be forced to choose sides. Turkey will almost surely side with the international consensus, whatever that will be—

and not with the consistently alarmist US/Israeli position—given Ankara's strong preference for internationally-sanctioned solutions on other issues.

Turkey was partner with Brazil in 2010 in seeking to broker an agreement with Iran on negotiations with the West over its enrichment program. Ankara believed it had Washington's blessing for such mediation, yet after Brazil and Turkey, quite unexpectedly, actually achieved the groundwork for an agreement and Iran agreed to talks, Washington then rejected the agreement out of hand in something of a rebuff to Turkey. Despite Washington's ultimate repudiation, this Brazilian-Turkish initiative represented nonetheless a new milestone in the architecture of international relations: two rising and respected medium powers had successfully used their good offices to reach an agreement with Tehran that Washington's blustering and threatening approach could not achieve. This event also suggests that medium-size world powers, not hobbled by imperial baggage, could assume a larger future role in seeking peaceful solutions through respecting the dignity of developing countries—as opposed to domineering western approaches and diktats. While the West may smirk at whether "dignity" has any real value in the world of power politics, it is proving to be an increasingly strong driver of many states and their populations who retain some anger at the ongoing history of western interventionism and who seek to restore the international balance.

Tehran, of course, cannot be allowed to simply sit by and pocket the concessions offered by neutral intermediaries and then raise the ante in some kind of *bazaari*-style bargaining. Tehran has proven itself an exceptionally prickly, wily, and exasperating interlocutor with nearly all intermediaries—including friendly ones—even as they have sought to negotiate on Iran's behalf. How far will Tehran feel that it can afford to allow neutral states of patently goodwill to fail in their attempts at mediation? Iran will increasingly face this problem in the years ahead as it seeks to break out of its isolation.

If Iran should eventually develop a nuclear weapons capability, Turkey will undoubtedly not be far behind. (So might Saudi Arabia.) But the purpose of such a capability would not likely be to intimidate the other. Joining the nuclear club is all about symbolism. Iran's prestige in the region would unquestionably rise, and its ability to impose its will in strategic confrontations would increase, as neighbors grow more wary. But the strategic situation in the Gulf would not be transformed as some believe it might.

Turkey would not welcome any major gain in prestige by Iran—even if Tehran is highly unlikely to threaten the use of nuclear weapons against Turkey. Indeed, NATO membership provides an umbrella to Turkey against such an attack. Furthermore, Turkey's agreement to host anti-ballistic missiles on its turf in September 2011 in principle would offer some theoretical protection against a potential Iranian nuclear threat by missile. But the fact is that Turkey sees little serious strategic benefit for itself in accepting the deployment of such NATO missiles on its soil; Ankara's decision was made almost exclusively as a sop to Washington on the heels of expelling the Israeli ambassador and other positions on regional issues at odds with Washington's preferences. The missile shield is a nod to NATO's interests, not a reliable shield against an Iranian attack that Turkey finds highly unlikely. Attack on Turkey from Syria, however, became far more conceivable since the outbreak of civil struggle there in 2011 (see Chapter 21).

The AKP government, and probably Turkey institutionally, favors linking Israel with Iran in future talks aimed at denuclearization of the entire region, Israel included. That view would be broadly supported across the Middle East. It would nonetheless be naïve to rule out all scenarios by which Iran might employ a nuclear weapon—the Iran-Iraq war being the primary case. That eight-year war, launched foolishly and aggressively by Saddam Hussein, came close to bringing down the new Iranian regime at its outset as it came under relentless Iraqi missile and chemical attack. There would seem to be little doubt that, if Iran had then possessed nuclear weapons at the time, under such desperate existential threat to the regime and the country, Tehran might well have used a nuclear weapon to defend its territory and regime. Conversely, some nuclear strategists argue that war becomes more dangerous—even perhaps unthinkable—when it involves two nuclear states. In other words, Saddam would not have even launched war against a nuclear Iran in the first place.

In my view, the chances are good that Turkey will itself eventually move towards the threshold of developing a nuclear capability—not in response specifically to Iran, but—much as in the spirit of the shah of Iran 40 years earlier—that Turkey's stature in the world calls for it to be "nuclear." Such a Turkish achievement would probably receive popular support at the public level in the Arab world. In the eyes of the Arab public, regional nuclear balance against Israel matters as much as a balance against Iran—again primarily in terms of the symbolism and trappings of Muslim geopolitical prestige.

The bottom line then, is that *for the region*, an Iranian nuclear weapon primarily possesses a political significance that cannot be dismissed. The military implications seem far greater for external powers that might choose to attack Iran's soil or intimidate it. And while some Gulf states, especially Saudi Arabia, would love to see the Iranian regime humbled, there are good indications that it too greatly fears the explosive regional consequences of an American or Israeli attack on Iran. They know that such an attack would be highly unlikely to eliminate the regime of the Iranian Islamic republic. Nor would any successor government—such as a nationalist-military regime in Tehran—be any more generously disposed to the Arab Gulf states, particularly if the Arabs had connived in encouraging an American/Israeli attack against Iran. The main hope of the Arab Gulf regimes is for its close ties with the US to discourage Iran from a bold political and rhetorical stance against their own regimes; they want the US to publicly have their back. None of them, including Saudi Arabia, really believes it could truly defend itself if it came to a military confrontation with Iran—and they probably do not believe that such a situation is in the cards.

In sum, nuclear issues in the Gulf have more to do with prestige and potential strengthening of Iran's stature in the region than it does with Shi'ism as a threat, or even the military aspects of nuclear negotiations. The Gulf Arab states were rightfully far more afraid of the Sunni regime of Saddam Hussein than they were of Iran. Indeed, if Iran were Sunni the geostrategic situation would scarcely be different, except that sectarian slogans could not then be invoked against Iran.

Shi'ite Minorities (and Majorities) in the Gulf

Up until the US overthrow of Saddam Hussein in Iraq, Iran stood as the sole Shi'ite state in the Middle East. (The Shi'a in Iraq constituted a clear majority but were excluded and suppressed by Saddam's Sunni regime.) Meanwhile the Gulf regimes remain worried about their own Shi'ite minorities (averaging about 10-15 percent). Bahrain is most exposed of all, since the Shi'a there constitute a significant majority—some two-thirds of the population—under a shaky, inflexible and inept Sunni *minority* regime. Bahrain for nearly two decades has been in a state of near-constant insurgency from the Shi'ite majority population that demands an end to discrimination and suppression, and seeks equal rights and political power proportional to their numbers; in the face of continuing repression and unresponsive attitudes over many years, the Shi'a have finally come to call for the overthrow of the Khalifa ruling family. After the reversal of the Sunni-Shi'a power balance in post-Saddam Iraq, a collapse of the Bahraini Sunni regime in favor of its Shi'ite majority would greatly increase pressures upon other Gulf regimes to liberalize and initiate reforms. Given the high degree of tensions and disorders there, Bahrain will likely be the first Gulf autocracy to fall. Saudi Arabia, too, faces an angry Shi'ite minority (some 15 percent of the population) where regime repression has only increased tensions and instability.

The Iranian Revolution of 1979 emboldened all Gulf Shi'a to protest the discrimination against them and to demand political change and greater political rights. After the formation of the first Shi'ite government in Iraq following the fall of Saddam in 2003, Riyadh quickly invoked the specter of a looming "Shi'ite threat" across the region—rather than deal with a democratic challenge to its own authoritarian and anti-Shi'ite order. Riyadh's determination by 2011 to overthrow the Asad regime in Damascus was directly linked to the "threat" emanating from Iran and its support to Damascus. The ugliest part of this course of events is Riyadh's choice to exacerbate extremist sectarian emotions, fanning a Sunni-Shi'ite struggle into unprecedented new levels of confrontation and even violence across the region. Riyadh has chosen to brand as "sectarian" most of the domestic challenges it faces, including calls for political reform and democratic institutions from both Shi'a and Sunnis. Worse, such exacerbation of sectarian antipathies gives free rein to jihadi extremism and intolerant Wahhabi views against the enemies of the kingdom.

Riyadh's mainstream support to the armed insurrection against Asad in Syria is first and foremost treated as a struggle against Shi'ism and Iran, although it is not so perceived in Syria itself. As a result of Saudi claims, Sunni jihadists became the primary beneficiary of the armed struggle in Syria. Riyadh also sought to enlist Jordan and, absurdly, Morocco, into this anti-Shi'ite, anti-Iranian crusade—two states with virtually no Shi'ite population. Riyadh also sought to ingratiate the kingdom with Washington by playing to its strong anti-Iranian policies as well. Yet the kingdom plays with fire through these tactics by intensifying sectarian passions and jihadi violence across the region. The campaign also reinforces the will of Gulf regimes to make no democratic concessions to their Shi'a population—or any other reformist groups. Shi'ite calls for democratization, and their efforts to gain equal political and social rights become, by Saudi definition, subversive and the product of "Iranian meddling."

Of course anti-Shi'ite prejudices exist in much of the Arab world. But they exist primarily where Shi'ite populations live side by side with Sunnis; Sunni prejudice is directed against "those people"—the community that lives on the other side of the tracks, whatever its name or designation might be, that is pushing for greater rights. One is reminded of white citizens in the American south that viewed black demands for reform and social justice as "uppity" and threatening to the dominant white status quo. Where there are no local Shi'ite communities present there is little serious anti-Iranian sentiment. Riyadh seeks to create or play on ethnic and religious stereotyping as a basic domestic and foreign policy tool. Thus it would be a mistake for the western analyst to perceive all of this as representing some kind of permanent and unbridgeable "sectarian divide."

The struggle of the Saudis to shore up Gulf monarchies has expanded into an effort to weaken Iran's political influence and ideology anywhere in the region. Egypt has been a key battleground going back for some time, despite the fact that Shi'a make up less than one percent of Egypt's population. As we noted earlier, the Muslim Brotherhood took a positive attitude early on in 1979 towards the Islamic character of the Iranian Revolution; it welcomed Tehran's attempt at creating a modern Islamist republic, it applauded Tehran's strong new support for the Palestinian cause and for the Sunni resistance movement Hamas, and its outspoken stance against western interventionist policies. Iran praised the 1981 assassination of Egyptian president Anwar Sadat by (non-Brotherhood) Sunni jihadi terrorists; Sadat had been broadly perceived by *both* Arab nationalists and Islamists as having sold out to the US and Israel in signing the Camp David peace agreement between Egypt and Israel—essentially removing Egypt from the front lines in opposing Israeli occupation of the West Bank and Gaza and splitting the Arab world.

Egyptian president Mubarak, as a US client, maintained a chilly relationship towards Iran, even hindering passage of Iranian ships through the Suez Canal. That changed with his fall and the emergence of a Brotherhood-led regime in Cairo in 2012. The new president Muhammad Mursi visited Tehran in 2012— attending a non-aligned meeting in Tehran—but the symbolism was significant and criticized by Washington. The Egyptian minister of tourism went to Tehran in 2013 to encourage desperately needed Iranian tourism to Egypt, yet Egyptian Salafis—virtually by definition anti-Shi'a—expressed fears that any ties with Iran, even via tourism, would lead to corruption of Sunni culture. Egyptian liberals feared that ties with Iran would only serve to strengthen religious forces in Egypt. The old Egyptian constitution does not even recognize Shi'ite Islam as a legitimate source of legislation. The Saudis attempted to use funding to sharply limit Mursi's contacts with Iran.[5]

Egypt's efforts to adopt a staunch anti-Shi'ite posture are awkward since one of the glories of Egyptian and Islamic history is the Isma'ili (Shi'ite) Fatimid Empire that ruled over most of the Arab world for 250 years starting in the 10th century. The Fatimids created some of the present glories of Islamic architecture in its capital Cairo, including the al-Azhar mosque and many other buildings and cultural accomplishments. Indeed, al-Azhar

University, a key center of Sunni Islam, was founded by the Fatimids over 1,000 years ago. In 1958 the Shaykh of Al-Azhar issued a *fatwa* declaring Iran's Shi'ite school of theology to be legitimate under Islam. He also worked to establish a Council for the Rapprochement of Islamic Theological Schools at the time. And in 1988 Tehran established a World Assembly for the Rapprochement of Islamic Schools. Thus the crude exploitation of sectarianism has never been so prominently displayed until much more recent times.[6] Indeed, Egyptians have little reason to fear or dislike Shi'ism. A Gallup poll of the Egyptian population in 2012 indicated that 56 percent of the population sees closer relations with the US as a bad thing, whereas 41 percent believed relations with Iran to be good for Egypt, while 60 percent saw relations with Turkey to be good.[7]

In demographic terms, the Gulf contains the greatest concentration of Shi'a in the Arab world, which helps explain the high degree of sectarian emotion. Historically the Gulf Shi'a represent one of the oldest Shi'ite urban and merchant communities anywhere, conquered only in the last few centuries by essentially Sunni bedouin nomadic tribes out of the Arabian desert. Riyadh's official Wahhabi ideology is of course harshly anti-Shi'ite on ideological grounds, apart from any demographic or political threat. In Bahrain, now a virtual protectorate of Saudi Arabia, the handwriting is on the wall for all to see: the Shi'a majority of two-thirds of the population will assume dominant political control of the country as soon as the al-Khalifa regime has been displaced or the country accepts democratic governance. This scares Riyadh since the Bahraini Shi'a maintain close family and clan links with the heavily Shi'ite al-Hasa province of eastern Saudi Arabia just a short way across the water (and the major zone of oil production.) These Saudi Shi'a, too, resent the hundreds of years of discrimination at the hands of Wahhabi power that oppresses them and has rendered them second-class citizens. Their culture and religious freedom is suppressed and their Shi'ite faith ridiculed as apostate in state textbooks. It is no surprise, then, that these Shi'ite minorities historically have been able to look only to Iran for external protection— whose response has generally been little more than rhetorical and lukewarm.

Turkey and Iran: Rivals or Pace-setters?
Turkey and Iran, along with Egypt, are historically the most deeply established states of the Middle East. Turkish and Persian cultural identities are also relatively clear and secure. Their borders are perceived as stable and durable. These powerful and significant non-Arab cultures both represent "stand-

alone" cultures; unlike Arab states they have no other immediate natural ethnic allies nearby.

Where does Iran fit into the calculus of regional change after the Arab Spring, and how does it relate to Turkey's own emerging role in the region? *Iran may ultimately be the single-most important country for Turkey in the Middle East.* After Turkey, Iran is arguably the second regional great power that is destined to grow stronger, not weaker, with time. Turkey and Iran together will exert greater influence than any other states in the region. Other potential rivals are floundering: Egypt is struggling to find itself in the midst of political turmoil under a new military regime and is unprepared to play a regional leadership role. Saudi Arabia is caught up in flagging defensive efforts to prop up regional monarchies against popular unrest from their own peoples and lacks vision for the future. But the Turkish relationship with Iran is of major importance with much impact on the rest of the region. How will it fare? Turkey's relations with Iran include important bilateral issues, especially huge energy deals, thorny shared third-party issues such as dealing with Kurds, Iraq, Syria, and sectarian struggles in the region. Iran represents a key stumbling block in Ankara's relations with Washington as long as Washington is unable to deal with Tehran.

In a region dominated by great swings of the power pendulum over time, the relationship between Turkey and Iran has actually remained remarkably stable for hundreds of years. And it is likely to remain that way, despite pressures from many sides, especially from the US, to break the relationship. At the same time, Turkey and Iran seem destined never be truly cordial towards one another. If overt hostility seems not in the cards between them, neither is a real alliance. They know each other too well for too long for that. Iran, for historical and cultural reasons, is suspicious and prickly in its views of the world in general, culturally condescending towards Turks and Arabs— although it has been compelled to acknowledge Turkey's pioneer role in the region in the 20th century. Iran's 30 years of isolation from the West has only intensified these instincts.

It wasn't always so. It's difficult to separate out Persians from Turks in the historical experience of both. The two peoples share a deeply interwoven past. Turks, in their grand migration of various tribes and clans out of Central Asia into Anatolia over centuries starting around AD 800, found themselves deeply engaged in the Persian cultural world as Turkic nomadic groups moved west, stopped and settled for long periods during which they became part of a Persian-Turkish political, social and cultural order. Turks were often the foot-soldiers of numerous Persian rulers and played a major role in administering the Iranian empire for long periods of time. Turkic peoples form an integral part of Persian history and they still make up a highly significant part of the modern Iranian state—particularly the Turkic Azeris. Large numbers of Persian words still stud everyday Turkish speech even if most Turks aren't aware of it. Turkey's (and the West's) most beloved poet, Rumi, lived most of his life in Turkey after migrating from Persia, even though he wrote most of his mystical Sufi poetry in Persian.

Less well known in the West is the fact that Iran—today the ultimate symbol of Shi'ism—had actually been a Sunni state throughout most of Islamic history. It was as late as 1500 when Sunni Iran was taken over by the Turkic-influenced Safavid dynasty in Iran that went on to adopt Shi'ism, throw out the old Sunni faith, and slowly convert the Iranian population to Shi'ism. This new Shi'ite state then proceeded to challenge the Ottomans— the center of Sunni Islam—whom they identified as the enemy of Shi'ism. As a result, the Middle East, from about 1500-1800, experienced one of history's great Cold Wars—occasionally hot—between Iran's Shi'ite Safavid Empire and the Sunni Ottoman Empire. This struggle was marked by immense ideological vituperation and denunciations, accompanied by numerous struggles over territory along their shifting borders in eastern Anatolia and Mesopotamia. This was the period in which the Iranian identity became newly and permanently identified with Shi'ism.

But despite the ideological quarrels and ongoing mistrust, by the 17th century serious territorial wars between these two warring states had drawn to an end. Frictions were never again to be translated into true territorial conflict or war. Relations between the two states instead came to be characterized by a cautious coexistence and grudging mutual respect. As a result, the two countries have enjoyed several hundred years of virtual peace. Unlike Turks and Arabs who often found themselves in opposing camps during the US-Soviet Cold War, Turks and Iranians were on the same side, both sharing an intense distrust of Russian territorial expansionism to which both had fallen victim over the centuries.

Iran's reformist shahs of the 20th century—Reza Pahlavi and Mohammad Reza Pahlavi—both modeled their reforms on Kemalist reformist programs in bringing top-down reforms to Iran, although far less skillfully. Probably the greatest ideological tensions between the two states in modern times came with the Islamic Revolution in Iran in 1979 when the first Islamist semi-democratic regime in modern Muslim history came to power in Tehran. The mullahs of Tehran proceeded to denigrate the secularist policies of the Kemalist revolution as anti-Islam and accused Ankara of kowtowing to western imperialism. But such ideological tensions had little practical effect upon their relations; pragmatism has since marked the views and actions of both sides. Turkey's Islamists have generally not been hostile to Iran. Shared Islamist suspicions of the hegemonic policies of the West and desire for Islam-influenced change clearly overrode sectarian concerns.

Turkey's essential goal in its relations with Iran is to maintain a stable regional environment and to maintain its significant trade with Iran— particularly in vital energy supplies. Until the Syrian crisis of 2011 the AKP fairly consistently opposed western military intervention or subversive operations against states in the region including Iran. Ankara is vividly aware of the devastating and destabilizing impact of US wars in Afghanistan and Iraq, of Israeli invasions of Lebanon, and Israeli expansionist policies in Palestinian territories. Ankara also declared its opposition to policies based on sectarianism that pit Sunnis against Shi'a. Davutoğlu has spoken of Turkey and Iran constituting a "backbone" of regional stability. Ankara believes that external military interventions in the region have consistently damaged Turkish interests at all levels—political, economic, sectarian and ethnic. Davutoğlu has called for regional solutions to regional problems, preferably reached through consensus and diplomacy. These principles have represented Turkish rock-bottom interests and goals.

What, then, are the key regional issues that dominate the Turkish relationship with Iran?

• Shared concern over Kurdish separatist movements in Turkey, Iran, Iraq and Syria (see Chapter 22 on the Kurdish Regional Web.)

• Concern for potential civil war in Iraq among Arab Shi'a, Arab Sunnis, Kurds, and Turkmen that would produce destabilizing disorders on Turkey's doorstep; Iranian policies directly affect those issues (see Chapter 20 on Shi'ism and Iraq).

• Sharply differing perspectives on the fate of the Asad regime in Syria and the character of any future regime there. A settlement of that crisis will greatly ease Ankara's relations with Tehran (see Chapter 21).

• Iranian nuclear policies and Washington's major efforts to enlist Ankara in isolating and destabilizing Iran.

• A shared desire to avoid Sunni-Shi'ite sectarian conflict in the region—that has major *internal* implications for Turkey as well;

• A desire to end conflict in Afghanistan and achieve removal of western forces;

• A manageable rivalry in Central Asia and a shared desire for the independence of the Central Asia states from both Russian and Chinese domination.

Washington has sought for decades to enlist Ankara in its struggle against Iran, only to find Turkey largely ignoring the assumptions and policy prescriptions coming from the US. Washington today still pressures Turkey to support policies designed to pressure Tehran—but with minimal success. Turkey has maintained ongoing and correct relations with Tehran through thick and thin despite some sharp exchanges, particularly over Syria. Ankara is in the first instance driven both by its need for energy imports from Iran, and by its opposition to any US or Israeli military strike against Iran that it views as deeply destabilizing. It simply does not view Iran as a major threat.

The western press, however, has maintained a series of differing and heady story lines towards Turkey's relationship with Iran. Take your pick—they're all inaccurate:

• Secular Turkey is locked in battle against fundamentalist Iran—Kemalism against the mullahs;

• Turkey represents the West in the grand struggle against Islamist Iran;

• Conversely, Turkey has joined Tehran in forming an anti-western, anti-Israeli axis—a view promoted by neoconservative observers;

• Sunni Turkey has joined with Saudi Arabia to take on Shi'ite Iran in a great Sunni regional coalition;

• Turkey is engaged in a massive and bitter rivalry with Iran for domination of the Middle East.

None of these self-contradicting cases can be seriously argued and reflect a western predisposition to see all issues in the region from a parochial US and Israeli perspective.

Economics and Energy

Understanding the dynamic of energy issues is key to understanding the strong bonds of mutual interest between Turkey and Iran today. The figures are striking: the Turkish Energy Market Regulation Board (EPDK) reported that Turkey depended upon Iran for 45 percent of its oil imports in 2010, followed by Iraq at 12 percent.[8] Turkey additionally imports about 30 percent of its annual gas needs from Iran and Iran is Turkey's second-largest source of gas after Russia. Turkey is investing in the further development of Iran's gas fields and plans to export Iranian gas across Turkish soil to Europe as well. Trade increased 10-fold between Turkey and Iran between 2000 and 2010 and is expected to triple again by 2014. Up to two million Iranian visitors come to

Turkey each year.[9] Turkey is thus unwilling to jeopardize this vital, long-term energy infrastructure in favor of short-term tactical maneuvers against Tehran. Ankara will not openly defy Washington, but it will make clear that its policies are firm, driven by its own interests, and subject only to cosmetic change.

Turkish trade with Iran, while significant, is less than one might expect and Ankara has targeted it for expansion. At present Iran meets only 5 percent of its import requirements from Turkey. Sweeping US sanctions in financial, energy and other major sectors are a significant factor here that have depressed bilateral trade, but Ankara is proceeding to intensify trade with barely a nod to US sanction policies. These ties are opening again fast to Washington's discomfiture even with initial negotiations between the US and Iran in 2014.

Trade is not just bilateral. Both states represent important entry points for each other: Turkey opens the door for Iran to the West, while Iran opens the door for Turkey to the East. According to the Foreign Economic Relations Board of Turkey, Turkey is gradually replacing Dubai as entrepôt for Iranian trade. "'The best of Iranian firms penetrate world markets through Turkey,' [an official] said, noting that cultural, historical and religious links go back hundreds of years as well as Iranian firms' interest in Turkey."[10] Reportedly, one out of three businessmen in Iran speaks Turkish (or the closely-related Azeri), greatly facilitating business ties. The number of Iranian firms operating in Turkey for trade to the West has hugely expanded under the AKP: in the whole 50 years before 2002 there were only 319 Iranian firms in Turkey; in the succeeding nine years the number leapt to 11,470. Turkish Airlines offers direct flights to five Iranian cities—Tehran, Tabriz, Isfahan, Kermanshah, and Mashhad—greatly facilitating business contacts. Ankara hopes to triple trade with Iran to US$30 billion by 2014 as more border-crossing points open up. Ankara also sees opportunities in utilizing good Iranian ties with Afghanistan and Tajikistan to create joint investment projects there.[11]

East of Tehran

With the collapse of the Soviet Union in 1991 and the emergence of eight new independent states south of Russia—six of them Muslim, five of them Turkic-speaking, one of them Persian-speaking—Turkey found new opportunities for the export of Turkish influence and role in Central Asia and the Caucasus. Iran perceived the same opportunities. Iran is, after all, a quintessentially Central Asian state whose culture—language, architecture, arts, food, music, philosophy—powerfully dominated Central Asia for millennia, far more so than Turkey. Washington initially backed Turkey heavily as a secular rival to

Iranian influence in Central Asia. In the end, it was Turkey's booming economy and its Gülen schools that enabled Ankara in the 2000s to achieve a strong position in the economic life of Central Asia. Iran understandably views Hizmet schools as a rival to its own influence and vision and is one of the few countries in the Middle East where no Hizmet schools yet exist. Tehran has so far turned them down, but Shi'ite students in Azerbaijan and elsewhere do attend Gülen schools where there are no "sectarian" problems.

As elsewhere Turkey has an informal rivalry with Iran in Central Asia, but it is not zero-sum, and both countries see areas for cooperation. As we noted above, Turkey needs Iran to help facilitate its land passage to Central Asia. Both countries share an interest in Central Asian and Caspian energy in which Iran will always be a natural transit route to the West. They both share a geopolitical interest in preventing the Central Asian and smaller Caucasian states from falling under complete Russian or Chinese domination—although China's clout is growing. Iran is also a natural player in the troubled regions of Afghanistan and Pakistan where Turkey also has long-standing ties and interests. Both Turkey and Iran seek a stable Afghanistan and are in a position to help develop the country after the departure of US/NATO forces and the inevitable subsequent domestic struggle for power there.

In the end, while there are some hardliners in Iran who view Turkey as a threatening rival to Tehran's interests, the mainstream establishments in both countries are pragmatic and believe they share more interests in the region than they contest.

The Turkish vs. Iranian "Model"

Both Turkey and Iran welcomed the events of the Arab Spring. Both believed the area was ripe for change and movement away from unpopular authoritarian regimes. Each believed it would itself benefit from this change. Iran has benefitted from its revolutionary image and its willingness to "stand up to the West" in the eyes of Middle East populations. But Iran's democratic and Islamic image suffered under the Ahmadinejad presidency—certain now to improve with the new more moderate presidency in Tehran and the opening of Iranian ties with the West. Ankara can still speak in the region about development, democracy and Islamic foreign polices more credibly than can Iran. When the choice comes for Arabs to find a model to emulate, Turkey offers far more than Iran ever could, even within an Islamic context. Thus Iran's appeal to the general public in the Middle East has notably declined relative to Turkey's growing role. Turkey, as viable and responsible democratic model in the Middle East, has essentially displaced Iran as challenger both to autocracy and to hardline Israeli policies in the Middle East.

Even in the Arab world Turkish and Iranian interests are not exactly zero-sum—one's gain is not automatically the other's loss. The Islamic Republic, which consistently sought to reduce western power and intervention in the Middle East, now finds that the Arab Spring is creating forces that in the end, even as they shift, will not benefit US power and position overall. Even Turkey's greater policy independence from Washington has served the longer-term Iranian goal of diminishing US clout in the region. Iran still sees regional events as moving essentially in the right direction, representing a net gain for Iran—except in Syria. The Middle East now enjoys arguably more regional autonomy than it has in centuries, although the process is messy and far from over. Iran finds grounds for satisfaction with these developments, but is distressed that events have not contributed to a palpable increase in Iranian power across the region (except dramatically in Iraq.) Worse, Saudi Arabia has declared sectarian war against Iran. But Riyadh's claim to be working to defend the region from the Shi'ite/Iranian threat will grow less credible.

As states of the Middle East achieve greater independence from western domination, the more Iran's symbol of defiance will ironically lose relevance and appeal. A just solution of the Palestinian problem would remove yet another card from the Iranian hand. While Turkey has not deliberately sought to reduce Iran's influence—and indeed insists on working closely with it to the extent possible—the course of events have largely benefitted Ankara at Tehran's expense. It is hard to imagine circumstances under which Iran would gain a major voice as a regional actor. But one such case cannot be excluded: if the smaller Gulf states were to be presented with a new and highly aggressive posture from either Iraq or Saudi Arabia, Iran ironically could play a significant balancing role against such a threat. Iraq under Saddam Hussein has already disastrously tried its hand at annexing Kuwait. More likely, however, is that a new revolutionary regime in Riyadh will itself one day threaten the independent existence of the small Gulf shaykhdoms, in a possible Wahhabi sweep towards "Manifest Destiny." Under such circumstances Iran and/or Iraq could quite plausibly serve as force to help check such an expansionist (Saudi) Arabia.

If the West is hoping for a major strategic split between Ankara and Tehran it will probably have to wait a long time. Neither Ankara nor Tehran wants it or needs it, and both know it. Promising new relations between Iran and the West open many new combinations for fresh geopolitical alignments that will differ from the frozen and fossilized relations of the past.

CHAPTER TWENTY

THE CHALLENGE OF SHI'ISM: IRAQ SHIFTS THE BALANCE

If Iran is the preeminent Shi'ite state of the world today, Iraq is a powerful cultural rival. In fact, in historical terms Iraq is more important to Shi'ism than is Iran: Iraq was the main seat of Shi'ite intellectual thought for more than a millennium. Shi'ism's single-most famous religious seminary (*hawza*) in the world is in Najaf in central Iraq, where the most important Shi'ite shrine of all—the tomb of 'Ali himself—is located. Formally speaking, of course, Iraq does not and will not declare itself as a Shi'ite state; Iraqi Shi'a, who represent two-thirds of the population, share the country with the remaining one-third Sunni population.

For 400 years, Iraq—or Mesopotamia—represented an important part of the Ottoman Empire. But it was also known to the Ottomans as a troublesome place. *Yanlış hesap Bağdattan döner* was a phrase well known to Ottoman bureaucrats: "Even miscalculation in Baghdad ends up back home." Indeed, the often rapid turnover of Ottoman governors in Baghdad revealed the problems of ruling it: Mesopotamia was territory contested with Iran over millennia. A large proportion of its population was Shi'ite (thus antipathetic to the Ottomans), and Kurds were isolated in the mountains and wanted to be left alone by the authorities; the region was a seat of latent Arab discontent with the shortcomings Ottoman rule. It was not until 1500 that Iran's new Safavid rulers abolished Sunnism to embrace Shi'ism, but Iran could not change the reality that the most sacred Shi'ite cities—particularly Karbala and Najaf—were both located in Ottoman Iraq. In its local administration in Iraq the Ottomans favored the Sunni community, while the Shi'a were left outside of mainstream society, creating a legacy of discontent among them. And then British imperialists decided to perpetuate Sunni dominance as they took over the country, a policy ultimately inherited by the rulers of Iraq's Ba'th Party and Saddam Hussein. Iraq's new Shi'ite rulers today retain vivid and angry memory of their political isolation over centuries and are determined that it will not recur.

This transfer of power from Sunni into Shi'ites after the US invasion and fall of Saddam Hussein in 2003 struck anxiety into the hearts of the Sunni Gulf, particularly Saudi Arabia and Bahrain. In terms of regional sectarian politics Iraq had just shifted out of the Sunni column and into the Shi'ite, recalibrating the balance of Iraqi domestic power and emboldening sidelined Shi'ite communities down the Gulf. Let's take a look at this Iraqi aspect of the story as constituting a key element in the new Shi'ite "threat" to the region.

The Question of Iraqi Identity

If "communal identity" lies at the heart of conflict, so too "national identity" is a question that occupies most states of the world. It has to do with self-perception, a state's "natural" links to the rest of the world; this self-perception reveals much about the character and nature of the state and where it sees itself going. We observe this phenomenon especially strongly in the Middle East where borders had been redrawn for the convenience of imperial powers; new states in effect had to determine who they now were, where their interests and natural allies might be and what shared goals might exist. Is Iraq a "Mesopotamian state" centered on that classical civilization? Or simply now an "Iraqi" state, however interpreted? How much of its identity is wrapped up in being a Muslim state? Or an Arab state, or a Sunni or Shi'ite state? Perhaps an Arab nationalist state, even a leftist state (at a time when the Iraqi communist party wielded great strength in the country). Or was its character set as a Ba'thist state (under Saddam)? States can shift elements of their identities over time in accordance with events and circumstances, and by choice of leadership. The public does not always have a decisive say in the character of the identity projected. And inevitably the character of the identity chosen empowers some, and disempowers others on the domestic scene.

Iraq's "Arab identity," however, has been the dominant identity over the past half a century. But even this is a relatively recent cultural development, beginning when Iraq became one of several key centers of Arab nationalism during the 20th century. And the idea of "Arab nationalism" itself needs clarification. Does it simply mean those who speak Arabic as their mother tongue—thereby excluding, for example, Arabized Kurds from participation in the national project? And what about religion? The history of Arab nationalism included Arab Christian figures who played vital roles in the evolution of the Arab nationalist concept in Syria and elsewhere. But Arab nationalism has always *unofficially* implied membership in "Muslim culture"; indeed, many Arab Christians would acknowledge themselves as being part of a broader "Muslim culture," even as Christian residents of the Middle East. But circumstances change; Arab Christians today find themselves fitting less comfortably into the Arab nationalist project, especially as the region has turned into a zone of conflict with predictable loss of tolerance. Muslim culture itself in Iraq almost invariably had a Sunni flavor to it as well, an assumption of participation in an essentially Sunni project, of which Shi'a were not always a part. (One of the reasons for the appeal of communist parties in the Middle East, especially in Iraq, was that they have no interest in whether their members are Christian, Muslim, Jewish, Sunni, or Shi'ite; communist parties everywhere regularly attract minorities.) And in today's Middle East, especially since the end of colonial rule—and even more since the wars of 9/11—society has grown more distraught, more tense, narrower, and less tolerant under the deteriorating conditions of conflict and war in its midst. When times are really bad, to whom do you flee for safety?

These issues may sound theoretical, but they do affect interaction among regional states today. Until the US invasion in 2003, Iraq was a stalwart member of the Arab nationalist bloc, along with Syria, and Libya (in its own quixotic fashion.) Egypt had been a founding member of the Arab nationalist movement, but during 30 years of Mubarak's rule had abandoned any meaningful leadership role in the region. Arab nationalists, however, mainly defined their foreign policy goals as strengthening the unity of the Arab world, resistance to Israeli domination of the Palestinians, and opposition to western exercise of hegemonic power in the region. While primarily a Sunni project in nature, it was not rigidly so: the 'Alawi regime of the Asads was among the most outspoken and activist in terms of the Arab nationalist cause, and large numbers of Shi'a in Iraq also supported it. But when the Sunnis in Iraq lost control of the state to the Shi'ite majority after the fall of Saddam, what would be the impact upon the Iraqi identity? Iraqis certainly had their own (diverse) ideas on the subject, but so did other states around Iraq; many in the Gulf were not at all sure that a Shi'ite-dominated Iraqi government with close ties to Iran could still form part of an "Arab world project"—one that the Saudis increasingly defined as Sunni. Of course there is no reason Shi'a too cannot just as much be part of that project, but when Sunnis drive them into a defensive posture, Sunni calls for "Arab unity" lose most appeal for Shi'a.

Recent history further complicated Iraq's identity issues. Transnational influences across Arab states have always been the norm, given largely arbitrary imposed colonial borders. During the long struggle against Saddam Hussein, opposition groups were forced to flee in exile around the region—to Iran, Syria, Saudi Arabia, and the West—in order to organize the anti-Saddam opposition movement. While out of the country they were exposed to different attitudes, ideas and influences from those states; now they are all back in post-Saddam Baghdad again but those earlier external influences and ties remain present. In addition, the US overthrow of Saddam and subsequent internal civil strife, turmoil and displacement of millions of Iraqis resulted in a new Iraqi diaspora in many of these same places, including Jordan, which stimulated further outside Arab influences on the orientation and thinking of many Iraqis.[1] The question remains: when will Iraqis enjoy the luxury of considering national identity—the nation as a whole—under more peaceful conditions instead of being driven by deep communitarian existential fears and a search for any port in a storm?

Iran and Iraq—a New Relationship

By far the most dramatic and sweeping change—180 degrees—in Iraq's recent foreign relationships has been with Iran. In modern history Iraq and Iran had nurtured hostility towards each other at least over the last half a century: Iraq was a Soviet client for long years while the shah of Iran was a stalwart western ally; Iran and Iraq hotly contested border issues; both manipulated each other's Kurdish population, and Saddam Hussein finally launched an unprovoked eight-year war against the new Islamic republic in Iran that cost both countries dearly, but especially Iran. With the Shi'a coming to power in Iraq after the US invasion, Iran immediately started to provide assistance to the new Shi'ite-dominated government which itself felt threatened by Sunni militias and under siege from Sunni jihadists; it therefore welcomed Iranian support, even during US occupation. Today Iran is a key supporter of the Iraqi government with major economic interests in the country. Iran is the prime beneficiary of the US debacle in Iraq, and is now no longer threatened by American power from Iraqi soil. Tehran will wish to keep Baghdad as friendly as possible towards Tehran as a priority policy goal. All of this has also been a major gain for overall Shi'ite power in the region.

These close new Iran-Iraq ties now feed Saudi fears of a doubled Shi'ite threat, which led to a near break in diplomatic relations between Riyadh and the new government in Baghdad. The Shi'ite government fears that Saudi Arabia will never truly acknowledge its legitimacy. The two countries have been on opposing sides of a proxy war in Syria; Baghdad supports the Asad regime while Saudi Arabia supports Sunni jihadis to overthrow it. Baghdad fears that Saudi Arabia may next try to target Iraq itself to attempt to restore Sunni power there, or to at least maintain ongoing Sunni jihadi attacks against the Iraqi government.

Still, it is simplistic to believe that just because Iran and now Iraq are both dominated by Shi'ite governments will guarantee permanently cordial relations between the two. It is entirely logical for Iraqi Shi'a at this point in Iraqi history to focus all attention on consolidating their majoritarian base of political power in the country; for that they need some degree of Iranian support. But over the longer run, Shi'ite and Sunni are not the only operative identities in the region that matter. Iraqi Shi'a are also Arabs and not Persians; they differ sharply in language and national narrative. Iraqi Shi'a view their own cultural expression of Shi'ism as more originally "Arab" than the later Persian cultural form. They speak of their Shi'ism as more oriented towards 'Ali the son-in-law of the Prophet while Iranians are more oriented towards the martyrdom of 'Ali's grandsons Hasan and Husayn. As Iraqi Shi'a come to feel more secure in the Iraqi political game they will certainly recognize that the interests of Iraq and Iran may differ in certain respects, and may even display elements of rivalry in the region. Baghdad will never welcome routine Iranian interference in Iraqi affairs and Iran will have to tread carefully in order not to overplay its hand in Iraqi affairs. The appearance of divisions between them cannot be far off.

Yet Shi'ite political dominance in Iraq is now a permanent reality, barring some kind of military coup by Sunni forces; in such an event the struggle for power would turn into genuine and bloody civil war, with Iran backing Shi'ite forces from a position of great advantage. Such an event also seems unlikely. Far more likely is a return to a modus vivendi, even if prickly, between Shi'a and Sunni in Iraq. Meanwhile all Iraqis ultimately share joint interests in the development of their country that transcend narrower sectarian interests. The country will ultimately be more stable now that the Shi'a have achieved their appropriate electoral voice in democratic politics as the majority. The Sunnis have no choice but to ultimately accept that reality. If the Shi'a, however, should now take advantage of their new position of power and seek to permanently disenfranchise the many Sunni voices in the country—as they have largely done under Prime Minister Nuri al-Maliki—the outlook will not be good. Sunni and Shi'a have many other interests than sectarian identity: restoring calm, playing in regional politics, building the economy, oil policies, Kurdish issues, and multiple other foreign policy interests. When domestic Iraqi politics become less existential to both communities, some degree of cooperation will return.

And how does this new Shi'ite power in Iraq affect the Shi'a down the Gulf? As long as Shi'ite communities in other Gulf states continue to be excluded or oppressed they will continue to struggle for equality of treatment—especially in Bahrain and Saudi Arabia, the two places of most egregious discrimination. In the past oppressed and impotent Shi'a indeed did look to Iran as the sole possible external source of support or representation of their cause. And in its more radical days Iran did support various violent Shi'ite groups in the Gulf, especially in countries like Kuwait and the UAE as those countries supported Iraq in its war against Iran. But today there is a new Shi'ite state force in the Gulf—Iraq. Iraq is in many ways closer to most Gulf Arab Shi'a than is Iran: they share a common Arabic language, family and community links, and a common Arab Shi'ite culture. Support to the Gulf Arab Shi'a from Arab *Baghdad* is more logical and credible than is support from Persian Iran, which opens up issues of *ethnic* rivalry as well. Thus Iraq, even with its large Sunni minority population, is now in a position to wield new influence on behalf of the Gulf Shi'a.

Baghdad will of course have more foreign policy interests in the Gulf than merely sectarian ones: oil policy, economic cooperation, and interest in common issues of leadership in the Arab world. Iraq is an Arab country with a tradition of support for Arab nationalist ideology and engagement in Arab nationalist causes. The quest for regional Arab leadership will not disappear; once sectarian rivalry in Iraq eventually reaches some equilibrium Iraq will surely acquire a more coherent Arab voice. Arab Shi'a have a strong sense of Arabness that Tehran cannot afford to forget. Iraq will gradually reassert greater interest and voice in Arab world affairs overall. It will be one of the three major Gulf states playing in Gulf geopolitics, along with Saudi Arabia and Iran. Iraq may end up ideologically adopting an anti-monarchical position—a role that may be "waiting for an actor" in the Gulf. Or, who knows, Iraq could even end up defending the Gulf monarchies against possible Iranian pressure down the road. Even more likely, Iraq may be in a vital position to balance a likely *Saudi* quest for Gulf hegemony among the small Gulf shaykhdoms in the future; these small states could be quite threatened and would look to some regional power, apart from the US, that could help them defend their sovereignty against a potentially aggressive Riyadh.

Forging some kind of regional security arrangements is an issue that has consistently divided the Gulf—the two major military powers of Iraq and Iraq on one side, Saudi Arabia and the small Gulf states on the other. As significant regional powers Iran and Iraq have both been hostile to western security guarantees and intervention in the Gulf; they have argued that the Gulf states should work out security arrangements among themselves as a regional bloc. Riyadh, on the other hand, has always depended upon the West and especially the US as its primary source of security in the event of Gulf crisis—partly because of the huge military power of the US, because Riyadh does not fully trust the loyalty, or capabilities, of its own armed forces, and has not wished to grant either Iran or Iraq a structural or organizational voice in Gulf security issues. Iraq and Iran may jointly now seek to develop an inclusive regional security organization—an expanded Gulf Cooperation Council—to handle security affairs, but Riyadh is likely to strongly resist such a plan, out of fear of the latent revolutionary or democratic character of Iran and Iraq—even in spite of Riyadh's dwindling confidence in the US as all-weather ally and protector.

In any case, Saudi efforts to portray the nature of regional politics as basically a sectarian struggle is overwhelmingly simplistic and masks the real geopolitical forces at work. The emergence of Iraq with a partially new identity that includes Shi'ite power creates complications in the power equation of the region; it is not yet fully clear just how that identity will affect Iraq's role in Arab world politics. Given Iraq's strong voice in Arab geopolitics in the past, it seems unlikely that it will now lapse into passivity under new Shi'ite domination, distant from Arab affairs. As Sunni voices gradually return to playing some role in governing Iraq, Baghdad is unlikely to fall henceforth into some predictable "Shi'ite column" in regional affairs. Growth of some new Sunni confidence in Iraq will likely hasten the return of Iraq to Arab politics.

Iraq and Syria

Iraq for the first time in modern history is now dominated by the Iraqi Shi'a, but they are not a monolithic group: some are secular, some follow various ayatollahs who do not agree with each other. They follow different secular ideologies, right and left; they have regional as well as class affiliations. Only an existential threat to them all on the basis of sectarianism is capable of uniting them. Saudi Arabia's regional campaign seems unintentionally designed to do just that. Thus Riyadh's determination to overthrow the secular 'Alawi (quasi-Shi'ite) Asad government in Syria has immediate direct negative implications for Iraq. It suggests that Riyadh will similarly hope to change the balance of sectarian power in Iraq, or at least maintain Iraq in turmoil. Sunni jihadi elements from Iraq, steeled in the armed anti-US insurgency there, have also joined the anti-Asad struggle in the name of sectarian war. Shi'ite elements from Hizballah in Lebanon and some Iraqi Shi'ite elements have also been drawn in to fight on the side of the Asad regime. The Syrian conflict only exacerbates sectarian passions inside Iraq. This is a new element in contemporary Arab geopolitics.

Turkey in the New Iraqi Politics

Ever since the founding of the Turkish republic in 1923 Ankara's primary interest in Iraq centered on a single issue: Kurds. Ankara feared any possible role Iraqi Kurds might play in exacerbating a Kurdish insurgency inside Turkey, for whom northern Iraq remained a safe haven. The Turkish army for decades periodically overran the Iraqi side of the border in hot pursuit of insurgents—not always with Baghdad's concurrence. (See Chapter 22 on the Regional Kurdish Web in Middle Eastern geopolitics.)

The eight-year war between Iraq and Iran launched by Saddam Hussein in 1980 also destabilized the region; it too had Sunni-Shi'a overtones, as well as ethnic Arab versus Persian elements. Throughout the conflict Turkey firmly resisted playing the "Sunni card"; Ankara remained neutral—and also profited considerably from huge war-time trade with both Iran and Iraq. Its main concern was about increased Iraqi Kurdish freedom of action in the border areas during the conflict. In 2003 Turkey opposed any US invasion of Iraq and Davutoğlu exerted major diplomatic efforts to prevent the outbreak of conflict, presciently fearing chaos as its inevitable aftermath. Ankara ultimately denied the US use of Turkish soil from which to invade Iraq. Turkey did seriously consider invading northern Iraq itself in the ensuing chaos after the overthrow of Saddam and the subsequent moves by Iraqi Kurds to establish greater autonomy. But this time Turkey expanded its vision and its range of interests in Iraq beyond preoccupation with Kurdish affairs to embrace a concern for the overall state of affairs in Iraq and their implications for regional stability. This was one of many elements in the positive transformation of Turkish relations with Iraq following the fall of Saddam.

With its new involvement in the region Turkey found it hard to avoid being drawn into issues of regional sectarianism that began to wrack the new Iraq. Erdoğan and Davutoğlu early on established an important and firm principle in Turkey's new foreign policy: to *stand above sectarian struggles and affiliations* and to work with all ethnic and sectarian elements in Iraq. In December 2010 on the supreme Shi'ite holy celebration day of Ashura, Erdoğan surprisingly announced that the "tragedy at Karbala 1330 years ago [the killing of 'Ali's grandsons Hasan and Husayn—a signal event of Shi'ism] affects all Muslims and should serve as a source of unity between Sunni and Shi'a." Erdoğan lent substance to this posture in a dramatic visit to Iraq in March 2011 during which he paid a highly publicized visit to the holiest Shi'ite city of Najaf where he prayed at the shrine of Imam 'Ali—reportedly the first Sunni leader ever to do so officially. He also went on foot through backstreets to visit the home of Grand Ayatollah 'Ali Sistani, arguably the most influential Shi'ite theologian in the world. Visits like this characterize the comfort and familiarity of both Erdoğan and Davutoğlu in incorporating the act of public prayer as powerful symbolism in their visits to mosques in the Muslim world as part of their diplomatic tool-kit. These new elements in Turkish foreign policy did not go unnoticed elsewhere in the Muslim world. Turkish policy has since consistently urged Iraq to establish an inclusive government to include broad Sunni as well as Shi'ite representation to ensure stability and international credibility for Iraq. Yet such advice was not welcome in Iraq under Shi'ite Prime Minister Nuri al-Maliki whose greatest goal was to ensure that political power in Iraq, finally acquired, never slip out of Shi'ite hands again. He has alienated most Sunni forces within the country and opened the door to international Sunni jihadi elements to engage in the civil strife.

The presence of a Türkmen minority in northern Iraq complicates Turkey's policies further. The Türkmen are ethnically closely related to Turks and some of Ottoman descent; they played a central role in the Ottoman administration in the past. They are centered around the northern city of Kirkuk where today they are ethnically squeezed by Iraqi Kurds who lay claim to Kirkuk, a significant oil region that the Türkmen view as their own capital. Turkey is committed to ensuring the welfare of the Türkmen and, in the early years of the American occupation, sought to limit Iraqi Kurdish power by keeping the city of Kirkuk out of any future Iraqi Kurdistan. Ankara still cares about the Türkmen but, as Turkish relations with the Iraqi Kurds have improved, the issue has become slightly less volatile. The Türkmen nonetheless remain a potential card Turkey can play against the Iraqi Kurds if need be and represent a significant domestic issue of much concern to Turkey.

Ankara's ties with the Iraqi government started to fray as Prime Minister Maliki increasingly narrowed his base of power to Shi'ite parties and began to exclude leading Sunnis from influence, sharpening sectarian tensions within the country and leading to the isolation of Maliki's Iraq from the broader Arab world. Ankara worked to overcome these divisions by inviting Iraqi Sunni and Shi'ite leaders to Istanbul for a conference in February 2012 to seek political reconciliation and establish dialog mechanisms to help heal the political-sectarian tensions inside Iraq. Turkey was to be represented by Mehmet Görmez, the president of Diyanet—again displaying the AKP's new uses of this office. In the end, the conference never came together. Shortly thereafter, in April 2012, the Organization of Islamic Cooperation (OIC), one of the largest international organizations in the world, began work to reinvigorate the Mecca agreement of 2006 by which, under OIC auspices, Iraqi factions and political parties agreed to a plan to bring political violence to an end. Significantly, the OIC was headed by a Turkish diplomat, Ekmeleddin İhsanoğlu, highlighting the strong Turkish interest in utilizing regional Muslim institutions to seek solutions to Muslim problems.

Turkey's keen interest notwithstanding, rhetoric unfortunately quickly deteriorated on both sides as Ankara continued to call for greater sectarian reconciliation in Iraq against Maliki's plans; Erdoğan gave refuge in Turkey to one of Maliki's leading Sunni opponents, Tariq al-Hashimi, the leader of the Muslim Brotherhood in Iraq, and one of the vice-presidents of the country; his safety was threatened in Baghdad when he was accused of backing sectarian killings and condemned to death. The charges were probably politically motivated but they also further revealed Erdoğan's particular sympathies for the Muslim Brotherhood in the region. In his characteristic blunt and emotional style, Erdoğan accused Maliki of fanning sectarian and ethnic tensions with "his self-centered ways." Maliki retorted that such statements represented "another flagrant interference in Iraqi internal affairs" by Turkey; he accused Ankara's own policies as revealing a "sectarian dimension," and a Turkish desire to establish "hegemony" in the region that would make Turkey "a hostile state for all."[2] Relations with Baghdad thus deteriorated quickly, undercutting years of earlier Turkish work to forge a new relationship with Iraq and Ankara's desire to avoid involvement in sectarian strife that had broader regional implications. By October 2013 Ankara made concerted diplomatic efforts to try to heal the breach; indeed both sides recognized that this quarrel was a political luxury that neither state could afford. It is unlikely to long dominate the future of relations between the two countries since Turkey is not playing a sectarian card in Iraq but rather seeks to maintain sectarian balance and harmony and benefit from close relations with all parts of Iraq.

The establishment of a first-ever Shi'ite government in Baghdad also dismayed many other parts of the Arab world, especially Saudi Arabia and the Gulf states, as Iran moved to give strong backing to Baghdad's new government. As we have noted, Riyadh chose to interpret many aspects of the Arab Spring in specifically sectarian terms: as an Iranian effort to destabilize Sunni regimes via manipulation of Shi'ite communities in the Gulf under the guise of calling for democracy. Iran's broad political calls in the 1980s for revolution against monarchies and pro-American rulers and "non-Islamic" regimes had been interpreted by Riyadh at the time as a purely sectarian call as well. Riyadh by 2011 had urged the entire Arab world to enlist in a broad struggle against Shi'ism and Iran. Turkey's self-declared sectarian neutrality angered Riyadh which has placed much pressure on Turkey to align with Sunni forces. And indeed, many Shi'a in the region believe that Ankara really is aligned with Sunni powers, despite its denials.

Ankara's problems with Iraq were further exacerbated when the Arab Spring hit Syria with uprisings against Asad's 'Alawi regime. (See Chapter 21, Shi'ite Revolution—Syria Tests the World.) Ankara increasingly supported the armed struggle against Asad—not on sectarian grounds but in support of a popular democratic uprising against authoritarian rule.

Turkey thus found itself in a deep dilemma. It sought to remain above sectarian rivalries and to reconcile such differences. Turkey aspires to something greater than playing champion of the Sunnis in the Arab world. Even the Ottoman Empire, after periodic serious clashes with Shi'ite Iran in the 16th-18th century, thereafter sought to play a role of supporting both Sunni and Shi'ite schools within Islam. But Erdoğan grew openly angry that his efforts to push Asad into concessions and reform in Syria had failed, causing Erdoğan to raise the ante and drift towards a de-facto alliance with Saudi Arabia and Qatar against Syria—interpreted by Maliki as a sign of Turkey's sectarian partisanship. As Ankara began to back away from military support for the overthrow of Asad, a major irritant in its relations with both Iran and Iraq began to ease.

Again, the test of sectarianism does not accurately capture the nature of the Iraqi political struggle. First, neither the Sunnis nor the Shi'a of Iraq constitute a monolithic bloc; there are significant personal, regional, ideological, ethnic, and political differences among them. One of the most important elements of division within the Shi'ite community is represented by the movement led by Muqtada al-Sadr, who stems from a distinguished, influential and powerful clerical family. While his political motivations are tactically complex, al-Sadr, himself a junior cleric, can perhaps best be summed up as representing a nationalist, even nativist, streak in Iraqi politics that is not driven exclusively by sectarian interests, but also by a desire for a strong and united Iraq, a desire to be a power broker with Sunni forces, and a populist concern for the economically impoverished segments of the population. Al-Sadr was a leading force in organizing early armed opposition against the American occupation of Iraq, along with Sunni jihadi forces. While he has been a part of Maliki's coalition government, Sadr opposed the narrow sectarian character of Maliki's circle, and sought a broad trans-sectarian foundation for national rule. As Maliki grew more unpopular and discredited, Sadr has become a leading candidate for eventual Shi'ite leadership. He is quite prepared to work with secular Sunni forces, and possibly with moderate Sunni Islamist elements as well, such as the Iraqi branch of the Muslim Brotherhood (the Iraqi Islamic Party). He has good ties with a number of Sunni clerics. He stands for an independent nationalist Iraq free of American influence, but also one that is not beholden to Iran, with whom he nonetheless maintains serious working relations. He also has good working relations with Turkey.

Al-Sadr is not the only dissident religious voice among the Shi'a. The Shi'ite Iraqi Da'wa party, of which Maliki is now head, once looked favorably upon the broader program of the Muslim Brotherhood and its vision of modern Islamist politics, despite being a Sunni movement. The renowned cleric Muhammad Baqr al-Sadr had espoused the principle of "the rule of the people" (*wilayat al-umma*) that was in sharp distinction to the reigning ideology in Iran of "clerical rule" (*wilayat al-faqih*). Ayatollah al-Sistani, the preeminent Shi'ite cleric in the world, has regularly indicated his dissatisfaction with the narrow basis of Maliki's government, and his failure to address the needs of the nation as a whole. Many in Maliki's own party have asked him, in vain, not to run for a third term out of concern that his sectarian orientation is not in the interests of the country. Maliki may still lose power in the next elections. If so, it could be a welcome victory for the diminished sectarianism that Iraq desperately requires.

Sunni forces in Iraq, furthermore, contain powerful influences from the Iraqi Muslim Brotherhood. The fact that Saudi Arabia and Egypt have declared virtual war on the (Sunni) Muslim Brotherhood movement in 2013, even as they oppose Shi'ism, suggests that the sectarian lines in Iraq are already quite blurred.

In early 2014 sectarian clashes still grew uglier and bloodier, as Iraq too became a proxy force in the international struggle over Syria. More disturbing was the growing strength of al-Qaeda in both Iraq and now Syria; the organization has even renamed itself locally as the Islamic State of Iraq and Greater Syria (ISIS), reflecting its rejection of the borders between the two countries in the quest for Islamic unification. (Any struggle against the US military in the Muslim world is of course an immediate and powerful magnet for international jihadi forces in keeping with al-Qaeda's determination to eliminate American interventionism in the Muslim world.) Iraq is unlikely to return to any degree of quiet as long as the Syrian struggle on its doorstep continues.

There are grounds for optimism, however, that the sectarian impasse in Iraq will not last forever. But relations between Maliki and Turkey are not solely a function of Maliki's government. He is also angry at Turkey's policies of dealing independently with Iraqi Kurdistan on oil pipelines going from Kurdistan to Turkey; he sees these policies as violating Iraqi sovereignty and taking sides in an internal Iraqi issue involving the status of the Kurds. Ankara has nonetheless tried to act from a set of principles—non-sectarianism, broad-based governance, and democratic process—which it hopes will bring about a more stable Iraqi political system. Ankara's insistence on these principles may bear fruit in the future even if it cannot be said that Ankara has zero problems with Baghdad today. Ankara remains stuck between many competing principles and desires: to remain above sectarian strife, to work with regional "realities", yet also to side with "the forces of history" and democratization; to solve issues on a regional basis, to maintain good working relations with all regional states, to act as an intermediary between problem states; to limit western military intervention into regional affairs; and to demonstrate to Washington that Ankara's approach to problems can be effective in solving regional issues.

Over the longer run, growing economic ties will strongly contribute to Turkish-Iraqi ties: Turkish goods and services; Iraqi energy resources; and a desire for stability in the region. Turkey's increasingly cordial relations with the Iraqi Kurds (see Chapter 22) should ultimately work to the benefit of both Baghdad and Ankara. Nor should a Shi'ite government in Baghdad necessarily fear a future Sunni regime in Damascus unless it is dominated by Salafi and jihadi forces. A Muslim Brotherhood-dominated regime in Syria, however, remains a distinct possibility; in such a case the Brotherhood is unlikely to play a strong anti-Iraqi card. The Brotherhood has not operated in strong sectarian ways in the past and has moved in that direction only when attacked. Arab *geopolitical* rivalries are more likely to dominate; recall that when Iraq, Syria and Egypt were all led by Arab nationalists, relations among them still often involved bitter rivalry. Syria under Ba'thi rule was a bitter enemy of Iraq under Ba'thi rule. Such issues of *leadership* rivalry could again reassert themselves between Iraq, Syria, and Egypt irrespective of sectarianism or ideology.

Are Turks and Iranians rivals in Iraq? Much American analysis—that tends to view the Middle East through the prism of its own confrontation with Iran—interprets the Turkish-Iranian relationship as a zero-sum game with absolute winners and losers. This is incorrect. Iranian influence in Iraq does not automatically come at the expense of Turkish interests, especially if Turkey does not position itself as primarily a protector of Sunni power. Turkey does not profit from ongoing sectarian turmoil in Iraq; Iran has benefitted from it to the extent that it threw the Iraqi Shi'a into Tehran's arms. But even Iran does not seriously gain from bloody sectarian rivalry and instability in Iraq. Ankara will urge any Shi'ite regime in Baghdad not to exclude and alienate the Sunnis in the interests of stability in the country and the region. Turkish influence does not have to translate into Iranian loss, especially if Tehran does not view Turkey as an instrument of US policy. Ankara's interests in Iraq are hobbled not by how much power the Shi'a have, but rather how that power is exercised—on economic, Kurdish, and other regional issues.

Thus Turkey and Iran are inevitably beginning a slow process of developing a new modus vivendi in Iraq. Iran's supreme goal is to prevent Iraq from being turned into a base for American power projection—a goal that has already slipped from Washington's hands. Turkey does not need or benefit from such an American presence there either—in fact Davutoğlu is likely to view an American military presence in Iraq as inherently destabilizing. Both Turkey and Iran will benefit from a stable and prosperous Iraq; Iran knows that it too will pay a price in the future if it is simply perceived as a champion of the Shi'a in Iraq.

CHAPTER TWENTY-ONE
THE CHALLENGE OF SHI'ISM: SYRIA TESTS THE WORLD

The Syrian face of the "Arab Spring" has presented the ugliest turmoil in the Arab world in decades. The popular uprising in Syria has lasted longer by far than any other Arab Spring revolution and cost vastly more lives—over 120,000 by early 2014, and counting. Tapping into latent national discontent over a long period, disaffected Syrians were inspired by the other uprisings of the Arab Spring to demonstrate for local demands from the Asad regime. An overly harsh government response, rather than intimidating citizens, created greater anger and caused the movement to spread; it soon took on a vicious sectarian character, and evolved into a proxy war by outsiders. There can now be no true winners on any side, regardless of outcome. The proxy war—at heart between Saudi Arabia and Iran, but also drawing in larger forces on all sides, including the US, Russia, and Turkey—attracted a large number of radical and violent foreign jihadis onto the scene, reminiscent of the Afghan conflict. The Syrian struggle has also created the greatest international crisis among all the disorders of the Arab Spring.

Syria is the third major state in the region in which the Shi'ite factor, or Shi'ite "threat", figures prominently. No state has gained from the conflict. Turkey in particular has been in the front seat of the three-year rollercoaster that has dealt serious damage to its overall foreign policy. No other country tested the policy precepts of AKP foreign policy as painfully as Syria has. These events also tested the policies of nearly all other regional players—Iran, Saudi Arabia, Iraq, Russia, Israel, the EU, and the US—as the country slid ever more deeply into a "lose-lose" struggle. In September 2013 Washington was on the verge of launching missile strikes against Syria because of its alleged use of chemical weapons against its population; a startling and unanticipated Russian initiative at the last minute to eliminate Syria's chemical weapons program surprisingly gained US agreement, enabling it to pull back from military action. Washington was compelled to acknowledge the major threat from international jihadi forces fighting against the Asad regime. The US policy shift also affected the nature of the internal war, perhaps fatally damaging the chances of the opposition to overthrow the Asad regime. The fighting may gradually grind to a halt, but a meaningful political settlement is still far off.

Syria: the Prickly Pear of History

What is it that makes Syria a particularly difficult challenge for the region? Some of the answer lies in the history of the country—the Greater Syria region—which demonstrates a fierce independence, a feistiness and a dislike of western powers going back 2,000 years. It has a strong sense of its centrality in Arab history unmatched by any other Arab state. Its demographically complex population requires subtle balances to rule, making it difficult to win over all elements to any one side.

Many countries of the Middle East are steeped in ancient histories but Damascus is the oldest continuously-inhabited city in the world with a powerful regional identity. Despite Syria's own complex ethnic and religious makeup, the impulse for Arab unity and Arab identity in modern times runs deeper in Syria than in any other Arab state. Syria has always been a cornerstone of regional (Levantine) nationalism—essentially the region of "Greater Syria," the Arab lands between Turkey and Egypt. Its strong regional identity forever plagued would-be conquerors and hegemons. Greater Syria has continuously been a fractious and prickly region at the crossroads of many empires that contested control over it. In the third and fourth centuries it was a rebellious border province of the Eastern Roman (Byzantine) Empire: a German historian notes that even then it was "strongly anti-western" (meaning anti-Byzantine and anti-Roman) and jealous of its own prerogatives. The great cities of Palmyra and Edessa in the Syrian desert, Syriac in language (closely related to Arabic), had a long history of revolt against Byzantine and Roman control. And it was greatly subject to influence from Persia even then.

Much of this provided the stuff of tales. In 269 CE legendary Queen Zenobia of the leading Syrian city of Palmyra launched a devastating military campaign against Roman rule; in the geopolitics of the day it is worth noting that Zenobia was descended from nobility in Carthage (today's Tunisia), another city that nurtured a deep historical hatred of its chief Mediterranean rival, Rome. Within a few years the forces of Palmyra conquered all of Syria, Egypt and half of Anatolia. Indeed, this "Palmyran Empire" was actually poised to succeed the Roman Empire in the East, an event that, if successful, would have perpetuated a Syriac/Semitic empire in the Eastern Mediterranean instead of the Byzantine Greek one. The famously beautiful Zenobia was finally defeated by Roman forces, reportedly wrapped in golden chains and sent to Rome where she was eventually pardoned and became a leading and exotic denizen of Roman society even after her empire had been crushed. Such tales convey the spirit of revolt as it ranged across great parts of Syria—

against Rome, and against Constantinople. Territorial rebellion was reinforced by ongoing *ideological and theological dissidence* against Rome in the Syrian city of Edessa that found itself regularly drawn to embrace Christian "heresies" condemned by Rome—first the Nestorian, and then the Monophysite doctrine about the true nature of Christ. Religion again serves as the banner and vehicle of grand political forces.

After Islamization and later incorporation into the Ottoman Empire, Greater Syria in one form or another represented something of a cultural unit; whoever ruled it generally ruled the rest of the Levant and parts of southern Mesopotamia and southern Turkey. It was only with the collapse of the Ottomans that the British and French broke up the province of Greater Syria between them and created several new states including Jordan and Palestine under British control alongside of a much-reduced Syrian rump state and the new state of Lebanon under French control—all an exercise in classic colonial divide and conquer. Syria thus still views itself as part of a greater Levantine cultural continuum over which it long presided. In 1948 Israel too was carved out of former Greater Syrian territory.

The idea of a Greater Syria never died. After World War I numbers of Syrian and Arab nationalists aspired to its restoration. In 1932 it was not a Muslim but a Greek Orthodox Syrian Christian who founded the Syrian Social Nationalist Party (SSNP) that was secular, nationalist and *pan-Arab* in character; it called for the reconstitution of a Greater Syria that would ambitiously embrace all of the Levant, even Kuwait, parts of southern Iraq and the Arab portions of western Iran. The movement initially had a right-wing nationalist character influenced by the German National Socialists—as were so many nationalist movements in this heyday of European fascism. Syria was later even willing to subordinate its national sovereignty to Egypt in 1958 when it agreed to establishing the United Arab Republic, a formal union of the two states, based on strong popular pan-Arab nationalist impulses and on admiration for Gamal Abdel Nasser in Egypt and his nationalist challenge to western dominance. (Handled with great ineptness by Egypt, this union collapsed in 1961.) The SSNP movement also eventually fell out with both Nasserist pan-Arabs and with Ba'th Arab nationalism, mainly on grounds of personalities and national rivalry rather than serious ideological differences.

But over and over again this theme of Arabism or pan-Arabism keeps emerging. Syria was the home of the first *Ba'th* (Renaissance) Party, a secular pan-Arab nationalist party, also founded by an Arab Orthodox Christian; it would later open a branch in Iraq and become the ruling ideology of Iraq for decades. Syria has thus been home to fully three variants of secular Arab nationalism that has operated across religious, sectarian and ethnic lines; these movements have usually interpreted "Arab" as a broad linguistic and cultural term rather than a narrow ethnic one. The Ba'th party in Syria continues to reflect these characteristics, albeit in an authoritarian order under the dominance of the Alawite minority—and more specifically the Asad family. The Ba'th Party's durability in Syria owes much to its historic roots in multi-religious and multi-ethnic ideals and a penchant for revolutionary rhetoric—not a narrow Alawite vision.

There is another important constant here as well: *all* nationalist parties in Syria have been anti-Zionist; it stems from sympathy with the Palestinian loss of their homeland, the perception of Zionism as a form of European settler colonialism, and anger at Israeli occupation of Syria's Golan Heights. Syria has prided itself on being one of the few remaining bastions of Arab resistance to Israeli power and the championing of the Palestinian cause. This posture garnered it much general sympathy among Arab populations of the region, especially when authoritarian rulers of Jordan, Saudi Arabia and Egypt were seen to be beholden to the US and quietly cooperated with Israel over the heads of public opinion.

The fact that "Syria" traditionally comprised the states of modern Syria, Jordan, Palestine, Lebanon and Israel has left another enduring legacy: what western states view as constant "Syrian meddling" in the affairs of neighboring states actually reflects the deep crisscrossing of historical, geopolitical, cultural, economic, ethnic and clan ties that still exist all across the "borders" of the new states. And of course the modern Syrian regime has been happy to manipulate these ties in an effort to maintain influence in the politics of Jordan, Palestine, and particularly Lebanon—always an integral component of Greater Syria. For better or for worse, Lebanese politics still remain unthinkable without a Syrian element. Syria is also close to Hizballah, the dominant Shi'ite movement in Lebanon. This movement has long enjoyed a positive image among Sunni populations (outside of Lebanon) for its bold and successful military resistance to Israel, especially in the 2006 Israeli attack on Lebanon in which Hizballah stood virtually alone against formidable Israeli firepower and emerged undefeated.

It's not surprising then, that Syria still represents in many ways the beating heart of modern Arab nationalism. As seasoned Israeli observer Uri Avnery points out, "A typical Syrian nationalist in Damascus was also a part of the Arab region, of the Muslim world and of the Sunni community—and the order of these diverse loyalties was never quite sorted out."[1] There are few other contenders today for that nationalist leadership. Even Egypt, which

307

played a major role as Arab nationalist leader in the 1960s under Nasser, in one sense only "discovered" its Arab national character in the mid-20th century. Iraq, too, has represented an important player in the Arab nationalist game but only since the 1960s, even though some important early theoreticians of Arab unity also came from Iraq. Nonetheless, Iraq will never be regarded as the "true" center of Arab nationalism even as it is acknowledged as a powerful Arab cultural force. Iraq's new Shi'ite-dominated government raises further questions in the mind of some Arab nationalists about Iraq's "true" Arab credentials.

What makes the phenomenon of Syrian Arab nationalism particularly striking is the diversity of its religious and ethnic makeup. Sunnis constitute about 73 percent of the population, while the ruling Alawites (quasi-Shi'tes) make up some 13 percent, various Christian sects form an additional 10 percent, and Druze 3 percent. There are ethnic divisions as well: 90 percent consider themselves Arab, 7 percent are Kurds, and some 2 percent Assyrian or Syriac. There remains a small community of Jews.

Despite, or perhaps because of this mixture, modern Syrian nationalism has been strongly secular, crossing Sunni-Shi'ite ('Alawi) religious lines even though the 'Alawite minority is in charge. In fact the ruling 'Alawis have arguably been more Arab nationalist than any other element: promotion of secular Arab nationalism has been the greatest source of Ba'th party and Asad clan's legitimacy in the region. More Sunni than the Sunnis one might say. The 'Alawi nature of the Syrian regime has been, until recently, largely irrelevant to most Arabs' perception of the state, otherwise viewed as a leader of the "Resistance Bloc" against Israel. Syria has given assistance to anyone who would make common cause in resisting Israel, whether Sunni or Shi'a. Syria's role as a flagship of the Arab nationalist cause in part accounts for the early hesitation and ambivalence among many Arab states and especially populations to call for the fall of the Asad regime starting in 2011.

The Pendulum Swings of Turkish Foreign Policy with Damascus

But Syria has been the graveyard of recent Turkish foreign policy—or at least the tripping stone from which it is still recovering. At the same time, Turkey has been more engaged than any other regional state in dealing with the whole series of changes in Damascus. With the collapse of the Ottoman Empire and Syrian "independence" (under French domination), Ankara's relations with Damascus deteriorated sharply. Syria had bad memories of harsh wartime Ottoman military rule during World War I in which the allies had sought to turn Syria into the heart of Arab revolt against Ottoman rule. Then in 1939

Turkey successfully maneuvered to annex the northern Syrian province of Alexandretta (Hatay) which Syria bitterly resented. Starting in the 1950s the two states found themselves operating on opposite sides of the Cold War. In the 1980s Syria began to give support to Kurdish insurgent movement (PKK) in Turkey and later gave refuge to the leader of the PKK. Syria found it useful to exploit the Kurds as a point of leverage against Ankara; the confrontation in the end nearly resulted in war between them at the end of 1990s.

Then in 1999 everything changed. Remarkably, after nearly a century of hostility, the tide turned as both sides decided to mend fences. Change began in 1999 when, under Turkish duress, Damascus yielded up the PKK leader-in-exile, leading to his eventual capture by the Turks with US assistance. Under the AKP starting in 2003 Davutoğlu began to court Syria, pulled troops back from the borders that had long been tense, removed the vast minefields in the border regions, lifted visa requirements, opened up the country to increased trade, worked on jointly rewriting the nationalist-tinged textbooks in each country that had vilified the other, and sought to negotiate outstanding problems between Syria and Israel. Erdoğan paid more than one high-profile state visit to Damascus and the two men declared deep friendship between the two countries. Turkey quickly gained huge popularity in Syria and Syrian tourists began to flow to Turkey. Recognition of old Ottoman ties were resuscitated. Significantly, Ankara began to work with the EU as a channel for a Syrian-EU dialog; the EU saw Damascus as a possible key to a future peace settlement and liberal economic change in the Middle East. These EU policies were in sharp distinction to US hostility to any Syrian rapprochement and its routine branding of Syria as a "rogue state." Ankara and the EU shared a vision that economic openings in Middle Eastern states could lead inevitably towards a gradual liberalization of the political order as well and encourage Syria to develop new economic and legal institutions in conformity with EU trade practices. The EU was persuaded that the Turkish model of change would prove more palatable and familiar in the Middle East than an imported western model.[2]

In numerous respects Syria's star was rising on the international scene in the 2000s and there was ground for optimism. Ties between Ankara and Damascus were flourishing. But in 2011 it all changed again. The pendulum swung back sharply as the disorders of the Arab Spring hit Syria. Early anti-regime demonstrations—poor economic conditions, lack of political reform, and Alawite domination of the regime—led to calls for immediate reform, and later even for even regime change, partly inspired by the changes in Tunisia, Egypt and Libya. In the event, Asad handled the initial disorders poorly. In the face of demonstrator violence, he made little effort at conciliation and instead employed harsh military and police countermeasures that resulted in mounting civilian casualties and further alienation of the public. Several thousand refugees soon fled cross the border into Turkey in the face of Syrian army reprisals. Since the outbreak of domestic disorders Davutoğlu had hoped he could persuade Asad to accept the need for concessions, to end one-party Ba'th rule, undertake reforms and democratization measures, to desist from killing civilians and to look towards more representative government. He had visited Damascus over 60 times starting in 2003. Asad repeatedly made personal promises to both Davutoğlu and Erdoğan that he would implement reform, but failed to live up to his word. Erdoğan, who had embraced Asad as a "brother" during visits, grew embittered at what he believed was a deliberate attempt by Asad to deceive Ankara about his intentions; Turkey's prominent efforts at mediation in Syria turned into an embarrassing failure. Erdoğan's "special relationship" with Asad that he had touted to the West had failed to deliver. Erdoğan responded angrily to what he felt was a personal betrayal and began to lend military and logistical support to external armed opposition forces, the Syrian National Council of resistance which took up residence in Turkey. Ankara did, however, stop short of direct Turkish military action and initially discouraged western armed intervention. The presence of eventually hundreds of thousands of Syrian refugees in temporary housing on the Turkish side of the border fueled further tensions, especially given the shared ethnic or religious ties that many refugees have with Turkish citizens of Arab origin, or with the Alevis.

Ankara faced unpalatable choices. It strongly hoped to avoid violence and to employ mediation and persuasion. But its mediation proved little more effective than anyone else's, including Arab League missions or Russian attempts to influence Asad. In the face of this impasse Ankara increasingly felt it must "go with the tide of history" in the uprising—as in the other countries of the Arab Spring and work to hasten Asad's collapse; Erdoğan began facilitating heavier arming of the Syrian opposition from external weapons sources and urgings to the West to do the same. But early confidence that Asad would fall quickly were stymied. Ankara then had to decide whether to contemplate a Turkish invasion of Syria itself to restore order and establish a new regime; it decided against it. The umbrella resistance organization, the Syrian National Council, proved to be badly divided and ineffective in fighting the Asad regime.

Regional factors added more complicating elements to the equation. First, much of Arab public opinion was originally sympathetic to the Arab nationalist policies of Damascus. But the Asad regime had been high on Washington's target list for overthrow for decades, perhaps not without some reason, but without success. US grievances included the realities that Syria housed and supported Hamas leadership, the Palestinian resistance movement, in Damascus; supported the Shi'ite Hizballah movement in Lebanon; facilitated Iranian assistance to Hizballah; has been historically a major player in internal Lebanese politics, sometimes supporting differing factions in Lebanon that oppose US strategies; and a belief that Syrian security forces were behind the 2005 assassination of Lebanese Prime Minister Rafiq al-Hariri, a protégé of both Saudi Arabia and former French President Jacques Chirac. Syria defied Washington's prescriptions for the region—including its rejection of 30 years of unproductive US peace process with Israel. Note that Syria also angered Washington for its support to Iraqi *Sunni* resistance against the US occupation of Iraq. Yet for all Syria's Arab nationalist credentials, Asad's bloody reprisals against his own citizens largely squandered his legacy of popular support and respect in the Middle East and the conflict began to attract international Sunni jihadi forces that had already been operating in Afghanistan and Iraq.

While most Syrian Sunnis felt that Asad simply represented minority Alawite power ruling the country, other Syrian minorities—Kurds, Christians, Jews, Druze—were not ready to overthrow Asad, for all his weaknesses. For them he represented a strong secular tradition and protection from fundamentalist Sunni views that might oppress them. Sectarianism does not adequately account for all the issues at work in Syria. The secular Asad regime had shared domestic power with the Sunnis in major respects: most of the major ministries including the prime minister were usually in Sunni hands; the sensitive security ministries, however, were controlled by 'Alawis. The merchant class is largely Sunni and greatly benefited from their relationship with the state. The extreme, radicalized and violent nature of the foreign jihadists fighting against Asad, often treating civilians as brutally as Asad's own forces, gave many Syrians grounds to fear the character of any successor Islamist regime. Even Washington had begun to dial back its assistance to the Syrian armed opposition as increasing evidence emerged that radical jihadis, including those even with links to al-Qaeda were beginning to dominate the anti-Asad war. In the event of Asad's fall, there could be no guarantee that a successor regime would be any better for the West and very possibly worse. And above all, US policy in Syria was driven even more by anti-Iranian motivations than anti-Asad motives—the desire to destroy Iran's chief Arab ally.

Turkey could only militarily intervene into this swirl of conflicting interests at much peril to itself including exposing itself to terrorist attacks that began to appear inside the Turkish border. In the end, Ankara was forced to acknowledge that the coalition to remove Asad was failing, and that Turkey was increasingly isolated in the project except for Saudi Arabia and Qatar and a wavering Israel. Meanwhile domestic opposition to Ankara's Syrian policies grew. The Syrian refugee flow into Turkey reached over 600,000 by early 2014 and is rising; more than 2 million Syrians have fled their country. If it had just been a crisis between Syria and Turkey it would have been simpler. But the entire Syrian issue was overtaken by the contesting forces of global geopolitical struggle, great power issues and a proxy war involving the US, the EU, Iran, Iraq, Saudi Arabia, Israel, the GCC, and Russia. Simple decisions became laden with major international repercussions. Maintaining an independent Turkish foreign policy under these circumstances became nearly impossible.

Saudi Arabia has grown ever more insistent that the Syrian crisis is first and foremost about the "Shi'ite threat" and Iranian power and influence in Syria. Yet this accusation rings hollow. Asad does not act as a sectarian Shi'ite except when he is threatened with overthrow for being sectarian. He has long identified himself closely with Sunni causes in the Arab world. Distinctive 'Alawi features to his policies, other than domestic favoritism, are hard to find, and even his long-standing good ties with Iran rest on a firm geopolitical basis including decades of shared common hostility to Saddam's Iraq—attitudes shared by many Sunni Syrians as well.

The reality is that a future Syrian regime—possibly dominated by the Syrian Muslim Brotherhood, but including secular Arab nationalists as well as Salafi and even jihadi elements—will be no more congenial to Washington, Tel Aviv or Riyadh than Asad has been. A democratic pro-western Syria with good ties to Israel is simply a pipe dream under almost any conceivable scenario.

The situation was a lose-lose for almost all parties concerned. Meanwhile the humanitarian aspects of the crisis continued to grow—massive refugee flows in all directions, growth of refugee camps, food and health crises, radicalization of refugees, and the negative impact on the internal politics of neighboring countries. The greatest hope is that multinational talks in Geneva will ultimately find some kind of unpalatable but stabilizing settlement that would allow the 'Alawi regime to stay in place, impose some greater degree of power sharing, with or without Asad, bring an end to the brutal conflict and remove foreign jihadis.

Post-Asad Regional Crises

Let's look at some of the key elements that create international disagreement over the *post-Asad* future.

•   *Any* democratic process will ultimately sharply shift the balance of power in Syria out of the hands of the 13-percent ruling Alawis and empower the 73-percent Sunni majority that seeks political power consonant with their numbers. But there will remain the political problem of "the tyranny of the majority"—a common transitional phase in newly democratic societies, as in Iraq.

•   The future of the Syrian-Iranian relationship will undoubtedly change, but not necessarily be severed. Since the Iranian Revolution in 1979 the Syrian-Iranian alliance has been the longest-lasting political alliance within the Middle East. New Sunni power in Damascus will no longer maintain that special alliance, but there are numerous geopolitical considerations that may cause Syria to maintain some significant ties with Iran as useful. The combination of Syrian Alawis, a Lebanese Shi'ite plurality, and an Iraqi Shi'ite majority all suggest some degree of permanent Iranian influence in the area that cannot be suppressed and does not have to be by definition entirely negative.

•   A power shift to the Sunnis in Syria directly impacts the new Shi'ite-dominated regime in Iraq. After a fall of Alawite power in Damascus, Baghdad will initially feel more insecure and isolated; at worst it could even become the object of attack by a new Sunni fundamentalist regime in Damascus backed by Riyadh. Such an event would tend to drive the Iraqi Shi'ite government still closer to Iran. But a Muslim Brotherhood-dominated regime in Damascus is not likely to be militantly anti-Iran.

•   More jihadi volunteers began to infiltrate Syria in 2013, including Sunni radicals who live in the West; Syria is now becoming a major international Sunni radical cause célèbre ranking with Afghanistan and post-Saddam Iraq. Jihadis have been responsible for some of the worst violence against Syrian civilians and have employed terrorist bombing inside Syria against the Asad regime. They will not be easily eliminated after any successful joint struggle against the Asad regime.

•   The 20-percent Alevi (quasi-Shi'ite) community in Turkey feels touched by the Syrian crisis. Even though the Turkish Alevi are somewhat distinct and their religious practices differ from the Syrian 'Alawis, they feel some kinship and are concerned for the fate of the 'Alawi community in Syria. Alevi discontent in Turkey, while not expressed through political violence, still

313

exists and is unnerved by Turkish state policies that seek to overthrow the 'Alawis in neighboring Syria. The flight of numerous 'Alawi refugees from Syria into Turkey after the fall of the Asad regime could intensify Turkish Alevi discontent and even spark sectarian clashes inside Turkey.

• The restive 7-10 percent Kurdish population in Syria has close ties to Kurdish clans inside Turkey; indeed, Syrian Kurds made up a significant part of the PKK—the separatist Kurdish guerrilla movement in Turkey. Many of these Syrian Kurds might be susceptible to recruitment into anti-state operations inside Turkey if peace talks between Ankara and the PKK should founder. Any territorial breakup of the Syrian state creates a major new regional crisis within the four-state Kurdish region of Turkey, Syria, Iraq and Iran. And Syrian Kurds fear that a future Arab nationalist or Salafi Sunni regime in Damascus could be even more anti-Kurdish than Asad has been.

• The Muslim Brotherhood of Syria is most likely the biggest long-term political winner in any regime change in Syria—as happened immediately after regime change in Tunisia and Egypt. Brotherhood strength in Syria affects the its standing in Egypt, Yemen, Jordan, and Iraq, as well as elsewhere in the Gulf and North Africa. Strikingly, Syria's Muslim Brotherhood Secretary General Muhammad Faruq Tayfur has described Turkey as a "model Islamic state." Saudi Arabia might now exert major efforts, however, to prevent the Muslim Brotherhood from acquiring a major voice in a future Syrian regime.

• The Asads' strong identification with the "Arab revolutionary tradition" has always made Arab monarchies nervous. That concern was intensified by Syria's political alliance with Iran. Saudi Arabia fears its own restive 10-percent Shi'ite population; for Riyadh, therefore, the overthrow of the Asad regime constitutes a blow to Shi'ite community in Saudi Arabia as well.

• Many in Lebanon fear regime change in Syria since it will upset the carefully-calibrated balance of power among Shi'ite, Sunni, various Christian sects, Druze, and other forces within Lebanon.

• The US has viewed Syria as a state hostile to its interests for well over half a century. Syria in turn has long felt threatened by the military and diplomatic power of Israel and has been determined to regain control over the Golan Heights—captured by Israel in the 1967 war. The US has consistently sought to blunt Damascus' regional influence and its leadership of Arab Resistance in the region. The US hoped (vainly) that the anti-Asad uprisings would provide that long-sought opportunity to shift the balance of power in favor of states seeking accommodation with Israel and US strategic goals.

• Israel dislikes the Asad regime, but the Asads have long been a known, even reliably predictable, quantity on the scene. Israel is even more nervous about what might follow the collapse of the Asad regime: most likely a state dominated by the Muslim Brotherhood with strong Salafi forces present, conducting policies that will be no less anti-Israeli, that will maintain close ties with other Muslim Brotherhood parties in the region, and that will enjoy greater domestic legitimacy than Asad. But Israel's concern over Iranian regional power seemingly overrides its coexistence with Asad, especially since Iran facilitates the flow of weapons to Hizballah in Lebanon, which constitutes a major military bulwark against Israel.

• If Turkey intervenes militarily into the Syrian situation it will likely create hostility among some Arab states and parties who will see it as either Turkish neo-imperialism or Turkish action as a surrogate for US policies in the region. Turkey's diplomatic status and independence, as well as its non-sectarianism posture in the region would be severely compromised. Direct Turkish intervention has become now quite unlikely.

Syria and Iran: What the Ties Are, and Are Not

The Syrian-Iranian relationship has been routinely dismissed for years as no more than a passing "marriage of convenience," but in reality that marriage is now one of the oldest and most durable geopolitical alliances in the entire Middle East; it rests on a quite solid long-term geopolitical foundation that will not easily be severed over the longer term.

After the Iranian Revolution in 1979, the new Islamic government in Tehran rejected the shah's policy of close cooperation with the US; it proceeded to proclaim its sympathy for the Palestinian cause and called for revolution against all dictatorships in Arab countries, particularly against rulers perceived to be under US control and protection. At this point Syria was a natural *ideological* ally for Tehran, not because it was Alawite but because it was *revolutionary*. Indeed, most Iranians scarcely consider 'Alawi practices to be a legitimate form of Shi'ism at all, since it embraces many non-Islamic elements. But to win greater support from Syria and to diminish the Asads' isolation, a prominent Iranian ayatollah, Musa al-Sadr (active in Lebanon in the shah's time in 1973), formally declared the 'Alawi faith to be "part of Shi'ism"—a major symbolic acknowledgment. The Asad family itself, furthermore, has long participated in Sunni rituals. The purely religious ties between Iran and Syria, then, are hardly strong. The Sayyida Zaynab shrine in Damascus, however, is a major pilgrimage site for Shi'a of the world, which raises Syria's

"Shi'ite image." (Egypt too has major Shi'ite mosques and buildings from the Fatimid dynasty that draw large numbers of Shi'a visitors.)

Shared ideology or religion does not guarantee political closeness, even between the Alawis and Iran. Note that even though Iraq and Syria were both ruled by Ba'th parties for some period, the two parties eventually became bitter enemies due to personality and state rivalry for regional influence. When Iraq's Saddam Hussein launched the long and brutal war against Iran in 1980, Iran naturally turned to Iraq's then bitter rival, Syria, for support. Indeed, Syria was virtually the only state in the world that supported the Iranians in their desperate battle to fight off Saddam's invasion, for which Tehran was grateful. Syria was again driven more by anti-Iraqi impulses than religious links. Syria continues to maintain the mantle of Arab Revolution which accords with Iran's own revolutionary ideology. Syria's ties with Iran have been important in softening Damascus' overall isolation—especially during the concerted US diplomatic efforts in the 2000s to intimidate or overthrow the Asad regime. After the first rumblings of the uprisings against Asad in 2011, Iran actually sought contact with the Syrian Muslim Brotherhood to see how the situation could be salvaged or resolved; Iran anticipated longer-term relations with the Brotherhood under any conditions. And finally, Syria also shares with Iran, along with Iraq and Turkey, concerns over Kurdish separatism within all their countries.

Iran, however, is suspicious of Turkey's game in Syria, and suspects it—incorrectly—of pressing a sectarian policy to strengthen Sunni power in the region. Tehran, with perhaps greater reason, believes that Ankara mainly seeks to please Washington on the Syrian issue, whereas in reality Iran itself is the primary target of US Syrian policy. The once-cordial ties between Ankara and Asad over nearly a decade of AKP policy demonstrate how well Turkey got along with this 'Alawi regime without any "sectarian differences" interfering—even while Syria was an ally of Tehran. Turkey is the only player that seeks resolution of the internal conflict in Syria *in principle*, out of concern for its destabilizing character as such, and not as part of any broader proxy war. If Asad had satisfied his political opposition early on, Ankara would have happily worked to facilitate it. And over the long run Turkey is not in a zero-sum relationship with Iran over Syria's future despite present tensions.

Syria's important and deep-rooted historical ties with Lebanon were also of great interest to Tehran, since it granted Iran greater access and regional clout with the Lebanese Shi'ite movement Hizballah. Even here, however, note that Syrian ties with Lebanese groups have at various times cut across *all* religious lines: Damascus has variously allied itself in turn with Greek Orthodox

Christians, Maronite Christians, Palestinians, Druze, Shi'a, Sunnis—virtually all elements of the internal rivalries of political power in Lebanon, depending on what was tactically most advantageous and working towards a balance of power. Syria has periodically even enjoyed decent working relations with Saudi Arabia, although that declined in the 2000s after a serious falling-out over conflicting interests in Lebanese politics.

Once again, sectarianism is a poor analytic tool by which to grasp the basic geopolitical and ideological struggles in the Middle East; it does not adequately account for Syria's actions. Early on after Saddam's fall, for example, Syria worked to support and strengthen *Sunni* guerrilla operations in Iraq against US forces, gave refuge to Iraqi Sunni guerrillas in Syria and allowed them to cross the borders freely, stirring anger in Washington. Syria was clearly not acting out of sectarian but rather ideological motives in opposing US power projection and dominance into the Middle East. Syria has been a close supporter of *Sunni* Hamas, the Palestinian branch of the Muslim Brotherhood. Maliki in turn had a soft spot in his heart for Damascus since it had granted him asylum in the long years of his struggle in exile against Saddam.

Finally, the forces of Arab geopolitics are complex, and shift like a mobile, constantly adjusting balances and creating new counterweight relationships as the world changes. Neither the US nor anti-Syrian Arab powers will be able to seize this mobile and set it permanently in the balance that they prefer. Syria at times has had close relations with Iraq and Egypt, at other times hostile. Similarly with Saudi Arabia. That evolving relationship is likely to continue with the leadership at any given moment. It is entirely conceivable that even a Sunni-led Syria might at some point work with Iran to weaken threats from a potentially aggressive Iraq. What is unthinkable today becomes suddenly quite thinkable tomorrow. Why should even a Sunni-run Syria permanently dedicate itself to hostile relations with Iran when there is virtually no threat from it, and when there might be gains to be had by maintaining relations with Tehran?

However complex, Syria is a central state of the region with which Ankara must deal. Prolonged internal sectarian rivalry inside Syria is certain: Sunni versus 'Alawi in the first instance, but also Muslim versus Christian, or Kurd versus Arab, Ba'th versus SSNP, secularists against Islamists, Brotherhood against Salafis or al-Qaeda, or even regionalism such as Aleppo versus Damascus—all create potentially destabilizing forces on Turkey's border that it neither wants nor needs.

Syrian Futures

Erdoğan and Davutoğlu remain committed to an independent Turkish foreign policy. So will any successor Turkish government, in general terms. Washington consistently measures Turkish policy against a narrow US-centric benchmark: every move is assessed as to whether Ankara is moving towards, or away, from support to Washington's policies at any given moment. In fact, Washington will not be the chief determinant or touchstone of Turkish policy; Turkey's own regional interests are.

Washington has experienced some eight years of angst over Turkey's new independence of foreign policy: Ankara has been variously described by some Washington observers as "having shifted over to the enemy column," or "straying off the reservation" (a really culturally-laden expression). Meanwhile, opposition critics in Turkey accused the AKP of having gone too far in burning its bridges with Asad, implementing risky policies when Asad's fall was far from assured, and for "implementing an American agenda" in Syria. More importantly, by March 2012 Washington's decision to back away from an aggressive posture to overthrow Asad left Turkey feeling isolated. Erdoğan was already overextended in his vocal opposition to the Asad regime, and had to backpedal and seek more diplomatic measures, including acceptance of Russian mediation, to bring an end to violence in Syria. By October 2013 Ankara and Tehran sought to overcome differences on Syria and Davutoğlu stressed again the importance of avoiding sectarian struggle in the Middle East. *A gradual move towards withdrawal from its disastrous Syrian policy will have major impact on two other key Turkish relationships: it will remove a major irritant in Ankara's relations with Iran as well as with Iraq.*

As for Syria, any successor regime will need close ties with Turkey, both out of necessity as well as respect for the Turkish body of experience. Turkey would be wise not to leave too heavy a thumbprint on regime change in Syria. Ankara has stood on principle in siding with "the future," but it needs to avoid accusations of exercising neo-Ottoman imperialism, or serving as executor of the West's bidding. Turkey's interests in Syria ultimately should survive any regime change in Damascus; Syria needs Ankara. What is less clear is how a post-Asad Syria itself would fit into the regional picture. It will almost certainly not be on the side of the counter-revolutionary forces of Saudi Arabia and the Gulf, but it also will likely be deeply dependent upon economic assistance from the Gulf. Overall Syria will be a critical swing state in determining the future face of the region—its supposed "Shi'ite character" will be of limited strategic importance in itself and should not too heavily color external analysis of events.

PART SIX

CHAPTER TWENTY-TWO

THE KURDISH REGIONAL WEB

Amidst all the chaos and destabilization of the Middle East over the last decade the number one winners may have turned out to be the Kurds. And, counter-intuitively, Turkey is probably the number one beneficiary of the Kurds' changing fortunes.

The Kurds of the Middle East—long forgotten, suppressed and excluded from national politics in every country in which they live, are probably the largest single ethnic group in the world with no state of their own. Their language (in several dialects) differs entirely from Turkish and Arabic, and is instead related to Persian. Total population figures are debated and politicized but the Kurds of the Middle East likely number at least 30 million souls. They occupy a roughly oblong area that embraces most of the Turkish southeast, moving south down through the Syrian-Iraqi-Iranian border regions. They are slowly edging their way back into the center of regional politics in a surprising new calculus of Middle East politics. They constitute important minorities of the populations of Turkey, Iran, Iraq, and Syria, alongside more modest Kurdish communities in Armenia, Azerbaijan, Lebanon and elsewhere. Their sense of common identity has never been greater in history than now.

Why has the time of the Kurds finally arrived? Two main reasons: their own expanding self-consciousness results from the increasing openness, political turmoil and even democratization under way to varying degrees in most of the countries in which they live, coupled with explosive new media that links them all as never before. Second, as Kurdish voices rise within these major states, competing *global* geopolitics across the region have dragged the Kurds into new political equations and increased their prominence.

The Kurds have seemingly been manipulated constantly as instruments by external powers against various Middle Eastern states: particularly by the UK, the US, Russia, and Israel as well as by most regional states against each other. The US famously used the Iraqi Kurds for decades as a weapon against regimes in Baghdad, then Tehran, and the game is still not fully over. In the past the Kurds usually ended up the losers—stirred up to rebellion against their local regimes only to be abandoned by the same outside powers when they had outlived their usefulness, only then to be vengefully crushed again by the regimes where they live. Only in the last decade or two have the Kurds actually begun to benefit from regional political disorder and change.

Ever since the founding of the modern Turkish state the threat of Kurdish separatism has ranked as Ankara's number one military-security preoccupation. Kurds in Turkey number roughly 14 million, making up some 18 percent of the population. Suppression of the Kurds and their resulting discontents have remained a running sore for most of the past century, creating internal tensions, spawning terrorism, guerrilla warfare, and brutal police and military repression by the state. Worse, the Turkish military consistently brandished the threat of Kurdish separatism as justification for its own domination of Turkish domestic policies.

The Ergenekon case (see Chapter 6) exposed a wealth of ugly details about the way radical groups within the Turkish military and security agencies exploited, provoked, and sometimes even sponsored terrorist acts in the Kurdish region and outside as an excuse to impose martial law, extend the army's powers over civilian government, and even to overthrow elected governments. Peaceful solution of the Kurdish problem is thus an essential prerequisite towards greater democratization and a permanent end to longtime military "supervision" over Turkish politics. It also marks a major ideological turning point in Turkey in the debate over what constitutes a "Turk" and a "Turkish citizen" in a multicultural society.

This near-obsessive focus upon Kurds similarly reduced Ankara's relations with neighboring states—Iraq, Iran and Syria—to a function of dealing with Kurds as a cross-border issue. That has now changed. Today the geopolitics swirling around the Kurds have become far more complex and nuanced. And for the first time in modern Turkish history, the AKP government has made pioneering efforts to resolve the Kurdish problem domestically, an approach that offers major promise at home and exerts significant impact upon the region.

The AKP government beginning in the early 2000s finally took the critical all-important first step essential to any resolution of the Kurdish problem: formal acknowledgement of the reality of the distinct Kurdish cultural and linguistic identity. That process had actually begun in quiet and indirect ways before the AKP came to power: a decade earlier several prominent Turkish leaders, including the important reformer President Turgut Özal and his Chief of the General Staff, had dropped hints that they just might partially share Kurdish blood themselves. Those steps were not easy. Early Turkish nationalists operating under the Kemalist vision had sought a unitary state, reminiscent of the French historical process, which denied and suppressed any alternative identities within the country other than "Turkish."

The Kemalist-statist argument ran as follows: if we are all seen as "Turks" in Turkey then we are all equal and there is no need to acknowledge any other ethnicity. The problem was that the Kurds did seek acknowledgment of their distinct identity, language and ethnicity, as well as calling for improved conditions in their neglected southeast region. The issue was not that a Kurd could not rise in Turkish society; they could and did rise to high places. They just couldn't openly acknowledge that they were Kurds. To do so would shatter the concept of a "unitary nation." The country was stuck in a kind of "don't ask, don't tell" dilemma. The claim was made that Turkish policy paralleled the US, Canada, or Australia, where everyone together, regardless of ethnic background, is called "American," "Canadian," or "Australian." Turkey is indeed a multiethnic state but the problem is that "Turk" is originally an ethnic and linguistic term. How can that word come to lose its ethnic and linguistic connotations to become a neutral, non-ethnic word like "American" or "Canadian?" Especially when Turkish nationalists prided themselves on the very racial character and cultural significance of the term "Turk." Atatürk himself had coined the phrase *Ne mutlu Türküm diyene*, "How happy is he who says 'I am a Turk.'" But did "Turk" mean an ethnic Turk? And hence not Kurd? Or did it just mean a citizen of Turkey? The phrase could be read differently, but for Kurds it smacked of exclusionism. Furthermore, a Kurd who assimilates as a Canadian does not thereby threaten the Kurdish homeland; but a Kurd *in the homeland* who abandons his identity is threatening the existence of the Kurdish homeland.

To deny or ignore—as Kemalist nationalist policy did—the reality of other ethnic groups, languages and cultures existing within the Turkish state was indeed to discriminate against Kurds and others who prize their own distinct linguistic and cultural identity within the country and wish to preserve it. Kurds consistently sought state acknowledgment of that reality—one of the causes behind numerous Kurdish rebellions in modern Turkish history. But it would be unfair simply to suggest that Kemalist nationalists were all just paranoid or racist. All citizens of Turkey know the history of past imperialist manipulations of various ethnic elements within the Ottoman state—Greeks, Serbs, Armenians, Kurds, and Arabs and others—by western powers designed to spark revolt and to weaken or destroy the Turkish or Ottoman state. The Kemalists justifiably sought to ensure that this manipulation of ethnicity by outsiders could never happen again. (We should note too that the heyday of

Turkish racial nationalism in the early 20th century paralleled an era of rampant racialism and ethno-nationalism across most of Europe.)

A third major factor facilitating progress towards a Kurdish solution lies in Turkey's aspirations to join the EU; such membership is contingent upon, among other things, acknowledgment of minority rights within the country. This EU requirement stipulated progress on dealing with the Kurdish reality. And finally, all Turks and Kurds were war-weary from long decades of brutal bloodletting that damaged the very democratic foundations of the Turkish state and in the end only stimulated feelings for the separatist cause.

In short, there has been every incentive for Turkey to resolve the Kurdish problem within the country. Today Turkey is no longer in official denial of the nature of the problem as it had been in an earlier period when even the very word "Kurd" was never uttered in public; the entire Kurdish issue used to be referred to as the "southeastern problem" and was constantly characterized as simply problems of banditry and lawlessness in the east. That was also the period when Kurdish aspirations were treated strictly as a security problem; as such the Turkish military had full license to resolve the problem by military means—leading to the deaths of tens of thousands of citizens—primarily Kurds—and only exacerbating the problem. Acknowledgment of the Kurdish reality—identity, language, culture, and the desire for some degree of Kurdish regional autonomy—is now underway, creating hope that a lasting resolution is on the doorstep. The moment of decisive breakthrough may be the landmark agreement between the PKK guerrilla movement and the Turkish government in April 2013: the Kurdish guerrilla movement agreed to cease military operations on Turkish soil and to withdraw their forces to Iraq in return for a political process that will grant them a high degree of their demands—formal acknowledgment of the Kurdish identity, cultural rights and some degree of regional autonomy. The terms are complex and are still to be fully worked out; indeed, the details of the resolution are vulnerable to exploitation by domestic Turkish politics. But nonetheless, a major, historic, and welcome step has undeniably been taken and most of the building blocks of a settlement are clear and in place. If not today, tomorrow.

Finally, a series of military conflicts in the region over the past two decades led to growing internationalization of the Kurdish problem. The US-led Gulf War in 1991 in response to Saddam Hussein's invasion of Kuwait first brought the issue of Kurds to major international attention as millions of Iraqi Kurds, who had sought greater autonomy as Saddam weakened, fled north to the Turkish border to escape Iraqi military reprisals; there they joined Turkish Kurds who were often part of the same clans. The word "Kurdish" at long last could no longer be kept out of the Turkish political vocabulary. The next psychological step came with the necessity that Ankara deal with the even more provocative term of "Kurdistan" as applied to northern Iraq. The Kurdish issue then further escalated with the US invasion and occupation of Iraq starting in 2003, marking the emergence of new Iraqi politics and a formal Kurdish regional entity. Finally, the outbreak of the Arab Spring and civil war in Syria raised the profile and role of two million (or more) Syrian Kurds and their future aspirations, still unresolved. Inevitably all these events impacted the seven million Kurds of Iran although Iran still maintains quite repressive control over its Kurdish region. Altogether these events broke open the Kurdish issue in nearly all its dimensions with incalculable effect on the future shape of Kurdish politics and their impact on the region. This new Kurdish challenge involves potentially sweeping domestic change in the four countries directly affected; it also has direct implication for the future handling of ethnic issues and political structure in all other states in the Middle East that have large minorities—and possibly even affecting their borders.

Syria and the Kurds

In the decades of Turkish-Syrian hostility before the AKP, Syria actively supported the Kurdish guerrilla movement in Turkey, the PKK, as a pressure point against Ankara. The year 1999 marked a milestone: the capture of Abdallah Öcalan, the leader of the PKK guerrillas who had long been sheltered in Damascus. With Öcalan's capture Syria decided to back away from support to the PKK that had nearly brought it to war with Ankara. But the Kurdish issue came back into play between the two countries again in 2011 as an angry and cornered Asad facing domestic uprisings threatened to renew support to the PKK in Turkey. Such a step could be easily accomplished since Syrian Kurds, some 9 percent of the Syrian population, maintain close clan links with the Kurds in Turkey just over their long mutual border. In fact, up to one-third of the members of the PKK are Syrian citizens whose ancestors a generation or two earlier had fled from Turkey's military repression of Kurds. At a time of sensitive Turkish government negotiations with Kurdish leaders inside Turkey, any possible new element of unrest sparked by Syria could greatly complicate Turkey's task of domestic reconciliation with the Kurds.

Yet the two issues cannot be completely separated. The Kurds of Syria, unhappy with their own second-class citizenship and denial of cultural rights there, began to debate whether or not to support the armed Syrian opposition movement against Asad. While Syrian Kurds hated their treatment at the hands of the Asad regime, they were equally wary of possible successor regimes, such as a majoritarian Sunni Arab nationalist regime, which might show even less tolerance for Kurdish distinctiveness—especially for the many Kurds who are not Sunni but 'Alawi. Ironically, by early 2012 Ankara found itself in the anomalous position of trying to *encourage* Kurdish rebellion within Syria to help overthrow the Asad regime. Ankara also operated on the belief that any post-Asad government would be politically beholden to Turkey, and would seek increased economic and investment ties with Turkey.

In short, Ankara's relationship towards the Syrian Kurds has been highly ambivalent. On the one hand it feared their ability to foster turmoil and violence among Turkey's own Kurds, and yet it sought their support to build a united Syrian front against the Asad regime. Turkey could not allow the Syrian Kurds to operate as a loose cannon in a complex struggle and thus sought direct control over the situation, dragging Ankara ever more deeply into the heart of Kurdish politics abroad. This situation places Turkey in a position of kingmaker in the evolution of the Kurdish future and welfare in Syria. The present situation, for the first time, casts Syria's Kurds too as a new autonomous player on the scene that must be part of future regional settlements. Will Iraqi Kurdistan join Turkey in helping direct and broker the future of the Kurds in Syria? Syrian Kurds tend to be unhappy with the more feudal character of some of the Iraqi Kurdish leadership.

The Iraqi Kurds—the Swing Factor

Of all the Kurdish communities outside of Turkey, it was Kurdish separatism in Iraq that constituted Turkey's greatest fear. Iraq functioned for decades as a de-facto safe haven and even a base of operations across the Turkish border for PKK guerrillas. Saddam repeatedly and brutally sought to crush Kurdish power in northern Iraq, including with the use of poison gas, but rarely communicated with Ankara on the issue. With the US invasion of Iraq in 2003 the Kurds quickly developed the foundations of autonomous regional governance, established the Kurdish Regional Government (KRG) and began a serious process of Kurdization of the north. Kurdish became the official language, the local economy began to boom, Kurds took over control of their own identity; the region became a quasi-independent state negotiating its own relations with Baghdad. Iraqi Kurds themselves now referred to their region officially as "Kurdistan"—a word that Ankara could not even bring itself to utter until the 1990s. And even Turkish Kurds traveling to Iraq admitted the thrill of seeing signs welcoming them to "Kurdistan" and hearing the use of Kurdish for official purposes.

In past years the emergence of any such Kurdish autonomy in Iraq would have sparked a military invasion by Turkey to crush it. Indeed, in the early years after the fall of Saddam, Turkey still seriously contemplated military invasion of Iraqi Kurdistan to eliminate the PKK and to nip in the bud any moves towards local Kurdish autonomy. But this time the conditions were different. Turkey slowly, uncomfortably but gradually began to adjust to the reality of the new Kurdish entity. Ankara realized that given the US occupation of Iraq, Turkey would not be allowed to militarily invade northern Iraq; the Kurds were close allies of Washington. Second, Ankara turned adversity into advantage by starting to embrace opportunities to establish new ties in Iraqi Kurdistan. The Turkish Kurds were well equipped to play that role, as well as to facilitate the economic entry of Turkish businessmen into the area. Within a few years Iraqi Kurdistan found itself bound by nearly inextricable ties in a profitable two-way relationship with the Turkish economy. The Iraqi Kurdish leadership played its cards shrewdly in opening up the region to large numbers of Turkish businessmen to invest and do business. Interestingly, this Turkish business interest in Kurdistan grew to involve members of nearly all Turkish political parties and leanings in Turkey, including Turkish nationalists. Road and air connections from Turkey to Iraqi Kurdistan expanded dramatically, and the major cities of Kurdistan began to look north rather than south to Baghdad in their economic orientation.

Kurdistan's oil became a major new factor in Ankara's relationship with the KRG. Turkey is building oil and gas pipelines from Iraqi Kurdistan into Turkey and investing in oil exploration, all of which can help meet some of Turkish domestic energy needs and lessen its dependence upon Iranian energy. But Baghdad is unhappy at the direct and unilateral Turkish energy negotiations with the Kurdish Regional Government that bypasses Baghdad; it sees this growing Turkish role as a direct challenge to Baghdad's sovereignty and ability to maintain control of affairs in Iraqi Kurdistan. The Turkish economic presence in Kurdistan, along with Turkish criticism of the narrow sectarianism of the Maliki regime, constitutes one of Baghdad's major grievances with Ankara.

Since the mid-1990s Turkish entrepreneurs linked with the Gülen (Hizmet) movement have opened over 20 elementary and middle schools throughout Iraqi Kurdistan; instruction is in English, with options for classes in Turkish, Kurdish and Arabic. They are all heavily subscribed. In 2008 Hizmet opened the University of Northern Iraq, the first Hizmet university in Kurdistan. Turkish and Turco-Kurdish culture now moves with ease both ways across the borders in the form of music in Turkish, Kurdish and Arabic, and there is a broad popular following on both sides of the border for Turkish films and TV programs. Turkish household appliances saturate the Kurdish and, increasingly, the Iraqi consumer market. Iraq now constitutes Turkey's second-biggest export market after Germany, with its sales reaching US$8 billion; indeed, it is scheduled soon to surpass Germany as Turkey's largest market. More significantly, about 70 percent of those exports go to Iraqi Kurdistan. By 2012 Kurdistan alone represented Turkey's eighth-biggest market in the world and it is still growing.[1]

Iraq and the Future of Kurdistan

The future of the Kurds in Iraq is intimately linked with the future and status of the Kurds in Turkey. Turkish Kurds are currently negotiating for considerable regional autonomy within Turkey, particularly in cultural and economic policies. As a matter of fact, regional administration across all of Turkey has been too long centralized in Ankara, affecting appointments and policies. Greater regional autonomy for the whole country is a desirable and even likely future development. The future of the Kurds in Turkey is furthermore hugely complicated by the dispersal of Kurds throughout the country. One can't simply speak of southeastern Turkey any longer as the home of Turkish Kurds: Istanbul itself now constitutes the biggest Kurdish city in the world. More Kurds in Turkey live outside of the southeast Kurdish region than in it. Kurds are deeply integrated into the Turkish social and economic order around the country and few would wish to give up that status and be forced to return to the Kurdish region that is still relatively isolated and undeveloped—although rapidly improving. The vibrant new economic development of Iraqi Kurdistan means that the Kurdish regions of Turkey are now no longer at the "end of the line" or "in Turkey's border regions" but rather foursquare on transportation and communication routes between Turkey and Iraq. They profit greatly from this position.

I have often observed that an "unhappy Diyarbakır" (the capital of the Kurdish region in Turkey) is forever destined to be the source of resistance and threat to Ankara, including even sparking guerrilla action; Kurdish discontent poses serious threat to Turkish stability and unity and renders Turkey vulnerable to manipulation by external enemies. On the other hand, a "happy Diyarbakır" turns the threat around and directs it towards neighboring countries with their own restive Kurdish minorities; a prosperous Turkish Kurdistan creates an economic and cultural magnet, a model to which Kurds in Iraq, Syria and Iran can aspire.

What, then, does this rise of a prosperous Kurdistan in Iraq mean for the Kurdish region? Does it offer the seeds of a broader solution to the Kurdish issue? Or, from a Turkish perspective, does it pose a threat, a heightened possibility of Turkish Kurds moving towards separatism and even ultimately seeking a unified Kurdish state?

Like it or not, Turkey's future is now inextricably tied to the future of the Kurdish people as a whole—not only inside, but also outside of, Turkey. If Ankara mishandles the relationship, it poses a threat to the entire country. Handled properly it will greatly empower Turkey's influence in the region and provide it with greater clout in domestic Iraqi, Iranian and Syrian politics. A Turkey that is an intimate partner in the future development of Iraqi Kurdistan has a great deal to offer, and to gain. A hostile Turkey will be faced with endless challenges to its power and prestige in the region, and will be threatened permanently with problems. Ankara possesses the democratic and governmental institutions to move towards a solution in a way that no other neighboring state is remotely yet capable of at this point. Indeed, Iraq, Iran and Syria already feel threatened by Ankara's new influence in Kurdish politics. But Turkey must move quickly to resolve its own domestic Kurdish demands if it is to benefit from its new position of power in the region. In short, Turkey can provide the model for treatment of large ethnic minorities in the Middle East in a way that no other regional state does.

Other Kurds in the region are themselves in no hurry to proclaim any kind of independence, although Mas'ud Barzani, the leader of the Kurdish Regional Government in Iraq, has on occasion admitted that a genuine independent and united Kurdish state represents a long-term ideal for most Kurds. Indeed, mere articulation of the idea now places certain useful pressures on Baghdad to more intelligently negotiate political and economic power-sharing with the Kurdish region. As for Iran, it maintains a dual policy: it has close, solid and growing economic, cultural and political relations with Iraqi Kurdistan, although they fall far short of Turkish influence and power there. But Tehran also continues to harshly repress any sign of movement towards greater autonomy among its own Kurdish population. Iran at this point represents the least progressive of all the four major regional states with large Kurdish minorities.

In a further sign of improving relations between Barzani and Turkey, Ankara now views the Iraqi Kurds as allies and pressure points in two respects. The KRG lends quiet but important diplomatic help to Turkey to help close down the PKK guerrilla war and to cooperate in finding a political resolution that will remove the chief element of confrontation between

327

Ankara and the KRG. Second, the Iraqi Kurds represent a useful Turkish pressure point against any future Baghdad government. Ankara wishes to see greater Sunni Arab and Kurdish participation in the Iraqi government, both to enhance Iraqi stability and to dilute strong Iranian influence that plays on Shi'ite-Sunni clashes. Iraqi Kurds and Sunni Arabs are natural partners in seeking greater ethnic and sectarian balance in Iraq in the face of the Shi'ite majority.

At the same time, both Washington and Ankara know that they are unlikely to enlist the Iraqi Kurdish Regional Government into an anti-Iran front. Iraqi Kurds know from long experience that Iran can exert major influence, for better or for worse, inside Iraqi Kurdistan. They need the balancing support that Iran can lend them against pressures from Baghdad and they have every reason to maintain good ties with Tehran. The Soranî dialect is the principal literary form of Kurdish in the KRG and shares an equal number of speakers on the Iranian side of the border. Iraqi Kurds follow the conditions of their brethren in Iran and are displeased with often harsh Iranian measures against Kurdish nationalist fighters there. But Tehran has often acted as a protector or supporter of Iraqi Kurds against Baghdad and will similarly seek good relations with the KRG in the future. Many Iraqi Kurdish leaders have spent much time in Iran, maintain personal ties there and speak Persian fluently. Iranian trade with the KRG has grown nearly 40 times in the last decade since the establishment of the KRG and now amounts to about US$4 billion a year, about half of Turkey's. This does not represent a win-lose situation for either Iran or Turkey in Iraqi Kurdistan; there is room for cooperation.[2]

Speculation about the future evolution of the Kurdish region poses many questions, but certain key trends and characteristics seem already evident:

• The somewhat feudalistic character of Kurdish society and governance in Iraq is being challenged by younger generations of Kurds. They demand change. Iraqi Kurds are now far less isolated and much more aware of regional politics as it affects them. They are full players in the game, and both Ankara and Baghdad have had to accept that reality.

• All Kurds now sense a greater potential for some ultimate grand unity of all Kurds into a united Kurdistan. One of the appeals of the PKK leadership, Marxist and authoritarian as it was, lay in its vision of a united Kurdistan in a way that local feudal leaders never understood and even feared as a challenge to their own local authority. The PKK now no longer enjoys a monopoly on those ideas. Still, none of this means that Kurds will be able to join forces or create a united Kurdistan in any foreseeable future. The obstacles are huge:

- Serious differences among four linguistic dialects among the Kurds in different regions that complicate common communication.

- The second language of Kurds differs totally from state to state: Turkish, Persian or Arabic have long been their primary languages of education and culture.

- The political socialization of the various Kurdish peoples differs markedly depending on the state in which they live. Turkish Kurds have had quite different historical experiences and cultural exposures than have Kurds in either Iran, Iraq, or Syria.

- Kurds also differ in their sectarian affiliations—Sunni, Shi'ite and Alevi.

Apart from differences among the Kurds from one state to another, political, personality, clan and ideological differences among them complicate internal politics as well. Concepts of Kurdish nationalism are in a state of evolution as new situations and opportunities present themselves. Kurdish nationalists within Iraq, for example, while recognizing the great commercial and economic benefits that Turkey has brought to the KRG, also worry about the new economic, political and cultural domination exerted by the soft power of the Turkish state. Turkish businesses represent half of the foreign investors in the KRG. And while Turkey needs and imports Kurdish oil, it represents only a small portion of Turkish energy imports; on the other hand those imports represent a huge portion of the KRG's income, so the KRG becomes increasingly economically dependent upon Turkey in ways that could influence future political relations. Class differences as well have increased as new prosperity hits Kurdistan and sparks calls for greater democratization of Kurdish politics. Pro- and anti-Turkish elements are likely to increase in Kurdish politics over time, especially as some kind of "Kurdish Spring" appears on the scene. In short, the major benefits of the new Turkish role in Iraqi Kurdistan have a few downsides as well in the eyes of many Iraqi Kurds. Indeed, some Iraqi Kurds worry that the power of Turkey's own Kurdish region could threaten Iraqi Kurdistan with vassalization.[3]

While political liberalization for the Kurds is emerging inside Turkey and in Iraq, neither Ankara nor Baghdad, much less Tehran, is willing to accept a move towards true independence by Kurds; those three states could conceivably even cooperate to stifle such an initiative as they have periodically in the past. While over the long run no one can predict what a future united Kurdistan might look like, most Kurds know that at best this is a very long-term project. Furthermore, they would risk exchanging a functioning and fairly desirable present situation for an uncertain and tempestuous future if some grand scheme of unification became the focus of their politics. Rivalries for leadership of a "united Kurdistan" would quickly develop and be vulnerable to manipulation by outside powers as well.

Any future "autonomous regions" or federative relations for Kurds naturally depends on the local politics of each country, but also on the future character of international borders themselves in a rapidly developing world. The EU model of state relations, while still evolving, has weakened formal borders and given birth to new regional associations across borders to make up rational new economic units. Spanish models of greater regional autonomy in places like Catalunya are evolving; if such ideas are successful in Europe, Turkey is likely to be influenced over the longer run by such ideas as well. Thus a highly autonomous Kurdish region in Turkey would pose less of a threat today than previously understood in the "old politics" of national borders with high walls of sovereignty.

Finally, some Turks still fear that greater Kurdish autonomy may be little more than a way station to an ultimate declaration of full Kurdish independence from Turkey. That possibility cannot be excluded. No one knows what direction events will take in this complex equation. But one thing is clear: Turkey can either adjust peacefully to evolution in the Kurdish regions, or it can try to prevent such evolution as it has in the past, including by force. The record suggests that force and violence in the end will only hasten the Kurdish thirst for separatism and create an ugly and deteriorating atmosphere. Such a call for separatism is far less urgent under the positive economic and political conditions offered by Turkey today.

In short, the Kurds are better off today than they probably have ever been in history. They have emerged from the recent turmoil of the Middle East as perhaps the number one winners. They have become overt political players in three major states already and will quickly challenge Iran as well if Tehran does not soon move to further accommodate Kurdish aspirations. Iran may soon emerge as the one state that has as yet yielded little to the Kurds. If Turkey should move out well ahead of Iran—as it now seems to be doing—in offering a generous settlement to Turkish Kurds—cultural freedom and some political autonomy—the pressure on Tehran will increase to make similar offers to its own Kurds. Such developments could even push Iran to try to sabotage Turkish political initiatives.

This gap in relative freedom will be a point of stress between Turkey and Iran. With luck and wisdom Iranian society may come to see Turkey as a model to meet Iran's own multicultural, multi-ethnic and multi-religious society. Meanwhile the relationship between Ankara and the KRG is growing and is fruitful for both. Turkey is on the right path towards resolution of the problem of the Kurds in Turkey, even though it still may take time to fully implement and there will be bumps along the way. The political trajectory of the Kurds in the future of Middle East politics has hardly yet stabilized, and indeed may only be in its early stages of evolution. But it will never be the same again.

CHAPTER TWENTY-THREE
THE ISRAEL FACTOR

Jews have seen more violence and persecution at the hands of the West than from any other source in their long history. The constant discrimination, harsh treatment, pogroms and ghettoization that Jews suffered living in the West went on for well over a millennium and a half, ultimately culminating in the huge crime of the Holocaust, the paradigm for modern industrialized genocide.

The emergence of the Zionist movement in the late 19th century was in many ways a natural product of these centuries of discrimination. It also reflected an era of nationalist movements across Europe, paralleling other nationalist movements in that same period—Slavic, Germanic, Turkic and others. But it was more than that: Zionism reflected the desire of Jews to find a safe haven in the form of a secure state of their own in the world—a response to a real existential threat, unlike the relatively more secure prospects confronting most other nationalist movements. The creation of the Israeli state, while immensely important for the preservation of Jewish physical security and culture, sadly also entailed major injustices against the deeply-rooted other Semitic inhabitants of the land that Israel came to occupy—the Palestinians. The tragedy of the Israeli state lies precisely in this: the discrimination, ghettoization, and lack of justice for the Palestinians that now creates a painful crisis of conscience for large numbers of Jews themselves as they sense the karma from the founding of the Zionist state. The repercussions of those events spread across the Middle East and the world. What began as primarily a Zionist effort to acquire land in Palestine for a new state became a struggle with Palestinians over land in Palestine, and ultimately took on ethnic, even religious overtones. The Zionist slogan that "Palestine was a land without people for a people without land" was not only preposterous, but a cruel and cynical rejection of the very existence and humanity of the huge Palestinian population displaced and turned into refugees in the ongoing process of ethnic cleansing.

Muslim views towards Jews present a complex picture. On the one hand, Islamic theology leaves no doubt that the mission of Moses and the message of Judaism constitute a vital and integral part of Islam. Abraham, Moses, Noah, Isaac and most other Old Testament prophets are all accepted as important prophets of God in Islamic theology; hundreds of given names commonly borne by Muslims have their origin in the Old Testament or the joint Semitic tradition. At the same time there remains a legacy of a few, quite time-and-place-specific, hostile references to Jews in the Qur'an that stem particularly from the time of Arab tribal warfare against the new Muslim community. The Qur'an relates how a few Jewish tribes in the early decades of the fledgling Muslim community were perceived to be working with the pagan enemies of the Muslims in Mecca to destroy the Muslim community. Jews are strongly condemned for those actions and hostile language against them from that period is preserved in the Qur'an. Otherwise Jews, along with Christians, remain "People of the Book" who are legally and theologically protected within Islamic society. Jews are known to have thrived in Islamic societies, vastly more than they ever did at any point in European history—most notably in Muslim Spain and later within the Ottoman Empire where they took refuge from the Spanish Inquisition. Muslim Spain represents the high point of medieval Jewish culture.

Ultimately, the creation of the state of Israel on Palestinian lands, the forcible expulsion of three-quarters of a million Palestinians in 1948 from the new state of Israel, along with ongoing Israeli land grabs from Palestinians in the occupied West Bank right down to the present—all illegal in international law—embitter Muslims worldwide and have cost Israel much sympathy globally. The unresolved and festering Palestinian issue lies at the heart of a great deal of the regional tension in the Middle East today. Nearly all Arabs sympathize deeply with the Palestinian plight as a symbol of injustice and oppression of fellow Muslims; increasingly other Muslims around the world have come to feel the same way on an issue now rife with symbolism. The case of Palestine is seen as but one prominent chapter of broader western domination of eastern peoples.

The Ottoman Empire was an early place of refuge for Spanish Jews starting in 1492—when King Ferdinand and Queen Isabella launched the Reconquista heralding the expulsion of all Jews and Muslims from Spain on pain of death. But Ottoman support for the Palestinians also goes back to the time when the Ottoman Empire held formal responsibility for the Holy Places in Jerusalem. The Ottoman sultan and caliph also bore responsibility for protecting Muslim societies from the West; thus the Ottoman government spoke of its specific concerns over both legal purchases and illegal land grabs by Zionist settlers in Palestine in the late 19th century when Palestinian notables came to Istanbul seeking Ottoman protection for their lands. Turks recall those events as part of their imperial history.

The problem was worsened by the *western colonial character* of the Zionist enterprise, specifically the arrival of large numbers of westerners—Jews from eastern and western Europe—into Palestine where they created essentially a western settler state outside of the West. The history of such distant settler states created by Europeans—including Boers and English in South Africa, and white English settlers in Rhodesia—has an unhappy history; it gives clear evidence that such western settler colonies inevitably face long-term resistance by the local people displaced by westerners who arrived, took up residence, and created a new state. It is the land—and not ethnicity or culture—that lies at the heart of the Palestinian issue. The Palestinians lost their lands in the process of the creation of the Israeli state and were forced to flee, creating a bleeding wound in Palestine that has not yet been treated. In fact it has grown worse as the Palestinians on the West Bank and in Gaza remain under Israeli military occupation for nearly half a century now with no relief in sight. Palestinians have responded in part with acts of terrorism against the Israeli occupation, and against Israeli apartheid policies that continue to oppress Palestinians and make them prisoner in their own homeland. Over time newer and sizable portions of the occupied territories have been seized and taken over by right-wing settlers or even non-ideological Israelis who were offered strong state financial inducements to settle there. There is no indication that large numbers of Israelis will ever willingly yield up any of this land back to the Palestinians. The likelihood of a two-state solution has now virtually disappeared in the face of such "facts on the ground" deliberately created by the Israeli state. Some observers within Israel itself now fear that this situation threatens the future existence of the Israeli state itself: we are looking at the prospect then of a single bi-national state that cannot easily remain a "Jewish state" unless yet millions more Palestinians are expelled.

The problem is compounded by a historic drift to the extreme right in Israeli politics which has led to hardening and racist policies opposed to the return of the occupied territories or the dismantling of growing illegal settlements, or the impounding of millions of Palestinians as virtual hostages for over 40 years within the occupied territories. The hardline and discriminatory nature of Israeli policies has been increasingly recognized by the world and has led to growing international isolation of the Israeli state. New Israeli insistence now on the "Jewish" character of the state does not sit well in a world where identification of a state in racial terms is no longer in keeping with a democratic multicultural world. (If Germany, for example, were to define itself as "the German state" there would be international outrage at the implications.)

Indeed, the well-known *New York Times* commentator Thomas Friedman—a good friend of Israel—referred in September 2011 to the Netanyahu government as "the most diplomatically inept and strategically incompetent government in Israel's history...[that] has also left the US government fed up with Israel's leadership but a hostage to its ineptitude, because a powerful pro-Israel lobby can force the administration to defend Israel at the UN, even when it knows Israel is pursuing policies not in its own interests or in America's."[1]

Politics in the Middle East after the foundation of Israel in 1948 was long defined by a defiant Arab bloc that initially rejected the "Zionist entity" in its midst and refused to recognize the state. Hostility on both sides remains palpable. Egyptian President Anwar Sadat's peace treaty with Israel at Camp David in 1978 broke the pattern, but remained the major exception to Arab hostility to Israel's policies, expansionism, and its abusive treatment of Palestinians. Jordan followed suit by recognizing Israel—both countries heavily dependent upon Washington for support. In each case it was the country's ruler and not the population that accepted such diplomatic settlements.

Turkey's relations with Israel, however, followed a very different pattern; they go way back to 1949 when Turkey became the first Muslim country to recognize the new state of Israel—partly reflecting Ankara's tendency in that era to follow the US lead in Middle East foreign policy. The two states were also pushed together in sharing the Cold War struggle against the Soviet Union, although Ankara also had no compunctions about officially recognizing the Palestinian state during the first *Intifada*, or Palestinian uprising, against Israel in 1987. There is a significant Turkish-Jewish community in Turkey that feels safe, quite well assimilated and enjoys prominent and respected roles in Turkish society and business—although there are pockets of anti-Semitism within Turkey as in other states.

The heyday of the official relationship between Israel and Turkey came in the mid-1990s at a time when it was driven strongly by a Turkish General Staff that valued Israel as a source of military equipment—particularly of items that Washington, for reasons of strategic sensitivity, often would not sell to Ankara. Second, the General Staff manipulated its demand for close ties with Israel in order to harass and constrain the Islamist predecessor of the AKP, the Refah party which was more outspokenly anti-Israel than the AKP. The General Staff at the time also maintained a hardline security view towards all its neighbors—Syria, Iran, Iraq, and Greece—whom Israel similarly regarded as shared enemies. Finally the General Staff was convinced that good relations with Israel would put them in good stead with the powerful pro-Israeli lobby in the US who would then support Turkey in the US Congress. The views of the General Staff, however, did not particularly reflect Turkish public opinion that has always shared a significant element of human sympathy for the plight of the Palestinians.

As Israeli politics moved ever further to the right over the years it was not surprising that Turkey, too, took an increasingly sharper line with Israel's policies, particularly following the ascent of the AKP to power. Prime Minister Erdoğan proclaimed an early desire to maintain Turkey's existing good relations with Israel, but grew disillusioned with the prospect of maintaining good ties with the expansionist, racist and narrowly defined "Jewish" character of Netanyahu's Israeli state. In particular, Erdoğan felt humiliated and betrayed when Israeli Prime Minister Olmert permitted him to continue brokering Israeli-Syrian negotiations in Israel in 2008 while all the while Israel was planning its imminent and ferocious "Cast Lead" operation against Gaza and its civilians mere weeks later, in which over a thousand Palestinians died—in a 10-to-one ratio over Israelis.

As tensions between Turkey and Israel rose, including Turkish criticism of Israeli invasions of both Lebanon and Gaza, Erdoğan finally publicly chastised Israeli President Perez in a public forum in Davos in January 2009, expressing his anger about how Israel was quick to routinely resort to overwhelming violence against the Palestinians—employing the provocative words "you know very well how to kill." This public rebuke raised Erdoğan's standing in Turkish opinion polls, reflecting a broader and growing anger among Turks themselves towards Israel. In 2010 Israel publicly and studiedly humiliated the Turkish ambassador to Israel by placing him in a low chair in a diplomatic meeting where everyone else sat higher and only the Israeli flag was displayed. As Turkish foreign policy in the Middle East diverged further from US policies, the Israeli lobby and neoconservative circles in Washington increasingly orchestrated strong attacks on Turkey itself in the press, suggesting that it had now "become the enemy" and that the Turkish government had fallen into the hands of "Islamic radicals."

There is no doubt that since the AKP came to power, anti-Israeli feelings have grown in Turkey. But such emotions are far from limited to Turkey; anti-Israeli sentiment has increased around the world in general over the past decade or so, based on specific condemnation of Israeli policies and not on mere "anti-Semitism"—that inevitably may also be present to some degree. Under Prime Minister Netanyahu Israeli politics have moved the country to the most unyielding position ever on the Palestinians; its hardline policies were buttressed by a foreign minister, Avigdor Lieberman, whose views are described as fascist and racist by many within Israel itself. These hardline Israeli personalities and policies also offended many in the West, even though western governments are invariably cautious about expression of any negative views towards Israel. This was also a decade in which Washington since 9/11 moved aggressively to launch military operations in nearly a half dozen Muslim countries, creating great anguish among Muslims everywhere. The resulting spectacle was over a million Muslims dead and several times more injured through the longest lasting American war in history in Afghanistan, as well as a long and brutal war in Iraq, and combat operations in Pakistan, Yemen, Somalia, Libya and elsewhere.

Under these conditions, it is not surprising that feelings against Israel, America's most intimate ally, have risen, not only in Turkey but in most of the rest of the world, and above all in the Muslim world which has long felt itself an impotent in the face of US and Israeli military power; Israel commands overwhelmingly the most powerful military force in the Middle East bar none. At the same time there is little doubt that ongoing hostility to specific Israeli policies can, and does over time, spill over into a more general anti-Semitic character as events multiply and emotions rise.

A general decline in Turkish-Israeli relations reached a nadir with the *Mavi Marmara* (Blue Marmara) incident, in which an international left-wing private relief flotilla in 2010 set sail from Turkey, with government knowledge, to Gaza with the intent of delivering food and medicines to Gaza and designed to peacefully break the Israeli blockade of Gaza. The *Mavi Marmara* was attacked and boarded on the high seas by Israeli commandos, leading to the death of 11 Turks. There was rage in Turkey over the event and Turkey's ambassador to Israel was recalled. Turkey set two demands for any restoration of normal ties: an apology from Israel for the incident, and compensation for the deaths of the Turkish victims of the attack. Turkey additionally said it planned to support legal action against Israel in both Turkish and international courts on the part of the families of the Turks who were killed on board. In addition Turkey planned to open a case with the International Court of Justice against the entire Israeli blockade of Gaza. What had been a bilateral issue thus took on international implications. In September 2011 Turkey also vetoed Israel's request to open an office in NATO, and refused to permit data gathered at NATO anti-ballistic missile radar stations on Turkish soil to be passed to Israel.

Nonetheless, the AKP government, while remaining strongly critical of Israel, has sought to avoid explicit anti-Semitic rhetoric. But critics point to a general rise in anti-Semitic expression in Turkey in this same period. There is no doubt that the AKP displays a higher degree of sympathy and solidarity with the Muslim world than any previous Turkish political party in power. Yet nearly all Turks have consistently demonstrated sympathy for the Palestinians over the years; Israel is broadly unpopular with the general public and there is little serious public criticism of AKP policy towards Israel. A notable exception is the religious movement of Fethullah Gülen who has been consistently cautious towards any criticism of Israel; Gülen was actually publicly critical of the AKP's support for the relief flotilla, deeming it to be provocative and counterproductive. Gülen's desire not to rock the boat with Israel resulted in some accusing him of being a "US agent."

The Deterioration of Relations
In a Middle East that has grown markedly more anti-American and anti-Israel since 2001, Ankara now seems to believe that maintenance of special ties with Israel has little justification for Turkey other than pleasing Washington. Ties to Israel in the past did buy Turkey some greater credit with the US Zionist lobby and the American Congress, but as the stakes shifted, and with the broad failures of US policy in the region, Turkey sharply downgraded the priority of its relations with Israel. Israeli strategists have concluded, probably correctly, that Turkey's ties with Israel will never regain the status they once had. But as US mainstream observer Fareed Zakaria pointed out, "the fact is that the old Israeli model—cutting deals with kings and dictators, getting Washington to lean on Turkey's generals—will not work anymore. And the fretting about Turkey's new attitude has missed a key effect: Turkey has utterly eclipsed Iran as the leader of the Arab street. "When Erdoğan visited Cairo on Sept. 12 and 13, he was greeted like a conquering hero. Cafés that once had photographs of [Iranian president] Mahmoud Ahmadinejad are replacing them with images of the Turkish leader."[2]

Indeed, Israel's position of strategic strength internationally has sharply eroded. It had been protected from the consequences of its expansionist and apartheid policies for a long time for several reasons: traditional western sympathies and guilt stemming from the Holocaust, support from western governments, the powerful funding activities and punitive capabilities of Zionist lobbies, lack of balanced public information on the Palestinian problem in the rigorously self-censored American media, and the absence of any mainstream news outlets in the West presenting a more balanced picture of the problem. The US press shies away from criticism of Israel, being unwilling even to reprint criticism of the Israeli government from the Israeli press itself. But in recent years much of the media, in the face of Israel's own intransigent policies and challenges to US presidents, has shown a slight shift in willingness to treat Israel more objectively, despite the financial hammerlock the Zionist lobby maintains on the US Congress. Younger American Jews, furthermore, are showing growing disillusionment with the absence of liberal sensibilities within the Israeli political system.

The AKP also displeased Washington and Tel Aviv with its insistence on maintaining relations with Hamas—the Palestinian version of the Muslim Brotherhood that is simultaneously a political movement, a political party, the legitimately elected ruling party in Gaza, and an armed wing for guerrilla operations against Israel. It has administered the Gaza strip since 2007 after it won elections in Palestine in 2006. Ankara—as do most other observers of the region—believes that inclusion of Hamas as a major Palestinian political player is indispensable to a final peace settlement. Top political operatives from Hamas have visited Ankara. Turkey has sought to mediate the political split between Hamas and Fatah leadership in the West Bank as part of an effort to build coherent negotiating parties on both sides. Yet Washington and Jerusalem insist that Hamas must be considered a purely terrorist organization, boycotted and even overthrown. While Washington and Israel have tried to overturn the rule of Hamas in Gaza they have not succeeded.

But Turkey did not spare blunt advice to Hamas either. In both 2006 and in 2011 President Abdullah Gül informed Hamas leader Khalid Mish'al that Hamas must come to recognize Israel's existence as part of any peace settlement. Then, starting in 2012, Turkey's special role as broker between the Fatah and Hamas entered a highly complicated new phase, first with the "return of Egypt" to Arab politics when, after the Muslim Brotherhood won the elections, Cairo itself took the lead in trying to bring the two Palestinian factions together. Turkey at that point lost its unique monopoly of diplomatic mediation that it once had in the face of Arab diplomatic paralysis and inaction. That changed again in 2013 with the coup against the government of the Brotherhood and the accession of military rule in Cairo which declared the Muslim Brotherhood in all its forms and branches to be a "terrorist" organization, including the Palestinian branch Hamas. Turkey at this point is somewhat isolated—at least for now—as the only major Muslim country to maintain ties with Hamas, but it will probably cling to principle and maintain those ties as being legitimate and necessary. Such a posture now riles both Cairo's military rulers and Saudi Arabia as well as Israel and Washington.

Some analysis by Israel and its supporters attribute the rising tensions in the Israeli-Turkish relationship to the AKP party and its Islamist roots. While there is no doubt that the AKP does have special interest and sympathy for the Muslim world and the Muslim Brotherhood, the AKP's position towards Israel enjoys broad support across the Turkish population. It is quite unlikely that any post-AKP government in Turkey will significantly reverse the nature of those relations. There are strong elements of nationalism on the part of the both the Nationalist Movement Party (MHP) and the People's Republican Party (CHP) that are similarly unsympathetic to Israel.

Turkey's trade with Israel is significant, but not vital to either party. Turkey accounted for about 3 percent of Israel's foreign trade in 2011, a 26 percent rise over the previous year. Turkey is Israel's sixth-leading export destination, primarily in chemicals and oil distillates. Loss of military sales and maintenance contracts with Turkey would deal a blow to Israel's aerospace sector.[3]

Other analyses from Israel have sensed—accurately in my opinion—a truly strategic shift in Turkish policies away from Israel, for all the reasons we have discussed above. These observers believe the decline in Turkish ties with Israel is a long-term trend unlikely to be reversed anytime in the foreseeable future. It believes that Turkey has no serious intentions of improving relations with Israel and primarily seeks to curry favor with the Muslim world. They then conclude, unwisely, that circumstances therefore call for a revamping of Israeli strategies in the region—including even a move to "contain" Ankara's new and assertive policies.[4] In what seemed either a foolish or a dangerously belligerent response to Turkey, Israeli Foreign Minister Lieberman in 2011 stated Israel's determination to "punish Turkey" by developing ties with the Kurdish rebel group PKK, and said it would work with the Armenian diaspora in the US to promote anti-Turkish resolutions in Congress on the issue of Armenian genocide. It would also have the Israeli foreign ministry promote news at the international level of Turkish domestic shortcomings in its minorities' problems such as the sensitive Alevi issue. While two can play at making humiliating demands of each other, such Israeli policies would be highly counterproductive, are guaranteed to intensify Turkey's extreme sensitivities on each of these issues and spark a harsh backlash. This will not benefit Israel nor produce greater Turkish flexibility; Israel has much more to lose than Turkey through this gambit.

Nonetheless, Cyprus became an immediate target of Israel's new anti-Turkish turn. Jerusalem expressed interest in developing the gas fields which lie off waters near Israel, Lebanon and Cyprus. Israel signed a joint agreement with the government of Cyprus—more accurately, the internationally recognized Greek-controlled part of Cyprus that is still contested by Turkey—

to drill for gas, employing an American company. Ankara took major exception to this since it believes there can be no unilateral drilling by the Greek-controlled portion of the island as long as the status of Greek and Turkish-controlled Cyprus has not been resolved. Turkey therefore quickly signed an agreement with the government of Northern Cyprus (dominated by Turkey and a government not recognized internationally) for drilling in the same area, and has threatened the use of its naval forces to prevent unilateral Greek prospecting for gas. Thus the foundations for a Greek-Cypriot-Israeli confrontation with Turkey might loom on the horizon.

Not surprisingly, Washington supports the Israeli-Cypriot gas deal. More surprisingly Russia also has so far supported the Cypriot case, reflecting the increasingly complex relationship between Moscow and Ankara. Russia has strong economic and strategic ties with Cyprus which it does not want jeopardized. While Moscow greatly values its strategic relationship with Turkey, it does not want the relationship to be taken for granted, nor would it welcome seeing Turkey as a potentially unrestricted new hegemon in the eastern Mediterranean.

In March 2013 US President Obama, while on a visit to Israel, finally persuaded Israeli Prime Minister Netanyahu to offer a much-touted formal apology to Turkey for its attack on the ship *Mavi Marmara*, thus fulfilling one of Ankara's major preconditions for the restoration of diplomatic ties with Israel. Yet those knowledgeable of the full dimensions of the Israeli-Turkish dynamic are skeptical that Netanyahu's apology really changed much between the two states, despite opening of negotiations on bilateral grievances. Israel greatly needs improved ties with Turkey, while Ankara will benefit in Washington through some cosmetic improvements in its relations with Israel. Perhaps the most important incentive for Turkey to improve its ties with Jerusalem is to regain its position as honest broker of the region. If Ankara cannot communicate effectively with Jerusalem its credibility is undermined. The civil conflict in Syria's civil war has opened communication between Jerusalem and Ankara on that issue, and Turkey does not wish to weaken its ties with Washington over Syria. But negotiations between Israel and Turkey remain prickly and no strategic change is in the offing. The broader trajectory of Israeli policies vis-à-vis the Palestinians and the region will almost certainly ensure a longtime coolness between the two. That situation will not significantly change with any successor government in Ankara.

The Future

Turkey's future relations with Israel directly impact the Palestinian-Israeli conflict. In historical perspective Turkey is inherently the least anti-Jewish of all Muslim states in the Middle East. But today Turkey is actually facilitating a regional shift in the balance of political power in the Middle East towards greater independence from western demands. The Palestinian conflict has been the paramount destabilizing and emotional issue in the region for over half a century. Until this situation receives equitable and acceptable resolution the problem will generate continuing turmoil. Such turmoil is likely to grow, not diminish, with greater democratization and the rise of public opinion as a greater factor in Arab foreign policy that had been suppressed under US-dominated autocratic rule.

How likely is a settlement, however? In a stunningly frank analysis of US hardball realpolitik, Lee Smith, who enjoys impeccable neo-conservative credentials, wrote in October 2013 (italics mine):

> [P]eace talks were primarily a device to advance American interests—a regional puppet show with Washington pulling the strings. With overwhelming political, diplomatic, and (most important) military support for Israel, Washington turned Jerusalem into a dependent client. It was also an invitation to the Arabs who, having despaired of any hope of defeating Israel in war, were forced to come to Washington on bended knee to secure concessions—like promises of withdrawals—from the Jewish state...
>
> [But]...in the absence of the familiar global Soviet threat, Americans were easily overwhelmed by cries for *a final peace deal that was arguably never in the American interest—since the perpetuation of the conflict by kicking the can down the road forever was the key to keeping both the Arabs and the Israelis firmly in the American fold.*[5]

This analysis helps explain what so many suspected—why indeed the "peace process" never went anywhere in 30 years and still does not, and why other observers, such as Turkey, have turned their back on it to try to broker independent channels. Israel is long familiar with irresponsible and demagogic rhetoric delivered against it by various rabble-rousing Arab dictators. But it is not accustomed to blunt criticisms leveled against it by credible, successful, democratic, globally-integrated mainstream governments and leaders like Turkey that are close to the West. The appearance of this kind of a state in the Middle East poses an exceptional challenge to Israel that cannot be simply written off as primitive, fanatic, ideological, anti-Semitic, authoritarian, irrational or anti-western. The blame for all the problems of the Middle East of course do not lie exclusively with Israel, but Israel over the past many decades is unaccustomed to receiving critique or pushback from any responsible quarter. There are many leaders in the West who significantly agree with the Turkish critiques of Israel but who feel constrained from speaking out, for multiple historical reasons. That situation is now changing and the Middle East is taking on a new strategic face.

The issue is not simply about Turkey or its AKP government. Sooner or later the Middle East was destined to witness the emergence of a credible spokesman to defend the Palestinians. Defense of the Palestinians is "a role in search of an actor" in the Middle East. That actor right now happens to be Turkey. But it is the *situation* that engenders the spokesman, not the spokesman engendering the situation; some kind of a spokesman will always emerge in the absence of a just settlement.

Events may now be moving towards a short- or long-term confrontation with Israel. Only if the extremist policies of Likud and Netanyahu come to be viewed inside Israel as negative, unproductive and ultimately harmful to Israel itself can the domestic political scene change, hopefully generating new leadership capable of bringing about bold new initiatives to extract Israel from the cul-de-sac in which it finds itself.

Turkey clearly will not seek war with Israel. It would not prevail militarily against an Israeli opponent in any case and it knows that. It has no intention of moving in that direction. But some degree of controlled tension is quite likely until the situation and policies shift within Israel—an event not now visible on the horizon. One small note of hope is that public opinion polls in Israel do indicate that the population is out ahead of the Likud party in terms of willingness to embrace a Palestinian state and UN recognition of such an entity. Meanwhile it is farfetched to believe that Turkey's ties with Israel could ever assume greater strategic importance for Ankara than its ties with the Arab world—in economic terms alone, much less cultural and emotional. Still, it is not in Ankara's interests to break its ties with Israel entirely. And, as mentioned, Israel needs Turkey more than Turkey needs Israel.

Conservative commentators in Israel and the US often claim that Turkey under the AKP (and its likely successors) has become a "threat" to Israel. In one sense there is an element of truth to this concern—at least in the political and diplomatic sense. Turkey will not likely become an ally of Israel again. As long as Israel pursues its present policy towards the Palestinians and the occupied territories, Turkey will not cease to hammer on this vocally; its objections will be treated seriously elsewhere in the world. Already Turkey's hostility to a strong Israeli presence in NATO is understood and even tacitly accepted by many NATO members who share in Turkey's critique of Israel.

Turkey will also reflect the Middle East public consensus on Israel and that will not be favorable to Israel.

What circumstances might change Turkey's view towards Israel, absent a major change in the character of the Jewish state and its policies? Only some overwhelming regional military and political threat that would drive Turkey to find strong regional allies. It is hard to imagine anything of that magnitude emerging from Iran, Russia or an Arab state bloc. Only Syria, domestically on fire, poses a threat to Turkey with its destabilized border and refugee flows; Israel is not in a position to change the internal dynamic in Syria in any case.

Turkey's new Islamically-oriented voice cuts more ice in the Muslim world than its former regional policies when Ankara worked more closely with Washington. Turkey is thus now in a position to play a more persuasive role in helping shift Arab views and policies towards Israel, if Israeli policy shifts should justify it. If anything, Turkey might be able to help prevent the confrontation from getting out of hand and moving onto a war footing. Despite its own tensions with Israel, Turkey can be the major spokesman for a Middle East bloc that will present a more united but moderate front in negotiating with Israel. Mechanisms such as the Arab League exist for this, and Turkey can work within that or other spheres. More likely Ankara will seek some other regional organization such as the Organization of Islamic Cooperation, or alter existing ones, that can deal with regional security issues that include both Israel and Iran.

It will take many years before the Arab world is able to establish some kind of functioning democracy and effective foreign policy mechanisms that reflect public opinion. And while Turkey can never speak for the Arab world—and Arabs do not want it to—Turkey can articulate views on the Arab-Israeli question which it believes are probably shared by public opinion within most of the region. Ankara is likely to pursue a strong legal line against Israel as long as it perceives justice is not served in Palestine. New and more representative Arab governments as they arise are increasingly likely to seek greater voice in the Palestinian situation at the political level. Turkey can take the initiative, perhaps in partnership with one or another Arab state, leading to international action towards a broader settlement. Turkey is likely to remain one of the preeminent voices in this respect, simply because its accomplishments and position lend it that kind of authority—in political, economic, military, cultural, and foreign policies.

CHAPTER TWENTY-FOUR
THE AKP AND THE FUTURE OF TURKEY

The remarkable 12-year rule of the AKP government in Turkey has taken place in the context of dynamic change domestically, regionally and globally. We see a new post-Kemalist Turkey, operating in the context of a new Middle East jolted by the turmoil of the Arab Spring, and all of this unfolding in an emerging new international order that is no longer dominated by the US. It is difficult to fully capture this dynamic that operates on so many different levels.

The present form of the AKP era already shows signs of serious wear resulting from the pressures of 12 years in office. Prime Minister Erdoğan has been the supreme architect of the new Turkey, benefitting additionally from the close collaboration of talented people around him, in particular President Ahmet Gül and Foreign Minister Davutoğlu. But for Erdoğan his era is statutorily drawing to a close. Despite earlier aspirations, he may think twice about running for the presidency of Turkey given the more recent tarnishing of his image through personal and party scandal. The AKP could still win the next parliamentary election in 2015, but the floundering opposition parties may be encouraged to pull themselves together by then and bring the AKP's government to a close.

What do we make of the era? By any standards of modern Turkish history it has overseen the greatest degree of democratization (despite some backsliding), enviable economic growth and prosperity, successful participation in economic globalization, a hugely expanded vision of Turkey's place in the world, the "domestication" and successful integration of an Islamic party into the democratic order, a major step towards resolution of the Kurdish issue, and an end to military domination of Turkish politics.

Do the party's Islamist roots make this a unique and passing moment in Turkish history that will now be reversed? Or can we expect Turkey to continue a roughly similar course down the road? Let's look at some major trends that will affect Turkey's own experience and its relevancy to a future Middle East.

The dramatic success of the AKP government in forcing the military back to the barracks is a milestone in Turkish history; it has also left an understandable legacy of anger and bitterness among some in the military from this sweeping reduction of its power and influence. For most Kemalists,

Kemalism is not just an ideology—it is the *equivalent of patriotism*. Many of them believe that the AKP political order has grievously weakened the values—and power—of Kemalism, resulting, in their view, in the end of Turkey's century of political and social progress towards secularism and marking a regression back to greater public expression of Islam. But the mentality of an older generation of many military officers and orthodox Kemalists is gradually passing from the scene; a page has almost certainly been turned. The most encouraging factor today is general public support for an end to military interference in civilian governance. Despite all the more recent demonstrations and anger with Erdoğan in the country and political turmoil resulting from party scandal, for the first time we hear no public calls from any quarter of *Ordu göreve!* (Army, do your duty!) that typified pre-coup situations in the past. This new public attitude reflects the emergence of a new political generation and a shift in the national consensus: that political crisis should be resolved via politics and not military intervention. While Atatürk's vital role in Turkish history as the heroic founder and modernizer of a new nation is secure, Kemalism—the ideology of his successors—is no longer regarded by the majority as a sacred national value.

If Atatürk, in his sweeping and authoritarian approach to reforms was a dynamic and progressive figure in his time, it becomes increasingly difficult to view Kemalism today as still representing the forces of "progress" and "westernism" that it once claimed to be. Indeed, it has actually become a reactionary force in one sense in seeking to cling to the past and resisting generational, demographic, democratic and intellectual change in Turkey and in the world. Kemalism, with its ubiquitous public portraits, statues, monuments and quotations of Atatürk, had become a cult of the personality not in keeping with the contemporary world—and not something that Atatürk himself would necessarily have supported. The stark symbols of the Kemalist era are increasingly challenged—or even ignored as irrelevant by a younger generation. We now see Islamic and Kurdish organizations protesting against the traditional Kemalist national pledge of allegiance that stipulates a secular identity, and glorifies "Turkishness" while ignoring the existence of other ethnic groups in the country.[1] Enforced identities are not part of the future multicultural world, religious or secular, Turkish or Kurdish. Significantly too in 2012 the AKP modified the militaristic-patriotic character of the 19 May celebrations that commemorate the 1919-1923 War of Independence by dispensing with the traditional parade of tanks and troops. This parade invariably struck a fiercely nationalistic—even chauvinistic—and militarist tone that Erdoğan said brought to mind "parades in the former Iron Curtain countries." He urged the new national holiday to be a "symbol of change and transformation." Do we interpret this shift as a reactionary, or progressive step?

Second, any return of the military to a supervisory role in governance—much less some kind of coup—would cost Turkey's international image and credibility dearly. All but the most fanatic anti-AKP elements know that. Finally, Turkey's national security faces few threats on the international scene that would call for a resuscitation of a powerful security state. The only major security question mark is the domestic Kurdish situation. If, unexpectedly, the present peace negotiations were to badly deteriorate through mistakes on both sides and degenerate into renewed civil conflict, violence and terrorism again, the public might well be more open to a stronger military role in domestic security policy. Indeed, some hardline military officers associated with Ergenekon had just such a scenario in mind in deliberately stimulating conflict on the Kurdish front. Certainly a desire to prevent a return of military supervision lies behind the growing eagerness of most Turks to achieve a peaceful political settlement with the Kurds as soon as possible. And the Ergenekon trials, some of which were perhaps carried too far, nonetheless revealed to the public that the military had long contained within it rogue elements ready to foster instability and a pro-coup mentality.

Critics of the AKP government also focus on what they see as an authoritarian streak in Erdoğan. He can be emotional and impulsive; he also sometimes stages his emotions to good political effect. He revels in a tough-guy image and has dealt increasingly roughly with political opponents. Both he and his political base thrive on combative approaches. In dealing with the press he harks back to methods employed by most governments before him, particularly in financial manipulation of the press. He has pressured pro-government newspaper owners to fire journalists he finds offensive. Erdoğan nonetheless is now longest-serving prime minister since Atatürk and may still remain the most popular candidate for that office. In the last few years, now at 60 years of age, he seems more prone to errors of political judgment. The financial scandals and irregularities have intensified his political intolerance of opponents, even paranoia about ubiquitous enemies. He is in danger of dismantling his own remarkable legacy and engineering his own political defeat under distasteful conditions that will retroactively harm his image and legacy as well as damage the party's future.

Erdoğan has also without question been the most powerful democratically-elected prime minister Turkey has seen: his successive electoral wins gave him a single-party government, a strong ruling majority in parliament, bolstered by a booming economy, the collapse of the army as a significant domestic political force, and the absence of a strong and credible opposition political party. But many liberal Turks, members of the Turkish opposition, and a number of western observers now express concern that Erdoğan could be adopting the authoritarian-lite features of a Vladimir Putin in Russia. While there are some elements of truth to these fears, overall they seem exaggerated and ignore both the growing power of informed public opinion in the country and the increasing power and solidity of political institutions that cannot be easily swept aside. Still, politics in Turkey can be a rough game at any time, and Erdoğan plays it to the full. This seems to reflect more a personal style than it is the result of his Islamist background or religious beliefs; as writer Mustafa Akyol remarks, "the AKP is not too Islamic, it is too Turkish." Anthropologist Jenny White notes: "In fact, the AKP is a very Turkish party: top down, hierarchical, authoritaran, patriarchal, etc., all the things that the other parties are as well, more or less."[2]

Erdoğan does not brook criticism well, but neither have many other Turkish leaders. This is, after all, a country where "insulting Atatürk" is still a criminal charge that can on occasion bring imprisonment. According to Article 301 of the old Turkish Penal Code, it is still illegal to "insult Turkey," Turkish ethnicity, or Turkish government institutions. Although these decades-old long-standing provisions are increasingly less implemented, they suggest that authoritarian holdovers from the past have not yet been fully eliminated.

A second key area of potentially creeping authoritarianism lies in the opposition's charge, often repeated in the West, that Erdogan has suppressed press freedoms. According to Reporters Without Borders, Turkey ranks incredibly low: 138th among 178 countries in terms of press freedoms. Yet to anyone who knows Turkey, this rating seems bizarre. First, the reality is that the press has always been a political football in Turkey, as in so many other countries. It has been dominated for long decades by a few blocs of powerful industrialists and press magnates, most of them associated with Kemalist institutions and the ruling party of the time. Governments have always enjoyed "special ties" with most of the press, provided patronage, and have been able to manipulate it through subventions and granting or withholding huge advertising revenues—devices familiar in many other countries. In the past the military created pro-military blocs within the press, and orchestrated political campaigns prior to, and after, military coups to justify their actions.

But to those who read the Turkish press, the character of public discussion in the country today has demonstrably never been bolder. Şahin Alpay, one of

Turkey's most distinguished, perceptive and balanced liberal commentators, has pointed out that the situation has two faces:

> We journalists and writers in Turkey are experiencing an increasingly conspicuous paradox. While on the one hand, the country is discussing its major problems in an increasingly free and lively debate, leaving no formerly taboo subjects intact—including the Kemalist ideology of the state, the political role of the military, the authoritarian character of Turkish secularism and the dark pages of Turkish history regarding the treatment of Armenians and Kurds—the number of journalists and authors who are being prosecuted and detained is on the rise.[3]

Some 50 journalists were under detention in 2012, but only a handful on charges related to violation of press laws. "The rest are detained either on allegations of involvement in plots to overthrow the elected government or for violating the draconian Counterterrorism Law (TMK)—with such a broad definition of terrorism that even individuals not involved in incitement to violence or violent acts are being prosecuted." [Alpay] The Ergenekon investigations indicted a considerable number of these journalists who were charged with actively colluding with military coup plotters to help create an environment through the media for a coup—for which there is much historical precedent. But the fact is that this old legislation—that enables these journalists (and others) to be detained before trial for months—emerges from the military-imposed 1982 Constitution that is still on the books.

Everyone acknowledges that the rewriting of the 1982 constitution is one of the urgent tasks of the nation in cleaning out the undemocratic vestiges of the past. This rewriting process is underway, but it is slow, complex and politically fraught. The AKP deserves criticism for not pushing more rapidly on this front. But until then the old measures still apply. In reality, however, the content of Turkish public discussion, radio, television, and book publishing today on sensitive issues is quite wide open. But press failure to adequately cover the fast-breaking Gezi riots was a dismaying event, and represents unacceptable and shameful press ethics and further sign of the continuing subordination of the press to government power—for long decades. Erdoğan's effort more recently to muzzle any kind of media reporting, including the internet, YouTube, and Twitter on the financial scandals is a considerable setback to civil liberties, even by past Turkish standards.

Not surprisingly, now that the shoe is on the other (AKP) foot, the tune changes. As Alpay notes:

> Finally, it needs to also be said that some journalists—most of them writing for the dominant Doğan Media Group, who have been ardent

supporters of the [Kemalist] bureaucratic tutelage regime and played key roles in legitimizing the political role of the military—nowadays run around the world complaining about the suppression of press freedoms and posing as the champions of freedom and democracy in Turkey. Surely this reflects nothing other than a shameful case of hypocrisy.

The Gülen movement is also seen by some as the lurking power behind judicial prosecution of journalists involved in the Ergenekon affair. The complaint is raised that the shoe is now on the other (Gülen) foot, that today it is those critical of Gülen who are singled out for jailing. Certainly some polarization of the press over the Gülen movement has emerged. Yet the reality is that the bookstores still contain plenty of publications, including newspapers, that attack Gülen. What is different now is that the threshold of judgment against Gülen and Islamists is higher than in the past when both groups were the routine, constant and unquestioning targets of mainstream media slander that crudely caricatured them as primitive and dangerous religious reactionaries.

By any standards the issue of freedom of the press deserves careful watching, especially in a country that aspires to show what a modern Islamic party can be. In any democracy it is the most influential institutions that bear the closest monitoring, particularly when the police and judicial powers are involved. The issue is not so much about Kemalists versus Islamists, as it is about exposing and reversing authoritarian legacies of the past. The tradition of the powerful state, going back to Ottoman times, is still strong; in societies around the world the state itself can take on a life and value of its own that is allowed to transcend even the social wellbeing of the population itself. Given Turkey's ability to face and overcome a range of daunting political crises over the past years and emerge the stronger, there are grounds for optimism that these press and civil liberty issues are moving slowly and bumpily towards some kind of resolution, and with much greater public awareness, participation and criticism than ever before. But a struggle is underway for a dominant voice in many of these judicial and security institutions, with each party concerned about state powers being used against it. Such fears will continue to exist until total independence of the judiciary and full depoliticization of the police is attained. Meanwhile, Erdoğan seems bent on controlling, rather than liberating, these institutions.

The AKP is aware that its early reform initiatives have slowed in recent years; in 2013 after the Gezi riots it announced plans to revivify the party's commitment by promoting an important new reform package to focus on religious minorities and further curtailment of military power in particular. For the Kurds, traditional Kurdish place names were to be restored in place of the imposed Turkish names and the oppressive "village guard" system (state-anointed vigilante groups) in Kurdish regions to be eliminated. Political parties could no longer be banned (Islamists, Kurds, and communists have consistently been the chief victims over the years.) Long pretrial detention would no longer be permitted. Greater freedom for public use of mother tongues would be granted. Alevis and non-Muslim religious organizations would receive official recognition. Electoral thresholds for political parties would be raised to enhance the chances of smaller parties to be elected to parliament. This democratization package, if implemented, will go some considerable way to meet some of the key opposition and minority grievances and should revivify the AKP's flagging image. Critics note that these are valuable first steps but more needs to be done to make the large Alevi population to feel as equals to Sunnis in state religious policies. Implementation of these reforms will be an important test of AKP future intentions, but an electoral period is not an environment conducive to such change. Prominent AKP officials have issued an appeal for minorities who had been forced to leave Turkey in the past, particularly Christians and Jews, to "come back to their home." A visitor to today's Istanbul cannot fail to be impressed with the hugely multicultural character of the city compared to several decades ago.

The Future of the AKP

The AKP grasped and embodied the spirit of the changing times in Turkey and the world; the other parties, in their personalities and public platforms, have not. Younger voters as well as experienced voters want something more than what the old parties, mired in the tired rhetoric of the past, have had to offer. And this very success of the AKP is part of Turkey's political problem right now: however successful it is, it needs competition and meaningful, creative challenge.

And when the AKP finally runs out of steam, who will succeed it? Among traditional Turkish parties, the most likely candidate could well be the default party, the People's Republican Party (CHP in Turkish), the oldest party in Turkey. The CHP has always been the classic Kemalist party but it has fared ever less well at the polls over the years as the public has come to perceive it as a tired elitist party out of touch with the times, believing it has a natural "right to rule" because it was founded by Atatürk. The CHP has shown condescension towards voters' views and considered their votes for the AKP as acts of ignorance. But under the CHP's new leader, Kemal Kılıçdaroğlu, the party has shown at least some willingness to reconsider its old paternalism, to alter its stereotyped and outdated Kemalist views, and to seriously cooperate with the AKP on the Kurdish issue—essential if the issue is to be successfully resolved. But will it have views fresh enough to win an election however?

In the meantime some observers discern the possibility that as the AKP runs out of energy, it could move towards some accommodation with elements of the Nationalist Movement Party (*Milliyetçi Hareket Partisi*, MHP). The MHP has long been a somewhat chauvinistic party of authoritarian inclinations in ways that the AKP never was. It is a mixed bag; it contains radical secularists of the Atatürk mold, but also nationalists who honor and respect the Ottoman tradition who have their counterparts in the AKP, and even a few who see Islam as part of the essential Turkish identity. It contains many elements paranoid and suspicious of the West. If the AKP should find itself losing support, one strategy is that it could turn in a more nationalist direction to win additional votes that are unavailable from the CHP on the "left." Such a fusion of Islamists with nationalists would likely be much less liberal, less democratic-minded, less tolerant on racial and ethnic issues, less accommodating to the Kurds, and less friendly to the West. Such a coalition could very well fall out with the Gülen movement; Hizmet is unlikely to abandon its message of dialog and tolerance across faiths and ethnicities.

Alternatively, the AKP could split into different wings, more religious and ideological versus more flexible and pragmatic, possibly reflecting Erdoğan and Gül wings of the party. If the CHP can cooperate with Erdoğan in forging a solution to the Kurdish issue, the AKP is much less likely to drift to the right.

Hizmet after Gülen?

What will become of Hizmet once Hoca Efendi departs from the scene? (He was 73 in 2014 and his health is not robust.) Basically no one really knows. The movement will continue to evolve as long as he is alive. Gülen's own personality has been the primary force and vision that has driven the movement for half a century; in that sense he is not replaceable. But his staff and chief counselors do play major roles as well in translating his vision into reality in diverse areas. That said, at this point there is no clear successor who commands charismatic support from the public or who has produced a body of writings and sermons that have lent Gülen such authority and following.

Gülen does not micromanage its daily affairs. His chief role is to provide overall vision. Some speculate that the movement could split along different lines and interests down the road. Already there is a powerful US contingent of the movement that operates under quite different conditions in North America than the organization working within Turkey with its own specific conditions and issues. Central Asian, Arab and South Asian elements of the movement could contribute to a further regionalization of Hizmet in the future. Such a development could be quite healthy in spreading the broad ideals of the movement while adapting to local conditions and needs.

Diverse perspectives could eventually emerge among its top figures who could take different directions with different emphases. Predictions about the movement post-Gülen are uncertain. But the spirit of the movement has been sustained for nearly a century, going back to the nature of the early roots in the Nursi movement. Such spirit provides meaning, purpose, and fulfillment to its members. The extensive corpus of Gülen's writings and speeches provides the philosophical foundation for continuing inspiration and guidance. These writings are not a blueprint but represent broad philosophical guidance on the place of faith and action in contemporary life.

New Trends in Islamism?

There are other Islamic trends in Turkey apart from the AKP or the Gülen movement. Turkey's Islamists—or neo-Islamists, or conservative democratic Muslims, or post-Islamists, however one wishes to describe the broader AKP phenomenon—have brought about change in public thinking about Islam, the nature of modern governance, and society in general. This change is welcome and will strengthen the rationalism and reality-tested realism of Islamist thinking.

While the AKP has created a strikingly successful model for economic progress, some elements within society feel left out. Nor are all Islamists comfortable with the status quo. A small but possibly growing group among a younger generation of Islamists is now adopting a more radical economic vision, one that is "anti-capitalist," expressing economic grievances, protesting against joblessness, low standards of living, corruption, inadequate worker safety, inadequate social insurance—all of which they blame on western-imposed "neo-liberalism" or the "Washington-IMF consensus" of economic reform. These views emerge in the context of a newly affluent Turkish society in which large numbers of new entrepreneurs—"nouveau riche" to some— have acquired much wealth over the past decade. The secular Left may criticize what it calls the social failures of AKP policies; the AKP is sensitive to such criticism since it resembles an Islamic critique seeking a framework of social justice. The AKP may eventually face growing challenge from some Islamists who call for an improved social safety net and greater expression of

Islamic concern for the poor. (We discussed the possible return of an "Islamic Left" in Chapter 13.)

In this area, the two other main opposition parties—the Kemalist CHP and the nationalist MHP—have *no strong grassroots tradition* of focus on social justice. Turkish Islamists, on the other hand, have long emphasized issues of economic justice, such as the former (Islamist) Welfare Party (*Refah Partisi*— overthrown and banned in 1997) whose slogan was "A Just Order" (*Adil Düzen*). Like many other Islamist parties in the Muslim world, the Welfare Party—and the AKP after it—gained much public support through its urban social programs at the neighborhood level: food programs, health services, educational programs, and social assistance. Kemalist critics of the Welfare Party accused these AKP programs of "buying votes." There is no doubt that social assistance programs helped win it support, but the social agenda of the party was solidly rooted in concepts of a just society at the economic ground level. Islamist competence at running smaller cities enabled them to win municipal elections in the big cities and eventually to attain national power. Of course its social programs help gain votes, but why was the AKP the only party doing this when even the powerful socialist-oriented Kemalist state did not? The answer lies in the grassroots character of the AKP that differs from the heavily statist and elitist traditions of its opposition.

Many old social categories are now fading. A new class is emerging with a younger generation that does not really fit the old "White Turk-Black Turk" (upper and lower class) dichotomy; it is made up instead of "hybrid Turks" who straddle the two social extremes. This group represents an encouraging development that could serve to reduce social polarizations of the past— represented by young women wearing blue jeans and headscarves, to put it in caricature.

> Hybrid Turks are a natural by-product of the new Turkey's sociological conditions. They are urbanized, well educated, and fluent in English, travel abroad, believe in democracy and pluralism and observe their religion as carefully as any other pious Muslim. They seem happy to have the best of both worlds…. [T]his group will help in determining how quickly the country can move towards full democratization, since the big transformation in Turkey is among the pious group, which is open to globalization.[4]

Muslimness—A New Identity?

We have often noted that an individual's Muslim identity in no way needs to contradict an Arab or Turkish identity at the same time. Indeed they can complement each other. (Only when religious identities are in direct competition with ethnic identities over power resources, as in competing political parties, do the two identities "clash.") The AKP is successfully integrating a *Muslim identity* with a Turkish identity—they are not mutually exclusive, nor were they back in the Ottoman era. And in the Arab context, we have seen that it may not be enough to be "Jordanian"; one may more strongly identify with being an "Arab" and even "pan-Arab" in inclination as well as being Muslim.

Anthropologist Jenny White has described this phenomenon in the Turkish context as "Muslim-ness" (*Müslümancılık*); this is a term that transcends the narrow *secular blood identity* of Turkishness, or the simple religious identity of being a "Muslim," to embrace an *Islamically-oriented cultural identity within Turkish culture* that can be as broad or as narrow as one wishes. The term is not meant to divide Muslim from non-Muslim so much as it is to broaden the cultural identity and sphere within one lives; it rises above the tired old secular-versus-religious dichotomy. Indeed, this term has powerful implications for Muslims everywhere who, apart from being Afghans or Algerians, for example, also share in the important quality of Muslimness. And while the concept suggests a kind of pan-Islamic linkage, it can also be quite culturally specific—so for Turks there is a strong sense of Islam making up part of their *Turkish* identity, and a pride in Turkish practice of Islam as a special, maybe even superior, form of practicing Islam. This concept of Muslimness then embraces a critical part of Turkish tradition not captured by a narrow secular-ethnic nationalism.[5]

Turkish Foreign Policy

For over a decade the AKP has placed a new stamp on Turkish foreign policy that has received general approval from a majority of the country that appreciates the country's new status and economic role in the world. Any successor party is unlikely to depart sharply from most of the precedents and principles set by the AKP, particularly the new orientation towards Asia and the Muslim world. These policies make sense economically and geopolitically and are largely in keeping with Turkish national interests.

But there are nonetheless ample grounds for criticism of AKP diplomacy. The key criticism has been of Ankara's risky and unsuccessful policy towards Syria beginning in 2011; the Turkish public fairly quickly became wary of involvement in the messy Syrian struggle and fears that Turkey has a lot to lose in the process. (No other country has managed Syria policy much better.) Kemalists are critical of what they call an "Ottoman" orientation in AKP policy—but no one is going to significantly reverse new Turkish engagement in the Middle East and the world. Turkey's Ottoman heritage and Muslim culture cannot be extricated from Turkish global outlook. A future Turkish government will likely have less sympathetic ties with organizations like the Muslim Brotherhood, but will not be able to ignore the significance of such Islamic movements in the future of the Middle East and will likely transcend the old Kemalist fear of dealings with them.

Some might criticize the AKP for its ideological support for democratic elements in threatened Middle Eastern regimes; such a policy has outraged Saudi Arabia and the Gulf, countries that are vital to Turkey's economic and investment policies. However these policies are implemented, it is clear that the AKP generally prefers to "err" on the side of what it sees as the "tide of history" while remaining pragmatic about ties with still-solid authoritarian regimes. Ankara's new activism has made Turks far more conscious of foreign policy than ever before, while the country's own multicultural character lends it greater awareness of regional forces. Even Syrian refugees into Turkey have now appeared as themes in recent Turkish soap opera as part of the current reality; many Syrians are likely to remain in Turkey and add one more color to the ethnic mosaic and demographics of the country.

Turkey's shift away from close alliance with Washington is likewise based on certain realities that are unlikely to change with any new party; there is a growing national consensus that reduction of the centrality of ties with the US accords with Turkey's larger interests. Washington, however, maintains a highly self-referential optic on Turkish developments; it has fretted that Turkey is somehow at some decisive "crossroads"; the touchstone is whether Turkey is "drifting away" or "coming back" to the US. This uniquely American optic is of little analytic use to understanding what is happening in the Middle East. Turks do not view themselves as being at any crossroads. They are not "Washington-indexed" but rather see themselves as progressing along a logical path of expanding their interests that are now governed by greater independence of action across a wider swath than ever before. Naturally Ankara will seek to maintain good working relations with Washington, but that is not the overriding consideration or priority except perhaps on a tactical basis.

From that perspective, Washington is bound to remain frustrated by Turkey's apparent inconsistency. It still tries to portray Turkey as part of a US "partnership" in a grander scheme for the region, yet Ankara does not really seek a partnership, nor are the benefits of such a partnership as defined by Washington at all clear, as opposed to well-known downsides. Ankara will not wish to tie its hands or be identified as acting within the framework of any other power either, although NATO membership still represents a valuable official place at the western table pending Turkish membership in the EU. Significantly, Ankara finds it appropriate to seek simultaneous membership in the Shanghai Cooperation Organization along with Russia and China where it has already been accepted as a "dialog partner."

The irony is that, while some in the West still speak in aggrieved tones of Turkey under the AKP as having "abandoned the West," the country itself sees the picture rather differently. Americans would be surprised to know that many Turks—Kemalists, nationalists, even staunch Islamists, and a minority in the AKP itself—believe the AKP actually to be in the pocket of the US, an instrument of US policy, Erdoğan as "Obama's man" carrying out American mandates in the region. Similarly many like to imagine Hizmet as a creature of the CIA or Mossad. A smaller group in the Middle East nurtures suspicions that Turkey is still pursuing a western agenda, partly on the basis of its NATO membership. And some old-style Arab nationalists like Muhammad Hasanain Haykal in Egypt express fears that the AKP is nothing more than a Turkish form of the international Muslim Brotherhood that, in combination with the Egyptian Muslim Brotherhood, represents a threat to the old Arab nationalist secular ideals. These views parallel other superficial and clichéd characterizations of Turkey as alternatively western, secular, moderately Islamic, a NATO ally, a maverick power, a Middle East power, and an Asian power. The AKP elephant is thus viewed quite differently by various blind men.

Turkey will remain Turkey as it deepens its own sense of historical identity in possibly unforeseen ways. No other country is likely to win Turkey over to its side as an ally. Turkey is serving own interests, but also has its own principled and credible vision of where the Middle East can go and should go. It is credible because it operates within the new framework of a post-US world, a multipolar world characterized by the rise of the BRICS along with other states that today make up essential elements of the new global political realities. Perhaps few in the US are comfortable with Turkey's independent approach—think France—but that's the way it will be. Given Turkey's history, political trajectory, experience, democratic character, its search for dialog, Muslim culture and its demonstrable success, it's hard to imagine a better model for the region as part of a balanced international order for all its transient political crises.

Nonetheless, AKP foreign policy achievements have fallen short of some of Davutoğlu's more grandiose visions. As one critic put it, "Turkey's often self-congratulatory over-conceptualization of its foreign policy behavior [read

Davutoğlu] has created 'a certain measure of cognitive dissonance in the foreign policy realm,' that has tarnished Turkey's external image.[6]

As we have seen in the course of this book, Turkey's foreign policy under Erdoğan and Davutoğlu has evolved through several distinct stages and in reaction to changing global events around it. That trajectory can be summarized as follows:

• An early shift away from status as "US ally" to one that emphasizes Turkey's independence, distinct regional interests, and frequent disagreement with US policies in the region.

• Hugely improved working ties with Russia and Eurasian states, but no desire to ally with them as such either.

• An early search to eliminate the causes of conflict with all of its neighbors and to improve country-to-country ties with them, regardless of US approval or disapproval. A willingness to work with all regimes and governments in the region, regardless of their character.

• During the long vacuum of leadership and vision in the Arab world, Turkey sought to serve as intermediary between conflicting parties in the Middle East and to encourage greater liberalization and democratization of governments.

• With the sudden new dynamism of the Arab Awakening, Turkey then sought to support the forces of democracy against embattled autocratic regimes: Tunisia, Egypt, Libya, Yemen (but not in Bahrain). In principle Ankara opposed western armed intervention into the Arab Spring (but was forced to accept it in Libya, and ended up actually embracing it in Syria).

• With the Syrian uprising Ankara continued its policy of encouraging reform and democratization but seriously miscalculated on the staying power of Asad. It thus shifted policies dramatically to support violent regime change in Damascus, and even to work with the West to that end, in contradiction to virtually all of its earlier policy principles.

• As a result Ankara became entangled in the Saudi game of fomenting sectarian division and conflict. Its support for violent regime change in Damascus, in partnership with Saudi Arabia, was directly responsible for significant deterioration of ties with Iraq and Iran.

• Burned by those deteriorating ties, Ankara retreated in isolation, abandoned even by a US avoidance of using force for change in Syria. The Syrian crisis essentially undercut nearly all of Ankara's policy positions.

• Counterrevolution in Egypt found Ankara back to supporting a key principle—insistence upon maintaining democratic process and opposing coups and counterrevolution; but it then stood isolated from the Gulf states on this stance as well.

• Cutting its losses in its Syrian policies Ankara has begun mending ties with Iran and Iraq.

• The beginnings of western reconciliation with Iran may now have major impact on Turkey's regional position which may find itself in a strategic shift working more closely with Iran on numerous issues.

Ankara indeed has completed nearly a full cycle—from bad relations with all neighbors, to good relations with all neighbors, and then back to bad relations again, leading to some degree of regional isolation. But the second stage of "bad relations" is qualitatively vastly different than the initial Kemalist phase of "bad relations" with neighbors inherited by the AKP. That Kemalist phase was characterized by a security mindset in which all neighbors posed "threats" to the Turkish state. Today's Turkey does not employ the language or mentality of "security threats"—the differences come primarily over how much to support a principled foreign policy which overall calls for dialog and democratization.

Yet we can find sharp critiques from the Arab left (erroneous in my view) that express this frustration with Turkey and the Arab Spring.

> As for Turkey, it completely lost its credibility in the Arab Spring. Over the course of the Syrian uprising, it has made an inelegant transition from a regional power that gradually built up its reserves of "soft power" into a party aligned with the Muslim Brotherhood and sharing a single regional agenda with Qatar. If Turkey fails in winning its share of the Iraqi pie because of Iranian cleverness, Kurdish resistance and the sectarian factor, then it will satisfy itself with military, political and economic hegemony over northern Syria, which lies on favorable ground in both a geographic and sectarian sense. …Turkey, whose political rhetoric over the last seven years stressed objection to foreign interference in regional affairs—apparently so that it could play the role of maestro—has gone back on itself. After the Syrian crisis exposed its limited capabilities, it invited foreign intervention to pave the way for a regional competition that would play to its advantage…[7]

By mid-2013 Ankara was forced to acknowledge that the old "zero problems" policy with neighbors was no longer an accurate description of affairs. Presidential advisor on foreign policy İbrahim Kalın, when questioned on Turkey's apparent growing isolation in support of the toppled Brotherhood government in Egypt, employed the unusual term "worthy solitude" (*değerli yalnızlık*)—a wry acknowledgment that Turkey was, for the moment, isolated in its stance but still standing on principle against the fast-moving and harsh gamble of the counterrevolutionary camp—Saudi Arabia, the Gulf monarchies, Egypt and Israel—to stifle change. Kalın emotionally defended Turkey's policies:

> But while the world remains silent in the face of coups and massacres, if we have to stand alone on the side of the right, we won't shrink from doing so. If you have to call this "isolation," it's a worthy solitude. This is not standing alone, but demonstrating an honorable stance.[8] "Since when did defending humanity, dignity, transparency and fairness become emotional foreign policy?" Kalın added.

In other words, Turkey seems unwilling to bow to the region's counterrevolutionary forces. But it will inevitably have to come to terms with the new counterrevolutionary bloc—it's too economically powerful to ignore or reject. But retreat from supporting the armed overthrow of the Asad regime should lead to an improvement of important ties with Iraq and Iran, as well as with the majority of Arab publics who do not identify with the counterrevolutionary bloc. Thus Ankara's "isolation" is a very different kind of "poor relations" with neighbors than before; it represents a new embrace of some key principles that many would argue represent the "direction of history" over the longer run in the Middle East. It also contains the option for quick improvement with regional political change down the road. Turkey is likely to win much support and admiration from Arab populations even while their authoritarian (or counterrevolutionary) leaders condemn Ankara. Turkey is still exploring its reengagement with the Muslim world, even as the Muslim world itself undergoes great change.

This book has attempted to show that Turkey, virtually unique among countries of the Middle East, has taken the lead towards seeking solutions to many of the region's most outstanding problems. All of this of course represents work in progress—when do political tasks of this sort ever achieve completion? But no other state in the region can claim even a small degree of this kind of success. From this perspective, Turkey has to be viewed as the most significant country in the Middle East, perhaps in the Muslim world, in terms of its evolution and development. It is recognized increasingly as a major player among medium-sized countries of the entire developing world. It has widened its vision of its place in the international order that is marked by self-confidence and growing ambition. Despite the transitory hopes of the early Arab Spring, there is still no other credible model of success worthy of emulation anywhere in the Muslim world at present.

Turkey has not rejected the West, but its once-dominant ties with the West have proportionally shrunk relative to the expansion of major new ties. Still, the emergence of Turkey as a strong new player in the region, however much admired, also upsets traditional balances of interests and power; this is particularly true at a time of turmoil and transition in the rest of the Middle East. That turmoil will not end soon, and indeed may just be beginning.

Davutoğlu's concept of zero problems with neighbors represents the soundest basis for Turkish policy in the region—at least as a body of principles. It is of course difficult to avoid being drawn into more complex imbroglios when violent and revolutionary events swirl on the doorstep. And much depends on wise tactical decisions. Yet it is instructive to note that China too, seeks to implement what is in effect zero problems with Middle East states: it enjoys close working political and economic ties with such diverse states as Iran, Syria, Turkey, Saudi Arabia, Egypt, and Israel simultaneously, despite the serious geopolitical differences among all those countries. Beijing declares a policy of non-intervention on regional struggles. Even more strikingly, however, China has come to declare that it is quite comfortable with Islamist movements—at least in the Middle East (even if not inside China among the Muslim Uyghur population where Islamist movements seek separatism.) During Premier Wen Jiabao's visit to the Gulf in January 2012 the *People's Daily* declared:

> [The Arab Spring] has changed the main color of the Arab political situation and formed a splendid "green" scene which worries or even scares the West. In fact, that is not a "backward" [retrogressive development] in the Arabs' course of modernization and secularization, but simply a retreat from the long-term excessive secularization of the toppled [old] regimes and a return to the traditional culture. It is also the common aspiration of the people ... Of course the world should have a broader and more open mind and wish these countries well. After all, it is the Arab people's own choice.[9]

Turkey's move in this direction does not simply represent a new willfulness or stubbornness. It is characteristic of medium powers to want to keep more powerful and distant players outside of their arena so as to maximize their own regional clout and influence. Turkey, no longer dependent on the West for strategic security, or even for economic security, thus no longer is compelled to follow the western lead. It must now balance the influence and power of external great power forces with its own regional interests—"the Middle East for Middle Easterners" if you will—not a radically new concept, even if an unwelcome one to external great powers.

Until US policy changes dramatically, it will continue to pursue a Middle East agenda that departs from the direction taken by most countries in the world including Russia and China. (Britain and France still remain mired in recurring imperial nostalgia.) But the promise of a US breakthrough in relations with Iran could have major implications for the US vision of its foreign policies in the Middle East and bring about a potential sea-change in recognizing regional realities. Otherwise, continuation of the same trajectory will find the US role increasingly marginalized in the region. Rapprochement with Iran does not readily square with deepened US support for Saudi Arabian plans to unify the GCC in an anti-imperial bloc. Similarly, virtually unqualified and unbroken US support for Israel will find increasingly limited echo even in the EU, much less in Moscow or Beijing, pending a dramatic change in character of Israeli policies of the last 10 to 15 years. Russia and China will be driven by a desire to limit the past impulses of US global intervention—especially military—as their key goal in the region, especially in the heartland of Asia. They will oppose war with Iran. Russia and China will be likely to support the status quo, and favor change only when it can be achieved peacefully. Russia will seek to maintain some kind of strategic foothold in the Middle East, which is not, in itself, threatening to Turkey or to the US. Both Russia and China have deep reasons to oppose jihadi Islamist forces that threaten their own countries. Russia has shown it is willing to work with Washington in disarming the Syrian conflict by removing chemical weapons from Syria with UN blessing. Russia and China will have no problem with regime change in places like Saudi Arabia as long as the oil flows—which it is likely to do under almost any leadership—but they will not press for regime change, or work to prevent it if it appears imminent. Turkey will probably find this approach more congenial than the US approach of the past 20 years. The new ideological polarity in the Middle East is more likely to be between Turkey's democratizing agenda and the counterrevolutionary forces of Saudi Arabia, Egypt and the Gulf.

In short, a natural form of cooperation or shared outlook on regional issues between Russia and China on the one hand, and Turkey on the other, is likely on a broad range of issues. Nonetheless, potential differences between them and Turkey can conceivably arise on issues relating to energy and Turkey's role as an energy hub, and disagreements over Russian and Chinese treatment of Muslim minorities in their own countries. Russia will wish to maintain its desire for a long-standing presence on Cyprus as well, which could bring it into differences with Turkey—and already has created some conflicts over energy exploration issues off Cyprus.

European Union
While Europe has resisted—often condescendingly—full Turkish membership in the EU, the chances are good over the longer term that it will accept Turkey. Turkey is too important a country for the EU to exclude,

especially given the Turkey's vigorous economy and dynamic geopolitical position. But Turkey is no longer begging at the EU door. By June 2012, public support for EU membership in Turkey had dropped below 50 percent for the first time ever, compared to 74 percent in 2005. Among youth the number *opposed* to EU membership rose to 30.8 percent. Feelings have grown across Turkey that the EU needs Turkey more than Turkey needs the EU; this is especially so given the travails of the euro, and the general sense among the Turkish public that Europe has treated a successful Turkey with insufficient respect, even with racism.

Membership in the EU would impose certain constraints on the independence of Turkish foreign policy, but the EU may find itself consulting closely with Ankara on many regional issues. EU interests in the Middle East come down to three basic issues: energy flows, which are not basically threatened; EU fear of uncontrolled illegal immigration from the Middle East, over which Turkey has minimal influence; and international crime and terrorism. In the field of terrorism Turkey is well equipped to work with other states on issues of Islamist extremism. It is also well equipped to offer one of the few successful models in the developing world towards democracy, economic success, and discovery of a deeper sense of its own identity.

If the West isn't really comfortable with the AKP, all of the opposition parties in Turkey are more nationalist, cooler to the West and the EU, and equally strong supporters of an independent Turkish foreign policy. Some would favor even stronger ties to Russia, China and the Middle East. Those parties might be less comfortable with the spread of Islamic values in Turkish society, but there will be no return to the cruder anti-religious impulses of classic Kemalism of the past. As long as Turkey faces no strategic threat on the horizon—and none is in sight—Ankara will have far less need of strategic alliance with the West, except in the economic sphere. These new impulses in Turkey reflect changing generations who have been socialized under new global conditions, who are comfortable with, but not in awe of, the West. At the same time they maintain a strong sense of a Turkish identity that now comfortably absorbs Turkey's Ottoman and Islamic heritage. This stronger identity generates a new self-confidence that is not likely to disappear.

In the meantime, the AKP seems slipping into decline at unpredictable speed—unless it is to be rescued by a new and gifted leader. Decline is never comfortable to watch. Indeed, the memory of a messy decline sticks in the memory more vividly than what precedes it. Messy decline even tends to erase recollection of earlier periods of gifted statesmanship. One recalls here Margaret Thatcher's gradual loss of political touch, decline and ignominious defeat. Those hostile to the AKP will rejoice in its decline, while its supporters will mourn it. But the accomplishments of the party represent the main food for political and historical analysis. For all its faults, the AKP's record accomplishments are what primarily mark the remarkable decade of its governance. That decade is all the more vivid when it is set against the major, often disastrous, events and turmoil in the Middle East and the world over that same period. That is what makes the record of the AKP decade in Turkey, and the Arab Spring, so important for decades to come.

CHAPTER TWENTY-FIVE

WHITHER THE MIDDLE EAST?

Future of Islamism in Middle East Politics

Many observers were quick to proclaim the military coup against the Muslim Brotherhood government in Egypt as heralding "the end of Islamism." Further credence was lent to the argument by the crackdowns against the Brotherhood in several Gulf states, as well as its weakening in Palestine (Hamas), Jordan (Islamic Action Front) and Tunisia. Such a view is quite limited, however, and lacks historical perspective. Islamism—more precisely its largest and most significant representative, the Brotherhood—for the moment has been excluded by force from the Egyptian political scene. While bruised, it still remains a powerful political and social force just beneath the surface and has no major rival in size or organizational terms in Egypt or in the Arab world. Many in Egypt will say the Brotherhood has already demonstrated its "failure" in Egypt, but the Brotherhood will only disappear from the scene when its millions of supporters reach the same conclusion. It is more accurate to say we have witnessed the end of a first round in the evolution of political Islam in Egypt—and elsewhere.

It is cautionary to look at the Algerian experience—a disastrous military bid to put an end to Islamism. In 1989 various Islamist movements in Algeria formed an umbrella organization, the National Salvation Front (FIS in French); in 1991 FIS competed in a parliamentary election in which it won a plurality in the first round. The Algerian military rulers panicked, then swiftly banned the FIS from competing in the final round of voting, denied it a role in governance, disbanded it by force, arrested large numbers of its members, and brutally suppressed the movement. A truly ugly civil struggle ensued in which multiple players—state security operatives, multiple Islamist organizations, self-appointed militias, criminals—all with multiple agendas ended up promoting a savage bloodbath that lasted a decade killing upwards of 100,000 people. Despite an uncomfortable truce in the country the FIS has yet to be restored to politics. Few observers would believe that the "Algerian solution" has been anything but disastrous: the massive damage to the country and loss of life exceeded any conceivable damage Islamists might have done to the state and society and ongoing volatile social scene. The military-backed Algerian regime today has again been unnerved by the Arab Spring, particularly in neighboring Tunisia, and has very likely supported Salafi forces there to weaken and defeat the moderate Muslim Brotherhood (Ennahda) government. Algeria will likely coordinate policies with Saudi Arabia on suppression of Islamist movements in North Africa. Yet Islamist forces still remain a powerful force on the sidelines in Algeria, waiting to bid for legitimacy again. (The Egyptian military cannot be unaware of this historical experience, yet now pursues a similar course.)

Similarly, Israeli and American efforts to crush the Hamas government in Palestine after it won free elections in Palestine in 2006 ended up only strengthening and legitimizing that branch of the Brotherhood. In an earlier era the shah of Iran had been unable to crush the political power of the Islamists who by 1979 managed to replace him. As of now, even if bloodied, Islamists in Egypt are still perceived by nearly half the population as a truly Egyptian political force and one of the most legitimate political elements in the region, and still the single-most successful political organization at the ballot box. They still have no meaningful organized popular political rival. Indeed, it would be better if they had—it would lead to a more balanced political order than the stark binary struggle simply between the military and the Islamists. Thus legal suppression and force will not defeat these movements. The most effective means of dealing with them is within the democratic process. Ideologies fail not because of repression or when abstract ideas lose favor, but because they fail to meet the concrete expectations of their supporters. Islamist parties, like all others, will be forced to examine their *political and managerial* (not so much ideological) failings, or they will collapse entirely.

Political Islam in the Middle East in all its various forms will likely undergo much more rapid evolution in the decades ahead. Islamist movements long enjoyed the luxury of criticism of the state without the responsibility of having to deal with burning issues of governance. That situation changed during the Arab Spring with short- or long-term Islamist resurgence in Tunisia, Libya, Egypt, Yemen, Morocco, and part of the official opposition in Jordan and Kuwait. Islamists are destined to gain greater power in a post-Asad Syria. Now more deeply involved in national electoral politics than ever, they will have to work harder to provide popular, meaningful and successful leadership. This guarantees new thinking on their part to meet the new conditions with new ideas—or perish with their old clichés.

Among the many glib anti-Islamist clichés in the West, one offered by former US Assistant Secretary of State Edward Djerejian was that Islamists only seek "one man, one vote, one time," that is, they will abolish democracy after achieving their electoral victory. While such an eventuality is distinctly possible, the reality is that *no nationally-elected* Islamist government has ever defaulted on democracy to date. It may well happen at some point, just as has happened repeatedly with elected *secular* officials who subsequently turned to authoritarianism. What we are really talking about here is not the weakness of political Islam as such, but of the character of *national political culture* in diverse countries of the world that lack democratic experience. The Brotherhood in Egypt was unfortunately not given enough time to decisively "fail" at the ballot box; in fact it was almost miraculously rescued by the military from such longer-term political self-reckoning.

But what of the poor—although differing—record of authoritarian Islamists in power in Sudan, Iran, or Afghanistan? It's important to remember that none of them took the reins *through elections*. In Sudan they achieved power via military coup; in Iran they eventually took control in the midst of chaotic civil struggle after the fall of the Shah; in Afghanistan the Taliban eventually prevailed after two decades of an anti-Soviet guerrilla war and a civil war *among Islamists*, and with major support from the Pakistani military. None of them qualify as examples of Islamists democratically elected. With Islamist governance now aborted in Egypt and Algeria, and on hold in Yemen and Tunisia, to date it is still only Turkey that meets these qualifications of successful democratic administration.

The AKP shows some sympathies for the Muslim Brotherhood; many in the leadership perceive it as the leading hope for the evolution of Islamist thinking towards modernity and democratic process in the Arab world. (This not to say the Brotherhood will succeed.) There are no other broad contenders for that role so far. The Brotherhood in Tunisia, Morocco, Yemen and Egypt and elsewhere all find in Turkey a desirable model for their own future development. But the AKP is still too secular for Brotherhood taste in the Arab context, and the Brotherhood is still too focused on the vague lure of Islamic law for the AKP's taste. Yet each sees a dynamism in the other that it believes represents the future of politics and Islam in the Middle East. This two-way affinity emphasizing democratic change is precisely why the counterrevolutionary bloc led by Saudi Arabia is angry with Turkey and its support for the Brotherhood in a call for change. Turkey is sufficiently modern and successful in other respects that even secular parties in the Arab world find much to admire in its political platform and accomplishments.

Scholars argue about whether the term "Islamist" should apply at all to the AKP, pointing out that the party itself rejects the term and describes itself strictly as a "conservative democratic party." Various other terms have been introduced such as "post-Islamist," or a "service party." The debate in fact involves much more than simple quibbling over definitions. Islamism or political Islam as a phenomenon represents a *spectrum* of views and behaviors. The term is not reserved only for violent and fanatic organizations and individuals. Such violent Islamist individuals and organizations very much do exist, but non-violent and more moderate Islamist groups far outweigh the jihadis. The reality is that the AKP—including many of its present top leadership—evolved out of a long series of Islamist/Islamic parties in Turkey; if these parties had described themselves as Islamist they would have been in violation of Turkish law. The AKP does not cease being "Islamic" or "having Islamic roots" simply because it is moderate, pragmatic, and successful. If it is not objectively described as Islamic/Islamist when its values spring from Islam, then what other name is appropriate for a successful moderate and pragmatic party on the Islamic spectrum? Turkish politics may find it uncomfortable to use the term Islamic/Islamist for well-known historical reasons, but much of the rest of the world does use it. Otherwise we are forced to define the term as applying only to the radical, violent and the fanatic. Indeed, the AKP's very evolution and trajectory within Islamism is what provides the *precedent* that such evolution is quite possible elsewhere. This phenomenon parallels the Left as it runs along a spectrum of communists, Italian Red Brigades, Pol Pot's Cambodia, Maoists, socialists, democratic socialists, and Christian socialists. "Left" does not automatically translate into fanatic, dogmatic and violent. We look for evolution towards greater moderation in most ideologies.

How "revolutionary" are Islamists likely to be once voted into power? That depends on the party and on local conditions; Islamists will indeed be constrained by local political realities. While Islamists are often perceived as radicals in the West, in fact they are usually quite conservative in social and economic spheres. Islamist parties across the Muslim world have not truly advocated genuine social revolution, make no appeal to class elements, do not aim to redistribute national income, and propose no major changes in land tenure policies. Economic policies have been decidedly "bourgeois" and pro-business in Turkey, Egypt, Pakistan, Jordan and elsewhere. It has rather been the *secular Arab nationalists* who have promoted radical change in economic and social policies. Only in Iran did the Islamic Revolution adopt radical economic and social policies, reflecting both its Shi'ite character as well as the infusion of Marxist concepts into much of Iranian Islamist thinking. These programs touched on a broad spread of education, especially expanded for girls, land reform, establishment of an elected parliament, and greater dispersal of wealth out of the hands of the old aristocracy, and concern for the "dispossessed."

Whatever the failures of the Arab Spring have been to date in transforming the political order, these events have nonetheless sparked rising popular expectations in the Middle East. There is a sense in the region that a new public spirit (even if unfulfilled) has emerged, and that the old order rests on ever shakier grounds. Regimes under challenge will have to resort to increasing repression, or else adopt greater flexibility and grant meaningful concessions to the people to survive. Such flexibility will require more populist economic policies, a reduction in ruling family corruption and systemic corruption, foreign policies more in keeping with popular desires, and a renewed sense of national dignity and sovereignty.

Forms of Islamism

Islamism comes in many forms, as we have seen. The Muslim Brotherhood still remains best positioned to make the breakthrough to competent rule in one place or another.

• *Tunisia's* Ennahda may emerge at the top of the list of potential successes, either alone or in coalition. This is much due to the experience, moderation, and political savvy of its head, Shaykh Rashid al-Ghannushi, who says he is inspired by the Turkish model. Unlike most other states, Tunisia lacks a tradition of military dominance in politics. Ennahda resigned from power in 2013 to avert national crisis after facing rising opposition from many sources including Salafis; it saw the establishment of a technocratic government until new elections can be held. It remains a potent player in parliament and sees itself as having been the first country to "export the Arab Spring."

• *Egypt's* Muslim Brotherhood may be banned but is far from gone from the scene, and will likely make a political comeback at some point, probably the wiser for its mistakes in its first foray at rule. Despite its inexperience at governance it remains one of the most seasoned Islamist movements.

• *Morocco's* Justice and Development Party is unofficially affiliated with the Brotherhood, and claims to be inspired by the AKP. It won a plurality in elections in Arab Spring reforms in 2011; the party's leader is currently prime minister in a coalition where it is gaining further governing experience. Its goals are moderate and focus primarily on secular needs of the country; it also calls for Arab and Muslim unity. Morocco is, of course, a monarchy and the party currently avoids mention of its Brotherhood affiliation amid the major anti-Brotherhood crusade conducted by Egypt and the Gulf states.

• *Libya's* new Justice and Development (or Construction) Party represents the much older Muslim Brotherhood movement in Libya, long banned under Qadhafi. It placed second in 2012 elections and is a significant political force, although the post-Qadhafi politics of the country remain fragmented, chaotic and unstable.

• The Brotherhood in *Algeria* avoided involvement with the Islamic umbrella organization FIS during the vicious civil strife in the 1990s; unlike FIS, it is still legal in Algeria, and is part of a moderate governing coalition.

• *Yemen's* Brotherhood movement *al-Islah* (Reform) remains a significant player on the political scene with close links to major tribal forces as well as intellectuals. It won nearly a quarter of the parliamentary seats in the last election; one-third of its seats in parliament are held by women.

The Brotherhood is now represented in virtually every Arab country with varying degrees of influence. The solidly-rooted Brotherhood is still likely to remain the primary Islamist trend in the Middle East in the future even as its skills, experience and opportunity vary greatly from state to state. It may assume a lower profile during the present ideological confrontation with Saudi Arabia and Egypt, but will not go away. From a western perspective the Brotherhood will remain "Muslim nationalist" at heart, mainly non-violent except for resistance to foreign occupation, but deeply suspicious of western influences.

The Muslim Brotherhood's strongest rival in the Middle East is the Salafis. They enjoy full Saudi financial backing as the weapon of choice in the Saudi and Egyptian campaign to eliminate the Brotherhood. A great danger is that many Islamists, frustrated at the failure of the Arab Spring to bring relief to current economic, social and political hardships, may now turn to the Salafis as an alternative, representing a more austere and rigorous version of Islamism compared to the more moderate, flexible and pragmatic positions of the Brotherhood. The Salafis promise to deliver the real thing—strict implementation of Shari'a as the solution (whatever that means)—despite the Salafis' absence of any track record in governance. The movement's ideological rigidities and near-total lack of political experience as a political party almost guarantee it to be unprepared to rule. It remains more potent as a negative force than a positive one. While Salafis are not necessarily violent, violent jihadi movements often emerge out of Salafi circles.

The New Fault Lines of Grand Ideological Struggle
The grand ideological polarity of past few decades was formed by Iran at one end, Saudi Arabia at the other, comprising the current Middle East Cold War.

Tehran will remain opposed to the projection of western power into the region, opposing monarchy, supporting the struggle against Israeli repression of the Palestinians, and exercising influence over Gulf politics consonant with Iran's size. It strongly opposes Saudi Arabia's role as champion of counterrevolution, of Sunni sectarianism, and claim to leadership of Gulf politics. It will probably view the Muslim Brotherhood with benign, even positive eyes as strengthening the forces of regional change and the desire to keep the West out. The struggle often contains more noise and heat than it does action however. The sectarian issue, as we have seen, is largely a red herring; it really applies to Gulf fears of greater activism on the part of oppressed Shi'a. On this issue time is against Saudi efforts to block democratization and greater Shi'ite rights. Furthermore, Iran is unlikely to pose serious military threat to the Gulf States and has not done so for a very long time. Riyadh had little time for even the shah of Iran many decades ago, a major US ally in the 1970s. With or without Iran, Saudi anti-Shi'ite policies and its own domestic stability will continue to be challenged. Iran may seek to exploit these "forces of history" but it did not create them and cannot end them.

But a new ideological polarity is now emerging in the Middle East, born of the Arab Spring. Turkey has become a far more serious—even ideologically dangerous—unspoken rival to the kingdom. It is dangerous to Saudi Arabia because it too is a powerful Sunni country, possesses historical and modern religious credibility, and represents a thriving, independent and successful democracy and economy in ways Iran does not. Turkey has good ties with the Brotherhood—an organization loathed and feared by Riyadh. Turkey opposes Saudi promotion of sectarianism which is damaging to regional stability and limits Ankara's flexibility. Turkey can operate in both East and West, speak with credibility in the world, and demonstrates elements of pragmatism in working with existing forces. Saudi Arabia and Turkey will struggle to maintain acceptable relations between them for the foreseeable future but the foreign policies and ideologies of the two countries are fundamentally incompatible.

The kingdom, apart from the power of the checkbook and its small Gulf allies, will find few other allies among Arab republics. Syria under almost any government is unlikely to embrace the Saudi role. In Iraq the Shi'a are likely to grow less sectarian with time, especially if sectarian strife in neighboring Syria can be controlled. Iraq will maintain suspicion of Saudi sectarian policies and intentions. Even Iraqi *Sunnis*, as they regain some voice within Iraqi governance, will show largely Arab nationalist colors and are unlikely to favor the Saudi strategy of vilifying Iran and supporting sectarianism. Algeria as a republic will have little use for Islamists of any stripe, and certainly not Saudi-supported Salafis. Palestinian Hamas, unless heavily bought off by Riyadh in the future, is ideologically cool to the Saudi counterrevolutionary camp.

On the Saudi side of the ledger stand all the monarchies. Jordan has no option but to follow the Saudi lead. Most of the Gulf monarchies, except Qatar and Oman, are likely to bow to Saudi policies on most regional issues. But all the monarchies will be fearful for their own independence from Saudi pressures and may look to outside powers to help balance Saudi power. Qatar will certainly maintain its somewhat independent stance from Riyadh and probably will maintain supportive relations with Muslim Brotherhood forces across the region and try to ride with the "forces of change." Its ties with Turkey will grow.

Leadership in the Middle East

A key theme of this book is the quest for leadership in the Middle East today: what is it, and who is likely to exercise it? The Arab world over several decades has witnessed a significant *leadership deficit*. Since Nasser there has been no leader who captured the attention and imagination of the broader Arab public—except, partially, Saddam Hussein who was at least perceived to be "tough" and defiant towards the West and Gulf shaykhdoms, but was also brutal and totalitarian at home. Ironically, *non*-Arabs, a few Iranian revolutionary leaders and Tayyip Erdoğan in Turkey, were perceived as closer to what much of the Arab public craved. The region is hungry for leaders of genuine vision to inspire a broader following in shaky modern Arab states. That is partly what the public fascination of al-Jazeera satellite TV has been all about: presentation of news and issues from a regional perspective that captures all the dilemmas, weaknesses and failures of most Arab leadership to date as well as uncensored coverage of western political and military intervention in the region. The Arab world has largely been frozen under dictatorship for three or more decades in ways that virtually suspended the workings of normal geopolitics among them. That is now changing. The old geopolitical rules are breaking apart; new forces and combinations of ideology and geopolitics are emerging in fresh ways. Above all, we see greater expression of public desires and demands, even when expressed through demonstrations and street violence—in the absence of any other more effective vehicles.

For a while it looked like the Arab Spring might bring new contenders into the ring for leadership in the Middle East. But three years later, no serious

Arab leader or leadership has emerged. Egypt, isolated for three decades, might have reclaimed that role after the overthrow of Mubarak. Egypt under Muslim Brotherhood leadership was poised to rethink the Mubarak legacy, and while it avoided radical actions, it thrashed around, torn between early cautious steps, inexperience, limited power to govern, a wide open free-for-all among all parties to write the new rules of the game in their own favor, and the need to reconcile Islamic concepts with realities on the ground with no time to do it. With Mursi's overthrow, Egypt has now returned to an even harsher authoritarian domestic order than Mubarak's, devoid of vision except for a heavy-handed determination to crush all political opposition; with so many of the faces and institutions of Mubarak's order now restored to power it is hard to perceive any net gains. The military will be heavily constrained by its economic dependency upon the Gulf States; it will not be able to pursue a dynamic domestic and foreign policy capable of capturing the imagination of the region. It lacks even a persuasive ideology to do so, except for a vague "Egyptianism" that has little to inspire at home and stops at the borders. More than any other of the countries of the Middle East it seems headed more determinedly against "the forces of history," and stifling moves towards popular, responsible and competent governance. Egypt is probably entering a period of unprecedented internal violence and regional isolation as it prepares for round two of a struggle among diverse popular forces—Islamist, Arab nationalist, and a weak liberal faction against the military.

Ironically, Saudi Arabia's desperate new measures as de facto leader of the counterrevolutionary bloc has lent it greater vigor than in many years; it is more publicly and unabashedly fighting its new ideological war against "terrorism," Shi'ism, Iran, and the Brotherhood, and more outspoken in its public criticisms of US policies. But this defensive posture does not constitute a true vision for the region, nor will it stir the public. The country is increasingly an anachronism. Under pressure, Saudi Arabia is now developing closer working ties with Israel against Islamist movements. Times are desperate when the leader of the reactionary camp embraces the regional enemy to save its skin. In doing so the kingdom loses all legitimacy in the eyes of the public. It is not a question of whether diplomatic relations with Israel can ever be appropriate for Arab states—of course they can be—but when they involve a self-serving counterrevolutionary alliance they are seen as hostile to the aspirations of the region.

Syria will require long years to recover from its brutal civil strife and will be unlikely to embark on any new foreign policy initiatives. No other Arab state leader poses a credible claim to leadership at this juncture. Things seem to be right back where we started as the Arab Spring began.

Shaykh Rashid al-Ghannushi in Tunisia may be the one exception on the scene: he represents a charismatic, visionary, sensible and progressive Islamist in the Arab world with leadership potential; he enjoys much respect, but he is not young. Tunisia is too small and unrepresentative to lead the Arab world, except perhaps by example. It nonetheless remains an important center of Muslim Brotherhood thinking and action; Ghannushi's branch of the Brotherhood has acted with restraint and even wisdom in the face of the turmoil of early democratic governance in the country.

Post-Saddam Iraq, despite its high level of violence, remains one potential new claimant for some role of significant regional influence, but only over the longer run; its new political order is still shaking down, its sectarian struggles are still unresolved, and it will of course remain dominated now by its Shi'ite majority with whom everyone will have to come to terms. Gulf rulers will need to undergo considerable change of heart before accepting Arab Shi'ites in any leadership capacity. Nonetheless we shouldn't forget that the non-Sunni Asads were acknowledged by all in the region for decades as powerful voices of the Arab nationalist cause. Iraq has always represented Arab nationalist impulses over many long decades and those impulses and traditions will not disappear. Sectarianism is not necessarily the permanent dominant feature of Iraqi politics. It will require a reworking of how Arab Shi'a think about the Arab nationalist cause. If Shi'a are rejected from the company of Arab nationalists then obviously they will not share in the ideology and will even be hostile to it; but if accepted, there is no reason why Iraq cannot be just as "Arab" as any other state. Its relations with Iran will be a key factor in where it sees its place (and is allowed by others to see its place)—potentially as ally, bridge, broker, or even rival down the road.

The ultimate task facing the region is not one of ideological choice, but of providing competent governance. Ruling competently is no easy task for any party of any ideological stripe, given the complexity and magnitude of problems, the decades of lost opportunity, and the increased expectations and impatience of a new generation of more informed citizens who themselves lack experience in democratic process. One thing is certain—the Arab Spring has generated new expectations and a demand for greater public voice in governance. In its absence the prospects of political explosion in an Arab Spring Round Two remain high. Autocrats can only ignore this at their peril.

Democracy and Social Strife

Authoritarian states have long stifled political expression, mainly out of self-preservation, but also to dampen intercommunal friction and domestic conflict. One stated goal was to impose social peace, even if by force. Yet sadly, experience has demonstrated that such repression does not truly eliminate social, ethnic and religious differences anywhere, it merely suppresses their manifestation. And when divisions and resentments are bottled up, they still remain, simply in a state of suspended animation, only to flare up with the old intensity as soon as the lid of the political pressure cooker is removed. This has been true the world over.

And while we should welcome the introduction of new democratization processes, they also open a wealth of new problems; rapid transition out of repressed authoritarian societies into more open political orders permits these long-contained political and social hostilities to explode. Feverish new competition among long-suppressed rivals suddenly emerges onto a new playing field where there are few known rules and no players with any experience. The process of putting grievances on the table and acknowledging them—however laden with emotion—may be a vital stage of *social reconciliation* in a process of accommodation and healing. Yet democracy as a process initially tends to intensify those divisions and strife among competing social groups, sects and ethnicities in a zero-sum race for votes.

We are talking about building eventual trust in the *state*. Communities facing deep threats tend to cling to the most *efficacious* social unit—clan, region, ethnic or religious community—that will provide its members the greatest sense of cohesiveness and security in times of danger. Who do you retreat to for safety when violence reigns? That is the ultimate touchstone of community. When you cannot depend upon "the state" to protect your welfare you look to the social grouping that can do so. Social units break down into smaller and more essentialist communities for survival. The smaller the group the more likely it is to provide the reliable identity, community, solidarity and self-protection. If this process is ever to be reversed, the state must attain a reliable degree of neutrality and competence before the general public will trust in its impartiality, fairness, and effectiveness in protecting all individuals and all communities. Who would give up clan protection for some bureaucratic fiction of a state that may be in the hands of another clan or group that is not really dedicated to the welfare of all its citizens—or even any of its citizens? Furthermore, trust in the state can never be total, anywhere, ever, and often breaks down under new pressures, causing reversions to "safer" and more trusted smaller social units. This is true even in developed societies under stress.

What does it take, then, to learn how to "just get along with each other?" Does the freedom of democracy permit social groups to gradually learn to compete peacefully and coexist? Perhaps the lesson is that only through learning the hard way, through thrashing out compromise under even chaotic democratic conditions, can social divisions begin to be overcome. But it takes time. And mishandled, free but violent expression of social grievances is highly destabilizing. Especially when outside powers manipulate them to their own ends.

And western states, particularly the US, indeed have represented an essentially negative or retrogressive force in the region, especially during the disastrous and brutal decade following 9/11 and still ongoing. Under the devastation of war and occupation, and the numbing fear of drone strikes, the region has few opportunities or mechanisms that permit it to settle down and attain some social calm. Radical conditions spawn radical responses. Violence and terrorism will remain key instruments for those driven by political anger against US policies and actions, coupled with frustration about domestic conditions. The US Global War on Terror has done little to end the phenomenon of terrorism—indeed terrorism is one quite rational response by the weak, the angry and the dispossessed to strike back. The War on Terror, while taking out some key leaders, has also helped spread and distribute the presence of radical jihadis over a broader region; the breakup of centralized terrorist planning has led to decentralized, localized, less organized and more spontaneous terrorist actions. Conflict zones—Iraq, Afghanistan, Somalia, Yemen, Syria—provide new breeding grounds for international jihadi action. US military instruments to defeat terrorism will only spawn more terrorist acts and destroy political environments that might be conducive to forces of moderation. As long as the original conditions that create terrorism remain— and they still remain—then terrorism will not diminish.

In the end it is only Muslim societies that will know how best to eliminate terrorism from their midst, but only through action by governments that are seen as legitimate. Note that Turkey has witnessed exceptionally little domestically-driven terrorism for well over a decade—precisely because there is public confidence that governance can work to resolve political problems. The public is generally angered by any terrorism—unlike in many other countries where citizens may secretly cheer terrorist acts against their governments that are perceived as repressive and unjust, or against the US. The US needs to end its War on Terrorism and the visitation of its internationally illegal violence, delivered at will, around the world. The struggle against terrorism has taken an obsessive center stage in US foreign policy and has served to deeply damage the country domestically and internationally. Terrorism cannot be ignored, but if the very techniques of combatting it lead to its exacerbation and the damage of vital American values, it is time for a rethink.

Adjudicating Identity

In the Middle East Turkey is so far the only state with a tradition of democratic practice of some duration. Elections in Turkey now do work to overcome major social fissures as issues are exposed to national debate. Issues of Kurds and Alevis have slowly entered a process of dialog and discussion. When confronted with strife over questions of Turkish and Kurdish identity, the AKP has suggested that "we all share an identity as Muslims together." This was, of course, the Ottoman approach to the many ethnic differences where actual ethnic identity was of little importance, it was the broader religious community that mattered. But Islam cannot provide a blanket identity to feasibly include Christians or Alevis as well.

In the mid-19th century a movement called The Young Ottomans proposed blanket Ottoman citizenship as the basis for political and social unity that would overcome all differences between ethnic and religious communities. But many non-Muslims did not sufficiently trust the Ottoman state to look out for their welfare. Many Christian groups had become infected with the 19th-century western virus of inflexible nationalism—that turned the Balkans into a tinderbox that has still not yet been fully resolved. Can the term "Muslim" today readily serve as an identity to include Shi'a and Alevis as well as Sunnis? And what about non-Muslims? Here the Gülen movement is seeking to raise the bar of inclusion above specific religions to seek service to higher human values than mere ethnicity or religious identity. There is a Sufi saying: "They drew a square and excluded me; I drew a circle and included them." That is the aspiration at least, even if it requires time and considerable change of consciousness in a fallible human world.

In the Arab World, can the term "Arab"—in a cultural sense—serve as the all-purpose word to bring people of diverse regional strains together under a broader concept? The problem is that all these words—Turk, Arab, Kurd— originally denoted specific *ethnic* groups; it is harder to translate them into new meanings denoting purely geographic or citizenship associations. Turkish liberals coined the term *Türkiyeli* (literally translated as "belonging to Turkey", "a Turkey-ite") to suggest common citizenship in the state of Turkey; this term in principle strips the word Turkey of specific exclusive ethnic connotation that once meant a home for ethnic "Turks." With this new word they seek to capture the neutral non-ethnic character of the terms "American," "Canadian" or "Australian" as they are employed in these immigrant cultures of the new world. The terms American, Canadian or Australian have the advantage of course that they never were *ethnic* terms (although there are some Americans for whom the term in their minds really only applies to white Anglo-Saxons or northern Europeans). How ready are Russians, French, Germans, Jews, and Turks to see the names of their homelands—derived from ethnic roots—be stripped of the historic ethnic and cultural designations they connote? Russia has created the term *Rossiski* that implies citizenship in the Russian Federation, and differs from the word *Russki* that denotes an ethnic Russian. Kazakstan uses the term "Kazakstani" to refer to a citizen of the multi-ethnic state; "Kazak" is an ethnic term. This shift of allegiance away from a shared ethnic and cultural group to a shared bureaucratic state is a difficult and complex process requiring a major growth of trust in the state that comes only slowly.

And, as in Turkey, the term "secular" does not refer simply to a theological or ideological posture; it also symbolizes class and power. Secularism is the founding ideology of the old westernized elites; it has legitimated the birthright of the elite to keep the country on the "correct" path. Such a paternalistic ideology in every case leads to authoritarian and non-democratic practice. "Secularism" for this elite comes to take on near-sacred value—on a par with Islam to Islamists; historically it has been the cover for autocracy. Of course neither "secularism" nor "Islam" should legitimate any government in and of itself. Indeed, we see how quickly so-called liberals in Egypt made common cause with the military to trash legitimate electoral results, to delegitimize and overthrow the elected Brotherhood government—all as part of a "liberal" project.

In the critical case of Tunisia, commentator Giuseppe Merone observes that the debate over power and legitimacy is really still only conducted *within* the ranks of the old elite, along with a few newcomer Islamists and middle class. The bulk of the population has been left out of the political dialog, and *feels* left out. Disgruntled and unemployed youth in particular bear the brunt of poor economic conditions that especially affect the lower class; this was the very source of the early spark that set off the Arab Spring in Tunisia. If economic life does not soon improve, these youthful elements will certainly dismiss both the old (and former regime) secular nationalists as well as the Islamists—all as elites who are failing the disadvantaged. They could turn to more extreme solutions that will no longer include the Brotherhood, but rather Salafis, and perhaps even violent jihadis in order to bring about violent change and "true" revolution.[1]

AKP and Middle East Islamists

With the rise of Islamists of various stripes to power across much of the Middle East over the next decade, the AKP was ideally better equipped to deal with them than were the secularists; its leadership is more familiar and comfortable with the Islamist environment and modes of thinking. Whether or not it favors specific policies proposed by other Islamic parties, the AKP possessed greater access and flexibility in dealing with them than almost any other political force. Those parties in other countries could find Turkey more understanding than western governments of their desire to work within an Islamic tradition. Even after a now beleaguered AKP leaves power, Turkey is likely to remain a more sympathetic and *knowledgeable* interlocutor within the Muslim world, with the Hizmet movement remaining on the scene to provide further balance. Turkey represents itself today as operating *within* the Middle East as part of the same culture, not as an outsider. That is why Davutoğlu argues that the problems of the Middle East "belong to *us*," to all of us in the region. His voice is *umma*-sensitive and clearly heard as representing sympathy, authenticity and experience—although many in the West find it preachy and irritating.

Despite the increasing complexity of tensions across the region, an annual poll of Turkey's standing in the Middle East in 2012 reported Turkey as perceived more positively than any other country in the world, with a 78 percent rating. The US received only 33 percent, well below China, Saudi Arabia, Egypt, France *and Iran*. Seventy-seven percent believed that Turkey contributes positively to regional peace compared to contributions from the EU, UN, Russia, the US, China or NATO in that order. Turkey was also perceived as a trusted interlocutor. Sixty-one percent saw Turkey as a model for the region. Turkey's high ratings in the poll were due particularly to its economic performance. Israel was perceived as the greatest *threat* to peace in the region (47 percent), followed by the US (24 percent), and then Iran (11 percent). Those polled overwhelmingly identified economic issues as their biggest problem, above political issues.[2] These polling figures hardly sketch a portrait of Middle East religious fanaticism.

Yet the events of the Arab Spring damaged even Turkey's standing in the region. Two years later in the same poll Turkey had dropped 10 points to a 59 percent positive perception, its standing most sharply affected by its continuing   support to the Muslim Brotherhood in Egypt after it was overthrown, and to its participation in efforts to overthrow the Syrian regime.[3]

Certainly such polls are transient and lack precision, but they demonstrate the shifting moods of publics. Turkey still fares quite well and stands only to benefit among Middle East *publics*, although certainly much less so among regimes, as regional tensions reduce. The weakening autocratic regimes of the region are threatened by Turkey's open call for more democracy. Turkey also represents a new force in the region (after a hiatus of a century), shaking up the old and stagnant geopolitical order and even rivaling other Middle East states for influence on foreign policy and issues of change. Here Turkey will have to tread carefully as it explores new turf between working with existing regimes and encouraging change. Yet, both the AKP and the Gülen movement have increased new understandings of Islamic values in democratic governance and social policy; this represents a powerful new challenge to older generations of Islamists who focused primarily on the religious negatives, forbidding the forbidden, and on defining what is *haram* (illicit) in life.

Islamic Economics, Ideology and the Absence of a Left

There is a hole in the middle of Middle Eastern politics: the absence of a Left. A political spectrum by definition must contain a right and a left. (By "left" I mean a group of ideas that includes a desire to promote change, greater economic egalitarianism, multiculturalism, broader social safety nets, a distrust of capitalism as the best means to meet major social needs, an appreciation of the role of the state in helping achieve these goals, a socialist leaning, and an anti-imperialist impulse.) The demand for social justice ranks very high in the Muslim world today and is invariably linked with parallel Islamic ideas. A Left will inevitably be revived in efforts to achieve greater social justice—and probably with an Islamic flavor.

A leftist program within Islam may be a key means by which Islamism gravitates away from a formal fixation on law (*fiqh*) as interpreted at least a thousand years ago—rulings on what is forbidden, and the hunt to root out "illegitimate views" within Islam—and instead looks instead towards distillation of the "essence" of Islam that is meaningful to contemporary governance and life. Many modernist Muslim thinkers have termed that essence as the *maqāsid*—the "aims" or "goals" of Islam as they relate to human existence and values today. "*Shari'a*" ("The Path") can be understood in various ways but the modern discipline of focusing upon Qur'anic-derived *maqāsid* centers upon *preservation of five basic spheres of human existence*: religion (commitment and exercise of faith); life (in all its facets including the total global and ecological environment in which it is lived); intellect (with its implied freedoms and pursuit of knowledge); property (and personal stewardship in the broadest sense); and family (offspring, upbringing, honor, personal dignity and worth.)[4] Many Islamist politicians who achieve office and responsibilities might find the *maqāsid* a more powerful guide to "applied contemporary Islam" to meet the needs of society than often ossified Islamic law. It is a safe bet that AKP leaders today are more driven by their understanding of *maqāsid* than by fiqh in their moral vision even if the term is not used in common parlance. The Islamist Left also focusses upon the *maqāsid* as well.

The Left has in fact been missing in Middle Eastern politics for many decades. The 1960s and 1970s represented its heyday with its strong Arab socialist, Marxist and communist groups. It was much influenced and stimulated by the existence of the Soviet Union and China whose ideologies in one form or another dominated "third world" politics for many decades. Socialist or communist ideas often served as a vehicle for nationalist politics as well. They all shared a common suspicion of the West. But the massive military defeat of the Arabs in the June 1967 Six-Day War at the hands of Israel discredited the Arab nationalist movement and its leadership; later on the fall of the USSR damaged the image and promise of the Left and communism—at least in its Russian version. And then China turned its back on Marxism and embarked on a new path of highly successful state capitalism. The Left seemed to have run out of steam.

But we have not heard the end of "leftist" ideology in the Muslim world. The "Left" is part of any political spectrum and is no less legitimate than the "Right." Ideas of the Left are likely to return and fill political and ideological needs, including in the Muslim world. These ideas had influence in the beginnings of the Islamic Revolution in Iran, and are now being expressed in Turkey within an Islamic context as we have seen. They may grow in power and influence. If that is happening in Turkey, it will certainly happen in the Arab world and beyond in the Muslim world.

But there was another reason for the weakening of the Left: the emergence of political Islam in the popular consciousness. Interestingly, many Middle Eastern communists broke with their own past around that time to become Islamists, finding considerable compatibility of views. Islamism, furthermore, was a genuine mass movement with mass appeal, unlike the more elitist leftists purveying borrowed western concepts. To be sure, many leftists leaned towards a more radical interpretation of "social justice" than was implicit in political Islam; many mainstream Islamists like the Brotherhood in Egypt were indeed nervous about leftist calls for redistribution of agricultural lands for example, and they generally opposed nationalization of land or redistribution of wealth as such. The same was true in Pakistan where Islamists still tended to support the old social—even feudal—order, even while critical of the state and of corruption. Islamists furthermore retained residual suspicion and fear of the secular aspects of socialism and especially of atheism as a foundation of communist ideology.

With weak or absent left-wing parties in the Arab world, Turkey and Iran, there is a vacuum waiting to be filled. Some liberal secular groups, too, speak of social justice, but they have gained little mass appeal. Nonetheless, in the June 2012 presidential race in Egypt a leftist candidate suddenly emerged with unexpected popular backing—perhaps a sign of things to come.

If the Turkish or world economy falls on harder times, and income gaps visibly increase, perspectives could rapidly change. Socialism in Turkey and across the Muslim world was (incorrectly) often linked with communist materialism and atheism. There is nothing inherently atheistic about socialism. Islam itself can generate ideas with "socialist" flavor without reference to western socialism or Marxism. The phenomenon gains strength when it draws ideas and principles from *within* Muslim culture and tradition rather than importing it, with all its political baggage, from the West. Indeed the West is seen in this context as *supporting systems of injustice* within the countries that imperialism once dominated. The Wall Street-induced global economic crises of the late 2000s reinforced the idea of socially and financially irresponsible western capitalism running amok. It seems that the years of policy errors by Washington in the Muslim world have now come home to roost: sadly, the benchmark for political legitimacy of so many parties often now resides in the degree of anti-Americanism they display.

Turkey as Magnet State
When a state can visibly demonstrate successful management of political, economic, social, cultural and international issues it often creates a force of attraction—a magnetic pull—that draws other states towards it into greater association. The EU has been one such model: numerous states are actually willing to yield up considerable elements of sovereignty to become part of the EU project. The euro has of course received setbacks in 2011 and 2012, and will likely face further crisis until the system is adjusted, probably in favor of greater centralized economic power in the EU itself. In any case, the model is evolving and historically powerful, perhaps not matched since the days of the

382

Roman Empire when outlying regions sought association with the empire's projects.

In the Middle East we see a similar persistence of yearnings for greater unity along with a desire for sovereign control. Arabs in particular still tend to feel that there is "something missing" or artificial in a nationalism directed, for example, towards any single truncated state like Jordan or Gulf states; they retain aspirations towards an ideal of a greater political whole that needs to be acknowledged. This call of greater Arab or Muslim unity persists, sometimes only beneath the surface but it is always present, cycling through a range of ideological visions in different regions over time: in visions of Islam, pan-Islamism, the caliphate, communism, Greater Syria, Arabism, Arab Socialism, Ba'thism, the Ottoman Empire, and Islamism. This idea of more intimate ties among Arab states is compelling, especially where modern borders are arbitrary and often impoverished in cultural perspective, providing little emotional gratification. The 19th-century western worship of the sacred "nation-state" is not really a model anymore; it ultimately led the 20th century to the ugliest series of wars the modern world has ever seen. Even Europe is backing off from its veneration of the "nation-state" in favor of new ties, new unions, and diminished sovereignty. Single "nation-states" are an even more inappropriate concept among Arab states.

Apart from the EU, other states, successfully managed, can be magnets. The Soviet Union, in principle, could have been a viable model, if it had been managed properly to bring together its component republics in a successful economic model. But it was abysmally, often brutally, managed. There is no reason why a new and inspired Russian leadership could not, in principle, create a magnet effect for outlying states in the former Soviet space, but the Soviet experience left too many lasting scars and Russia is still struggling to improve even its own domestic rule, hardly yet a model for anything. Nonetheless Russia seeks to create a Eurasian Economic Community. China may also be in a similar process with its huge economic drawing power and far greater claim to success. Brazil may serve the same function in Latin America. Why not Turkey in the Middle East? There is a considerable likelihood that Middle Eastern states—especially if their brittle authoritarian structures are reformed—will seek closer voluntary association with Turkey in some form or other, perhaps a kind of resuscitation of the *geopolitical space* of an Ottoman Empire in economic and cultural terms, as long as it is voluntary and makes concrete economic and political sense. The former Islamist Welfare (*Refah*) Party under Erbakan sought such a D-8 economic project among developing Muslim states. Of course, any such undertaking is now little more than a glint in the eye for some; it will take many years before the full potential of such a new regional market based on common economic and cultural ties in the Middle East might emerge. But no other state in the Middle East is as well poised to organize it as Turkey whose increasingly industrialized and globalized economy is complementary to Arab world economies. And if Turkey's political crises and scandals of 2013-2014 are resolved through democratic process and the ballot box—as it most likely will be—that makes its political order all the more impressive.

Egypt might have been a possible partner in such a new political vision with the liberation of the grassroots power of the Muslim Brotherhood at the ballot box. Just before his election to the presidency, newly elected Brotherhood leader Muhammad al-Mursi commented:

> [My plan] is to establish relations with all countries of the region to revive Egypt's identity in the region through economic cooperation among the Arab countries and making certain reforms in the Arab league to activate its role on the international arena—and, besides that, supporting the Palestinian nation in its legitimate campaign for realizing its rights.[5]

Mursi did not remain in power long enough to even begin to think about implementing such a project. And now Egypt has a great deal of compelling domestic business to attend to over the next years. Nonetheless the ideal and the ambitions for an Arab project have been firmly planted; it could enthuse many Arabs. Mursi did not mention Turkey—but can we doubt that his words are anything but welcome to Ankara's ears? The speaker was not merely the new president of Egypt, but the leader of the key wing of an international Islamist organization, whose words and longer-range ambitions affect other states. These are clear indicators of a search for a potential new order underway. It may well be that the Islamists in many states will founder—or have foundered—and will be voted out of office in later elections. But the vision is not alien to politicians of most other ideological backgrounds and it will not go away.

The Islamists do not represent the sole wave of the future. Indeed, they may have only a short window of opportunity if they do not quickly learn how better to govern, and to expand the basis of the state for greater inclusiveness of all citizens. The secular state—one that sits above specific religious identities of its citizens and operates as an impartial arbiter—is certainly the foundation of future governance; but there is no reason why that secular state cannot operate in a Christian or Muslim cultural environment and be inspired by the universal values of those faiths. The Gülen movement is one such organization that aspires in this direction. "Secularists" may clash with

"Islamists" but what they are really clashing over is control of the power of the state; neither trusts the other. But the grander process is underway.

New horizons are wide open. What is called for is a transformation of imagination and of mental maps; this requires the transcendence of nearly 100 years of unproductive isolation of the Middle East in order to restore community, cultural and economic ties that were broken by imperial ruling patterns. Europe after World War II, after all, began to back off from the old model of conflicting nation-state borders in favor of a higher social, economic and even political order. In the Middle East unfortunately it had often been conceived as a goal to be attained by force. And it was at that time invariably accompanied by bad rule. That need not be the permanent case at all.

The region that historically comprised Greater Syria, in particular, is central to the complex of Middle Eastern politics. Even with its borders truncated by colonialism, Syria is likely to remain—at least in its ambitions and vision—a larger player than its present reduced size and agonizing civil struggle suggests. If contemporary states like Iraq, Lebanon, Syria, Jordan, the Palestine region—the Levant taken together—or the Arabian Peninsula should sink into civil wars or collapse, new combinations of states and regional associations could emerge, washing away the old colonial state order that has uncomfortably existed over the past century. That may not happen, and a process of reconceiving and restructuring the political landscape of the Middle East would be fiercely chaotic. Nonetheless the results of colonial history are still working themselves out. Furthermore, the appeal of Arab unity, although quite tarnished through bad historical experience, will always be able to stir Arab souls if the right leader(s) comes along with a vision for a new future. It is not the vision as such that is flawed; it has been *flawed political orders and flawed leadership* that destroyed efforts to implement those ideas in effective ways.

As the late great *New York Times* journalist Anthony Shadid put it a year before his untimely death in 2012,

> As the Arab world beyond the border struggles with the inspirations and traumas of its revolution—a new notion of citizenship colliding with the smaller claims of piety, sect and clan—something else is percolating along the old routes of that empire, which spanned three continents and lasted six centuries before Ataturk brought it to an end in 1923 with self-conscious revolutionary zeal. ...
> It is probably too early to define identities emerging in those locales. But something bigger than its parts is at work along imperial connections that were bent but never broken by decades of colonialism and the cold war. The links are the stuff of land, culture, history, architecture, memory and imagination that remains the realm

of scholarship and daily lives but often eludes the notice of a journalism marching to the cadence of conflict.[6]

Is the present turmoil of the Arab Spring part of the long-drawn out birth pangs of some kind of new Middle East order? What lessons or insights have been gained in the process? Turkey would so far appear to be a leading candidate as a source of inspiration and leadership and accomplishment. Even with its shortcomings its institutions would be the envy of all its neighbors. For the first time in a century Turkey would seem ready.

Notes

Chapter Two

[1] Pilling, David, "Why Americans should learn to love the renminbi," *Financial Times*, 12 October 2011. http://www.ft.com/intl/cms/s/0/3aa54f1a-f3fe-11e0-b221-00144feab49a.html#axzz1vZB87hYn

[2] UNDP 2013 Human Development Report, http://hdr.undp.org/en/

[3] Makdisi, Ussama, "Ottoman Orientalism", *The American Historical Review* Vol. 107, Issue 3, 2011. http://www.historycooperative.org/journals/ahr/107.3/ah0302000768.html

[4] Makdisi, ibid

[5] Aydin, Cemil, *The Politics of Anti-Westernism in Asia*, Columbia University Press, NY, 2007, p. 191-192.

Part Two

[1] Avnery, Uri, "Butterflies in Damascus," *Outlook India*, 7 June 2013, http://www.outlookindia.com/article.aspx?286019

Chapter Three

[1] Beck, 4 Feb 11.

[2] Remarks by President Bush before the National Endowment for Democracy on the War on Terror, October, 2005.

[3] Özcan, Azmi, *Pan-Islamism: Indian Muslims, the Ottomans and Britain (1877-1924)*, Brill, Leiden, 1997, p 1-5.

[4] Özcan, 11-13.

[5] Özcan p. 27.

[6] Özcan p. 28.

[7] Özcan p. 37.

[8] Urdu Akhbar, 17 August 1876, quoted by Özcan, p. 65.

[9] Kramer, Martin, *Islam Assembled: The Advent of the Muslim Congresses*, Columbia University Press, NY 1986, p.9.

[10] Özcan p. 61

[11] Davutoğlu, Ahmet, "Principles of Turkish Foreign Policy and Regional Political Structuring," Tepav, April, 2012. http://www.tepav.org.tr/upload/files/1334845338-5.Principles_of_Turkish_Foreign_Policy_and_Regional_Political_Structuring.pdf

Chapter Four

[1] "The Farewell Sermon of the Prophet Muhammad", Islamicity.com. http://www.islamicity.com/articles/articles.asp?ref=IC0107-322

Chapter Five

[1] Hanioğlu, M. Şükrü, *Atatürk: An Intellectual Biography*, Princeton University Press, Princeton, 2011, p. 32.

[2] Hanioğlu, *Atatürk: An Intellectual Biography*, p 34, 41.

[3] Hanioğlu, *Atatürk*, p. 37.

[4] Hanioğlu, M. Şükrü, *A Brief History of the Late Ottoman Empire*, Princeton University Press, Princeton, 2008, p. 148.

[5] Wikipedia: The 1980 Turkish coup d'état

[6] Dağı, İhsan, "The Fall of the Generals," *Today's Zaman*, 8 April 2012.
http://www.todayszaman.com/columnist-276811-the-fall-of-the-generals.html

Chapter Six
[1] Cengiz, Orhan Kemal; Oğur, Turgay; Özipek, Bekir Berat, "Ergenekon is our Reality," Human Rights Agenda Association, Young Civilians, Ankara, June 2010.
[2] For a strong and detailed rebuttal of Ergenekon see Jenkins, Gareth, "Ergenekon, Sledgehammer and the Politics of Turkish Justice: Conspiracies and Coincidences," Gloria Center, Herzliyya, Israel, 29 August 2011.
http://www.gloria-center.org/2011/08/ergenekon-sledgehammer-and-the-politics-of-turkish-justice-conspiracies-and-coincidences/
[3] Birand, Mehmet Ali, "Evet, genlerimizde darbecilik vardı," (Yes, a coup mentality has resided in our genes), Posta, 19 May 2011.
http://www.posta.com.tr/siyaset/YazarHaberDetay/%E2%80%9C___Evet_genleri
mizde_darbecilik_vardi___%E2%80%9D.htm?ArticleID=73145
[4] http://ec.europa.eu/enlargement/pdf/key_documents/2010/package/tr_rapport_
2010_en.pdf
[5] Mahcupyan, Etyen, "End of the Story," *Today's Zaman*, 1 September 2011.
http://www.todayszaman.com/columnist-255486-end-of-the-story.html

Chapter Eight
[1] *The Economist*, "What a Prime Minister's Funeral Says About Democracy and Islam," 3 March 2011. http://www.economist.com/node/18289145
[2] Alpay, Şahin, "İslami Kemalizm'in kökleri nerede?," (Where are the roots of Islamic Kemalism?), *Zaman*, 19 April 2012.
http://www.zaman.com.tr/yazar.do?yazino=1275771
[3] Alpay, ibidem.
[4] Index Mundi, "Turkey Economy Profile," 2012.
http://www.indexmundi.com/turkey/economy_profile.html
[5] Mahcupyan, Etyen, "A Headscarved Woman at the April 24 Commemoration, *Today's Zaman*, 3 May 2012. http://www.todayszaman.com/columnist-279331-a-headscarved-woman-at-the-april-24-commemoration.html]
[6] Zıbak, Fatma Dişli, "Not State's Job to Raise People According to Religion,' *Today's Zaman*, 12 February 2012.
http://www.todayszaman.com/newsDetail_getNewsById.action?newsId=271162
[7] Taşpınar, Ömer, "Turkey: The New Model?", Brookings Institution, April 2012.
http://www.brookings.edu/research/papers/2012/04/24-turkey-new-model-taspinar
[8] Interview with Abdullah Gül by Nathan Gardels, Christian Science Monitor, 29 May 2012. http://www.csmonitor.com/Commentary/Global-Viewpoint/2012/0529/
Interview-with-Turkey-s-Abdullah-Gul-Egypt-should-embrace-secularism

Chapter Nine
[1] Sunier, Landman, van der Linden, et al., "Diyanet: The Turkish Directorate for Religious Affairs in a Changing Environment," VU University Amsterdam, Utrecht University, January 2011.
[2] Pigott, Robert, "Turkey in radical revision of Islamic texts," BBC News, 27 February 2007.

[3] Jones, Gareth, "Turkey Explains Revision of Hadith Project," Reuters, 7 March 2008, http://blogs.reuters.com/faithworld/2008/03/07/turkey-explains-revision-of-hadith-project/

[4] Jones, ibid.

[5] Jones, ibid.

[6] Donovan, Jeffrey, "Turkey: Islamic Reformers Look Back To Future," RFE/RL, 29 November 2006. http://www.rferl.org/content/article/1073078.html

[7] Sunier, et al, ibid.

[8] Birch, Nicholas, "How the AKP is Using Islam to Transform Turkey in a Global Power," *The Majalla*, 06 July 2011. http://www.majalla.com/en/cover_story/article467067.ece

[9] Akyol, Mustafa, *Islam Without Extremes: A Muslim Case for Liberty*, W. W. Norton and Company, New York, 2011.

[10] Esposito, John, "Racing Backwards Into the Future: Saudi Arabia and Kuwait," Huffington Post, 14 May 2012. http://www.huffingtonpost.com/john-l-esposito/racing-backwards-into-the-future-saudi-arabia-and-kuwait_b_1507134.html

[11] "Turkish Religion Officials Rule Out Haram Fatwa for Protests," *Hürriyet Daily News*, 8 May 2012. http://www.hurriyetdailynews.com/turkish-religion-officials-rule-out-haram-fatwa-for-protests.aspx?pageID=238&nID=20227&NewsCatID=356

[12] "Turkey to Help Rebuild Mosques in Gaza Strip," *Hürriyet Daily News*, 12 Jan 2012. http://www.hurriyetdailynews.com/turkey-to-help-rebuild-mosques-in-gaza-strip.aspx?pageID=238&nID=11286&NewsCatID=338

[13] Idris, Hamza, "Africa: Turkey - Shouldering the Pains of Muslims on Continent," Daily Trust, 6 December 2011. http://allafrica.com/stories/201112060858.html

[14] "Head of Turkish religious establishment meets with Russian Muslim leaders," *Today's Zaman*, 30 November 2011. http://www.todayszaman.com/news-264366-head-of-turkish-religious-establishment-meets-with-russian-muslim-leaders.html

[15] "Bosnian grand mufti praises Turkey's regional power," *Today's Zaman*, 04 October 2011.

Chapter Ten

[1] Anadolu Agency, 26 April 2012

[2] Göktürk, Gülay, "Davutoğlu o sözlere açıklık getirdi," (Davutoğlu clarifies his remarks,") 5 May 2012, http://gundem.bugun.com.tr/davutoglu-o-sozlere-aciklik-getirdi-191595-haberi.aspx

[3] Doğan, Yonca Poyraz, "Anthropologist: Turkish Muslimhood replacing Islamism," *Today's Zaman*, 1 July 2012.

[4] Bacık, Gökhan, "Erdoğan, Gül and Davutoğlu: the inner bargain on Turkish foreign policy," *Today's Zaman*, 27 May 2012. http://www.todayszaman.com/columnist-281620-erdogan-gul-and-davutoglu-the-inner-bargain-on-turkish-foreign-policy.html

[5] Gül, Abdullah, "Eğer yetkisi olsaydı Uludere'yi DDK'ya tereddütsüz inceletirdim," *Star Politika*, 28 Mayıs Pazartesi. http://www.stargazete.com/politika/eger-yetkisi-olsaydi-uludereyi-ddkya-tereddutsuz-inceletirdim/haber-589998

[6] Baban, Mehmet, "Whither Axis Shift: A Perspective from Turkey's Foreign Trade," SETA, Report #4, Ankara, November 2010.

[7] Enginsoy, Ümit, "Islamic Trade Tops Turkish Defense, *Hürriyet*, 28 May 2012. http://www.hurriyetdailynews.com/islamic-trade-tops-turkish-defense.aspx?pageID

=238&nID=14586&NewsCatID=344

[8] "NATO Defense Official: Turkey Plan to Purchase Chinese Weapons System Would Implant 'Virus' Into NATO Command and Control System," *The Tower Magazine*, 15 October 2013. http://www.thetower.org/turkey-china-missile-deal-virus

[9] İhsanoğlu, Ekmeleddin, *The Islamic World in the New Century*, Columbia University Press, New York, 2010, pp. 6-10.

[10] İhsanoğlu, p. 17.

[11] Kardaş, Şaban "No Boutique State: Understanding the Debate on Turkey's Involvement in Afghanistan," German Marshall Fund, 13 April 2012

Chapter Eleven

[1] Life Positive, "The Dervish and the King" http://www.lifepositive.com/Mind/Inspirations/The_Dervish_and_the_king112010.asp

[2] Mardin, Şerif, *Religion and Social Change in Modern Turkey*, Suny, Albany, 1989, p. 59.

[3] Birch, Nicholas, "Sufism in Turkey: The Next Big Thing?," Eurasianet, 22 June 2010, http://www.eurasianet.org/node/61379

[4] See the Nursi website in English: http://www.risaleinur.us/

Chapter Twelve

[1] Oxford Analytica, "Gulen Inspires Muslims Worldwide," *Forbes Magazine*, 2 Jan 2008. http://www.forbes.com/2008/01/18/turkey-islam-gulen-cx_0121oxford.html

[2] See http://www.fethullahgulen.org/

[3] http://www.fgulen.org/about-fethullah-gulen/gulens-thoughts/1294-the-new-man-and-woman.html

[4] Seufert, Günter, "Is the Fethullah Gülen Movement Overstretching Itself?", SWP Research Paper, Stiftung Wissenschaft und Politik (German Institute for International and Security Affairs), Berlin, January 2014, p. 14, http://www.swp-berlin.org/en/publications/swp-research-papers/swp-research-paper-detail/article/turkey_the_fethullah_guelen_movement.html

[5] Seufert, p. 25

[6] www.todayszaman.com

[7] Michel, Thomas, S.J., "Sufism and Modernity in the Thought of Fethullah Gülen," *The Muslim World*, Special Issue, July 2005 - Vol. 95 Issue 3.

[8] Michel, ibid.]

[9] Ahmet Kuru, "Searching for a Middle Way between Modernity and Tradition: The Case of Fethullah Gülen," cited in M. Hakan Yavuz and John L. Esposito (editors), *Turkish Islam and the Secular State: The Gülen Movement*. Syracuse: Syracuse University Press, 2003, p.117. Kuru's citation of Gülen is taken from Fethullah Gülen, *Prophet Muhammad: The Infinite Light*, London: Truestar, 1995, pp. 200-201. Both sources as cited in Michel.

[10] Michel, Thomas, S.J., "Sufism and Modernity in the Thought of Fethullah Gülen," The Muslim World, Special Issue, July 2005 - Vol. 95 Issue 3]

Chapter Thirteen

[1] "Turkish corruption probe deepens," Europost, 10 January 2014. http://www.europost.bg/article?id=9432

[2] Samanyolu Haber, "Taraf Ankara'yı karıştıracak şok belgeler yayınladı!" ("Taraf Newspaper Publishes Shocking Documents that Shake up Ankara!"), 9 December 2013. http://www.samanyoluhaber.com/gundem/Taraf-Ankarayi-karistiracak -sok-belgeler-yayinladi/1035465/]

[3] For an excellent discussion of these issues see Balcı, Bayram, "Turkey's Gülen Movement: Between Social Activism and Politics," Carnegie Endowment, 24 October 2013. http://carnegieendowment.org/2013/10/24/turkey-s-g%C3%BClen -movement-between-social-activism-and-politics/gr8q?reloadFlag=1#

[4] Gürsel, Kadri, "Gülenist-AKP Clash Is Now in the Open," Al-Monitor, 16 August, 2013. http://www.al-monitor.com/pulse/originals/2013/08/turkey-erdogan-akp-gulenism-the-service-power-struggle.html##ixzz2mwDFJ3KW

[5] See, for example, Çakır, Rüşen, "Gülen cemaati parti kurar mı?", ("Will the Gülen Community Found a Political Party?"), Vatan, 23 January 2014. http://haber.gazetevatan.com/gulen-cemaati-parti-kurar-mi/602960/4/yazarlar

[6] Taştekin, Fehim, "Turkey's Sunni Identity Test, Al-Monitor, 21 June 2013. http://www.al-monitor.com/pulse/originals/2013/06/turkey-sunnism-sectarian-rhetoric.html##ixzz2kE6SlALt

[7] Gürsel, Kadri, "Gülenist-AKP Clash Is Now in the Open," Al-Monitor, 16 August 2013. http://www.al-monitor.com/pulse/originals/2013/08/turkey-erdogan-akp-gulenism-the-service-power-struggle.html##ixzz2mwDFJ3KW

[8] Europost, "Turkish corruption probe deepens," 10 January 2014. http://www.europost.bg/article?id=9432

[9] Gültaşlı, Selçuk, "The 'grand theory' and the corruption scandal in Turkey," EU Observer, 7 January 2014. http://euobserver.com/opinion/122641

[10] "Erdogan Declares War On Gulen's 'Empire Of Fear'," Agence France Press, 15 January 2014. http://news.yahoo.com/erdogan-declares-war-gulen-39-39-empire-fear-144757124.html]

[11] Ibidem.

[12] Öğret, Özgür, "Young Party Seeks New Perspective For Turkish Politics," Hürriyet Daily News, 6 December 2010. http://www.hurriyetdailynews.com/default.aspx?pageid=438&n=young-party-aims-to-bring-a-brand-new-perspective-to-turkish-politics-2010-12-06

[13] Güsten, Susanne, "Pious Turks Push for Labor Justice," New York Times, 9 May 2012. http://www.nytimes.com/2012/05/10/world/middleeast/pious-turks-push-for-labor-justice.html?ref=world&pagewanted=print

[14] http://www.economist.com/blogs/charlemagne/2013/07/turkish-politics

[15] Çolak, İbrahim, etc., "Mesele söz söylemek değil; Mesele zamanın sözünü söyleyebilmek!", ("The issue isn't just about speaking out but about addressing the issues of our time!", Racon Dergisi, 23 July 2011. http://ihsaneliacik.blogspot.com/2011/07/mesele-soz-soylemek-degil-mesele-zamann.html

Chapter Fourteen
[1] Çandar, Cengiz, "'Sıfır Sorun'dan' Herkesle Sorun'a Geçerken," ("From 'Zero Problems' to 'Problems with Everybody"), Hürriyet, 23 September 2011. http://hurarsiv.hurriyet.com.tr/goster/printnews.aspx?DocID=18805750

Chapter Fifteen
[1] Arab News, Riyadh, 28 November 2002. http://www.arabnews.com/Article.asp?ID=20711

Chapter Sixteen

[1] Younis, Ahmed and Younis, Muhammad, "Egyptians Sour on U.S., Eye Closer Ties to Turkey, Iran," 23 March 2012. http://www.gallup.com/poll/153401/Egyptians-Sour-Eye-Closer-Ties-Turkey-Iran.aspx?utm_source=alert&utm_medium=email&utm_campaign=syndication&utm_content=morelink&utm_term=World

[2] Esposito, John, al-Jazeera, 15 Jul 13. http://www.aljazeera.com/indepth/opinion/2013/07/2013715105014165446.html

[3] "In Egypt, the 'Deep State' Rises Again," *The Wall Street Journal*, 12 July 2013. http://online.wsj.com/news/articles/SB10001424127887324425204578601700051224658

[4] "Egypt Overview," World Bank, September 2013. http://www.worldbank.org/en/country/egypt/overview

[5] Salman, Talal, "Protesters Show Awareness Of Egypt's Historic Role," Al-Monitor, 3 July 2013. http://www.al-monitor.com/pulse/politics/2013/07/egypt-brotherhood-protests-arabism.html#ixzz2YO5GkVzz

[6] Daragahi, Borzou, "Egypt's leftwing populist draws broad support," *Financial Times*, 21 May 2012. http://www.ft.com/intl/cms/s/0/f29ce774-a356-11e1-988e-00144feabdc0.html#axzz1vZB87hYn

[7] "Erdoğan slams West for not calling Egypt army intervention a 'coup,'" *Today's Zaman*, 5 July 2013. http://www.todayszaman.com/news-320102-erdogan-slams-west-for-not-calling-egypt-army-intervention-a-coup.html;
Bhadrakumar, M. K. "Turkey's sultan deplores the pharaoh's fall," *Asia Times*, 9 July 2013. http://www.atimes.com/atimes/Middle_East/MID-01-090713.html

[8] Turkish Ministry of Foreign Affairs Bulletin, 4 July 2013, "Foreign Minister Davutoğlu remarks on the latest developments in Egypt." http://www.mfa.gov.tr/foreign-minister-davutoglu-remarks-on-the-latest-developments-in-egypt.en.mfa

[9] Springborg, Robert, "Sisi's Islamist Agenda for Egypt," *Foreign Affairs*, 28 July 2013. http://www.foreignaffairs.com/articles/139605/robert-springborg/sisis-islamist-agenda-for-egypt?page=show

[10] al-Dhayidi, Mishari, "The Revolution of the Muslim Brotherhood 'Caliph'", Asharq al-Awsat Online in Arabic, 24 July 2012; http://www.asharqalawsat.com/

[11] Kirkpatrick, David D., "Egyptians Say Military Discourages an Open Economy," New York Times, 18 February 2011. http://www.nytimes.com/2011/02/18/world/middleeast/18military.html?pagewanted=all

[12] Gümüşçü, Şebnem "Political Islam in Turkey and Egypt," Changing Turkey, 3 June 2010. http://changingturkey.com/2010/06/03/political-islam-in-turkey-and-egypt-by-dr-sebnem-gumuscu/

[13] Kirkpatrick, David D., "Premier of Turkey Takes Role in Region," *New York Times*, 12 September 2011. http://www.nytimes.com/2011/09/13/world/middleeast/13egypt.html?_r=0

[14] Mirenzi, Nicola, "Erdoğan and Secularism," Reset Doc, 27 September 2011. http://www.resetdoc.org/story/00000021750

[15] Al-Majid, Hamad, "Egypt's Brotherhood: Follow the Turkish Example," Asharq Al-Awsat, 2 April 2013. http://www.aawsat.net/2013/04/article55297585

[16] Shadid, Anthony, "Turkey Predicts Alliance With Egypt as Regional Anchors," *New York Times*, 18 September 2011. http://www.nytimes.com/2011/09/19/world/middleeast/turkey-predicts-partnership-with-egypt-as-regional-anchors.html?pagewanted=all

[17] Samir, Samir Khalil, "Egyptian Imams and intellectuals: Renewing Islam towards modernity," *Asia News*, 26 January 2011. http://www.asianews.it/news-en/Egyptian-Imams-and-intellectuals:-Renewing-Islam-towards-modernity-20609.html

[18] http://arabist.net/blog/2014/3/2/civilian-military-relations-in-egypt

[19] Telhami, Shibley, "Egypt's Identity Crisis," *The Washington Post*, 16 August 2013. http://www.washingtonpost.com/opinions/egypts-identity-crisis/2013/08/16/70d1459c-0524-11e3-88d6-d5795fab4637_story.html

[20] Maziad, Marwa, "Egypt's security solution," Al Jazeera, Aug. 21, 2013. http://www.aljazeera.com/indepth/opinion/2013/08/2013821121826242832.html

[21] Merone, Guiseppe, "Tunisia and the divided Arab Spring," Open Democracy.net, 9 August 2013. http://www.opendemocracy.net/giuseppe-merone/tunisia-and-divided-arab-spring

[22] http://www.amnesty.org/en/news/egypt-three-years-wide-scale-repression-continues-unabated-2014-01-23

Chapter Seventeen

[1] Noureddine, ibid.

[2] Şenerdem, Erisa Dautaj, "Turkey and Gulf countries to foster trade ties," SES Türkiye, 10 February, 2012. http://turkey.setimes.com/en_GB/articles/ses/articles/features/departments/economy/2012/02/10/feature-01

[3] Noureddine, Mohammad, "Turkish President Opens New Chapter in Relations with Gulf States," al-Monitor, 3 February 2012. http://www.al-monitor.com/cms/contents/articles/politics/2012/02/turkish-gulf-honeymoon.html

[4] Al-Shayji, 'Abdullah, "A bolder GCC Can Tackle Regional Challenges Better," *Gulf News*, downloaded February 2012. http://gulfnews.com/opinions/columnists/a-bolder-gcc-can-tackle-regional-challenges-better-1.983207]

[5] Brown, Jonathan A. C., "Dim Prospects for Egypt's Salafis," Council on Foreign Relations, 19 July 2013 http://www.cfr.org/egypt/dim-prospects-egypts-salafis/p31127

[6] Marroushi, Nadine, "Persisting Brothers," interview with Amr Darrag, secretary of foreign relations with the Muslim Brotherhood's Freedom and Justice Party, Mada Masr, 8 September 2013. http://madamasr.com/content/persisting-brothers

[7] R4BIA Song. http://www.r4bia.com/en/content/r4bia-song

Chapter Nineteen

[1] Burr, William, "The history of Iran's nuclear energy program," Bulletin of the Atomic Scientists, 19 January 2009, http://www.thebulletin.org/web-edition/op-eds/the-history-of-irans-nuclear-energy-program

[2] MK Bhadrakumar, "Iran urges India to cherish friendship," May 16, 2012. http://indrus.in/articles/2012/05/16/iran_urges_india_to_cherish_friendship_15766.html

[3] 2010 Arab Public Opinion Poll: Results of Arab Opinion Survey Conducted June 29-July 20, 2010, Brookings Institution, Washington DC. http://www.brookings.edu/reports/2010/0805_arab_opinion_poll_telhami.aspx

[4] Kibaroğlu, Mustafa and Çağlar, Barış, "Implications of a Nuclear Iran for Turkey," Middle East Policy Council, 2011. http://www.mepc.org/journal/middle-east-policy-archives/implications-nuclear-iran-turkey?print

[5] "The Shiites are coming, The Shiites Are Coming," Egyptian Chronicles, 5 March 2013. http://egyptianchronicles.blogspot.co.uk/2013/03/the-shiites-are-coming-shiites-are.html

[6] Cerić, Shaykh Mustafa (former Grand Mufti of Bosnia), "Sunni-Shia relations the key to regional stability," 3 September 2013. http://www.commongroundnews.org/print_article.php?artId=33180&dir=left&lan=en&sid=2

[7] Younis, Ahmed and Younis, Mohamed, "Egyptians Sour on U.S., Eye Closer Ties to Turkey, Iran," Gallup Poll, 23 March 2012. http://www.gallup.com/poll/153401/Egyptians-Sour-Eye-Closer-Ties-Turkey-Iran.aspx?utm_source=alert&utm_medium=email&utm_campaign=syndication&utm_content=morelink&utm_term=World

[8] "Almost Half of Turkey's Oil Needs Supplied by Iran," *Fars News*, 19 September 2011, http://english.farsnews.com/newstext.php?nn=9006230520

[9] Omidi, Ali, "The Ultra-Importance of Turkish AKP's Parliamentary Victory for Iran," *Foreign Policy Journal*, June 17 2011. http://www.foreignpolicyjournal.com/2011/06/17/the-ultra-importance-of-turkish-akps-parliamentary-victory-for-iran/

[10] Kurtaran, Gökhan, "Iranian firms break into world markets via Turkey," *Hürriyet Daily News*, 18 April 2011. http://www.hurriyetdailynews.com/n.php?n=iranian-firms-break-into-world-markets-via-turkey-2011-04-18

[11] Kurtaran

Chapter Twenty

[1] Stansfield, Gareth; Kinninmont, Jane; and Sirri, Omar, "Iraq On The International Stage: Foreign Policy And National Identity In Transition," Chatham House, UK, July 2013. http://www.chathamhouse.org/publications/papers/view/192895

[2] Donat, Gözde Nur; Cengiz, Sinem, "Iraq on brink of disintegration as rift with Turkey deepens," *Today's Zaman*, 29 April 2012. http://www.sundayszaman.com/sunday/newsDetail_getNewsById.action?newsId=278894

Chapter Twenty-One

[1] Avnery, Uri, "Butterflies in Damascus," June 8, 2013. http://www.opednews.com/articles/Butterflies-in-Damascus-by-Uri-Avnery-130608-428.html

[2] Islam, Rana Deep, "Politics of Dilemma: Turkish and EU Approaches toward Syria," AICGS Transatlantic Perspectives, American Institute for Contemporary German Studies, June 2011.

Chapter Twenty-Two

[1] Hemming, Jon, "Middle East turmoil draws Turkey and Iraqi Kurds closer," Reuters, 1 Feb 2012, http://uk.reuters.com/article/2012/02/01/uk-turkey-iraq-kurds-idUKTRE8101Z620120201

[2] Richards, George, "Iran influence in Iraqi Kurdistan," *The Guardian*, 21 November 2013. http://www.theguardian.com/world/2013/nov/21/iran-influence-iraqi-kurdistan

[3] Natali, Denise, "Iraqi Kurds Criticize Growing Turkish Influence," Al-Monitor Iraq Pulse, 4 June 4 2013.

http://www.al-monitor.com/pulse/originals/2013/06/iraqi-kurds-critical-turkish-influence.html?utm_source=&utm_medium=email&utm_campaign=7425#ixzz2VM meGQLE

Chapter Twenty-Three
[1] Friedman, Thomas, "Israel: Adrift at Sea Alone," *New York Times*, 18 September 2011.
[2] Zakaria, Fareed, "The Storm Before the Calm," *TIME*, 3 October 2011. http://www.time.com/time/magazine/article/0,9171,2094387,00.html#ixzz2T98xtT Yj
[3] Ynetnews, 4 September 2011. http://www.ynetnews.com/articles/0,7340,L-4117793,00.html
[4] Bhadrakumar, M.K., "Israel turns tables on Turkey", *Asia Times*, 29 August 2011. http://www.atimes.com/atimes/Middle_East/MH27Ak05.html
[5] Smith, Lee, "The Arab-Israeli Peace Process Is Over. Enter the Era of Chaos," *The Tablet*, 30 October 2013. http://www.tabletmag.com/jewishnews-and-politics/150744/without-peace-enter-chaos

Chapter Twenty-Four
[1] Vela, Justin, "Is Turkey Turning Its Back on Atatürk?," Eurasianet, 20 June 2012. http://www.eurasianet.org/node/65576
[2] Doğan, Yonca Poyraz, "Anthropologist: Turkish Muslimhood replacing Islamism, *Today's Zaman*, 1 July 2012. http://www.todayszaman.com/news-285170-anthropologist-turkish-muslimhood-replacing-islamism.html
[3] Alpay, Şahin, "Paradox of press freedom in Turkey," *Today's Zaman*, 23 May 2011. http://www.todayszaman.com/columnist-244740-paradox-of-press-freedom-in-turkey.html
[4] Akarçeşme, Sevgi, "A new class of Hybrid Turks emerging between White and Black Turks," *Today's Zaman*, 5 August 2012. http://www.todayszaman.com/news-288628-a-new-class-of-hybrid-turks-emerging-between-white-and-black-turks.html
[5] White, Jenny, *Muslimness and the New Turkish Nationalism*, Princeton University Press, Princeton NJ, 2012.
[6] Afrasiabi, Kaveh L, "Misstep in Turkey's neighborly ties," *Asia Times*, 12 October 2011. http://www.atimes.com/atimes/Middle_East/MJ12Ak03.html
[7] Al-Labbad, Mustafa, "Arab World Is Loser in Syrian war," al-Monitor, 9 September 2013. http://www.al-monitor.com/pulse/politics/2013/09/syria-crisis-arab-exodus-history.html
[8] Alperen, Tahir, "Yalnız değiliz ama yalnızlığı göze alacak kadar ilkeliyiz," (We're not alone, but we are principled enough to risk standing alone," *Stargazete*, 26 August 2013. http://haber.stargazete.com/guncel/yalniz-degiliz-ama-yalnizligi-goze-alacak-kadar-ilkeliyiz/haber-783839#ixzz2gEGDsNNW
[9] Quoted in Bhadrakumar , M.K., "China weighs in on 'right side of history' in Gulf," *Asia Times*, 18 January 2012. http://www.atimes.com/atimes/China/NA18Ad02.html

Chapter Twenty-Five
[1] Merone, Giuseppe, "Tunisia and the divided Arab Spring," Open Democracy.net, 9 August 2013. http://www.opendemocracy.net/giuseppe-merone/tunisia-and-divided-arab-spring

[2] "Turkey remains popular for Middle Eastern nations, TESEV study finds," *Today's Zaman*, 2 February 2012. http://www.todayszaman.com/news-270290-turkey-remains-popular-for-middle-eastern-nations-tesev-study-finds.html

[3] Akarçeşme, Sevgi, "Turkey's approval rating in Middle East down 10 percent from 2012," *Today's Zaman*, 3 December 2013. http://www.todayszaman.com/newsDetail_getNewsById.action;jsessionid=4E84F76 66AD9110363848FDC461BB477?newsId=333047&columnistId=0

[4] See, for example, Hathout, Dr. Hassan, "Basics of Sharia," http://www.islamicity.com/voi/transcripts/Shariah.htm; see also "Maqasid" [Goals of Shari'a] in Wikipedia for a discussion of the evolution of this line of thought from the 12th century into contemporary thought where it is gaining influence.

[5] cited in Bhadrakumar, Melkulanangara, "Egypt's Brothers and New Middle East (II)," Strategic Culture Foundation, 29 June 2012. http://www.strategic-culture.org/news/2012/06/29/egypt-brothers-and-new-middle-east-ii.html

[6] Shadid, Anthony, "Can Turkey Unify the Arabs?," *New York Times*, 28 May 2011, http://www.nytimes.com/2011/05/29/weekinreview/29ottoman.html

INDEX